The Yom Kippur Anthology

Publication of this book
was made possible through a gift by
Mr. & Mrs. Howard J. Rubenstein.

PHILIP GOODMAN

The Yom Kippur Anthology

The Jewish Publication Society

Philadelphia   Jerusalem
5752/1992

Copyright © 1971 by The Jewish Publication Society of America
First paperback printing, 1992
Introduction © 1992 by The Jewish Publication Society
All rights reserved   Manufactured in the United States of America
Designed by Sidney Feinberg

Library of Congress Catalog Card Information
The Yom Kippur Anthology. Philip Goodman, comp.
  1971, 1992.
Cloth, ISBN 0–8276–0026–7   Paper, ISBN 0–8276–0409–2
1. Yom Kippur. I. Goodman, Philip, 1911–
BM695.A8G66   296.4'32'08   72-151312

The editor herewith expresses his sincere appreciation to the following publishers and authors who have kindly granted permission to use the material indicated:

ACUM Ltd., Societe d'Auteurs, Compositeurs et Editeurs de Musique en Israel, Tel Aviv, Israel: "Innocent," by Levin Kipnis, trans. by Israel M. Goodelman.

Ben Aronin, Chicago: "*Kol Nidre*," from *Jolly Jingles for the Jewish Child*, by Ben Aronin, Behrman House, New York, 1947.

Bantam Books, Inc., New York: "Every Day Is a Day of Atonement," from "The Dybbuk," by S. Anski, THE DYBBUK AND OTHER GREAT YIDDISH PLAYS, ed. and trans. by Joseph C. Landis. Copyright © 1966 by Bantam Books, Inc.

A. S. Barnes & Company, Inc., Cranbury, N. J.: "The Miracle on the Sea," by Isaac Loeb Peretz, from *Yisroel: The First Jewish Omnibus*; rev. ed., ed. by Joseph Leftwich, Thomas Yoseloff, New York, 1963.

Basic Books, Inc., New York: commentary on "Forgiven," from PRAYER IN JUDAISM by Bernard Martin, Basic Books, Inc., Publishers, New York, 1968.

Beacon Press, Boston: "We Stand before Our God," by Leo Baeck, from *The Dynamics of Emancipation: The Jew in the Modern Age*, ed. by Nahum N. Glatzer, 1965, and reproduced in *The Judaic Tradition*, ed. by Nahum N. Glatzer, 1969.

Behrman House Inc., New York: "*Kol Nidre*," from *Jolly Jingles for the Jewish Child*, by Ben Aronin, 1947; selection from *The Talmudic Anthology*, ed. by Louis I. Newman and Samuel Spitz, 1945; "The *Tzaddik*'s Defense," from *The Wedding Song: A Book of Chassidic Ballads*, by Rufus Learsi, 1938.

Dr. Samuel Belkin, New York: "The Sinner and His Penitence," from *In His Image: The Jewish Philosophy of Man as Expressed in Rabbinic Tradition*, by Samuel Belkin, Abelard-Schuman, New York, 1960. Copyright © 1960 by Samuel Belkin.

Bloch Publishing Co., New York: commentary on "God, That Doest Wondrously" and "The Import of the *Kapparot* Ceremony," from *Jewish Feasts and Fasts*, by Julius H. Greenstone, 1945; selections from *Rejoice in Thy Festival: A Treasury of Wisdom, Wit and Humor for the Sabbath and Jewish Holidays*, by Philip Goodman, 1956; "Never Too Late to Repent," from *Menorat ha-Maor*, by Israel ibn Al-Nakawa, ed. by H. G. Enelow, 1931; "The Revelation of *Neilah*," from *The Unknown Sanctuary: A Pilgrimage from Rome to Israel*, by Aimé Pallière, trans. by Louise Waterman Wise, 1928; "The Tear of Repentance," from *The Story of Jewish Holidays and Customs for Young People*, by Dorothy F. Zeligs, 1942; "Atonement" and "A Dream," from *Around the Year in Rhymes for the Jewish Child*, by Jessie E. Sampter, 1920.

B'nai B'rith Commission on Adult Jewish Education, Washington, D. C.: "Franz Rosenzweig's Self-discovery," by Nahum N. Glatzer, from *Great Jewish Thinkers of the Twentieth Century*, ed. by Simon Noveck, 1963.

Board of Jewish Education, Chicago: "Atonement," by Alexander M. Dushkin, from *The Tree of Life: Sketches from Jewish Life of Yesterday and Today in Drawing, Prose and Verse*, by Enrico Glicenstein and Alexander M. Dushkin, L. M. Stein, Chicago, 1933.

Mrs. Ruth F. Brin, Minneapolis: "Atonement," from *Interpretations for the Weekly Torah Reading*, by Ruth F. Brin, Lerner Publications Co., Minneapolis, 1965.

Bruce Humphries, Somerville, Mass.: "Yom Kippur Eve," by Constantine A. Shapiro, from *Gems of Hebrew Verse: Poems for Young People*, trans. by Harry H. Fein, 1940.

Central Conference of American Rabbis, New York: "Prayer for Yom Kippur" and "We Stand before Thee on This Day," from *The Union Prayer Book for Jewish Worship: Newly Revised Edition: Part II*, 1962.

Clarendon Press, Oxford, England: selections from *The Mishnah*, trans. by Herbert Danby, 1933. Reprinted by permission of Clarendon Press, Oxford.

Commentary, New York: "The Paradox of *Kol Nidre*," from "The Curious Case of *Kol Nidre*," by Herman Kieval. Reprinted from *Commentary* by permission of the author and publisher. Copyright © 1968 by the American Jewish Committee; "Yom Kippur," by Howard Harrison. Reprinted from *Commentary* by permission of the publisher. Copyright © 1955 by the American Jewish Committee.

Community, Paris, France: "Why Do You Fast on Yom Kippur?," trans. from "Pages Retrouvées," by Edmond Fleg, *Evidences*, no. 23 (January, 1952), published by the American Jewish Committee.

Dorrance & Company, Philadelphia: "*Erev* Yom Kippur," from *How Fair My Faith and Other Poems*, by Mollie R. Golomb, 1968.

Doubleday & Company, Inc., New York: "Community Confession," from THIS IS MY GOD by Herman Wouk. Copyright © 1959 by The Abe Wouk Foundation, Inc. Reprinted by permission of Doubleday & Co., Inc.; "Yom Kippur in Old San Francisco," from 920 O'FARRELL STREET by Harriet Lane Levy. Copyright © 1937, 1947, by Harriet Lane Levy. Reprinted by permission of Doubleday & Co., Inc.

Feldheim Publishers Ltd., Jerusalem, Israel: "Means to Repentance," from *The Gates of Repentance*, by Yonah ben Avraham of Gerona, trans. by Shraga Silverstein, 1967.

Harvard University Press, Cambridge: "The Sabbath of Sabbaths," reprinted by permission of the publishers, Harvard University Press, Cambridge, Mass. and THE LOEB CLASSICAL LIBRARY from *Philo*, Volume VII, F. H. Colson, translator.

Hebrew Publishing Company, New York: "Repentance Makes Atonement," from *Maimonides' Mishneh Torah*, ed. and trans. by Philip Birnbaum, copyright 1967 by Hebrew Publishing Company; "Meditation before *Kol Nidre*," "All Vows," "The Confession," "May Our Entreaty Rise to Thee," "Like the Clay in the Hand of the Potter," "We Are Thy People," and "Thou Stretchest Out a Helping Hand," from *The High Holyday Prayer Book*, trans. by Ben Zion Bokser, copyright 1959 by Hebrew Publishing Company.

Herzl Press, New York: "Yom Kippur," by Aaron David Gordon, from *The Zionist Idea: A Historical Analysis and Reader*, ed. by Arthur Hertzberg, 1959.

[v

by Schocken Books Inc.; "Out of the Depths," by S. Y. Agnon, trans. by Yoram Matmor, reprinted by permission of Schocken Books Inc. Copyright © 1967 by Schocken Books Inc.

E. S. Schwab, London, England: "Yom Kippur in Frankfort," from *Memories of Frankfort*, by Hermann Schwab, Jewish Post Publications, London, 1955.

Levi Shalit, Johannesburg, S. A.: "*Kol Nidre* in the Dachau Concentration Camp," by Levi Shalit, Munich *Unzer Velt*, October 12, 1948; translated in *High Holy Days Program*, Mizrachi Women's Organization of America, September–October, 1954.

The Soncino Press Limited, London, England: "The Death of the Righteous Atones," from *Zohar*, trans. by Harry Sperling and Maurice Simon, 1931–1934; "I Have Forgiven," from *Judaism Eternal: Selected Essays*, by Samson Raphael Hirsch, trans. by I. Grunfeld, 1956; selections from *Midrash Rabbah*, trans. under the editorship of H. Freedman and Maurice Simon, 1939–1951; selections from *The Babylonian Talmud*, trans. under the editorship of Isidore Epstein, 1935–1950. All rights reserved by The Soncino Press Limited.

Rabbi Alexander Alan Steinbach, Hollywood, Fla.: "Compassionate Father," from *Supplementary Prayers and Meditations for the High Holy Days*, prepared by Alexander Alan Steinbach, Temple Ahavath Sholom, Brooklyn, N. Y., 1961.

Twayne Publishers and Dr. Azriel Eisenberg, New York: "Forgiven," by Judah Steinberg, from *The Bas Mitzvah Treasury*, ed. by Azriel Eisenberg and Leah Ain Globe, 1965.

Union of American Hebrew Congregations, New York: "Yom Kippur in an East European Town," from *The Jewish Festivals: From Their Beginnings to Our Own Day*, by Hayyim Schauss, trans. by Samuel Jaffe, 1938; "A Little Hero of Long Ago," from *Hillel's Happy Holidays*, by Mamie G. Gamoran, 1939.

The University of Chicago Press, Chicago: "Yom Kippur in the Second Temple," from *The Apocrypha*, trans. by Edgar J. Goodspeed, published by The University of Chicago Press. Copyright 1938 by Edgar J. Goodspeed. All rights reserved.

Vallentine, Mitchell & Co. Ltd., London, England: "Why Fast?" and commentaries on "Like the Clay in the Hand of the Potter," "May God Remember," and "The Martyrdom of the Ten Sages," from *A Guide to Yom Kippur*, by Louis Jacobs, Jewish Chronicle Publications, London. Copyright 1959 by Louis Jacobs.

The Viking Press, Inc., New York: "The Search" by Sholom Aleichem, translated by Norbert Guterman, and "*Neilah* in Gehenna" by Isaac Loeb Peretz, translated by A. M. Klein, from A TREASURY OF YIDDISH STORIES edited by Irving Howe and Eliezer Greenberg. Copyright 1954 by The Viking Press, Inc. Reprinted by permission of The Viking Press, Inc.

Yale University Press, New Haven: selections from *The Fathers according to Rabbi Nathan*, trans. by Judah Goldin, 1955; "The Day of Atonement of the Falashas," from *Falasha Anthology*, by Wolf Leslau, 1951; selections from *Pesikta Rabbati: Discourses for Feasts, Fasts and Special Sabbaths*, trans. by William G. Braude, 1968; selections from *The Midrash on Psalms*, trans. by William G. Braude, 1959.

Yeshiva University, New York: "The Jewish Concept of *Teshuvah*," from "Sacred and Profane: *Kodesh* and *Chol* in World Perspectives," by Joseph B. Soloveichik, *Gesher*, vol. 3, no. 1 (June, 1966), published by Student Organization of Yeshiva.

Zionist Organization Youth and Hechalutz Department, Religious Section, Jerusalem, Israel: "Yom Kippur in Persia, 1944," by H. Z. Hirschberg, *Igeret Lagolah*, no. 28 (August, 1946); "A Day of Festivity," from *The Modern Jew Faces Eternal Problems*, by Aron Barth, trans. by Haim Shachter, 1965.

Michael Zylberberg, London, England: "Yom Kippur in the Warsaw Ghetto," by Michael Zylberberg, London *Jewish Chronicle*, no. 4,196 (September 23, 1949).

מוקדש
לנכדי
משה חיים
בן הרב יצחק ויהודית רובין

PREFACE

It is again my pleasant privilege to thank many friends who have been most helpful in editing this book. Dr. Joseph Gutmann, professor of art history, Wayne State University, and Cantor Max Wohlberg, professor of *hazzanut*, Cantors Institute, Jewish Theological Seminary of America, both of whom wrote for *The Rosh Hashanah Anthology*, kindly responded to my request and prepared, respectively, the chapters on "Yom Kippur in Art" and "The Music of the Yom Kippur Liturgy." Among others who have graciously extended their wholehearted cooperation are Dr. I. Edward Kiev, librarian of the Hebrew Union College—Jewish Institute of Religion, New York; Sylvia Landress, director of the Zionist Archives and Library; Rabbi and Mrs. Herbert Parzen; Bernard Postal, associate editor, *The Jewish Week and The American Examiner;* Rabbi Irving Rubin of Congregation Kesher Israel, West Chester, Penna.; Jacob and Ruth Schreiber, Kibbutz Heftzibah, Israel; Dora Steinglass, chief of the Jewish Division, New York Public Library. Dr. Chaim Potok and Lesser Zussman, editor and executive director, respectively, of The Jewish Publication Society of America, are responsible for initiating this anthology and making possible its publication. Kay Powell, the Society's copy editor, gave invaluable assistance in preparing the manuscript for press.

A special word of appreciation is due to Dr. Sidney B. Hoenig, professor of Jewish history, Yeshiva University, who painstakingly examined the entire manuscript and generously gave me the benefit of his vast scholarship and his constructive criticism. I am also greatly indebted to Dr. Alexander Alan Steinbach, editor of *The Jewish Book Annual* and of *In Jewish Bookland,* poet and literary critic, for his sincere interest and zealous cooperation in editing parts of the manuscript. *Aharon aharon haviv:* my wife, Hanna, gave of herself unstintingly in the creation of this volume.

PHILIP GOODMAN

New York City
Nisan 27, 5730 [1970]

INTRODUCTION

Yom Kippur, the Day of Atonement, is the holiest day in the Jewish calendar. The Bible calls it *Shabbat Shabbaton*, the "Sabbath of Sabbaths" (Lev. 23:26–32); the Talmud, simply, "the Day." During this day of complete fasting, Jews devote themselves to individual and communal repentance, *teshuvah*, returning to the right path. Occurring on the tenth day of the Jewish month of Tishrei, Yom Kippur climaxes a long period of self-examination and atonement, beginning with a month of spiritual preparation during Elul and then becoming more intensive between Rosh Hashanah, which falls on the first of Tishrei, and Yom Kippur, the tenth of the month. During these ten days, known as *aseret yeme teshuvah*, individuals are encouraged to make amends for wrongs committed against their fellow human beings and against God during the previous year.

The chief feature of Yom Kippur is a twenty-five hour fast, beginning just before sundown and culminating the next day about an hour after sundown, when the shofar is sounded in one long, final blast, marking the end of the holy day. During this twenty-five hour period, all Jews over the age of thirteen (except those whose health might be jeopardized by fasting) are obligated to refrain from all physical pleasures—specifically, eating and drinking, bathing, anointing the body with oil, wearing leather shoes, and engaging in sexual activity.

The medieval poet Yehudah Ha-Levi observed that by fasting and refraining from other earthly pleasures on this day, Jews become as pure as angels, liberated from worldly needs. Temporarily freed from material concerns, human beings can be sustained solely by prayer and closeness to God's Presence; they can devote themselves to their souls, take spiritual inventory, *heshbon ha-nefesh*, and thus atone for previous shortcomings and sins. On this day, many traditional Jews wear a white kittel, a simple white garment in which one will ultimately be buried, symbolizing both the transience of the flesh and the purity of the soul.

Yom Kippur begins with the evening service of Kol Nidre ("all vows"), during which the liturgy introduces the main themes of the day: communal confession of sins, individual atonement, and divine compassion. Throughout the day, these themes are voiced repeatedly. The unique traditional and contemporary Yom Kippur liturgy contains many special additions: biblical excerpts describing the ancient scapegoat ceremony performed by the High Priest on this day; the inspiring hymn *unetanneh tokef*, affirming at its close that "repentance, prayer and righteousness *(tzedakah)* annul the severity of the divine decree"; the Martyrology, recounting the sufferings of the Jewish people from ancient times to the Holocaust in our own time; the Yizkor memorial service; and a description of the awesome ritual once performed by the High Priest, who on this one day of the year would enter the Holy of Holies in the Jerusalem Temple and utter the Four-Letter Name of God, emerging to declare that God had once again forgiven the people's sins. Since the theme of repentance is central to the Book of Jonah, this book is recited during the afternoon Minhah service.

In ancient Israel, young women would dress in white on the afternoon of Yom Kippur and dance in the fields; young men would meet them there and choose brides (Ta'anit 4:8). This ancient custom may have given rise to the practice of reading about forbidden sexual relations during the afternoon Torah service on Yom Kippur (Lev. 18).

Because Yom Kippur marks the end of this special forty-day period of repentance, it is characterized by a sense of urgency and solemnity. The phrase, "Write us in the Book of Life," which is recited throughout Rosh Hashanah, is changed on the evening of this day to "Seal us in the Book of Life." The final service of *Ne'ilah* reminds worshipers that the Gates of Compassion are about to close. The day ends with a long blast of the shofar, sounding a final appeal for God's forgiveness as well as proclaiming the hope for messianic redemption. Similar to the conclusion of the Passover seder, the day ends with the proclamation: *"L'shana ha-ba'ah bi-Yerushalayim!"*—"Next Year in Jerusalem!"

It is traditional to hammer the first nail into one's sukkah immediately after the end of Yom Kippur to symbolize the link between these two festival periods and to affirm the continuity of life, for once confession has been made and atonement achieved, each individual must resume with renewed vigor the holy task of caring for and repairing our as-yet-unredeemed world.

The eighteen sections of *The Yom Kippur Anthology* provide valuable resource materials for teachers, rabbis, parents, students, and newcomers to Judaism. The first five sections—"Yom Kippur in the Bible," "Yom Kippur in Postbiblical Writings," "Yom Kippur in Talmud and Midrash," "Yom Kippur in Medieval Jewish Literature," and "Yom Kippur in Jewish Law"—present traditional texts for study and historical background. The next two sections—"Selected Prayers" and "The Paradox of *Kol Nidre*"—provide valuable source material to enhance one's appreciation and understanding of the *Mahzor*, the special High Holyday prayerbook. In this section can be found the texts of many classic Yom Kippur prayers, with commentaries by such noted scholars as Rav Kook, Hermann Cohen, Louis Jacobs, Max Arzt, and Morris Silverman. Other sections—"Yom Kippur in Many Lands," "Pre-Yom Kippur Feasting," and "Yom Kippur Miscellany"—provide fascinating background information about Yom Kippur observances throughout the world, in both ancient and modern times. These selections include folklore, customs, and historical anecdotes that testify to the powerful influence this holiday has exercised on Jewish communities for centuries. Joseph Gutmann's "Yom Kippur in Art" and Max Wohlberg's "The Music of the Yom Kippur Liturgy" demonstrate the rich aesthetic heritage inspired by this holiday. The volume also includes numerous illustrations and photographs that depict scenes and artifacts representative of traditional observances of this holiday.

One of the unique features of this anthology is the abundant selection of both secular and religious literature written on the themes of Yom Kippur. These include Hasidic tales and teachings, culled from the rich treasury of lore once so popular in the Eastern European shtetl and today enjoying a remarkable revival in America, as well as essays by such noted writers as Franz Rosenzweig, Samson Raphael Hirsch, Herman Wouk, S. Anski, and Joseph Soloveitchik. An additional section features short stories by such famous masters as Martin Buber, I. L. Peretz, Shmuel Yosef Agnon, and Sholom Aleichem.

Parents and teachers will find in this anthology two sections especially designed for children. There are classic stories such as Sadie Rose Weilerstein's "How K'tonton Was Forgiven on Yom Kippur" and Howard Fast's "Haym Salomon—Son of Liberty" as well as a number of children's poems appropriate for various age groups. Teachers and parents can also adapt selections from "Yom Kippur in Many Lands" and "Yom Kippur Miscellany" for classroom or home use.

The Bible recounts that when Moses descended Mount Sinai after receiving the Ten Commandments and found his people worshiping a Golden Calf, he shattered the tablets in great anger. Later, he ascended Mount Sinai a second time to receive a new set of tablets. According to Jewish tradition, it was on the first of Elul that he went up the mountain, and it was on Yom Kippur that he returned with the new tablets. During the forty days that Moses was gone, the people fasted from sunrise to sunset and, on the fortieth day, from sunset to sunset. When Moses finally came down the mountain carrying the new Tablets of the Law, he found the people weeping, and he too wept. Only then did God accept their repentance for the sin of the Golden Calf, declaring the tenth of Tishrei a Day of Atonement for all future generations (Eliyahu Zuta 42).

Another tradition teaches that the people of Israel kept both sets of tablets in the ark as they traveled through the wilderness and that these two sets remained in the Holy of Holies once the Temple was built in Jerusalem.

Symbolically, these two sets of tablets represent several ideas: that our hearts, whether whole or broken, are always holy in God's eyes; that we are a people capable of both sin and faithfulness; that our history contains transcendent moments as well as moments of great shame; that we have much repair work to do, both within ourselves and within the world.

All these themes are sounded on Yom Kippur. The Baal Shem Tov, founder of Hasidism, taught that there are many keys to unlock the gates of repentance, but that the ax—that is, the sincere prayer of a broken heart—is the mightiest key of all, capable of shattering even the strongest gate. Similarly, Rabbi Nahman of Bratzlav taught that nothing is as whole as a broken heart. On Yom Kippur we knock with urgency and trepidation on heaven's gate, hoping that our forty days of soul-searching and atonement have been sincere enough to qualify as true *teshuvah*, returning to the right path, turning away from old habits of mind and character. Each of us carries within us both the broken tablets of our past misdeeds and the newly hewn tablets of God's forgiveness. As the shofar sounds its final *tekiah gedolah* at the end of Yom Kippur, we release our angel and come back to earth to wrestle with our imperfections and wayward hearts. And we hope that our angel has left us a blessing.

ELLEN FRANKEL

Philadelphia
1992/5752

CONTENTS

Preface XIII
Introduction XV
List of Illustrations XXXI

I   YOM KIPPUR IN THE BIBLE   3

     A Sacred Occasion   4
     Proclamation of a Jubilee   5
     The Temple Ritual on the Day of Atonement   5
     The Purpose of Fasting   7
     The Book of Jonah   9

II   YOM KIPPUR IN POSTBIBLICAL WRITINGS   12

     Yom Kippur in the Second Temple   13
         from *Ben Sira*
     The Institution of Yom Kippur   15
         from *Book of Jubilees*
     The Sabbath of Sabbaths   16
         by Philo of Alexandria

III   YOM KIPPUR IN TALMUD AND MIDRASH   20

     The Origins   21
     The Observance   22

Atonement of Sins   24
The Fast   30
Acts of Loving-kindness   31
The High Priest's Preparations   32
Prayers   35

IV   YOM KIPPUR IN MEDIEVAL JEWISH LITERATURE   36
The Fast of a Pious Man   37
   by Judah Halevi
The Reason for the Fast of Atonement   38
   by Moses Maimonides
The Rebuke to the Sinner   38
   by Abraham Bar Hiyya
A Means to Repentance   39
   by Jonah ben Abraham Gerondi
Never Too Late to Repent   40
   by Israel ibn Al-Nakawa
The Death of the Righteous Atones   41
   from the *Zohar*

V   YOM KIPPUR IN JEWISH LAW   43
Repentance Makes Atonement   44
   by Moses Maimonides
Laws for the Eve of the Day of Atonement   45
   by Solomon Ganzfried
Laws for the Day of Atonement   46
   by Solomon Ganzfried

VI   SELECTED PRAYERS   48
The Father's Blessing on the Eve of Yom Kippur   49
Prayer for Yom Kippur   50
   from *Union Prayer Book*
We Stand before Our God   52
   by Leo Baeck
      Commentary   53

Meditation before *Kol Nidre*   53
   by Abraham Isaac Kook

All Vows   54
        Commentary by Max Arzt   55

The Confession   56
        Commentary by Hermann Cohen   59

May Our Entreaty Rise to Thee   60
        Commentary by Morris Silverman   61

"Forgiven"   62
   by Yom Tov ben Isaac of York
        Commentary by Bernard Martin   63

Like the Clay in the Hand of the Potter   64
        Commentary by Louis Jacobs   65

Hear Our Voice   65
        Commentary by Max Arzt   66

We Are Thy People   66
        Commentary by Max Arzt   67

May God Remember   68
        Commentary by Louis Jacobs   68

The Martyrdom of the Ten Sages   70
        Commentary by Louis Jacobs   72

Thou Stretchest Out a Helping Hand   73
        Commentary by Max Arzt   74

God, That Doest Wondrously   75
   by Moses ibn Ezra
        Commentary by Julius H. Greenstone   76

Open unto Us the Gate   77
        Commentary by Max Arzt   77

Lord, I Remember   78
   by Amittai ben Shefatiah
        Commentary by Max Arzt   79

Lord, Thine Humble Servants Hear   79
   by Judah Halevi

The Declaration of Faith   80
        Commentary   80
    We Stand before Thee on This Day   82
        from *Union Prayer Book*

VII   THE PARADOX OF *KOL NIDRE*   84
        by Herman Kieval

VIII   THE MUSIC OF THE YOM KIPPUR LITURGY   99
        by Max Wohlberg
    Musical Examples   103

IX   HASIDIC TALES AND TEACHINGS   113

X   YOM KIPPUR IN MODERN PROSE   124
    Every Day Is a Day of Atonement   124
        by S. Anski
    A Day of Festivity   125
        by Aron Barth
    The Import of the *Kapparot* Ceremony   126
        by Julius H. Greenstone
    Why Fast?   128
        by Louis Jacobs
    Why Do You Fast on Yom Kippur?   130
        by Edmond Fleg
    The Distinguishing Characteristic of the
        Days of Awe   133
        by Franz Rosenzweig
    Repentance in Judaism   134
        by Bernard J. Bamberger
    "I Have Forgiven"   136
        by Samson Raphael Hirsch
    Community Confession   137
        by Herman Wouk

The Jewish Idea of Atonement   139
     by Leo Baeck
The Sinner and His Penitence   141
     by Samuel Belkin
The Jewish Concept of *Teshuvah*   142
     by Joseph B. Soloveichik
Go to Nineveh   146
     by Hayim Greenberg
Yom Kippur   150
     by Aaron David Gordon
Franz Rosenzweig's Self-discovery   152
     by Nahum N. Glatzer
The Revelation of *Neilah*   153
     by Aimé Pallière

XI   YOM KIPPUR IN ART   156
          by Joseph Gutmann

XII   YOM KIPPUR IN MANY LANDS   163
     Yom Kippur in the Days of the Second Temple   163
          by Solomon ibn Verga
     Marranos and the Day of Purity   166
          by Cecil Roth
     The Day of Atonement of the Falashas   167
          by Wolf Leslau
     The Atonement Day of the Bene-Israel   168
          by Haeem Samuel Kehimkar
     With the Jews of Libya   170
          by Devora and Menahem Hacohen
     Atonement Day among Persian Jews   171
          by Devora and Menahem Hacohen
     Yom Kippur in Persia, 1944   172
          by H. Z. Hirschberg

Yom Kippur in an East European Town   173
    by Hayyim Schauss
Day of Atonement in Vitebsk, Russia   179
    by Bella Chagall
Yom Kippur in Kasrielevky   186
    by Maurice Samuel
Yom Kippur in Frankfort   188
    by Hermann Schwab
The Great White Fast in the London Ghetto   189
    by Israel Zangwill
Yom Kippur in Old San Francisco   192
    by Harriet Lane Levy
Yom Kippur in Brownsville   199
    by Chaver Paver
The Two-Day Yom Kippur in Japan   201
    by David Kranzler
Yom Kippur in the Warsaw Ghetto   204
    by Michael Zylberberg
Kol Nidre in the Dachau Concentration Camp   208
    by Levi Shalit
Yom Kippur in Korea   212
    by Billy Rose
Yom Kippur at the Viet Front   214
    by Barry Cunningham
Yom Kippur in Moscow   215
    by Elie Wiesel

XIII   YOM KIPPUR IN POETRY   219

Erev Yom Kippur   219
    by Mollie R. Golomb
The Tzaddik's Defense   220
    by Rufus Learsi
Kol Nidre   225
    by Zeev Falk

Yom Kippur   226
     by Israel Zangwill
Yom Kippur   228
     by Jessie E. Sampter
Atonement   232
     by Ruth F. Brin
Confession   233
     by Solomon ibn Gabirol
Day of Atonement   235
     by Gustav Gottheil
Day of Atonement   236
     by Abraham Vieviorka
Compassionate Father   236
     by Alexander Alan Steinbach
Day of Atonement   237
     by Charles Reznikoff
Yom Kippur   238
     by Howard Harrison
Yom Kippur   240
     by Ben A. Sochachevsky
Neilah   241
     by Fania Kruger

XIV   YOM KIPPUR IN THE SHORT STORY   243

The Prayer Book   243
     by Martin Buber
The Boy's Song   247
     by Meyer Levin
Out of the Depths   249
     by Shmuel Yosef Agnon
Three Who Ate   256
     by David Frishman
The Miracle on the Sea   262
     by Isaac Loeb Peretz

Neilah in Gehenna   269
      by Isaac Loeb Peretz
A Savior of the People   276
      by Karl Emil Franzos
Yom Kippur   283
      by Eliezer David Rosenthal
The Day without Forgiveness   297
      by Elie Wiesel
The Call   303
      by Victor Barwin
The Search   312
      by Sholom Aleichem

xv   PRE-YOM KIPPUR FEASTING   319

xvi   YOM KIPPUR MISCELLANY   323

Names   323
Two Days of Yom Kippur   324
The Minor Yom Kippur   324
Parallels in Islam   325
"Next Year in Jerusalem"   325
The *Shofar* at the Western Wall   326
Yom Kippur Likened to Wedding Day   327
Candles for Yom Kippur   327
Forty Days and Nights of Silence   329
The Number Ten   329
A Deceptive Appearance   329
An Emergency Decree   330
An Order to Eat   330
Nut Games   330
Yom Kippur Balls   330
A Yom Kippur Blood Libel in New York   331
Yom Kippur in the *Kibbutz*   332

xvii CHILDREN'S STORIES FOR YOM KIPPUR 336

How K'tonton Was Forgiven on Yom Kippur 336
    by Sadie Rose Weilerstein
I'm Sorry 341
    by Sadie Rose Weilerstein
Innocent 343
    by Levin Kipnis
A Little Hero of Long Ago 346
    by Mamie G. Gamoran
The Tear of Repentance 350
    by Dorothy F. Zeligs
Haym Salomon—Son of Liberty 351
    by Howard Fast
Forgiven 355
    by Judah Steinberg
The Day of Decisions 359
    by Ruben Rothgiesser

xviii CHILDREN'S POEMS FOR YOM KIPPUR 368

Kol Nidre 368
    by Ben Aronin
Fasting 369
    by Sadie Rose Weilerstein
Atonement 369
    by Jessie E. Sampter
A Dream 369
    by Jessie E. Sampter
Yom Kippur Eve 370
    by Constantine A. Shapiro
Atonement 371
    by Alexander M. Dushkin

Notes 374
Glossary of Yom Kippur Terms 385

Bibliography   387
General References   387
Yom Kippur in Jewish Law   391
The Liturgy of Yom Kippur   391
Yom Kippur in the Short Story   392
Children's Stories and Descriptions of
    Yom Kippur   394
Collections with Yom Kippur Music   397
Recordings   398
Program and Audio-Visual Materials   398

ILLUSTRATIONS

1. *Mahzor.* Germany. 14th century. Library of the
   Hungarian Academy of Sciences, Budapest, Ms.
   A 387, fol. 350. Courtesy of the Hungarian Academy of Sciences.   17
2. *Mahzor.* Germany. Circa 1320. University Library, Leipzig, Ms. V 1102/II, fol. 74v. Courtesy
   of Karl Marx University, Leipzig.   33
3. *Mahzor.* Germany. Early 14th century. University
   Library, Breslau (Wroclaw), Ms. Or. I, fol. 89v.   51
4. *Mahzor.* Ulm, Germany. 1459–60. Bayerische
   Staatsbibliothek, Munchen, Ms. Hebr. 3/I, fol.
   48. Courtesy of Bayerische Staatsbibliothek,
   Munchen.   69
5. *Mahzor.* Germany. Circa 1320. University Library, Leipzig, Ms. V 1102/II, fol. 164v. Courtesy
   of Karl Marx University, Leipzig.   81
6. *Mahzor.* Germany. Circa 1320. University Library, Leipzig, Ms. V 1102/II, fol. 129v. Courtesy
   of Karl Marx University, Leipzig.   97
7. White tablecloth with gold brocade appliqué.
   Oberzell, Germany. 1781. Strauss-Rothschild Collection of the Cluny Museum, Paris. Courtesy of
   Cluny Museum. Picture from Photographic Archive of The Jewish Theological Seminary of
   America, New York, Frank J. Darmstaedter.   145
8. Belt buckle for Yom Kippur. Silver. Poland. 19th

century. Harry G. Friedman Collection, The Jewish Museum, New York. Courtesy of Jewish Museum. Picture from Photographic Archive of The
Jewish Theological Seminary of America, New
York, Frank J. Darmstaedter.   161

9. Belt buckle for Yom Kippur. Silver. Eastern Eu-
    rope. 19th century. Courtesy of Museum of the
    Hebrew Union College-Jewish Institute of Reli-
    gion, Cincinnati.   161

10. Torah shield. Silver. Poland. Late 18th century.
    Courtesy of Museum of Hebrew Union College-
    Jewish Institute of Religion, Cincinnati.   177

11. Yom Kippur scenes. From *Kirchliche Verfassung
    der heutigen Juden*, by Johann C. G. Boden-
    schatz, Erlang, 1748. Picture from the Pho-
    tographic Archive of The Jewish Theological
    Seminary of America, New York, Frank J.
    Darmstaedter.   193

12. Yom Kippur scenes. From *Der Juden Glaube und
    Aberglaube*, by Friedrich A. Christiani, Leipzig,
    1705. Picture from New York Public Library.   209

13. "The Prayer." Sculpture. By Jacques Lipchitz.
    1943. Collection of the Philadelphia Museum of
    Art. Photograph by A. J. Wyatt. Courtesy of
    Jacques Lipchitz and Philadelphia Museum of Art.   231

14. Yom Kippur scenes. From *Juedishes Ceremoniel*,
    by Paul C. Kirchner, Nuremberg, 1726. Picture
    from Photographic Archive of The Jewish Theo-
    logical Seminary of America, New York, Frank
    J. Darmstaedter.   239

15. "*Kol Nidre* Eve." Painting. By Moritz Oppenheim
    (1800–1882). From *The Jewish Year . . . Paint-
    ings by Professor Moritz Oppenheim*, Philadel-
    phia, 1895. Picture from New York Public Li-
    brary.   257

16. Yom Kippur in a synagogue in Amsterdam. From
    Cérémonies et coutumes religieuses, by Ber-
    nard Picart, Amsterdam, 1723. Picture from
    Photographic Archive of The Jewish Theologi-
    cal Seminary of America, New York, Frank J.
    Darmstaedter.   273

17. "The Cantor." By Marc Chagall. Reprinted by permission of Schocken Books Inc. from *Burning Lights*, by Bella Chagall, with drawings by Marc Chagall. Copyright © 1946 by Schocken Books Inc.   289

18. "Jews at Prayer on the Day of Atonement." Oil painting on canvas. By Maurycy Gottlieb (1856–1879). Courtesy of Tel Aviv Museum, owner. Photograph by I. Zafrir, Tel Aviv.   305

19. *Kapparot.* Courtesy of Ministry for Foreign Affairs, State of Israel.   321

20. The meal before the Yom Kippur fast. Courtesy of Ministry for Foreign Affairs, State of Israel.   339

21. Blessing the children on the eve of Yom Kippur. Courtesy of Israel Information Services, New York.   353

I

YOM KIPPUR IN THE BIBLE

As the keynote of Yom Kippur, the Bible emphasizes self-denial, which the rabbis later interpreted in several ways, including fasting. The prophet Isaiah elucidates the ultimate purpose of a fast day.

During the periods of the Temple the predominant feature of the Day of Atonement was the elaborate Temple ritual, as recorded in the Bible. On this day only the high priest entered the holy of holies to make atonement for his sins and for those of the Israelites.

The Book of Jonah, identified in the Talmud (Taanit 15a) with fasting and stressing God's mercy to those who repent, is therefore a most appropriate Scripture reading for the Day of Atonement.

A SACRED OCCASION

The Lord spoke to Moses, saying: Mark, the tenth day of this seventh month is the Day of Atonement. It shall be a sacred occasion for you: you shall practice self-denial, and you shall bring an offering by fire to the Lord; you shall do no work throughout that day. For it is a Day of Atonement, on which expiation is made on your behalf before the Lord your God. Indeed, any person who does not practice self-denial throughout that day shall be cut off from his kin; and whoever does any work throughout that day, I will cause that person to perish from among his people. Do no work whatever; it is a law for all time, throughout the generations in all your settlements. It shall be a sabbath of complete rest for you, and you shall practice self-denial; on the ninth day of the month at evening, from evening to evening, you shall observe this your sabbath.

Leviticus 23.26–32[1]

On the tenth day of the same seventh month you shall observe a sacred occasion when you shall practice self-denial. You shall do no work. You shall present to the Lord a burnt offering of pleasing ódor: one bull of the herd, one ram, seven yearling lambs; see that they are without blemish. The meal offering with them—of choice flour with oil mixed in—shall be: three-tenths of a measure for a bull, two-tenths for the one ram, one-tenth for each of the seven lambs. And there shall be one goat for a sin offering, in addition to the sin offering of expiation and the regular burnt offering with its meal offering, each with its libation.

Numbers 29.7–11

And this shall be to you a law for all time: In the seventh month, on the tenth day of the month, you shall practice self-denial; and you shall do no manner of work, neither the citizen nor the alien who resides among you. For on this day atonement shall be made for you to cleanse you of all your sins; you shall be clean before the Lord. It shall be a sabbath of complete rest

for you, and you shall practice self-denial; it is a law for all
time. The priest who has been anointed and ordained to serve
as priest in place of his father shall make expiation. He shall
put on the linen vestments, the sacral vestments. He shall
purge the innermost Shrine; he shall purge the Tent of Meeting
and the altar; and he shall make expiation for the priests and
for all the people of the congregation.

This shall be to you a law for all time: to make atonement for
the Israelites for all their sins once a year.

Leviticus 16.29–34

PROCLAMATION OF A JUBILEE

You shall count off seven weeks of years—seven times seven
years—so that the period of seven weeks of years gives you a
total of forty-nine years. Then you shall sound the horn loud;
in the seventh month, on the tenth day of the month—the Day
of Atonement—you shall have the horn sounded throughout
your land and you shall hallow the fiftieth year. You shall proclaim liberty throughout the land for all its inhabitants. It shall
be a jubilee for you: each of you shall return to his holding and
each of you shall return to his family.

Leviticus 25.8–10

THE TEMPLE RITUAL ON THE DAY OF ATONEMENT

The Lord said to Moses:

Tell your brother Aaron that he is not to come at will into the
Shrine behind the curtain, in front of the cover that is upon
the ark, lest he die; for I appear in the cloud over the cover.
Thus only shall Aaron enter the Shrine: with a bull of the herd
for a sin offering and a ram for a burnt offering. He shall be
dressed in a sacral linen tunic, with linen breeches next to his
flesh, and be girt with a linen sash, and he shall wear a linen
turban; they are sacral vestments. He shall bathe his body in
water and then put them on. And from the Israelite community

he shall take two he-goats for a sin offering and a ram for a burnt offering.

Aaron is to offer his own bull of sin offering, to make expiation for himself and for his household. Aaron shall take the two he-goats and let them stand before the Lord at the entrance of the Tent of Meeting; and he shall place lots upon the two goats, one marked for the Lord and the other marked for Azazel. Aaron shall bring forward the goat designated by lot for the Lord, which he is to offer as a sin offering; while the goat designated by lot for Azazel shall be left standing alive before the Lord, to make expiation with it and to send it off to the wilderness for Azazel.

Aaron shall then offer his bull of sin offering, to make expiation for himself and his household. He shall slaughter his bull of sin offering, and he shall take a panful of glowing coals scooped from the altar before the Lord, and two handfuls of finely ground aromatic incense, and bring this behind the curtain. He shall put the incense on the fire before the Lord, so that the cloud from the incense screens the cover that is over [the Ark of] the Pact, lest he die. He shall take some of the blood of the bull and sprinkle it with his finger over the cover on the east side; and in front of the cover he shall sprinkle some of the blood with his finger seven times. He shall then slaughter the people's goat of sin offering, bring its blood behind the curtain, and do with its blood as he has done with the blood of the bull: he shall sprinkle it over the cover and in front of the cover.

Thus he shall purge the Shrine of the uncleanness and transgression of the Israelites, whatever their sins; and he shall do the same for the Tent of Meeting, which abides with them in the midst of their uncleanness. When he goes in to make expiation in the Shrine, nobody else shall be in the Tent of Meeting until he comes out.

When he has made expiation for himself and his household, and for the whole congregation of Israel, he shall go out to the altar that is before the Lord and purge it. He shall take some of the blood of the bull and of the goat and apply it to each of the horns of the altar; and the rest of the blood he shall sprinkle on it with his finger seven times. Thus he shall cleanse it of the uncleanness of the Israelites and consecrate it.

When he has finished purging the Shrine, the Tent of Meeting, and the altar, the live goat shall be brought forward. Aaron shall lay both his hands upon the head of the live goat and confess over it all the iniquities and transgressions of the Israelites, whatever their sins, putting them on the head of the goat; and it shall be sent off to the wilderness through a designated man. Thus the goat shall carry on him all their iniquities to an inaccessible region; and the goat shall be set free in the wilderness.

And Aaron shall go into the Tent of Meeting, take off the linen vestments that he put on when he entered the Shrine, and leave them there. He shall bathe his body in water in the holy precinct and put on his vestments; then he shall come out and offer his burnt offering and the burnt offering of the people, making expiation for himself and for the people. The fat of the sin offering he shall turn into smoke on the altar.

He who set the goat for Azazel free shall wash his clothes and bathe his body in water; after that he may re-enter the camp.

The bull of sin offering and the goat of sin offering whose blood was brought in to purge the Shrine shall be taken outside the camp; and their hides, flesh, and dung shall be consumed in fire. He who burned them shall wash his clothes and bathe his body in water; after that he may re-enter the camp.

Leviticus 16.2–28

THE PURPOSE OF FASTING*

Cry aloud, spare not,
Lift up thy voice like a horn,
And declare unto My people their transgression,
And to the house of Jacob their sins.
Yet they seek Me daily,
And delight to know My ways;

* From the *haftarah* for Yom Kippur morning.

As a nation that did righteousness,
And forsook not the ordinance of their God,
They ask of Me righteous ordinances,
They delight to draw near unto God.

"Wherefore have we fasted, and Thou seest not?
Wherefore have we afflicted our soul, and Thou takest no
        knowledge?"—
Behold, in the day of your fast ye pursue your business,
And exact all your labours.
Behold, ye fast for strife and contention,
And to smite with the fist of wickedness;
Ye fast not this day
So as to make your voice to be heard on high.
Is such the fast that I have chosen?
The day for a man to afflict his soul?
Is it to bow down his head as a bulrush,
And to spread sackcloth and ashes under him?
Wilt thou call this a fast,
And an acceptable day to the Lord?
Is not this the fast that I have chosen?
To loose the fetters of wickedness,
To undo the bands of the yoke,
And to let the oppressed go free,
And that ye break every yoke?
Is it not to deal thy bread to the hungry,
And that thou bring the poor that are cast out to thy house?
When thou seest the naked, that thou cover him,
And that thou hide not thyself from thine own flesh?
Then shall thy light break forth as the morning,
And thy healing shall spring forth speedily;
And thy righteousness shall go before thee,
The glory of the Lord shall be thy reward.
Then shalt thou call, and the Lord will answer;
Thou shalt cry, and He will say: "Here I am."
If thou take away from the midst of thee the yoke,
The putting forth of the finger, and speaking wickedness;

And if thou draw out thy soul to the hungry,
And satisfy the afflicted soul;
Then shall thy light rise in darkness,
And thy gloom be as the noonday;
And the Lord will guide thee continually,
And satisfy thy soul in drought,
And make strong thy bones;
And thou shalt be like a watered garden,
And like a spring of water, whose waters fail not.

                                        Isaiah 58.1–11[2]

THE BOOK OF JONAH*

The word of the Lord came to Jonah son of Amittai: Go at once to Nineveh, that great city, and proclaim judgment upon it; for their wickedness has come before Me.

Jonah, however, started out to flee to Tarshish from the Lord's service. He went down to Joppa and found a ship going to Tarshish. He paid the fare and went aboard to sail with the others to Tarshish, away from the service of the Lord.

But the Lord cast a mighty wind upon the sea, and such a tempest came upon the sea that the ship was in danger of breaking up. In their fright, the sailors cried out, each to his own god; and they flung the ship's cargo overboard to make it lighter for them. Jonah, meanwhile, had gone down into the hold of the vessel, where he lay down and fell asleep. The captain went over to him and cried out, "How can you be sleeping so soundly! Up, call upon your god! Perhaps the god will be kind to us and we will not perish."

The men said to one another, "Let us cast lots and find out on whose account this misfortune has come upon us." They cast lots and the lot fell on Jonah. They said to him, "Tell us, you who have brought this misfortune upon us, what is your business? Where have you come from? What is your country, and of what people are you?" "I am a Hebrew," he replied, "I

* Read as the *haftarah* on Yom Kippur afternoon.

worship the Lord, the God of Heaven, who made both sea and land." The men were greatly terrified, and they asked him, "What have you done?" And when the men learned that he was fleeing from the service of the Lord—for so he told them—they said to him, "What must we do to you to make the sea calm around us?" For the sea was growing more and more stormy. He answered, "Heave me overboard, and the sea will calm down for you; for I know that this terrible storm came upon you on my account." Nevertheless, the men rowed hard to regain the shore, but they could not, for the sea was growing more and more stormy about them. Then they cried out to the Lord: "Oh, please, Lord, do not let us perish on account of this man's life. Do not hold us guilty of killing an innocent person! For You, O Lord, by Your will, have brought this about." And they heaved Jonah overboard, and the sea stopped raging.

The men feared the Lord greatly; they offered a sacrifice to the Lord and they made vows.

The Lord provided a huge fish to swallow Jonah; and Jonah remained in the fish's belly three days and three nights. Jonah prayed to the Lord his God from the belly of the fish. . . .

The Lord commanded the fish, and it spewed Jonah out upon dry land.

The word of the Lord came to Jonah a second time: "Go at once to Nineveh, that great city, and proclaim to it what I tell you." Jonah went at once to Nineveh in accordance with the Lord's command.

Nineveh was an enormously large city, a three days' walk across. Jonah started out and made his way into the city the distance of one day's walk, and proclaimed: "Forty days more, and Nineveh shall be overthrown!"

The people of Nineveh believed God. They proclaimed a fast, and great and small alike put on sackcloth. When the news reached the king of Nineveh, he rose from his throne, took off his robe, put on sackcloth, and sat in ashes. And he had the word cried through Nineveh: "By decree of the king and his nobles: No man or beast—of flock or herd—shall taste anything!

They shall not graze, and they shall not drink water! They shall be covered with sackcloth—man and beast—and shall cry mightily to God. Let everyone turn back from his evil ways, and from the injustice of which he is guilty. Who knows but that God may turn and relent? He may turn back from His wrath, so that we do not perish."

God saw what they did, how they were turning back from their evil ways. And God renounced the punishment He had planned to bring upon them, and did not carry it out.

This displeased Jonah greatly, and he was grieved. He prayed to the Lord, saying, "O Lord! Isn't this just what I said when I was still in my own country? That is why I fled beforehand to Tarshish. For I know that You are a compassionate and gracious God, slow to anger, abounding in kindness, renouncing punishment. Please, Lord, take my life, for I would rather die than live." The Lord replied, "Are you that deeply grieved?"

Now Jonah had left the city and found a place east of the city. He made a booth there and sat under it in the shade, until he should see what happened to the city. The Lord God provided a ricinus plant, which grew up over Jonah, to provide shade for his head and save him from discomfort. Jonah was very happy about the plant. But the next day at dawn God provided a worm, which attacked the plant so that it withered. And when the sun rose, God provided a sultry east wind; the sun beat down on Jonah's head, and he became faint. He begged for death, saying, "I would rather die than live." Then God said to Jonah, "Are you so deeply grieved about the plant?" "Yes," he replied, "so deeply that I want to die."

Then the Lord said: "You cared about the plant, which you did not work for and which you did not grow, which appeared overnight and perished overnight. And should not I care about Nineveh, that great city, in which there are more than a hundred and twenty thousand persons who do not yet know their right hand from their left, and many beasts as well!"

Jonah 1.1–2.2, 2.11–4.11[3]

II

YOM KIPPUR IN
POSTBIBLICAL WRITINGS

▼▼▼

From about 330 B.C.E. to about 200 C.E., Diaspora Jewry created a number of outstanding literary works in the Greek language, among them the Septuagint, a Greek version of the Pentateuch translated by Jews in Alexandria. The other books of the Bible were translated later. The present text of the Septuagint contains additional, or "hidden," books known as the Apocrypha. The selection below is from the Apocryphal Ben Sira *(Ecclesiasticus in Greek).*

The Book of Jubilees, *considered a significant source of Jewish law, was composed during the second century B.C.E. A pseudepigraphical work, it is a commentary, or midrash, on Genesis and parts of Exodus.*

Among other significant postbiblical writings are the works of Philo of Alexandria (c. 20 B.C.E. to c. 50 C.E.), who sought to merge contemporary Hellenistic philosophy with a literal, pious acceptance of Scripture.

▼▼▼

YOM KIPPUR IN THE SECOND TEMPLE

It was Simon, the son of Onias, the great priest,
Who in his lifetime repaired the house,
And in his days strengthened the sanctuary.
He laid the foundation for the height of the double wall,
The lofty substructure for the temple inclosure.
In his days a water cistern was hewed out,
A reservoir in circumference like the sea,
He took thought for his people to keep them from calamity,
And fortified the city against siege.
How glorious he was, surrounded by the people,
As he came out of the sanctuary!
Like the morning star among the clouds,
Like the moon when it is full;
Like the sun shining forth upon the sanctuary of the Most High;
Like the rainbow, showing itself among glorious clouds,
Like roses in the days of first fruits,
Like lilies by a spring of water,
Like a sprig of frankincense, on summer days,
Like fire and incense in the censer,
Like a dish of beaten gold,
Adorned with all kinds of precious stones;
Like an olive putting forth its fruit,
And like a cypress towering among the clouds.
When he assumed his glorious robe,
And put on glorious perfection,
And when he went up to the holy altar,
He made the court of the sanctuary glorious.
And when he received the portions from the hands of the priests,
As he stood by the hearth of the altar,
With his brothers like a wreath about him,
He was like a young cedar of Lebanon,
And they surrounded him like the trunks of palm trees,
All the descendants of Aaron in their splendor,
With the Lord's offering in their hands,

Before the whole assembly of Israel;
And when he finished the service at the altars,
To adorn the offering of the Most High, the Almighty,
He stretched out his hand to the cup,
And poured out some of the blood of the grape;
He poured it out at the foot of the altar,
A fragrant odor unto the Most High, the King of All.
Then the descendants of Aaron shouted;
They sounded the trumpets of beaten work;
They made a great sound heard,
For a reminder, before the Most High.
Then all the people made haste together,
And fell upon their faces on the ground,
To worship their Lord,
The Almighty, the Most High.
The singers too praised Him with their voices;
They made sweet music in the fullest volume.
And the people intreated the Lord Most High,
With prayer before Him who is merciful,
Until the worship of the Lord should be finished,
And they completed His service.
Then he came down and lifted his hands
Over the whole assembly of the descendants of Israel,
To pronounce the blessing of the Lord with his lips,
And to exult in His Name.
And they prostrated themselves a second time,
To receive the blessing from the Most High.
   Now bless the God of all,
Who in every way does great things;
Who exalts our days from our birth,
And deals with us according to His mercy.
May He give us gladness of heart,
And may there be peace in our days
In Israel, and through the days of eternity.
May He intrust His mercy to us,
And let Him deliver us in our days.

Ben Sira 50.1–24[1]

THE INSTITUTION OF YOM KIPPUR

He [Jacob] sent Joseph to learn about the welfare of his brothers from his house to the land of Shechem, and he found them in the land of Dothan. And they dealt treacherously with him, and formed a plot against him to slay him, but changing their minds, they sold him to Ishmaelite merchants, and they brought him down into Egypt, and they sold him to Potiphar, the eunuch of Pharaoh, the chief of the cooks, priest of the city of Elev. And the sons of Jacob slaughtered a kid, and dipped the coat of Joseph in the blood and sent [it] to Jacob their father on the tenth of the seventh month. And he mourned all that night, for they had brought it to him in the evening, and he became feverish with mourning for his death, and he said: "An evil beast hath devoured Joseph"; and all the members of his house were grieving and mourning with him all that day. And his sons and daughters rose up to comfort him, but he refused to be comforted for his son. And on that day Bilhah heard that Joseph had perished, and she died mourning him, and she was living in Qafratef, and Dinah also, his daughter, died after Joseph had perished. And there came these three mournings upon Israel in one month. And they buried Bilhah over against the tomb of Rachel, and Dinah also, his daughter, they buried there. And he mourned for Joseph one year, and did not cease, for he said, "Let me go down to the grave mourning for my son." For this reason it is ordained for the children of Israel that they should afflict themselves on the tenth of the seventh month [Yom Kippur]—on the day that the news which made him weep for Joseph came to Jacob his father—that they should make atonement for themselves thereon with a young goat on the tenth of the seventh month, once a year, for their sins; for they had grieved the affection of their father regarding Joseph his son. And this day has been ordained that they should grieve thereon for their sins, and for all their transgressions and for all their errors, so that they might cleanse themselves on that day once a year.

Book of Jubilees 34.10–19[2]

THE SABBATH OF SABBATHS

PHILO OF ALEXANDRIA

The feast held after the "Trumpets" is the Fast. Perhaps some of the perversely minded who are not ashamed to censure things excellent will say, What sort of a feast is this in which there are no gatherings to eat and drink, no company of entertainers or entertained, no copious supply of strong drink or tables sumptuously furnished, nor a generous display of all the accompaniments of a public banquet, nor again the merriment and revelry with frolic and drollery, nor dancing to the sound of flute and harp and timbrels and cymbals, and the other instruments of the debilitated and invertebrate kind of music which through the channel of the ears awaken the unruly lusts? For it is in these and through these that men, in their ignorance of what true merriment is, consider that the merriment of a feast is to be found. This the clear-seeing eyes of Moses the ever wise discerned and therefore he called the fast a feast, the greatest of the feasts, in his native tongue a Sabbath of Sabbaths, or as the Greeks would say, a seven of sevens, a holier than the holy. He gave it this name for many reasons.

First, because of the self-restraint which it entails; always and everywhere indeed he exhorted them to show this in all the affairs of life, in controlling the tongue and the belly and the organs below the belly, but on this occasion especially he bids them do honor to it by dedicating thereto a particular day. To one who has learned to disregard food and drink, which are absolutely necessary, are there any among the superfluities of life which he can fail to despise, things which exist to promote not so much preservation and permanence of life as pleasure with all its powers of mischief?

Second, because the holy day is entirely devoted to prayers and supplications, and men from morn to eve employ their leisure in nothing else but offering petitions of humble entreaty in which they seek earnestly to propitiate God and ask for remission of their sins, voluntary and involuntary, and entertain

1. *Mahzor*. Germany. 14th century. Library of the Hungarian Academy of Sciences, Budapest. See Chapter XI.

bright hopes looking not to their own merits but to the gracious nature of Him who sets pardon before chastisement.

Third, because of the time at which the celebration of the fast occurs, namely, that when all the annual fruits of the earth have been gathered in. To eat and drink of these without delay would, he held, show gluttony, but to fast and refrain from taking them as food shows the perfect piety which teaches the mind not to put trust in what stands ready prepared before us as though it were the source of health and life. For often its presence proves injurious and its absence beneficial. Those who abstain from food and drink after the ingathering of the fruits cry aloud to us with their souls, and though their voices utter no sound, their language could hardly be plainer. They say, "We have gladly received and are storing the boons of nature, yet we do not ascribe our preservation to any corruptible thing, but to God the Parent and Father and Savior of the world and all that is therein, who has the power and the right to nourish and sustain us by means of these or without these. See, for example, how the many thousands of our forefathers, as they traversed the trackless and all-barren desert, were for forty years, the life of a generation, nourished by Him as in a land of richest and most fertile soil; how He opened fountains unknown before to give them abundance of drink for their use; how He rained food from heaven, neither more nor less than what sufficed for each day, that they might consume what they needed without hoarding, nor barter for the prospect of soulless stores their hopes of His goodness, but taking little thought of the bounties received rather reverence and worship the bountiful Giver and honor Him with the hymns and benedictions that are His due."

By order of the law the fast is held on the tenth day. Why on the tenth? As has been shown in our detailed discussion of that number, it is called by the learned the all-perfect, and embraces all the progressions, arithmetical, harmonic, and geometrical, and further the harmonies, the fourth, the fifth, the octave and the double octave, representing respectively the ratios 4:3, 3:2, 2:1 and 4:1, and it also contains the ratio of 9:8, so that it sums up fully and perfectly the leading truths of musical science, and for this reason it has received its name of the all-perfect. In ordaining that this privation of food and drink should be based on the full and perfect number ten, he intended to prescribe the best possible form of nourishment for the best part of us. He did not wish anyone to suppose that as their instructor in the mysteries he was advocating starvation, the most intolerable of sufferings, but only a brief stoppage in the influx which passes into the receptacles of the body. For this would ensure that the stream from the fountain of reason should flow pure and crystal-clear with smooth course into the soul, because the constantly repeated administrations of food which submerge the body sweep the reason away as well, whereas if they are checked, that same reason stoutly fortified can in pursuit of all that is worth seeing and hearing make its way without stumbling, as upon a dry, firm causeway. Besides, it was meet and right when everything has shown abundance as they would have it, and they enjoy a full and perfect measure of goodness, that amid this prosperity and lavish supply of boons, they should by abstaining from food and drink remind themselves of what it is to want, and offer prayers and supplications, on the one hand to ask that they may never really experience the lack of necessities, on the other to express their thankfulness because in such wealth of blessings they remember the ills they have been spared.

The Special Laws II, 193–203[3]

III

YOM KIPPUR IN
TALMUD AND MIDRASH

In this chapter are selections characterized by incisive ethical insights for modern living. They derive from the vast storehouse of talmudic and midrashic literature, representing a veritable ocean of law, commentary, exegesis, legends, principles of morality and rectitude, and the like.

Although one finds references to the Day of Atonement throughout the Talmud, Tractate Yoma is devoted by and large to this Sabbath of Sabbaths, especially the preparations for the Day of Atonement services in the Temple in Jerusalem. The eighth and last chapter prescribes the laws that are a guide for observance. A basic source for rich interpretation material on Yom Kippur is the Midrash Rabbah. Pesikta Rabbati, most likely edited during the seventh century C.E., *is an aggregation of instructive homilies and discourses for special Sabbaths, festivals, and fasts. The ethical religious book Eliyahu Zuta was composed at the end of the tenth century. Among the midrashic texts is Midrash Tehillim ("Midrash on Psalms"), a book of homilies that was compiled during the period from the third to the thirteenth century* c.e. *The selections quoted below are not necessarily from the earliest sources, as the later ones are generally more descriptive.*

THE ORIGINS

From the very beginning of the world's creation the Holy One, blessed be He, foresaw the deeds of the righteous and the deeds of the wicked. *And the earth was desolate* alludes to the deeds of the wicked; *And God said: Let there be light,* to those of the righteous; *And God saw the light, that it was good,* to the deeds of the righteous; *And God made a division between the light and the darkness*: between the deeds of the righteous and those of the wicked; *And God called the light day* alludes to the deeds of the righteous; *And the darkness called He night,* to those of the wicked; *And there was evening,* to the deeds of the wicked; *And there was morning,* to those of the righteous; *One day*: the Holy One, blessed be He, gave them one day, and which is that? It is the Day of Atonement.

Genesis Rabbah 3.10[1]

And God called the light day (Genesis 1.5) symbolizes Jacob; *and the darkness He called night,* Esau; *and there was evening* —Esau; *and there was morning*—Jacob. *One day* teaches that the Holy One, blessed be He, gave him one [unique] day: and which is that? the Day of Atonement.

Genesis Rabbah 2.3

When the children of Israel received the Ten Commandments on Shavuot, Moses ascended Mount Sinai and remained there forty days to receive the tablets of the Law. On the seventeenth day of Tamuz he descended and, seeing the people worshiping a golden calf, broke the tablets. Then, for forty days Moses placed his tent beyond the camp, and the people mourned. On the first day of Elul, Moses again ascended the mountain to receive the second tablets. During this period the Israelites fasted daily from sunrise to sunset. However, on the fortieth day they fasted from sunset to sunset. This day was the tenth of Tishri. When Moses returned in the morning, the Israelites went forth to meet him. He saw that they were weeping and he too wept as he became aware of their repentance. Then God said: "Your repentance is acceptable to me, and this day will remain the Day of Atonement throughout all generations."

Eliyahu Zuta 4[2]

Of the three hundred sixty-five days in the year, the Only One of the universe already had designated one of them as His very own. And what day was that? R. Levi and R. Isaac differed. R. Levi said that it was the Day of Atonement: *Is such the fast that I have chosen, The Day for a man to afflict his soul?* (Isaiah 58.5). R. Isaac said, however, that it was the Sabbath day.

Pesikta Rabbati 23.1[3]

THE OBSERVANCE

There were no happier days for Israel than the fifteenth of Ab and the Day of Atonement, for on them the daughters of Jerusalem used to go forth in white raiments; and these were borrowed, that none should be abashed which had them not; hence all the raiments required immersion. And the daughters of Jerusalem went forth to dance in the vineyards. And what did they say? "Young man, lift up thine eyes and see what thou wouldest choose for thyself: set not thine eyes on beauty, but set thine eyes on family; for *Favor is deceitful and beauty is vain, but a woman that feareth the Lord shall be praised* (Proverbs 31.30)."

Taanit 4.8[4]

It is quite right that the Day of Atonement [should be an occasion for dancing] since it was a day of forgiveness and expiation for Israel, and the day upon which the second tablets [of the Law] were given.

Lamentations Rabbah 33

On the Day of Atonement, eating, drinking, washing, anointing, putting on sandals, and marital intercourse are forbidden. A king or a bride may wash their faces and a woman after childbirth may put on sandals.

Yoma 8.1[5]

They do not cause children to fast on the Day of Atonement, but they should train them therein one year or two years before they are of age, that they may become versed in the commandments.

If a pregnant woman smelled [food and craved it], they may give her food until she recovers herself. He that is sick may be given food at the word of skilled persons; and if no skilled persons are there, he may be given food at his own wish, until he says, "Enough!"

Yoma 8.4–5[6]

A sick person is fed at the word of experts. R. Jannai said: "If the patient says, 'I need [food],' whilst the physician says: 'He does not need it,' we hearken to the patient. What is the reason? *The heart knoweth its own bitterness* [Proverbs 14.10]. But that is self-evident? You might have said: The physician's knowledge is more established; therefore the information [that we prefer the patient's opinion]. If the physician says: 'He needs it,' whilst the patient says that he does not need it, we listen to the physician. Why? Stupor seized him [so that he does not feel the lack of food]."

Yoma 83a[7]

R. Phinehas said: There is a story of a pious man in Rome who used to honor the holy days and Sabbath. On the eve of a Sabbath—some say it was the eve of the Great Fast [Yom Kippur]—he went up to the market to buy something, and he found nothing except one fish. Now the governor's servant [was there and he] also wanted the fish. And the one bid up for it, and so did the other. In the end the Jew bought the fish at a denar a pound. At mealtime, the governor said to his servant: There is no fish. The servant replied: Today only one fish was brought to the market, and a Jew bought it at a denar a pound. The governor asked: You know him? And the servant replied: Yes. The governor said: Go forth and summon him, for apparently the Jew owns a treasure which properly belongs to the king. The servant went forth and summoned the Jew. The governor asked: What are you? The Jew replied: I am a Jew. The governor asked: What is your work? The Jew replied: I am a tailor. The governor asked: But is there a tailor who can afford to eat food at a denar a pound? The Jew said: My lord, if permission be given me, I would say something to you in my defense. The governor said: Speak. The Jew said: We Jews have one day which is more precious to us than all the other days of the year. That day atones for all the sins which we have committed during the year so that they are forgiven us. Therefore we honor it more than any other day of the year. The governor then said: Since you bring reason for what you have done, you are free to go.

How did the Holy One, blessed be He, requite the tailor? He caused him to find in the fish a gem of purest ray, a pearl, and on the money he got for it he sustained himself all the rest of his days.

Pesikta Rabbati 23.6[8]

ATONEMENT OF SINS

If a man said, "I will sin and repent, and sin again and repent," he will be given no chance to repent. If he said, "I will sin and the Day of Atonement will effect atonement," then the Day of Atonement effects no atonement. For transgressions that are between man and God the Day of Atonement effects atonement, but for transgressions that are between a man and his fellow the Day of Atonement effects atonement only if he has appeased his fellow. This did R. Eleazar b. Azariah expound: *"From all your sins shall ye be clean before the Lord* (Leviticus

16.30)—for transgressions that are between man and God the Day of Atonement effects atonement; but for transgressions that are between a man and his fellow the Day of Atonement effects atonement only if he has appeased his fellow." R. Akibah said: "Blessed are ye, O Israel. Before whom are ye made clean and who makes you clean? Your Father in heaven; as it is written, *And I will sprinkle clean water upon you and ye shall be clean* (Ezekiel 36.25)."

Yoma 8.9[9]

If one says, "I shall sin and then repent," he is given no opportunity to repent. If one says "I shall sin and the Day of Atonement will atone," then the Day of Atonement does not atone. If one says "I shall sin and the day of death will purge me of sin," the day of death does not purge him of sin.

If one sins and repents and continues uprightly, he is forgiven before he stirs from the spot. But if one says, "I shall sin and then repent," he is forgiven up to three times, but no more.

The Fathers according to Rabbi Nathan 40[10]

The Holy One, blessed be He, said to Israel: Remake yourselves by repentance during the ten days between New Year's Day and the Day of Atonement, and on the Day of Atonement I will hold you guiltless, regarding you as a newly made creature.

Pesikta Rabbati 40.5[11]

It was with regard to the four categories of atonement that Rabbi Mattiah ben Heresh went to call upon Rabbi Eleazar Hakkappar at Laodicea. And he asked him: "Hast thou heard what Rabbi Ishmael used to teach in regard to the four categories of atonement?"

"I have heard," Rabbi Eleazar replied, "but they are three, and along with each of these there must be repentance.

"Now how is all this to be understood?

"If a man transgressed a positive commandment and repented, he is forgiven on the spot, before he has so much as stirred from his place. Of such it is said, *Return, ye backsliding children* (Jeremiah 3.22).

"If a man transgressed a negative commandment and re-

pented, repentance suspends the sentence and the Day of
Atonement atones. Of such it is said, *For on this day shall
atonement be made for you* (Leviticus 16.30).

"If a man transgressed commandments punishable by ex-
tirpation or by death from the courts and repented, repentance
and the Day of Atonement suspend the sentence, and his sufferings during the remaining days of the year atone. And of such
is said, *Then will I visit their transgression with the rod* (Psalms
89.33).

"But when one profanes the name of heaven, there is no
power either in repentance to suspend his sentence or in sufferings to cleanse him of his sins or in the Day of Atonement to
atone. Rather, repentance and sufferings suspend the sentence,
and death, along with these, cleanses him of his sins. And of
such it is said, *Surely this iniquity shall not be expiated by you
until ye die* (Isaiah 22.14)."

The Fathers according to Rabbi Nathan 29[12]

R. Bibi b. Abaye said: "How should a person confess on the
eve of the Day of Atonement? He should say: 'I confess all the
evil I have done before Thee; I stood in the way of evil; and as
for all the evil I have done, I shall no more do the like; may it
be Thy will, O Lord my God, that Thou shouldst pardon me for
all my iniquities, and forgive me for all my transgressions, and
grant me atonement for all my sins.' This is indicated by what
is written, *Let the wicked forsake his way, and the man of iniquity his thoughts* (Isaiah 55.7)." R. Isaac and R. Jose b.
Hanina [each gave a simile]. R. Isaac said: "It is like a man
fitting together two boards, and rejoining them one to another."
R. Jose b. Hanina said: "It is like a man fitting together two bed
legs and joining them one to another." [These similes probably
describe how perfectly and harmoniously man becomes joined
to God when he genuinely repents.]

Leviticus Rabbah 3.3

Said R. Eleazar: "The scriptural text reads, *From all your sins
[shall ye be clean] before the Lord* [Leviticus 16.30]. [This

teaches us that] the Day of Atonement expiates sins that are
known to the Lord alone."

Keritot 25b

It is customary that if a man knows that he has to appear in
court for trial, he wears black clothes and lets his beard grow,
as he does not know what his verdict will be. However, the
children of Israel do not act thus. On their day of judgment
they don white clothes, trim their beards, eat, drink, and rejoice, for they have confidence that the Holy One, blessed be He,
will perform miracles for them.

Jerusalem Rosh Hashanah 1.3

There was a province that owed arrears to the king, and the
latter came to collect them. When he was within ten miles the
nobility of the province went out and greeted him with praise;
so he freed them of a third of their tax. When he was within
five miles the middle-class people of the province came out and
praised him; so he freed them of another third. When he
entered into the province all the people—men, women, and
children—came out and praised him; so he forgave them the
whole sum. The king said to them: "Let bygones be bygones;
from now we shall commence a new account." In a similar
manner, on the eve of New Year the leaders of the congregation fast, and the Holy One, blessed be He, absolves them of a
third of their iniquities. From New Year to the Day of Atonement private individuals fast, and the Holy One, blessed be
He, absolves them of a third of their iniquities. On the Day of
Atonement, everyone fasts—men, women, and children—and
the Holy One, blessed be He, says to Israel: "Let bygones be
bygones; from now on we shall begin a new account."

Leviticus Rabbah 30.7

As a child before it reaches maturity is not held responsible
for its misdeeds, so the children of Israel are not held responsible for any of the sins wherewith they have soiled themselves
throughout the days of the year: The Day of Atonement cleanses

them, as it is said, *On this day shall a cleansing be appointed for you* (Leviticus 16.30).

Midrash on Psalms 15.5[13]

Just as if a nut falls into some dirt you can take it up and wipe it and rinse it and wash it and it is restored to its former condition and is fit for eating, so however much Israel may be defiled with iniquities all the rest of the year, when the Day of Atonement comes it makes atonement for them, as it is written, *For on this day shall atonement be made for you, to cleanse you* (Leviticus 16.30).

Song of Songs Rabbah 6.11

Satan comes on the Day of Atonement to accuse Israel and he specifies the iniquities of Israel, saying: Master of the Universe, there are adulterers among the nations of the earth; so, too, among Israel. There are thieves among the nations of the earth; so, too, among Israel. But the Holy One, blessed be He, specifies the just deeds of Israel. Then what does He do? He suspends the beam of the scales and looks to see what the balance or imbalance is between the iniquities and the just deeds. And as they are weighed—the iniquities against the just deeds, these against those—the two pans of the scale balance exactly. Thereupon Satan goes out to fetch more iniquities to put in the pan of iniquities and bring it down. What does the Holy One, blessed be He, do? Even while Satan is going about seeking iniquities, the Holy One, blessed be He, takes the iniquities out of the pan and hides them under His royal purple. Then Satan comes and finds no iniquity on the scale, as is said *The iniquity of Israel shall be sought for, and there shall be none* (Jeremiah 50.20).

Pesikta Rabbati 45.2[14]

Who is like God, a teacher of sinners that they may repent? They asked Wisdom, what shall be the punishment of the sinner? Wisdom answered: *Evil pursueth sinners* (Proverbs 13.21). They asked Prophecy. It replied: *The soul that sinneth shall die* (Ezekiel 18.4). They asked the Law. It replied: *Let him bring a sacrifice* (Leviticus 1.4). They asked God, and He replied: Let him repent and obtain his atonement. My children, what do I ask of you? Seek Me and live.

Pesikta Kahanah 158b

May God's name be praised and His title exalted! For in His tender regard of Israel, He ordained the Ten Days of Repentance for them, so that if even only one of the congregation of Israel resolves repentance, his repentance is accepted as though it were the repentance of an entire congregation. Therefore all Israel should take hold of repentance and hold on to it. Let them make peace with one another and forgive one another on the eve of the Day of Atonement, in order that the Holy One, blessed be He, in His own presence, accept their repentance and prayer in reconciliation and with special love. Indeed, we find the power of peace among men to be so great that for its sake the Holy One, blessed be He, Himself revises the words a person has uttered. For example, in the passage *And Sarah laughed within herself, saying . . . "Shall I have pleasure, my lord being so old?"* (Genesis 18.12), *but unto Abraham the Lord said: "Wherefore did Sarah laugh, saying: Shall I of a surety bear a child, old as I am?"* (ibid. 13). Note that Sarah uttered the words *my lord being so old*, but the Holy One, blessed be He, revised her words, having her say *old as I am*, in order that no bad feelings should rise between Abraham and Sarah because of her calling him old.

Pesikta Rabbati 50.6[15]

The numerical value of the letters in *ha-Satan* [the Satan], "the Adversary," is three hundred and sixty-four, which is one short of the number of days in the year. Thus the Adversary is given the authority to make accusations against the children of Israel on all the days of the year, except on the Day of Atonement, when the Holy One, blessed be He, says to him: "Thou hast no authority to touch them. Nevertheless, go forth and see wherein they busy themselves." Then the Adversary, going forth, finds all of them at fasting and prayer, dressed in white

garments and cloaked like the ministering angels, and forthwith
goes back in shame and confusion. The Holy One, blessed be
He, asks: "What hast thou found out about My children?" And
he answers: "Verily, they are like the ministering angels, and I
am unable to touch them." Thereupon, the Holy One, blessed be
He, chains the Adversary and declares to the children of Israel:
"I have forgiven you."

Midrash on Psalms 27.4[16]

THE FAST

Whence then does R. Ishmael derive the rule that an addition is to be made from the profane on to the holy? From what
has been taught: *And ye shall afflict your souls on the ninth day
of the month in the evening from evening to evening, shall ye
keep your Sabbth* (Leviticus 23.32). I might think literally on
the ninth day. It therefore says, *In the evening.* If in the evening,
I might think, after dark? It therefore says, *on the ninth day*
[and after dark would be on the tenth]. What then am I to
understand? That we begin fasting while it is yet day; which
shows that we add from the profane on to the holy. I know
this so far only in regard to the inception of the holy day; how
do I know it in regard to its termination? Because it says, *from
evening to evening.* So far I have brought only the Day of
Atonement under the rule, how do I know that it applies to
Sabbaths also? Because it says, *ye shall rest.* How do I know
that it applies to festivals? Because it says, *your Sabbath.* How
am I to understand this? That wherever there is an obligation to
rest, we add from the profane on to the holy.

What then does R. Akiba make of this, *and ye shall afflict
your souls on the ninth day*? He requires it for the lesson learnt
by R. Hiyya b. Rab from Difti. For R. Hiyya b. Rab from Difti
learnt: "*And ye shall afflict your souls on the ninth day.* Do we
then fast on the ninth day? Is it not on the tenth day that we
fast? We do; but the use of this word indicates that if a man
eats and drinks on the ninth day, the Scripture accounts it to
him as if he fasted on both the ninth and the tenth days."

Rosh Hashanah 9a–b

It was related of R. Akiba that he never said in the house of study, "It is time to cease studying," except on the eve of Passover and the eve of the Day of Atonement. [He wanted to leave early] on the eve of Passover, because of the children, so that they might not fall asleep [before the *seder*], and on the eve of the Day of Atonement, in order that they should give food to their children.

Pesahim 109a

One Yom Kippur R. Hana went to visit R. Haggai who was feeling weak. The latter said, "I am thirsty." R. Hana replied, "Drink some water." He then left him and returned an hour later. When he inquired of R. Haggai if he had satisfied his thirst, the reply was: "When you granted me permission to drink, I was no longer thirsty."

Jerusalem Yoma 6.4

David prayed: *Let none that wait on Thee be ashamed; they shall be ashamed who act deceitfully with respect to their emptiness* (Psalms 25.3)—that is, men who fast without repentance shall be ashamed.

Midrash on Psalms 25.5[17]

ACTS OF LOVING-KINDNESS

Once as Rabban Johanan ben Zakkai was coming forth from Jerusalem, Rabbi Joshua followed after him and beheld the Temple in ruins.

"Woe unto us!" Rabbi Joshua cried, "that this, the place where the iniquities of Israel were atoned for, is laid waste!"

"My son," Rabban Johanan said to him, "be not grieved; we have another atonement as effective as this. And what is it? It is acts of loving-kindness, as it is said, *For I desire mercy and not sacrifice*" (Hosea 6.6).

For thus we find concerning Daniel, that greatly beloved man, that he was engaged in acts of loving-kindness.

Now, what were the acts of loving-kindness in which Daniel was engaged? Canst thou say that he offered burnt offerings and sacrifices in Babylon? What then were the acts of loving-kindness in which he was engaged? He used to outfit the bride and make her rejoice, accompany the dead, give a *perutah* to the poor, and pray three times a day—and his prayer was received with favor.

The Fathers according to Rabbi Nathan 4[18]

When the Temple stood, a man used to bring his shekel and so make atonement. Now that the Temple no longer stands, if they give for charity, well and good, and if not, the heathens will come and take from them forcibly. And even so it will be reckoned to them as if they had given charity.

Baba Batra 9a

Mar Ukba had a poor man in his neighborhood to whom he regularly sent four hundred zuz on the eve of every Day of Atonement. On one occasion he sent them through his son, who came back and said to him, "He does not need your help." "What have you seen?" his father asked. "I saw that they were setting old wine before him." "Is he so delicate?" the father said; and he sent back his son with double the usual amount.

Ketubot 67b

The merit of a fast day lies in the charity dispensed.

Berakhot 6b

THE HIGH PRIEST'S PREPARATIONS

Seven days before the Day of Atonement the high priest was taken apart from his own house unto the counselors' chamber and another priest was made ready in his stead lest aught should befall him to render him ineligible. R. Judah says: Also another wife was made ready for him lest his own wife should die, for it is written, *He shall make atonement for himself and for his house* (Leviticus 16.6); "his house"—that is his wife. They said to him: If so there would be no end to the matter. . . .

They delivered unto him elders from among the elders of the court and they read before him out of the prescribed rite of the

2. *Mahzor*. Germany. Circa 1320. University Library, Leipzig. See Chapter XI.

day; and they said to him, "My lord High Priest, do thou thyself recite with thine own mouth, lest thou hast forgotten or lest thou hast never learnt." On the eve of the Day of Atonement in the morning they make him to stand at the Eastern Gate and pass before him oxen, rams, and sheep, that he may gain knowledge and become versed in the Temple service.

Throughout the seven days they did not withhold food and drink from him; but on the eve of the Day of Atonement toward nightfall they did not suffer him to eat much, since food induces sleep.

The elders of the court delivered him to the elders of the priesthood and they brought him up to the upper chamber of the House of Abtinas. They adjured him and took their leave and went away having said to him, "My lord High Priest, we are delegates of the court, and thou art our delegate and the delegate of the court. We adjure thee by Him that made His Name to dwell in this house that thou change naught of what we have said unto thee." He turned aside and wept and they turned aside and wept.

If he was a sage he used to expound the Scriptures, and if not, the disciples of the sages used to expound before him. If he was versed in reading the Scriptures he read, and if not, they read before him. And from what did they read before him? Out of Job and Ezra and Chronicles. Zechariah b. Kabutal says: Many times I read before him out of Daniel.

If he sought to slumber, young members of the priesthood would snap their middle finger before him and say to him, "My lord High Priest, get up and drive away [sleep] this once [by walking] on the [cold] pavement." And they used to divert him until the time of slaughtering drew near.

Yoma 1.1, 3–7[19]

He [the high priest] then came to the scapegoat and laid his two hands upon it and made confession. And thus he used to say: "O God, Thy people, the House of Israel, have committed iniquity, transgressed, and sinned before Thee. O God, forgive, I pray, the iniquities and transgressions and sins which Thy people, the House of Israel, have committed and transgressed and sinned before Thee; as it is written in the law of Thy servant Moses, *For on this day shall atonement be made for you to cleanse you: from all your sins shall ye be clean before the Lord* (Leviticus 16.30). And when the priests and the people which stood in the Temple Court heard the Expressed Name come forth from the mouth of the high priest, they used to kneel and bow themselves and fall down on their faces and say, "Blessed be the name of the glory of His kingdom for ever and ever!"

Yoma 6.2[20]

PRAYERS

This was the prayer of the high priest when he departed in peace from the sanctuary on Yom Kippur:

"May it be Thy will, O Lord our God and God of our fathers, that exile shall not be our lot—neither on this day nor in this year. But if exile be decreed for us either today or this year, let our exile be to a place where Torah is studied. May it be Thy will, O Lord our God and God of our fathers, that we have no deficiency—neither on this day nor in this year. But if a deficiency be decreed for us either today or this year, let it be a deficiency caused by the performance of good deeds. May it be Thy will, O Lord our God and God of our fathers, that this year will be a year of plenty, a year of trade, a year of rain, warm weather and dew, and that Your people Israel will not be dependent on one another."

Jerusalem Yoma 5.3

R. Hamnuna said: "My God, before I was formed, I was of no worth, and now that I have been formed, it is as if I had not been formed. I am dust in my life, how much more in my death. Behold I am before Thee like a vessel full of shame and reproach. May it be Thy will that I sin no more, and what I have sinned wipe away in Thy mercy, but not through suffering." That was the confession of sins used by Rab all the year round, and by R. Hamnuna the younger, on the Day of Atonement.

Yoma 87b

IV

YOM KIPPUR IN MEDIEVAL
JEWISH LITERATURE

*Outstanding works of philosophy, poetry, and scholar-
ship enriched medieval Jewish literature and are the subject of
study and a source of inspiration to this day. Among the major
philosophical writings of this period are Judah Halevi's* Kuzari
and Maimonides' Moreh Nevukhim *("Guide for the Perplexed").
The foremost Hebrew poet of the Middle Ages, Judah Halevi
(1085–1142), affirmed the superiority of Judaism over other
universal religions in his philosophic work* Kuzari. *Moses ben
Maimon (1135–1204), popularly called Maimonides and noted
as a philosopher, codifier, and physician, sought in the* Moreh
Nevukhim *to harmonize philosophy and religion.*

*Abraham Bar Hiyya, a twelfth century Spanish Jewish scholar
who wrote many scientific works in Hebrew, also authored the
ethical treatise* Hegon ha-Nefesh *("Meditation of the Soul").
The Talmudist Jonah ben Abraham Gerondi of Spain (1180–
1263) is best known as the author of* Shaare Teshuvah *("Gates
of Repentance"), which exerted a profound influence on later*

Jewish ethical literature. Israel ibn Al-Nakawa (died 1391) of Spain was the author of Menorat ha-Maor *("Lamp of Light"), an exhaustive religioethical work which summarized all phases of practical religious life.*

Generally attributed to Simeon ben Yohai of the second century, the Zohar *first appeared during the thirteenth century through Moses ben Shemtob de Leon. Recognized as the basic work of Kabbalah, the* Zohar *presents discursive commentaries on the Bible and teachings on mysticism.*

These classical medieval volumes are concerned with various phases of Yom Kippur, as is evident from the following selections.

THE FAST OF A PIOUS MAN

JUDAH HALEVI

The pious man attends the Three Festivals and the Great Fast day, on which some of his sins are atoned for. His soul frees itself from the whisperings of imagination, wrath, and lust, and neither in thought or deed gives them any attention. Although his soul is unable to atone for sinful thoughts—the results of songs and tales heard in youth, and which cling to memory—it cleanses itself from real sins, confesses repentance for the former, and undertakes to allow them no more to escape his tongue, much less to put them into practice, as it is written: "I am purposed that my mouth shall not transgress" (Psalms 17.3). The fast of this day is such as brings one near to the angels, because it is spent in humility and contrition, standing, kneeling, praising, and singing. All his physical faculties are denied their natural requirements, being entirely abandoned to religious service, as if the animal element had disappeared. The fast of a pious man is such that eye, ear, and tongue share in it, that he regards nothing except that which brings him near to God. This also refers to his innermost faculties, such as mind and imagination. To this he adds pious works.

Kuzari 3.5[1]

THE REASON FOR THE FAST OF ATONEMENT

MOSES MAIMONIDES

The reason for the Fast of Atonement is self-explanatory, that is, it provides the idea of repentance. It is the day on which the master of the prophets descended [from Mount Sinai] with the second set of tablets of the Law and communicated to the people forgiveness for their great sin. This day became forever a day of repentance and true worship. On it are forbidden all corporeal pleasure, every burden and care of the body; that is to say, work is not done. Only confessions are permitted so that one will confess his sins and repent of them.

Guide for the Perplexed 3.43

THE REBUKE TO THE SINNER

ABRAHAM BAR HIYYA

As for those who endeavor to subdue their inclination but have difficulty in conquering it, if their faith is sufficiently strong they subdue it and are rescued from their iniquity—and the forgiveness of their wickedness is their ultimate reward. But if they are not sufficiently strong to overcome their iniquity, their fasting will serve only as a reminder of their iniquity. Nobody who is dominated by his evil inclination deserves to have his fast accepted unless he repents of his evil ways; as it says "Ye shall not fast as ye do this day, to make your voice to be heard on high" (Isaiah 58.4), i.e., if that is the nature of your fast, your voice will not be heard. This is the rebuke to the sinner who is dominated by his evil inclination but yet appears at Divine service, and to all such haughty hypocrites. It asks those who are insincere (Isa. 58.5): "Is such the fast that I have chosen? A day for a man to afflict his soul? Is it to bow his head like a bulrush and to spread sackcloth and ashes under him? Wilt thou call that a fast and an acceptable day to the Lord?" The fast that God desires is not that a man humble himself, cast down his eyes, spread dust and ashes beneath him and appear to be mourning and grieving, while God knows that he is a deceiver and liar and that, while he restrains his mouth from food and drink, he is not restraining his heart and tongue from evil meditation. An act of affliction is not called "fast" or "an acceptable day to the Lord." The proper form of fast is indicated in the next verse: "Is not this the fast that I have chosen? To loose the bands of wickedness, to undo the heavy burdens, to let the oppressed go free and that ye break every yoke?" It speaks here about the man who is overcome by the evil inclination, and is subdued by it at the time of the fast, and it does not let him direct his heart. This is the person meant when it says: "Behold ye fast for strife and debate," and they are the ones of whom it says: "They say 'I sin and afterwards I will repent,' but God does not give them the opportunity to repent." Similarly, God is angry with those who say "I sin and the Day of Atonement will make the repentance."[2]

A MEANS TO REPENTANCE

JONAH BEN ABRAHAM GERONDI

In the Ten Days of Repentance the heart of one who fears the word of God will tremble within him in the knowledge that all of his deeds are being inscribed in a book and that during that period God brings into judgment every deed concerning every hidden thing, whether good or evil. For a man is judged on Rosh Hashanah and his judgment is sealed on Yom Kippur. If a man knows that his judgment is being brought before a king of flesh and blood, will he not be seized with a great trembling and take counsel with himself and, with all manner of diligence, hasten to his defense? It will never occur to him to turn to the right or to the left and to occupy himself with other matters. He will not concern himself with the plowing and harrowing of his ground and he will not turn to the path of the vineyards. . . . How foolish are those who go out to their work and to their labors until evening in the Days of Awe, the days of justice and judgment, not knowing what their judgment will be. It befits everyone who fears God to curtail his activities, to be fearful in his mind, to set aside times in the daytime and in the evening to be alone in his chambers and to search and investigate his ways, to rise at the night watches, to busy himself in the ways of repentance and in the perfection of his deeds, to pour forth his plaint, present prayer and song, and make supplication, the time being one of acceptance, in which prayer is attended to, as it is said, "In an acceptable time have I answered thee, and in a day of salvation have I helped thee" (Isaiah 49.8). It is a positive commandment of the Torah that a man awaken his spirit to repentance on Yom Kippur, as it is said, "From all your sins shall ye be clean before the Lord" (Leviticus 16.30). The Torah instructs us to cleanse ourselves before the Lord through repentance so that He might grant us atonement on this day and cause us to be clean.[3]

NEVER TOO LATE TO REPENT

Israel ibn Al-Nakawa

It is never too late to repent; though a man repent in his hour of death, the Lord will forgive him and have mercy upon him. Perfect repentance, however, depends upon the relinquishment of the unethical life, upon frank confession and promise to mend one's ways, and upon inner resolve actually to fulfill one's promise. Also, it depends upon recognition of the principle that one's social sins can be forgiven only if one has righted the wrong one has done to another. Else even the Day of Atonement is of no avail. Confession is a good part of penitence in matters affecting one's relation to others; in personal matters, however, there is no need for one's confessing aloud and publishing one's sins; on the contrary, it is impertinence to do so.

Having fulfilled the conditions, the penitent will naturally conduct himself in a spirit of humility, but he must not regard himself as inferior to others, and so carry about a sense of shame. It is not so. He is beloved and cherished and prized, and his worth is greater than ever, in accord with the old teaching that those who have repented occupy a place such as those who have never failed cannot enjoy. It is one of the distinctions of repentance that it knits closer the bonds between man and God.

Acts of communal repentance are commendable and are always appropriate. But neither the individual nor society should make the efficacy of penitence an occasion for unethical conduct. One should not make the abundance of divine mercy an excuse for misbehavior. There is such a thing as too much repenting, which, according to an old teacher, is one of the things that cannot be forgiven. Nor should one make penitence a matter of physical self-affliction, such as abstaining from meat and wine and wearing rough wool. The root of penitence is that one should repent with all one's heart, just as sin originates in the heart.[4]

THE DEATH OF THE RIGHTEOUS ATONES

When the righteous are removed from the world, punishment is removed from the world, and the death of the righteous atones for the sins of the generation. Therefore we read the [scriptural] section dealing with the death of the sons of Aaron on the Day of Atonement that it may atone for the sins of Israel. God says: Recount the death of these righteous ones, and it will be accounted to you as if you brought an offering on that day to make atonement for you. For we have learnt that so long as [the people of] Israel are in captivity, and cannot bring offerings on that day, the mention of the two sons of Aaron shall be their atonement. It has been taught in the name of R. Jose that on this Day of Atonement it has been instituted that this [scriptural] portion should be read to atone for Israel in captivity. Hence we learn that if the chastisements of the Lord come upon a man, they are an atonement for his sins, and whosoever sorrows for the sufferings of the righteous obtains pardon for his sins. Therefore on this day we read the portion commencing "after the death of the two sons of Aaron," that the people may hear and lament the loss of the righteous and obtain forgiveness for their sins. For whenever a man so laments and sheds tears for them, God proclaims for him, "thine iniquity is taken away and thy sin purged" (Isaiah 6.7).

Zohar Ahare Mot 56b, 57b[5]

V

YOM KIPPUR IN JEWISH LAW

Moses ben Maimon (1135–1204), popularly known as the Rambam or Maimonides, codified the prodigious body of Jewish law in his Mishneh Torah. Some three centuries later the Shulhan Arukh, accepted up to our own day as the authentic code for traditional Jewish practice, was prepared by Joseph Karo (1488–1575), considered the last great codifier of rabbinical Judaism. An abridged and popular version, known as Kitzur Shulhan Arukh, was prepared by Solomon Ganzfried (c. 1800–1886).

REPENTANCE MAKES ATONEMENT

Moses Maimonides

At this time, when the Temple no longer exists, and we have
no atonement altar, there is nothing left but repentance. Repentance atones for all transgressions. Even if a man was
wicked throughout his life and repented at the end, we must
not mention anything about his wickedness to him, as it is
written: "A wicked man's wickedness shall not bring about his
downfall when he gives up his wickedness" (Ezekiel 33.12).
Yom Kippur itself atones for those who repent, as it is written:
"Atonement shall be made for you on this day" (Leviticus 16.30).

Perfect repentance is where an opportunity presents itself to
the offender for repeating the offense and he refrains from
committing it because of his repentance and not out of fear or
physical inability. . . . If, however, one repents only in his old
age, when he is no longer able to do what he used to do, his
repentance, though not the best, will nevertheless do him some
good. Even if a person transgressed all his life and repented on
the day of his death and died during his repentance, all his
sins are pardoned, as it is written: "Before the sun grows dark,
and the light goes from moon and stars, and the clouds gather
after rain" (Ecclesiastes 12.2), that is, the day of death. This
implies that if he remembers his Creator and repents before
death, he is forgiven.

Repentance and Yom Kippur effect atonement only for sins
committed against God, as when one has eaten forbidden food;
. . . for sins committed against a fellow man, as when a person
either injured or cursed or robbed his neighbor, he is never
pardoned unless he compensates his neighbor and makes an
apology. Even though he has made the compensation, the
wrongdoer must appease the injured person and ask his pardon.
Even if he only annoyed him with words he must apologize and
beg for forgiveness. . . .

One must not show himself cruel by not accepting an
apology; he should be easily pacified, and provoked with difficulty. When an offender asks his forgiveness, he should forgive

wholeheartedly and with a willing spirit. Even if he has caused him much trouble wrongfully, he must not avenge himself, he must not bear a grudge. This is the way of the stock of Israel and their upright hearts.

Mishneh Torah, Laws of Repentance 1.3, 2.1, 9, 10[1]

LAWS FOR THE EVE OF THE DAY OF ATONEMENT

Solomon Ganzfried

It is a religious duty to eat and drink sumptuously on the day preceding Yom Kippur, for he who does so for the sake of fulfilling a commandment is regarded as if he fasted also on that day.

It is customary for the master of every household to have a candle made for his home, because on the Day of Atonement Moses descended Mount Sinai with the second set of the tablets of the Law, and the Torah is called light. Another candle is made to memorialize the souls of his deceased parents and to atone for them. It is customary that the candle lit in the home should burn until *Havdalah* time so that the *Havdalah* ritual may be recited over it. The other candle is lit in the synagogue.

It is customary to wear Sabbath clothes when attending the synagogue afternoon service.

The confession should be recited while standing with head bowed. With the mention of each sin one beats against his heart with clenched fist, as if to say: You caused me to sin. All must recite the complete confession as written in the prayer book. If one is aware of a sin he committed that is not mentioned in the confession, since he is saying it inaudibly, it is proper for him to acknowledge his guilt with grief and tearfulness. One who committed a sin specified in the confession should experience an inner pang when reciting it.

Even though aware that he did not commit again the sins expiated on the previous Day of Atonement, he reiterates confessing them. This is praiseworthy, as it is said, "And my sin is ever before me" (Psalms 51.5).

A *kittel* [white shroud], which is the raiment for the dead, is usually worn as a symbol of a humble and contrite heart. Women garb themselves in clean white clothes in honor of the day, but they should not be bejeweled because of the reverential awe of [the Day of] Judgment.

It is customary for parents to bless their children before entering the synagogue. By that time the sanctity of the day is established and the gates of mercy are already open.

Kitzur Shulhan Arukh 131

LAWS FOR THE DAY OF ATONEMENT

SOLOMON GANZFRIED

The following are prohibited on the Day of Atonement: partaking of food, drinking, washing, anointing, wearing shoes, and sexual intercourse. It is also forbidden to do any manner of work and to carry objects, as on the Sabbath. Since it is necessary to add from the profane to the sacred, all these are forbidden shortly before twilight, and also briefly after the appearance of the stars terminating the Day of Atonement.

One who is ill, even if not in danger, may wash in his usual manner. A bride within thirty days of marriage may wash her face so as not to be repulsive to her husband.

The laws pertaining to a woman about to give birth and also to a person dangerously ill who may require food, drink, and the desecration of the Day of Atonement by partaking of food are in the same status as the laws governing the desecration of the Sabbath. Even though several physicians prescribe that a patient does not necessarily require food and drink and might even suffer ill effects by eating and drinking, if the patient says that, although not yet dangerously ill, he may further jeopardize his health by refraining from food, he is heeded and fed [on Yom Kippur]. In the matter of eating and drinking the patient's judgment is more reliable, since he knows in his heart the bitterness of his symptoms.

Departed ones are memorialized on the Day of Atonement, [first] because remembering our dead invokes a mood of humility, and [second] because even the deceased are in need of atonement. It is written in *Sifri*: "Atone for Your people Israel —this refers to the living; whom You redeemed—this refers to the dead. This teaches that the departed require expiation; therefore charity should be pledged in their name."

Immediately upon the conclusion of the Day of Atonement, those who scrupulously observe the commandments begin to build a *sukkah*, to fulfill the verse: "They go from strength to strength" (Psalms 84.8).

Kitzur Shulhan Arukh 133

VI

SELECTED PRAYERS

The Yom Kippur liturgy reflects considerable Jewish thinking on God and man, as formulated by the prophets and psalmists, by the rabbis of the Talmud and medieval hymnologists. Indeed, the Day of Atonement Mahzor includes psalms and prayers from the time of the Temple, anthems and poetic offerings of liturgical poets of the Middle Ages, and compositions of recent centuries. Thus the Yom Kippur prayer book is a collection of selections from the Bible, Talmud, Midrash, and medieval literature. They make up a compendium of devotionals through which the worshiper deepens his communion with God and reaffirms the eternal and challenging verities which are still valid in this modern era.

The liturgy of Yom Kippur, "a Day of Atonement" (Leviticus 23.28), emphasizes that man's alienation from God, resulting from sin, may be altered through repentance. But repentance must be more than remorse for evil perpetrations; it must include confession, restitution, and inner change. Through prayers and resolutions, the worshiper seeks to fashion within himself a new spirit and expresses his confidence that, as he has true repentance, the God of justice and mercy will forgive and pardon his sins.

Yom Kippur is initiated with the chant of Kol Nidre, *which sets the mood for the solemnity that characterizes this most holy and awesome day in the Jewish calendar. The prayers are concluded with the* Neilah *service, recited only on this day.*

The selections from the Mahzor *in this chapter are followed by modern commentaries which explain their source and meaning. Also included are some examples of prayers from modern Jewish literature.*

THE FATHER'S BLESSING ON THE EVE OF YOM KIPPUR

May God make you like Ephraim and Manasseh. May it be the will of our heavenly Father to instill in your heart His love and His fear. May the fear of God be with you throughout your life, that you sin not. May you be diligent in the study of Torah and zealous in the fulfillment of the commandments. May your gaze ever be straightforward, your mouth speak wisdom, your heart meditate on fear. May your hands be occupied in good deeds and your feet fleet to perform the will of your heavenly Father. May God grant you virtuous children who will occupy themselves with Torah and commandments all their lives. May the stock from which you stemmed be blessed [so that you may rejoice in family life]. May He grant you abundant sustenance in tranquillity from His generous hand so that you will require no support from your fellow man but be free to serve God. May you be inscribed and sealed for a good, long life among all the righteous of Israel. Amen.

Hayye Adam 144

PRAYER FOR YOM KIPPUR

In deep humility, and contrition I make supplication unto Thee, my God and my Father, on this holiest of days. Conscious of my frailties and my shortcomings, I seek Thee with the hope in my heart that I shall find forgiveness for my sins, for I know that Thou art merciful and loving, long-suffering and abundant in pardoning.

As I ponder upon the years that lie behind me, I recognize how I have failed to make them count in Thy service and the service of my fellow men. I have often been selfish when I should have been self-sacrificing, harsh when I should have been gentle, hard when I should have been kind, thoughtless when I should have been considerate. Day after day I have sought my own pleasure and gain without a thought of the higher purpose of my life. Again and again I have turned a deaf ear to the promptings of my better nature and have permitted the evil inclination to swerve me from the path of purity and right.

I know how often I have chosen the worse, conscious though I was of the better. I confess this before Thee in this hour of self-searching and self-examination. I know how frail I am. . . .

Help me and I shall be helped, save me and I shall be saved. I yearn to undo the evil I may have done consciously or unconsciously, to correct fault and failing, to change bitter to sweet, to bring light where there is darkness, truth where there is falsehood, and good where there is evil. I would make atonement for all the lapses from the right of which I have been guilty. Open mine eyes that I may see clearly where I have gone astray. Give me the courage to ask forgiveness of all whom I have wronged. Remove from my heart all rancor and hardness, that I may forgive freely even as I hope to be forgiven. Accept Thou with favor my prayer for forgiveness, my confession which I make before Thee. May the words of my mouth and the meditation of my heart be acceptable before Thee, my Rock and my Redeemer. Amen.

Union Prayer Book[1]

3. *Mahzor*. Germany. Early 14th century. University Library, Breslau. See Chapter XI.

WE STAND BEFORE OUR GOD

Leo Baeck

In this hour all Israel stands before God, the judge and the
    forgiver.

In His presence let us all examine our ways, our deeds, and
    what we have failed to do.

Where we transgressed, let us openly confess: "We have
    sinned!" and, determined to return to God, let us pray:
    "Forgive us."

We stand before our God.

With the same fervor with which we confess our sins, the sins
    of the individual and the sins of the community, do we,
    in indignation and abhorrence, express our contempt for
    the lies concerning us and the defamation of our religion
    and its testimonies.

We have trust in our faith and in our future.

Who made known to the world the mystery of the Eternal, the
    One God?

Who imparted to the world the comprehension of purity of
    conduct and purity of family life?

Who taught the world respect for man, created in the image of
    God?

Who spoke of the commandment of righteousness, of social
    justice?

In all this we see manifest the spirit of the prophets, the divine
    revelation to the Jewish people. It grew out of our
    Judaism and is still growing. By these facts we repel
    the insults flung at us.

We stand before our God. On Him we rely. From Him issues
    the truth and the glory of our history, our fortitude
    amidst all change of fortune, our endurance in distress.

Our history is a history of nobility of soul, of human dignity. It
    is history we have recourse to when attack and grievous
    wrong are directed against us, when affliction and
    calamity befall us.

God has led our fathers from generation to generation. He will
     guide us and our children through these days.
We stand before our God, strengthened by His commandment
     that we fulfill. We bow to Him and stand erect before
     men. We worship Him and remain firm in all vicissi-
     tudes. Humbly we trust in Him and our path lies clear
     before us; we see our future.
All Israel stands before her God in this hour. In our prayers, in
     our hope, in our confession, we are one with all Jews
     on earth. We look upon each other and know who we
     are; we look up to our God and know what shall abide.
"Behold, He that keepeth Israel doth neither slumber nor sleep"
     [Psalms 121.4].
"May He who maketh peace in His heights bring peace upon us
     and upon all Israel."

Translated by Nahum N. Glatzer[2]

COMMENTARY

*In 1935, when anti-Semitism was clearly evident throughout
Germany, Rabbi Leo Baeck (1873–1956), who was president of
the representative organization of German Jewry, wrote a
prayer that was distributed to all rabbis in the country for
reading at* Kol Nidre *services. When the Nazis found a copy of
the text, they arrested Rabbi Baeck and placed him in a S.S.
prison. This prayer which the Nazis had prohibited on Yom
Kippur in 1935 was made a part of the trial record of Adolf
Eichmann that took place in Jerusalem in 1961.*

MEDITATION BEFORE *KOL NIDRE*

ABRAHAM ISAAC KOOK

     Take away my shame,
     Lift my anxiety,
     Absolve me of my sin
     And enable me to pray before Thee

With gladness of heart,
To pursue Thy commandments and Thy Torah
In the joy of holiness.
Grant me
To bring happiness to all Thy children,
To exalt and ennoble Thy faithful,
To spread goodness and mercy
And blessing in the world.
Humble the arrogant
Who have tried to pervert me with falsehood
While I sought my happiness in serving Thee.
Save me from weakness
And from faltering
And from every evil trait,
Illumine my eyes
With the light of Thy deliverance.
Help Thy people,
Imbue the heart of Thy people with reverence
And with awe before Thy majesty.
Strengthen them with Thy love,
Guide them to walk in the path of Thy righteousness,
Kindle in their hearts
The light of the holiness of this Day of Holiness
And bring them to possess the inheritance
Thou hast set for them,
Speedily, speedily, in our time, soon.
Amen.

Translated by Ben Zion Bokser[3]

ALL VOWS

KOL NIDRE

All vows, renunciations, promises, obligations, oaths, taken rashly, from this Day of Atonement till the next, may we attain it in peace, we regret them in advance. May we be absolved of them, may we be released from them, may they be null and void and of no effect. May they not be binding upon us. Such vows shall not be considered vows; such renunciations, no renunciations; and such oaths, no oaths.

And may atonement be granted to the whole congregation of Israel and to the stranger who lives among them, for all have transgressed unwittingly.

Forgive the sins of this people in accordance with Thy great mercy, as Thou hast continued to forgive them from the days of Egypt until now.

As we have been promised: And the Lord said, I have forgiven, in accordance with Thy plea.

Translated by Ben Zion Bokser[4]

COMMENTARY: *Max Arzt*

For us today, Kol Nidre can symbolize the need to deepen our sensitivity toward the resolutions which we make in our finest moments of spiritual decision. A feeling of discontent may, in a solemn moment of self-examination, prompt a person to resolve to change his ways. But too often he lacks the tenacity needed for effecting a radical break with strongly entrenched habits. Kol Nidre can serve us as a reminder that only by resolute will and by severe self-discipline can we hope to lessen the distance between what we are and what we ought to be. . . .

Rabbi Moshe Mordecai Epstein (1863–1933), head of the yeshiva of Slabodka, offered an interesting reinterpretation of the concluding words of the Kol Nidre. He suggested that we should regard them as a confession of our lack of moral constancy. The self-righteousness and smugness which stand in the way of our spiritual growth need to be dispelled by a confession, in utter humility, that so often the vows we make are no vows, our resolves no resolves, and our oaths no oaths. When accompanied by such a meditation, the recital of Kol Nidre *prepares us for the soul-cleansing experience of the Yom Kippur day.*[5]

THE CONFESSION

VIDDUI

Our God and God of our fathers, pardon our sins on this Day of Atonement. Let our sins and transgressions be removed from Thy sight. As Thou didst promise: It is I who erases your transgressions, for Mine own sake, and I will recall your sins. And Thou didst further promise: I have blotted out your transgressions and they are gone, as a cloud, and your sins, as a mist; return unto Me, for I have redeemed you. And it is further promised: On this day shall atonement be made for you to cleanse you; of all your sins shall you be cleansed before the Lord. Make us holy through Thy commandments and grant that we may have a portion among those who devote themselves to Thy Torah. Satisfy us with Thy goodness, and cause us to rejoice in Thy deliverance. And purify our hearts that we may serve Thee in truth. Thou art He who forgives Israel and pardons the community of Yeshurun in every generation. We have no other King to grant us forgiveness and pardon.

Praised be Thou, O Lord, who forgives and pardons our sins and the sins of the household of Israel, who cancels out our wrongdoings year by year. Thou King over all the earth sanctifiest Israel and the Day of Atonement. . . .

We have offended, we have strayed, we have robbed, we have spoken basely;

We have been devious, mean, arrogant, violent, false;

We have counseled evil, we have deceived, we have scoffed;

We have been rebellious, we have provoked, we have disobeyed, we have been impulsive, we have been contemptuous, we have been oppressive, we have been obstinate;

We have been insolent; destructive, dishonorable, misleading.

We have turned away from Thy goodly commandments and judgments; and now we face the consequences of our folly. Thou art just in all that has come upon us. Thou hast acted in accordance with the truth, but we have done evil.

What can we tell Thee, O Thou who abidest in eternity, what

can we tell Thee, Thou who reignest in the endless spaces of the universe? All things hidden as all things open, Thou knowest everything.

Thou knowest the mysteries of the universe, and the things hidden from mortal eyes. Thou searchest out our innermost secrets; Thou knowest the unspoken meditations of the heart. Nothing is hidden from Thee, nothing is veiled from Thine eyes.

And now, O our God and God of our fathers, may it be Thy will to forgive all our sins, to pardon all our iniquities, and to grant us atonement for all our transgressions.

For the sin we committed before Thee under compulsion or of our own free will,

For the sin we committed before Thee by stubbornness of heart,

For the sin we committed before Thee in ignorance,

For the sin we committed before Thee with the utterance of our lips,

For the sin we committed before Thee by unchastity,

For the sin we committed before Thee openly or secretly,

For the sin we committed before Thee consciously and deceitfully,

For the sin we committed before Thee by word of mouth,

For the sin we committed before Thee by deceiving a neighbor,

For the sin we committed before Thee in the meditation of the heart,

For the sin we committed before Thee by licentiousness,

For the sin we committed before Thee by insincere confessions,

For the sin we committed before Thee by disrespect for parents and teachers,

For the sin we committed before Thee deliberately or unintentionally,

For the sin we committed before Thee by violence,

For the sin we committed before Thee by defaming Thy name,

For the sin we committed before Thee by unclean lips,

For the sin we committed before Thee by foolish speech,

For the sin we committed before Thee by evil passions,

For the sin we committed before Thee knowingly and un-knowingly,

For all these, O God of forgiveness, forgive us, pardon us, grant us atonement.

For the sin we committed before Thee by deception and falsehood,

For the sin we committed before Thee by bribery,

For the sin we committed before Thee by mocking,

For the sin we committed before Thee by slander,

For the sin we committed before Thee in our business dealings,

For the sin we committed before Thee in eating and drinking,

For the sin we committed before Thee by usury,

For the sin we committed before Thee by arrogance,

For the sin we committed before Thee by gossiping,

For the sin we committeed before Thee by wanton looks,

For the sin we committed before Thee by haughty eyes,

For the sin we committed before Thee by insolence,

For all these, O God of forgiveness, forgive us, pardon us, grant us atonement.

For the sin we committed before Thee by casting off the yoke of Thy Torah,

For the sin we committed before Thee by false judgments,

For the sin we committed before Thee by betraying a neighbor,

For the sin we committed before Thee by envy,

For the sin we committed before Thee by levity,

For the sin we committed before Thee by being obstinate,

For the sin we committed before Thee by rushing to do evil,

For the sin we committed before Thee by talebearing,

For the sin we committed before Thee by false oaths,

For the sin we committed before Thee by unjust hatreds,

For the sin we committed before Thee by a breach of trust,

For the sin we committed before Thee by confusion of mind,

For all these, O God of forgiveness, forgive us, pardon us, grant us atonement. . . .

O my God, before I was created I was nothing, and now that I have been created, what am I? In life I am dust, and more so when I fall prey to death. When I measure my life in Thy presence, I am confused and I am ashamed. Help me, O God and God of my fathers, to steer clear of sin. And as for my past sins, purge me of them in Thy great mercy, but, I pray, not through severe and painful disease.

Translated by Ben Zion Bokser[6]

COMMENTARY: *Hermann Cohen*

The confession of sin *constitutes the central point of the liturgy of the Day of Atonement. To begin with, one should consider that this is not the exclusive prerogative of the Day of Atonement; in the prayer at the hour of death it is the last refuge.*

But even this fundamental use does not circumscribe sufficiently the distinctive character of the confession of sin on the Day of Atonement. For all prayers on every day are pervaded by the confession of sin, although merely in the general atmosphere of the basic idea. One might believe that the distinctive character of confession on the Day of Atonement replaces this basic element of the daily liturgy. However, in this may perhaps be found a distinctive mark of pure monotheism.

In order to bring out this distinctive mark we ask another question: Should confession of sin be made in the midst of the community at all, and therefore in its public worship? The Talmud reports a difference of opinion as to whether confession should be made individually and in solitude or in the chorus of the community. The decision was made for the community, for public confession. And through this decision the Talmud may well have saved the purity of monotheism in its ritual profundity. For, in the first place, the public nature of the confession shows trust in God's forgiveness. Moreover, the act of confession, analogous to punishment, implies a demand to carry it out within the community. Now, however, we are guided by the point of view of trust in God's forgiveness, which takes away from the individual a false sense of public shame.

Confession and remorse merge into one another. Thus remorse is already fully active when confession breaks forth. How can one shrink from and avoid the community of the fellow guilty, or the fellow confessors? . . .

It is at the same time also the public expression of trust in God, before whom the sin of man does not endure. Hence the question asked above is clearly answered. Properly speaking, the confession of sin belongs to public worship alone, and that worship in general has its center of gravity in this confession to the good God.

It is, further, a very valuable sign of the inwardness of the intention which inspired the institution of this prayer ritual that in this confession of sins, so far as they are specified, only purely moral transgressions *between man and man are explicitly mentioned. To be sure, the rabbis, and particularly the teachers of the Mishnah, not only knew the distinction between purely moral and ritual commandments but distinguished their specific values. And the rabbis or their successors introduced into the daily morning prayer one such midrash concerned with this distinction. However, in spite of this they were convinced of the unity of the Torah and, therefore, of the lack of difference between the moral laws and the ritual. These builders of traditional monotheism are the more to be admired and esteemed because they avoided, without exception, an express formulation of all the ritual transgressions in the great confession of sins on the Day of Atonement, although they were convinced of the sinfulness of these transgressions.*

Translated by Simon Kaplan⁷

MAY OUR ENTREATY RISE TO THEE

YAALEH TAHANUNENU

May our entreaty rise to Thee at evening time,
May our cry come before Thee in the morning,
And may our song be received by Thee at the dusk.

May our voices rise to Thee at evening time,
May our uprightness reach Thee in the morning,
And may our redemption come from Thee at dusk.

May our fasting rise to Thee at evening time,
May our penitence come before Thee in the morning,
And may our plea be heard by Thee at dusk.

May our trust in Thee rise up at evening time,
May it rise for Thine own sake in the morning,
And may atonement come from Thee at dusk.

May our deliverance be decreed by Thee at evening time,
May our cleansing come before Thee in the morning,
And may Thy grace be conferred on us at dusk.

May our remembrance come to Thee at evening time,
May our assembly win Thy favor in the morning,
And may our adorations reach to Thee at dusk.

May our knocking at Thy gates be heard at evening time,
May our joy be ours in the morning,
And may our petition be granted at dusk.

May our supplication rise to Thee at evening time,
May it come before Thee in the morning,
And may it win Thy mercy at dusk.

Translated by Ben Zion Bokser[8]

COMMENTARY: *Morris Silverman*

The theme of this well-known poem, Yaaleh, *the author of which is unknown, was suggested by the twenty-four-hour service of the Day of Atonement which begins with the* Kol Nidre *in the evening, is resumed early at dawn, continues throughout the entire day, and culminates at dusk. The author, using the inverted alphabetical acrostic [in the Hebrew], makes a poetical and soul-stirring plea that the prayers of Israel ascend to heaven at nightfall, arrive before God's throne at dawn, so that salvation and reconciliation may come at dusk.*[9]

"FORGIVEN"

"SALAHTI"

YOM TOV BEN ISAAC OF YORK

Ay 'tis thus   evil us   hath in bond;
By thy grace   guilt efface   and respond,
           "Forgiven!"

Cast scorn o'er   and abhor   th' informer's word;
Dear God, deign   this refrain   to make heard,
           "Forgiven!"

Ear in lieu   give him who   intercedes;
Favoring   answer, King,   when he pleads,
           "Forgiven!"

Grant also   the lily blow   in Abram's right;
Heal our shame   and proclaim   from thine height,
           "Forgiven!"

Just, forgiving,   mercy living,   sin condone;
List our cry,   loud reply   from Thy throne,
           "Forgiven!"

My wound heal,   deep conceal   stain and flake,
Now gain praise   by Thy phrase   "For My sake,
           "Forgiven!"

O forgive!   Thy sons live   from Thee reft;
Praised for grace,   turn Thy face   to those left—
           "Forgiven!"

Raise to Thee   this my plea,   take my pray'r,
Sin unmake   for Thy sake   and declare,
           "Forgiven!"

Tears, regret,   witness set   in sin's place;
Uplift trust   from the dust   to Thy face—
           "Forgiven!"

Voice that moans,	tears and groans,	do not spurn;
Weigh not flaws,	plead my cause,	and return,
		"Forgiven!"

Yea, off-rolled,	as foretold,	clouds impure,
Zion's folk,	free of yoke	O assure,
		"Forgiven!"

*Day** by day	stronghold they	seek in Thee,
Good One! let	stronger yet	Thy word be
		"Forgiven!"

Translated by Israel Zangwill[10]

COMMENTARY: *Bernard Martin*

Included in the evening service of Yom Kippur is this stirring poem. The Hebrew original is in the form of an alphabetical acrostic, and Israel Zangwill's celebrated English rendering given here retains the acrostic scheme as well as the rhythm of the original. Though Zangwill indulged perforce in some poetic license in translating the Hebrew and employed a number of archaisms which may be somewhat jarring to the contemporary ear, his version is remarkably faithful, both in content and style, to the original.

The Omnam Ken *was written by Rabbi Yom Tov ben Isaac who lived in the city of York in England in the twelfth century. . . .*

The author begins his poem with the rueful admission that evil (the yetzer ra*) has taken man captive, and pleads with God therefore to exercise His grace and mercifully confirm the sinner's pardon by responding "Forgiven!" This becomes the refrain of each of the poem's verses.*

*God is then implored to abhor the word of the "informer" and to listen rather to him "who intercedes." Jewish folklore pictured Satan as the prosecutor (*kategor*) at the heavenly assizes, which were believed to take place during the High Holy Day season; he reminds God of all the sins of Israel and urges that they be*

---

* The first words of the last two lines establish the author of the poem as Yom Tov—*Yom* (day) and *Tov* (good).

punished. Opposing Satan, however, is a good angel who serves as Israel's intercessor or defender (sanegor) *and advocates their acquittal.*

The puzzling seventh line in Zangwill's version, "Grant also the lily blow in Abram's right," reads in the original Hebrew, "Let also the merit of the home-born son bloom for the lily." The home-born son is the patriarch Abraham, and the lily, which is mentioned in Songs of Songs 2.1–2, is understood in the rabbinic interpretation of those verses as symbolizing the people of Israel.[11]

LIKE THE CLAY IN THE HAND OF THE POTTER

KI HINNEH KA-HOMER

Like the clay in the hand of the potter
Who thickens or thins it at his will,
So are we in Thy hand, gracious God,
Forgive our sin, Thy covenant fulfill.

Like a stone in the hand of the mason
Who preserves or breaks it at his will,
So are we in Thy hand, Lord of life,
Forgive our sin, Thy covenant fulfill.

Like iron in the hand of the craftsman
Who forges or cools it at his will,
We are in Thy hand, our Keeper,
Forgive our sin, Thy covenant fulfill.

Like the wheel in the hand of the seaman
Who directs or holds it at his will,
So are we in Thy hand, loving God,
Forgive our sin, Thy covenant fulfill.

Like the glass in the hand of the blower
Who dissolves or shapes it at his will,
So are we in Thy hand, God of grace,
Forgive our sin, Thy covenant fulfill.

Like the cloth in the hand of the tailor
Who smoothens or drapes it at his will,
So are we in Thy hand, righteous God,
Forgive our sin, Thy covenant fulfill.

Like silver in the hand of the smelter
Who refines or blends it at his will,
So are we in Thy hand, our Healer,
Forgive our sin, Thy covenant fulfill.

Translated by Ben Zion Bokser[12]

COMMENTARY: *Louis Jacobs*

In this hymn of unknown authorship God is described as a craftsman shaping man's destiny. He is compared to the potter who molds the plastic clay into various shapes; to the mason hewing the block of stone; to the smith bending the rigid steel; to the glassblower fashioning his vessels out of glass; and to the silversmith removing the dross from the precious metal.

It is worthy of note that in all the illustrations given, the craftsman, no matter how skilled he may be, cannot produce a thing of beauty unless his raw material is good. It is sound Jewish teaching which thinks of God helping us to make our lives dignified and worthy. We have to provide Him, as it were, with the raw material. We have to give Him something to work on.

Seen in this light our abasement before God on Yom Kippur is to fall before Him that He may elevate us. It is the submission of the clay to the potter who can fashion it into a thing of beauty, of the silver to the refiner to purge it of its dross, of the ship to the pilot to guide it on its way.[13]

HEAR OUR VOICE

SHEMA KOLENU

Hear our voice, O Lord our God,
have mercy and compassion on us,
and receive compassionately, and acceptingly
this our prayer.

Return us, O Lord, to Thee, and we shall return:
renew our days as of old.

Hear our speech, O Lord,
our meditation comprehend.

Cast us not from before Thee,
and Thy holy spirit take not from us.

No, cast us not away, when we grow old;
when our strength expires forsake us not.

Forsake us not, O Lord our God;
be not far from us.

For to Thee, O Lord, have we aspired;
Thou shalt reply,
O Lord our God.

Translated by Jacob Sloan[14]

COMMENTARY: *Max Arzt*

The order of the Selihot *follows the rule that the praise of God
must be concluded before petitionary prayer is offered (Berakhot
32a). After reciting verses depicting God's steadfast mercy, we
proceed in* Shema Kolenu *to pray that ours be the will to return
to God in wholehearted repentance, that we may be forgiven
and reinstated in His good favor, as we return to Him sincerely
and wholeheartedly.*[15]

WE ARE THY PEOPLE

ANU AMMEKHA

Our God and God of our fathers, forgive us, pardon us, grant
us atonement.
For we are Thy people and Thou art our God,
We are Thy children and Thou art our Father,
We are Thy servants and Thou art our Master,
We are Thy congregation and Thou art our Heritage,
We are Thine inheritance and Thou art our Portion,

We are Thy flock and Thou art our Shepherd,
We are Thy vineyard and Thou art our Keeper,
We are Thy dependents and Thou art our Deliverer,
We are Thy beloved and Thou art our Friend,
We are Thy treasure and Thou art our Dear One,
We are Thy subjects and Thou art our King,
We are pledged to Thee and Thou art pledged to us,
(But yet how we fail to measure up to Thee!)
We are arrogant and Thou art merciful,
We are stubborn and Thou art slow to anger,
We are bound in sin and Thou aboundest in compassion.
Our days are as a passing shadow and Thy years are
 endless.

Our God and God of our fathers, may our prayer come before
Thee, and do not ignore our entreaty. We are not so arrogant
and stubborn as to declare before Thee that we are wholly
righteous and without sin. Surely we have sinned.

       Translated by Ben Zion Bokser[16]

COMMENTARY: *Max Arzt*

*These expressions of intimacy between Israel and God are culled
from various parts of the Bible. The epithets of endearment
reach their climax in a declaration of mutual fealty: "We are
pledged to Thee and Thou art pledged to us," based on the verse
"Thou hast avouched [affirmed] the Lord this day to be thy
God. . . . And the Lord hath avouched [affirmed] thee this day
to be His own treasure" (Deuteronomy 26.17–18).*

*At this point there is a sharp change from a tone of con-
fidence and elation to one of abject contrition. The contrast is
now drawn between man's insolence and God's graciousness,
between man's obstinacy and God's forbearance, and between
man's ephemeral life and God's eternity. Nevertheless, we venture to make entreaty to God because, despite our sinfulness,
there is a redeeming quality to our life, in that we confess our
sins.*[17]

MAY GOD REMEMBER

YIZKOR

May God remember the soul of —— who has gone to his (her) eternal home. I pledge charity in his (her) behalf and on account of this may his (her) soul be bound up in the bond of eternal life among the souls of Abraham, Isaac, and Jacob, Sarah, Rebekah, Rachel, and Leah, and all the righteous men and women in paradise. Amen.

COMMENTARY: *Louis Jacobs*

The idea of praying for the souls of the departed is ancient. In the second book of Maccabees (12.43–45) it is said that Judah collected the sum of two thousand drachmas of silver and sent it to Jerusalem as a sin offering for those who had died "in that he was mindful of the resurrection. For if he had not hoped that they that were slain should have risen again, it had been superfluous and vain to pray for the dead. And also in that he perceived that there was great favor laid up for those that died godly, it was an holy and good thought. Whereupon he made a reconciliation for the dead, that they might be delivered from sin."

That the living can atone by their charity for those who have died is found in a number of passages in the rabbinic literature. Arising out of this belief it became customary to recite prayers for the dead and to donate to charity on their behalf on Yom Kippur. At first these prayers were recited on Yom Kippur only (the Torah reading for Yom Kippur morning begins with the words: "And the Lord spake unto Moses after the death of the two sons of Aaron . . .").

In the order of prayers known as Mahzor Vitry (1208) refer-ence is made to memorial prayers on Yom Kippur, not on the other festivals. But at a later date the custom arose of reciting these prayers on all festival days on which the portion of the Torah dealing with the duty of supporting the poor is read,

4. *Mahzor*. Ulm, Germany. 1459–60. Bavarian State Library, Munich. See Chapter XI.

namely, on the last days of Passover and Pentecost and on the eighth day of Tabernacles.

The central idea behind the memorial service is that a person's life does not come to an end with the death of his body. His soul lives on in two ways. First, Judaism teaches that the soul of man is immortal, that after his bodily death it continues to exist and that therefore what we do with our lives is of eternal significance. And second, the soul of a man who has influenced others lives on, here on earth, even when he has gone to his eternal rest. By remembering their parents in the memorial prayer, sons and daughters keep their memory alive by resolving to follow in their teachings.[18]

THE MARTYRDOM OF THE TEN SAGES

ELEH EZKERAH

These things I do remember: Oh, I pour
My soul out for them. All the ages long
Hatred pursueth us; through all the years
Ignorance like a monster hath devoured
Our martyrs as in one long day of blood.
Rulers have risen through the endless years,
Oppressive, savage in their witless power,
Filled with a futile thought: to make an end
Of that which God had cherished. There was once
A tyrant searching in the Book of God
For some word there to serve him as a sword
To slay us; and he found the line which spake:
"He that doth steal a man and selleth him,
He shall surely be put to death." That king,
That dark-designing servant of false gods,
Summoned to him ten sages of the Law,
Saying: "Pervert the truth not with your lies,
But judge this thing: What if a man be found
Stealing his brother—one of Israel's sons—
And making merchandise and selling him?"

And the ten sages spake: "That thief shall die."
"Your fathers," said the tyrant, "where are they,
That sold their brother to a company
Of Ishmaelites? Lo, ye shall now receive
Justice of heaven upon you; for if they
Were now in life, then ye yourselves should judge;
But now ye bear on your fathers' sin."
"If we have sinned," they said, "then we shall bear
His sentence, whose compassion fills the world."
"Give us three days," they spake. And they all looked
Unto the high priest, Rabbi Ishmael,
Saying, "Arise, arise, pronounce the Name;
Know from our God if this be His decree."
Then Rabbi Ishmael, in purity,
Pronounced the Name, and rising up on high,
Made question of the angel clothed in white,
Who spake: "O righteous! O beloved! I,
Hearkening within the sacred region, heard
That ye indeed be captured." Thus he spake,
And Rabbi Ishmael, descending, told
His fellows all their doom.

And that dread king
Bade the ten sages to be slain in woe
And torture. Lo! I saw them all:
They stepped out of the ages, and they walked
Before the deathless spirit that is mad
With hunger for destruction of God's own. . . .

Thus were the princes of the Law brought low,
The cornerstones jeweled with precepts. Now
Rabbi Akiba was led forth to die;
Hananiah, too, who was Teradyon's son,
Torn from his place; and yet he held the scroll
Fast in his arms—O God, blot out their pain.

Mourn, O my people, not yet widowed;—still
As in a vision, for a worthless whim

I see your holiest slaughtered; see their blood
Shed in the name of heaven. . . .
Here were ten righteous men; lo, they are slain.

This hath befallen us. All this I tell
As I beheld it passing through the years
Of bygone ages. And subdued and crushed,
We pour our hearts out supplicating Thee.
Lord, Lord, give ear; O pitying, merciful,
Look from Thine height upon the blood outpoured
Of all Thy righteous. Make an end of blood
Poured out and wasted; wash the stain away,
God, King, who sittest on a gracious throne.

Translated by Nina Davis Salaman[19]

COMMENTARY: *Louis Jacobs*

The Roman Emperor Hadrian, resolved to stamp out Judaism ruthlessly, engaged in a bloody persecution during which many of Israel's sages perished. In those days numerous Jewish families gave their lives for the Sabbath, circumcision, and other Jewish institutions. Tradition records that ten great sages were slain during the Hadrianic persecutions. Later legend describes how they were all killed on the same day, though this is historically incorrect. This dirge in the Yom Kippur liturgy is based on a late midrash and describes the martyrdom of the ten sages in detail.

No mention is made of the Hadrianic persecutions. Instead it is said that the emperor, after reading in the Torah the account of Joseph and his brothers, asked the sages the punishment for one who steals a man. When they answered that he was to be sentenced to death, the emperor ordered them to be put to death to expiate the sin of Joseph's brothers, their ancestors. Ishmael inquired in heaven if this were indeed to be their fate and was told that they must be prepared to die. The theology of the dirge is inconsistent with the general Jewish view that descendants do not suffer for the sins of their ancestors. Because of this difficulty and the anachronisms in the dirge Dr.

*H. J. Zimmels is of the opinion that the whole lament is a veiled
attack on the Church which persecuted the Jews.*

*Among the ten martyrs were Akiba, who died with a smile
on his lips in obedience to the verse: "And thou shalt love thy
God with all thy life" which Akiba interpreted to mean: "Even
if thy life is demanded," and Hananiah ben Teradyon who was
burned at the stake with a Sefer Torah wrapped round his body
and who said that he saw "the parchments burning but the
letters of the Torah flying aloft."*[20]

THOU STRETCHEST OUT A HELPING HAND

ATAH NOTEN YAD

Thou stretchest out a helping hand to transgressors, and Thy
hand is ever open to receive the penitent. Thou didst teach us,
O Lord our God, to confess our sins before Thee, and to cease
committing evil, so that we may be accepted by Thee in full
penitence, as Thou didst promise. Endless are the deeds of
expiation we ought to perform in atonement of our guilt, numberless are the offerings we ought to bring as tokens of our
remorse. But Thou who knowest our frailty, Thou art abounding
in forgiveness. What are we? What is our life, our kindness,
our uprightness, our helpfulness, our strength, our heroism?
What claims can we make before Thee, O God and God of our
fathers? The mighty men are as nothing before Thee, and re-
nowned men as though they had never been, and wise men as
though without knowledge, and discerning men as though without understanding. For in comparison with Thee, the deeds of
mortal men are as vanity and their years on earth are as
nothing. Indeed, before Thy perfection, even the preeminence
of man over the beast is naught, for we are all so very trivial.

Thou didst, nevertheless, distinguish man from the very beginning, and Thou didst deem him worthy to stand before Thee.
Who can inquire of Thee: What doest Thou? And even if man
be righteous, what can he give Thee? Out of Thy love for us
didst Thou give us this Day of Atonement, to put an end to

unrighteousness, and to grant forgiveness and pardon for all
our sins, so that we may cease to do evil and return to Thee
and perform the ways of Thy will with a whole heart. In Thine
abundant mercy, have mercy upon us, for Thou desirest not
that the world be destroyed. As it is written (Isaiah 55.6,7):
"Seek the Lord while He may be found, call ye upon Him when
He is near. Let the wicked forsake his way, and the evil man
his thoughts, and let him return to the Lord, and He will have
compassion upon him, and to our God, for He will abundantly
pardon." For Thou art a forgiving God, gracious and merciful,
slow to anger, abounding in compassion, truth, and goodness.

Translated by Ben Zion Bokser[21]

COMMENTARY: *Max Arzt*

*Judaism is distinctive not only in what it teaches about God,
but also in what it teaches about man. These two prayers, which
in the* Neilah *service replace the* Al Het, *reflect Judaism's conception of God and of man's relation to Him. God is kind and
compassionate, and not vindictive: "Thou stretchest out Thy
hand to transgressors and Thy right hand is stretched out to
receive the repentant."*

*But with a realism as sobering as it is sublime, the prayer
proceeds to state that the magnanimity of God's forgiveness is
necessitated by man's creatureliness and moral fragility. Even
men of renown and of power are woefully defective in spiritual
constancy, moral courage, and wisdom. . . .*

*This derogation of man aims to humble, but not humiliate us.
It is balanced by the next prayer: "Thou didst distinguish man
from the very beginning," which depicts man as God's most
favored creation, singled out and set apart from other creatures.*

*Judaism's affirmation of man's uniqueness is to be contrasted
with the debasing pessimism which would reduce the barrier
between man and animal life to one of degree and not of kind.
In such a view, man's actions are deemed to be conditioned by
the "struggle for existence," and his moral values to be solely
derived from biological, environmental, and historical factors.*

In the face of this reduction of man to a helpless creature of impulse and circumstance, Judaism reaffirms its belief that man is "made in the image of God" and that every human being is of incalculable worth. Man's distinctiveness lies in the fact that he contemplates the universe with wonder. He is potentially greater than his own limited understanding of himself. His is the capacity to transcend himself and to reach out for the Reality behind reality and to establish what ought to be as the measuring scale of what is. He alone must come to terms with death which, of all creatures, he alone knows to be inescapable. An irresponsible "scientific" determinism tends to focus man's attention on his animal heritage, as if directing him to look back to his lowly origin. Judaism also reminds man that he comes from a putrid drop (Avot 3.1), but the purpose of this is not to equate him with other living things, but to remind him that his moral accountability is the differential that sets him apart from other creatures. In effect, Judaism says to man: "Look back and ponder your creatureliness, and then look up and realize the divine image in which you are fashioned. By doing so, your life will be one of service as God's collaborator in the continuing process of transforming chaos into creation."[22]

GOD, THAT DOEST WONDROUSLY

EL NORA ALILAH

MOSES IBN EZRA

> God, that doest wondrously,
> God, that doest wondrously,
> Pardon at Thy people's cry,
> As the closing hour draws nigh!

> Few are Israel's sons, and weak;
> Thee, in penitence, they seek.
> Oh, regard their anguished cry,
> As the closing hour draws nigh!

Souls in grief before Thee poured,
Agonize for deed and word;
"We have sinned. Forgive!" they cry,
As the closing hour draws nigh!

Heal them! Let their trust in Thee
Turn aside wrath's dread decree;
Doom them not, but heed their cry,
As the closing hour draws nigh!

Mercy, grace, for these low-bowed!
But upon the oppressor proud,
Judgment for his victims' cry,
As the closing hour draws nigh!

For our fathers' righteousness,
Save us now in our distress;
Make us glad with freedom's cry,
As the closing hour draws nigh!

Join, O Shepherd, as of old,
Zion's with Samaria's fold;
Call Thy flock with tend'rest cry,
As the closing hour draws nigh!

Elijah, Michael, Gabriel,
Come! the hoped-for tidings tell;
Let "Redemption!" be your cry
As the closing hour draws nigh!

God, that doest wondrously,
God, that doest wondrously,
Pardon at Thy people's cry,
As the closing hour draws nigh!

Translated by Solomon Solis-Cohen[23]

COMMENTARY: *Julius H. Greenstone*

*Perhaps the most popular melody among the Sephardim is the
one used in connection with a hymn beginning with the words
El Nora Alilah, chanted just before the Neilah service. The*

hymn is the work of the Spanish Jewish poet Moses ibn Ezra,
and consists of eight stanzas which are sung with much vim
and gusto by all the members of the congregation. The tune is
spirited and buoyant, and the manner in which it is chanted is
indicative of the confidence of the people in the mercy of God
who has listened to their prayers and has granted them all
another year of life and health, of spiritual growth and religious
progress.[24]

OPEN UNTO US THE GATE

PETAH LANU SHAAR

Open unto us the gate
at the time of closing the gate,
now that the day is turning.

The day is turning,
the sun is setting and turning.
O let us enter in Thy gate.

Translated by Nahum N. Glatzer[25]

COMMENTARY: *Max Arzt*

The realism with which the liturgy recalls the rites held in the
Temple on Yom Kippur is demonstrated by the name of the
fourth service: Neilah. Neilah (closing) preserves the name of
the concluding ceremony in the Temple when, at the end of the
day, before closing the gates of the Temple, the priests dismissed
the people. The Mishnah refers to Neilah as Neilat Shearim—
"The closing of the gates" (Mishnah Taanit 4.1). The Palestinian
Talmud speaks of it as Neliat Shaare Shamayim, "The closing
of the gates of heaven," rather than as Neliat Shaare Hekhal,
"The closing of the gates of the Temple." This distinction is
made because the usual time for the Neilah service on Yom
Kippur is at sunset when "the gates of heaven close"—which is
an hour later than the closing of the gates of the Temple. We
are informed in the Palestinian Talmud that it was Rab's prac-
tice to ask that his cloak be fetched "when the sun is seen over

the top of the trees" so that he might then begin to recite the Neilah prayers and prolong his prayers till "the closing of the gates of heaven" (Jerusalem Taanit 67c).

The image of the "closing gates" is the theme of a number of piyyutim in the Neilah liturgy. They allegorize the "gates of heaven" in the light of a homily by Rabbi Eleazar, to the effect that, although the gates of prayer have been closed since the Temple was destroyed, the "gates of tears" (i.e., fervent prayer) are never closed (Berakhot 32b). The most impressive of these "closing of the gates" hymns is "Open unto Us the Gate," . . . a deeply moving twilight hour appeal. As the gate is about to close, we ask that it be opened wide, so that, cleansed of our sins, we may be reinstated in the divine favor.[26]

LORD, I REMEMBER

EZKERAH

AMITTAI BEN SHEFATIAH

Lord, I remember, and am sore amazed
   To see the cities stand in haughty state,
And God's own city to the low grave razed—
   Yet in all time we look to Thee and wait.

Spirit of mercy! rise in might! awake!
   Plead to thy Master in our mournful plaint,
And crave compassion for thy people's sake;
   Each head is weary, and each heart is faint.

I rest upon my pillars—love and grace,
   Upon the flood of ever-flowing tears;
I pour out prayer before His searching face,
   And through the fathers' merit lull my fears.

O Thou who hearest weeping, healest woe!
   Our tears within Thy vase of crystal store;
Save us; and all Thy dread decrees forgo,
   For unto Thee our eyes turn evermore.

Translated by Nina Davis Salaman[27]

COMMENTARY: *Max Arzt*

The author, Rabbi Amittai ben Shefatiah, whose name Amittai [in Hebrew] is the acrostic formed by the first letters of the four stanzas, lived in Italy in the beginning of the tenth century. Sorely depressed, he compares the devastated city of Jerusalem and its abandoned ruins with the cities of other lands and other peoples which had been rebuilt after being devastated. But as he invokes the Thirteen Attributes and the merit of the patriarchs, he is fortified by the belief that God will treat His people with tender mercy.[28]

LORD, THINE HUMBLE SERVANTS HEAR

YAH SHEMA EVYONEKHA

JUDAH HALEVI

> Lord, Thine humble servants hear,
>   Suppliant now before Thee;
> Our Father, from Thy children's plea
>   Turn not, we implore Thee!
>
> Lord, Thy people, sore oppressed,
>   From the depths implore Thee;
> Our Father, let us not, this day,
>   Cry in vain before Thee.
>
> Lord, blot out our evil pride,
>   All our sins before Thee;
> Our Father, for Thy Mercy's sake,
>   Pardon, we implore Thee.
>
> Lord, no sacrifice we bring,
>   Prayers and tears implore Thee;
> Our Father, take the gift we lay,
>   Contrite hearts, before Thee.
>
> Lord, Thy sheep have wandered far,
>   Gather them before Thee;
> Our Father, let Thy shepherd love
>   Guide us, we implore Thee.

Lord, Thy pardon grant to all
That in truth implore Thee;
Our Father, let our evening prayer
Now find grace before Thee.

Lord, Thine humble servants hear,
Suppliant now before Thee;
Our Father, from Thy children's plea
Turn not, we implore Thee!

Translated by Solomon Solis-Cohen[29]

THE DECLARATION OF FAITH

Hear, O Israel, the Lord is our God, the Lord is One [recited once].

Blessed be the name of His glorious kingdom forever and ever [recited three times].

The Lord, He is God [recited seven times].

COMMENTARY

As Neilah *comes to a close, the congregation joins with the reader in a final, stirring declaration of faith. The classic formulation of God's unity—Shema Yisrael (Hear, O Israel)—is pronounced once, for any immediate repetition might be construed to imply that there is more than one Deity. Then the kingship of God—"Blessed be the name of His glorious kingdom forever and ever"—is proclaimed thrice to stress that His sovereignty spans the past, the present, and the future. This proclamation, recited daily after the first verse of the* Shema, *indicates an acceptance of the "yoke of the kingdom of heaven." The sevenfold affirmation—"The Lord, He is God" (1 Kings 18.39)—symbolically emphasizes the universal supremacy of God who dwells "above the seven heavens which God opened before the children of Israel at Mount Sinai to show them that there is none beside Him."*

5. *Mahzor*. Germany. Circa 1320. University Library, Leipzig. See Chapter XI.

Rabbi Elie Munk in his The World of Prayer *wrote that, when these passages are recited, "Israel acknowledges again its eternal task and pledges itself anew to the faithful execution of its calling among the nations and in history. It is a solemn pledge of allegiance which shines over the parting hour of Yom Kippur on which Israel has been reconciled with its God, and it is under the impact of these sacred vows that Israel, purified, uplifted, and strengthened, enters anew upon the task of daily living."*[30]

WE STAND BEFORE THEE ON THIS DAY

Our God and God of our fathers, we stand before Thee on this day, as the community of Israel. We feel Thy nearness to us yet we are deeply conscious of our disloyalty to Thee. We realize, alas, how remiss we have been as a community in upholding Thy name and sanctifying it before men. We confess that we have often failed to rise to the responsibility of glorifying Thee by our conduct and of vindicating by our lives the precious belief that we are Thy people.

We have glorified in proclaiming Thy unity before men. And yet, how often have we desecrated Thy Name by showing our indifference to faith, to the duty of worship, and to the knowledge and the love of Thee which are the supreme bliss of life.

We have declared to the world that we were sent by Thee to teach justice and loving-kindness, brotherhood, and peace. And yet, even in our own household, prejudices, class enmities, and the envious conflicts for the prizes of worldly gain have not ceased. They have not been overcome by the belief that Thou art our Father, that Thou hast created us all, and that therefore we should not deal treacherously one man against his brother. Preaching peace to the world, we have not established it, even in the midst of Israel.

We have, by Thy grace, taught the world the sanctity of a weekly day of rest, and that the Sabbath is the sign of the tie that binds us to Thee. And yet, we have denied our teaching by refusing to hallow the week of toil with hours of rest and worship. Thus we are discrediting ourselves as ministers of the Lord, as a kingdom of priests and as a holy people, called by Thee to give light to the world.

We confess also before Thee that what should have been the most powerful challenge to our soul, calling forth the best in us, of humility, of duty, of self-sacrifice, was often turned by our erring minds into an excuse for our sins. We know only too well that what should have made us most scrupulous in self-searching helped us rather to self-indulgence and self-justification. We have proclaimed to the world, even as lawgiver and prophet taught, that we were Thine own treasure, a chosen people, Thy servant, upon whom Thou didst put Thy spirit. But we have not always lived so as to show ourselves worthy of this high and holy charge. Alas, we have contemned our holy heritage and made it minister to our own pride. Our sacred obligations we have turned into an oblation of incense to our own vanity. . . .

Turn our hearts to Thee, O God and Father, that we may serve Thee in sincerity and in truth. And serving Thee, may our example help to lead many to Thee. O Thou who hast founded the world on love, may this Atonement Day, by Thy grace, become a spiritual power to unite us with our fellow men, in reconciliation, in forgiveness, and in love. Praised be Thy name, O Holy One of Israel, who hast sanctified us for Thy service and hast consecrated us as a messenger of glad tidings to mankind. Amen.

Union Prayer Book[31]

VII

THE PARADOX OF *KOL NIDRE*

HERMAN KIEVAL

In our time, the best-known ritual of the High Holy Day
services—not only among Jews but among Christians as well—
is unquestionably *Kol Nidre*. Highlighted by its strategic location at the very inauguration of the twenty-four-hour Fast of
Atonement and chanted in a traditional melody of great spiritual
force, *Kol Nidre* exerts an enormous impact. Yet few of the
millions who experience that impact every year are aware of the
paradoxical and controversial history of the *Kol Nidre* rite. The
first of these paradoxes lies in the fact that *Kol Nidre* is not
even a prayer, but rather a legal formula for the annulment of
certain types of vows. The Name of God is never mentioned.
The language is a curious mixture of Aramaic—the Jewish
vernacular of the talmudic period—and of Hebrew, the language
of classical Jewish prayer. The style is prosaic, the wording
technical. Moreover, although *Kol Nidre* has become virtually
synonymous with the Day of Atonement, it is not, strictly
speaking, part of the Yom Kippur liturgy; it is a prefatory

84]

declaration which must be recited before the sunset which
ushers in the holy day.

Even more paradoxical, in view of its enormous popularity,
Kol Nidre has had to survive centuries of powerful and per-
sistent opposition, expressed not only by enemies and detractors
of Judaism but even by eminent rabbis who have challenged
the very principle underlying its recitation—the concept of a
blanket annulment of sacred vows. In response to these criti-
cisms the text of *Kol Nidre* has been amended to such an extent
that the version in most common use today defies the laws of
logic and syntax alike.

That a disputed formula like *Kol Nidre* should eventually
have won a central place in the standard liturgy is a phenomenon that defies complete comprehension. . . .

No one has been able to determine just where and when *Kol
Nidre* originated and under what special circumstances, if any.
We do not know who the author was, whether the original
language was Hebrew or Aramaic, nor exactly when or how its
long struggle for acceptance into the Yom Kippur liturgy was
won. There are many theories—some so dramatic as to border
on fantasy—which attempt to solve the mysteries, but none is
conclusive.

One of the mysteries is why the ritual for the dispensation of
vows should have, in the first instance, been associated with
the Day of Atonement. Actually the talmudic passage which
provides the legal basis for *Kol Nidre* speaks, not of Yom Kippur,
but of Rosh Hashanah: "He who desires that none of his vows
made during the year shall be valid, let him stand at the
beginning of the year [Hebrew, *Rosh Hashanah*] and declare,
'every vow [Hebrew, *kol neder*] which I may make in the
future shall be null.'" Pious Jews still follow a procedure
based on this original practice: after the morning worship on
the day preceding Rosh Hashanah, they petition a "court" of
three learned men to hear declarations pertaining both to vows
unwittingly neglected during the past year and those which
might be improperly taken during the year about to begin.
However, the procedure originally established for the day before

Rosh Hashanah was shifted to the eve of Yom Kippur sometime during the posttalmudic period. The medieval authorities explain that this was done in order to accommodate the rank-and-file worshipers who did not come to the synagogue on the day before New Year but did so on the eve of the Atonement worship. Here is one of those many curious accidents which rescued *Kol Nidre* from obscurity and helped to transform a dry legal formula, written in a confusion of tongues and tenses, and plagued by both legal and ethical problems, into the most prominent ritual of the High Holy Days.

The vow (*neder*) is one of the earliest forms of prayer known to Scripture, but a growing religious sophistication over the centuries led to a downgrading of this primitive form of prayer. The Pharisees, for example, took a dim view of candidates for their fellowship who were prone to the making of vows. Indeed, the Torah itself discourages vowing: "When you make a vow to the Lord your God, do not put off fulfilling it, for the Lord your God will require it of you, and you will have incurred guilt; whereas you incur *no guilt if you refrain from vowing*" (Deuteronomy 23.21–23). The Torah further provides for the annulment of certain vows, notably those made by females who are legally within the jurisdiction of their father or husband (Numbers 30). And Scripture, generally, cautions against vows lightly taken: "Be not rash with your mouth, and let not your heart be hasty to utter a word before God . . . better it is that you should not vow, than that you should vow and not pay. Allow not your mouth to bring your flesh to guilt . . . but fear God" (Ecclesiastes 5.1,4,6).

The postbiblical moralists shared this attitude and tried to dissuade Jews from resorting to vows as a demonstration of piety. In the period of the Mishnah, the habit of making vows was held to be a mark of low breeding. Some of the rabbis permitted the use of vows as a means of reinforcing resolutions to replace bad habits with good ones, but others disapproved. A favorite talmudic maxim says, "It is sufficient for you [to limit yourself] to that which the Torah forbids." In third century Babylonia, the distinguished Amora Samuel derogated those who, like the

Nazarite, adopted vows of abstinence: "Even though he fulfills [the vow], he is called wicked." The Palestinian authorities were inclined to be more indulgent than their Babylonian colleagues in the matter of vowing; yet it was a Palestinian Tanna, Rabbi Nathan, who said: "One who vows is as though he built a high place, and he who fulfills it as though he sacrificed thereon."

Despite such injunctions, not every Jew could resist the habit of centuries of oriental vow-making. Thus the legal authorities in the talmudic period had to cope with the dilemma of preserving the sanctity of the pledged word in a society that continued to make ill-considered vows. The problems—legal and moral—which perplexed the most eminent rabbis in the matter of the dispensation of the many types of vows, oaths, etc. are so complex and subtle that it is impossible to discuss them here in detail. Two entire tractates of the Talmud (*Nedarim* and *Shevuot*) deal directly with these issues, to say nothing of discussions in other tractates. Chief Rabbi Hertz, in his commentary on the Pentateuch, gives this vivid summary:

> Altogether aside from imbecile and rash minds, men in time of danger or under momentary impulse would make vows which they could not fulfill. . . . In such cases, the rabbis would consider it their duty to afford a man the facility, under certain definite conditions and restrictions, of *annulling* his thoughtless or impossible vows. Such annulment could never be effected by himself, but only by a *Bet Din* of three learned men in the Law, after they had carefully investigated the nature and bearing of the vow, and had become convinced that its purpose was not, on the one hand, self-improvement, nor did it, on the other, infringe upon the rights of others. For not all vows or oaths could be absolved. A vow or oath that was made to another person, even be that person a child or a heathen, could not be annulled except in the presence of that person and with his consent; while *an oath which a man had taken in a court of justice could not be absolved by any other authority in the world.*

The practice of annulling vows which had been made by *individuals* through the agency of a legal expert or an *ad hoc* "court" of three laymen originated in Palestine; but the first

references to a specific *Kol Nidre* formula for *collective* use are
found in the legal responsa of the Babylonian geonim, beginning
in the eighth century. These powerful authorities, however, far
from approving the practice familiar to them from "other
lands," violently condemned it, with outstanding geonim—
Yehudai, Natronai, Amram, and Hai, the son of Nahshon—
going so far as to forbid the recitation of *Kol Nidre*. Amram's
historic "Order of Prayers," composed about 870, preserves a
complete text of *Kol Nidre* (largely in Hebrew) but he prohibits
its use, calling it *minhag shtut*, "a foolish custom" (he was
probably quoting Natronai here).

What prompted the Babylonian authorities to take such a
negative attitude? On the surface, the objections appear to be
purely legalistic; but the passion, which is only partially hidden
by their technical language, suggests that the geonim were
fighting a losing battle against a highly popular practice. Both
Salo W. Baron and Cyrus H. Gordon believe that the geonic
opposition to *Kol Nidre* was connected with an opposition to
magic. Gordon points out striking parallels between the Aramaic
text of *Kol Nidre* and texts in the same language inscribed on
magical incantation bowls which were popular in Babylonia
around 500 C.E. According to this view, the function of *Kol
Nidre* was "the annulment of curses or oaths (originally *not* in
the sense of promises or contractual obligations) that touch
off evil forces in the community."

But the geonic opposition to *Kol Nidre* was not monolithic. A
difference of opinion existed—at least during certain periods—
between the two great Babylonian academies, the authorities at
Pumbedita taking a more lenient view, probably in response to
popular clamor, than those at Sura. By the time of Hai Gaon
(son of Sherira Gaon), who flourished in Pumbedita about the
year 1000, some form of *Kol Nidre* declaration appears to have
gained general acceptance throughout Babylonia and the far-
flung Jewries which accepted geonic authority. Unfortunately,
the liturgical writings of Hai, the most influential of the geonim
of Pumbedita, have been lost and the quotations in later
medieval writers are often inaccurate. We do not know, there-

fore, the exact wording of the *Kol Nidre* formula approved
by Hai.

But what we do know is the principle underlying the Babylonian compromise on a permissible *Kol Nidre* formula. The
geonim rejected the concept that vows might be annulled either
retroactively or in advance, a practice which had been permitted
in Palestine under carefully controlled conditions. Fearful of
the moral implications of such procedures, the geonim permitted
only a *Kol Nidre* formula which achieved the purely religious
purpose of seeking divine "pardon, forgiveness, and atonement"
(*mehilah, selihah, ve-kapparah*) for the sin incurred in failing
to keep a solemn vow (or possibly for having made a vow in the
first instance). This purely religious function of the *Kol Nidre*
declaration was made explicit by the closing formula: "as it is
written in Thy Torah, 'The whole Israelite community and the
stranger residing among you shall be forgiven, for it happened
to the entire people through *error*' " (Numbers 15.26). The
period of time covered by the declaration was always the year
just concluded; consequently the characteristic phrase of the
geonic *Kol Nidre* is, "from the previous Yom Kippur until this
Yom Kippur."

The Babylonian version of *Kol Nidre*, however, is not the
familiar formula which is used in the overwhelming majority
of Jewish communities today. The Jewries of Western and
Northern Europe, which did not recognize the hegemony of
Babylonia, also did not accept the *Kol Nidre* text of the geonim.
In the twelfth century a further major change was to be introduced into this ritual by the Tosafists ("Supplementers") of
France and Germany, from whom the Ashkenazic rite eventually derived. These influential scholars, reverting to the original
practice of Palestinian Jewry as recorded in the Mishnah, recast
the *Kol Nidre* formula as an *anticipatory* cancellation of vows,
oaths, etc., which might be taken "from *this* Yom Kippur until
next Yom Kippur." They excluded vows taken during the *past*
year because the Talmud rules that vows already contracted
cannot be annulled unless the votary explicitly states the content of his vow and voices penitence for his change of heart

(*haratah*) before a legal expert or a court of three knowledge-
able laymen. None of these conditions was required in the *Kol
Nidre* formula accepted by the Babylonian geonim. One of the
most important of the Tosafists, Rabbenu Tam, desired, indeed,
to transform all the verbs of the old *Kol Nidre* formula from
the past to the future tense. His lack of success on this point
has bequeathed to the Ashkenazic posterity a grammatical mon-
strosity: the time period mentioned is "from *this* Yom Kippur
until *next* Yom Kippur," yet all the verbs ("which we have
vowed," etc.) are in the *past* tense. Later efforts to remove these
contradictions—from R. Mordecai Jaffe of Prague, in the late
sixteenth century, to R. Wolf Heidenheim, in early nineteenth
century Germany—have been conspicuously unsuccessful.

The legal arguments of Rabbenu Tam and his father, R. Meir
ben Samuel, were not accepted uncritically by later Ashkenazic
authorities. Such distinguished rabbis as R. Mordecai Jaffe, the
Vilna Gaon, and R. Jacob Emden took issue with some of the
legalistic assumptions on which the new *Kol Nidre* was based.
Nevertheless, Rabbenu Tam's version (also known as the Aramaic version) has remained the standard *Kol Nidre* in Ashkenazic congregations to this day. This is not to say that the older
(or Hebrew) version of the Babylonian geonim was entirely dis-
placed. The Romanian (Balkan) rite, which has long been
obsolete, and the Italian rite, preserved today in only a handful
of congregations, retained the old geonic *Kol Nidre* in its
Hebrew form. The Sephardim of the West recite only part of the
geonic text, notably its concentration on the vows of the past
year, while the oriental Sephardim and the Yemenites have
compromised by adding the emendations of Rabbenu Tam to
the older geonic version.[1]

Not all the opposition to *Kol Nidre* has come from within
Jewish ranks or from sectarian groups (like the Karaites).
Throughout the Middle Ages in Christian Europe, *Kol Nidre*
was seized upon as a prime weapon in the continuing campaign
to vilify the character of the Jew. Accusations were constantly
leveled against the "perfidious" children of Israel whose religion
permitted them to perjure themselves in their dealings with

Christians and then—on the holiest of festivals—clear their
consciences simply by reciting the *Kol Nidre*. It was on the basis
of such accusations that the notorious "Jew's oath" was instituted by Christian courts.

Kol Nidre made trouble for the Jews in other ways too. Several
public disputations between learned rabbis and churchmen in
the thirteenth century included controversy over the legitimacy
of *Kol Nidre*. In the seventeenth century Manasseh ben Israel,
the famed rabbi-statesman of Amsterdam, had to defend the
ethical character of *Kol Nidre* in the course of negotiating with
Oliver Cromwell to permit the return of Jews to England
(whence they had been expelled in 1290). The governmental
machinery of tsarist Russia was likewise concerned with the
legitimacy of *Kol Nidre*. On October 25, 1857, after repeated
complaints from unfriendly quarters to the Russian authorities
touching on the rights of Jews in the province of Kurland, the
authorities issued an order prescribing a special Hebrew introduction to *Kol Nidre*, which stated explicitly that the declaration was valid only for vows exclusively involving the person
who made them but no other human being.

The Jewish defense of *Kol Nidre* always was that the declaration applied only to the relations between man and God, not to
contractual obligations between man and man: "For transgressions between a man and his fellow man, Yom Kippur does not
effect atonement until he shall have first appeased his fellow
man" (*Yoma* 9.9). Yet many defenders of *Kol Nidre* were themselves uneasy about it, haunted by the well-known criticism of
illustrious rabbis, both Sephardic and Ashkenazic. Thus in
twelfth century Spain, R. Judah ben Barzillai declared the recitation of *Kol Nidre* to be dangerous, since ignorant Jews might
erroneously conclude that all their vows and oaths were annulled through this declaration and, consequently, would take
obligations upon themselves without due caution. In thirteenth
century Italy, R. Zedekiah ben Abraham Ha-Rofe opposed the
practice of absolving vows and cited the opinion of some
authorities "that *Kol Nidre* was intended only for *impulsive*
vows which the Mishnah deems to be not binding, so that people

might learn that even in such matters our yea must be yea
and our nay, nay." R. Jeroham ben Meshullam, of fourteenth
century Provence, attacked "those fools who, trusting to the
Kol Nidre, make vows recklessly." Even the *Shulhan Arukh*, the
standard code of Jewish law, recognizes that the legality of
Kol Nidre rests on precarious foundations.

Against this centuries-old background of controversy, it is
not surprising that *Kol Nidre* was one of the early targets of
the Reform movement which arose in nineteenth century Germany. In 1844 the first conference of Reform leaders decided
to expunge the ancient ritual entirely from the Yom Kippur
liturgy, and several attempts were subsequently made by both
German and American Reformers to substitute an acceptable
prayer in its place. Abraham Geiger's Breslau prayer book
(1854) contains an original prayer, *Kol pesha'ai* ("All my iniquities, etc."). The Berlin prayer book and the older editions
of *The Union Prayer Book* (of the American Reform movement) substituted the 130th Psalm, a most appropriate selection
since it had introduced the Yom Kippur evening service in
ancient Palestine long before there ever was a *Kol Nidre*. But
once again, the incredible resilience of the traditional *Kol Nidre*
ritual made itself felt: in the most recent edition of *The Union
Prayer Book* (1962), *Kol Nidre* has been restored.

In the United States, also, the Reconstructionist movement
attempted to abolish the recitation of *Kol Nidre*. But the movement's founder, Rabbi Mordecai M. Kaplan, later reinstated the
ritual, with an emendation specifying that *Kol Nidre* refers only
to the annulment of vows made in such a way "as to estrange
ourselves from those who have offended us, or to give pain to
those who have angered us. . . . These our vows, and these only,
shall not be vows. . . ." This revised *Kol Nidre* text was incorporated into the Reconstructionist High Holy Day prayer
book (1948) and is used in a small number of congregations.

It should be obvious that the phenomenal capacity of *Kol
Nidre* to withstand so many vicissitudes over the centuries
cannot be explained in purely rational terms. Due regard must
be given to other factors, foremost among them the powerful

folk tradition that has long associated *Kol Nidre* with Jewish martyrdom, especially at the hands of the Spanish Inquisition. The fact that this deeply rooted tradition cannot be substantiated by firm historical evidence has not in the least dimmed the mystical aura with which it has surrounded an otherwise undramatic legal formula of dubious provenance.

The legendary association of *Kol Nidre* (and its various musical settings) with Jewish martyrdom was given some scholarly underpinning in 1917 by Joseph S. Bloch, who attempted to trace the origin of the ritual to the persecution of Jews in seventh century Spain by the Visigoths. According to Bloch, these barbarian conquerors, themselves freshly converted to Christianity, forced the Jews of their Spanish domains to renounce their religion and vow their acceptance of the Christian faith. But the forced converts remained secretly faithful to their ancestral religion, and when Yom Kippur came, they would observe it surreptitiously. Nevertheless, feeling they had broken the solemn oath given, albeit under duress, to their Christian persecutors, they recited *Kol Nidre* to voice grief over their apostasy and simultaneously to seek God's forgiveness for, and absolution from, their unwilling vows. This, Bloch suggests, is the reason that *Kol Nidre* is recited before the prayers of Yom Kippur proper begin. Bloch further argues that Jews suffered similar persecution in the Byzantine Empire (700–850) and utilized *Kol Nidre* in the same fashion, as also did the Marranos who secretly practiced Judaism after being forcibly converted by the Spanish Inquisition (1391–1492).

Though Bloch's theory has not won scholarly acceptance, it is probably true that "secret Jews," in various times and places, did utilize *Kol Nidre* as a means of absolving themselves from vows made under coercion. In any case, there is a very long history in Jewish writings, going back to ancient rabbinic literature, of explaining innovations and peculiarities in worship and ritual in terms of persecutions at the hands of a variety of enemies. Whatever the merits or demerits of any particular theory of this type, the overall effect has generally been further to endear the prayer in question to the Jewish

people. Thus, Bloch's theory is reputed to have moved a number
of European synagogues to restore *Kol Nidre* after it had been
dropped from the service.

The plaintive melody of *Kol Nidre* has been scarcely less
important than the martyrdom tradition as a factor protecting
the embattled formula against its critics and enemies. Indeed,
the music itself has been associated by popular tradition with
persecution and martyrdom. For this notion there is no historical basis whatsoever, yet the myth dies hard. The history of the
Kol Nidre music is as obscure as that of the words; and, as with
the text, there are a number of versions. To name only the best
known, there is the familiar Ashkenazic melody and the two
current Sephardic melodies: one for the Western and the other
for the oriental communities, both based on the mode of *Selihot*
(prayers of penitence) and both quite different from the
Ashkenazic.

The earliest reference to a *Kol Nidre* melody comes, ironically,
from one of the ritual's enemies, the Karaite Judah Hadassi of
twelfth century Jerusalem. The procedure, still current, of
chanting the *Kol Nidre* formula three times is recorded in
Mahzor Vitry, a thirteenth century record of the liturgical
practices of Old-French Jewry. Each of the repetitions was intended to convey particular thoughts and emotions, and it is
probable that the early *hazzanim* improvised in order to express
these ideas. In the course of time certain melodies must themselves have become traditional. For example, we know that in
the early fifteenth century R. Jacob Moelin (Maharil), the
father of the Ashkenazic mode of worship, had his own special
melody for *Kol Nidre*. And so well entrenched was the melody
used in Prague at the end of the sixteenth century that the
codifier R. Mordecai Jaffe could write: "Most of the text of
Kol Nidre, as it is now printed in the *Mahzorim*, makes no
sense and is quite unintelligible; the only thing that gives it
substance and meaning is the melody. But they [the cantors] do
not know or understand what they are reciting. Many times
have I attempted to correct the wording and teach my improved
version to the *hazzanim*; but they were unable to incorporate

the changes in the course of their chanting because they are too
attached to the old melody which fits the familiar text."

Since *Kol Nidre* is neither a prayer nor a hymn, it is difficult
from a purely liturgical standpoint to understand why such an
elaborate chant should have been provided for it in the first
instance. The great Jewish musicologist A. Z. Idelsohn conjec-
tured that the *hazzanim* were obliged to improvise a melody
because of certain legalistic and practical considerations: they
had to begin *Kol Nidre* while it was still daylight and prolong
its recitation until sunset; moreover, in order to enable the
latecomers among the congregation to hear *Kol Nidre*, they
would have to repeat it several times. In the course of time,
an elaborate melody evolved.

The *Kol Nidre* chant has captivated Christians as well as
Jews. Long before the advent of the ecumenical age, it had
become routine for Christians to visit synagogues on *Kol Nidre*
night to hear the melody which Tolstoy once described as "one
that echoes the story of the great martyrdom of a grief-stricken
nation." This melody has also found its way into the work of
such non-Jewish composers as Beethoven (the penultimate
movement of the G Minor Quartet, opus 131, and the first movement of the Trio, opus 9, no. 3) and Bruch (the well-known
composition entitled "Kol Nidre").

The setting of the *Kol Nidre* service has perhaps been no less
instrumental than the melody in establishing its wide appeal.
The details vary from one regional or local rite to another, but
the general pattern is similar. In every case, *Kol Nidre* is recited
as a prelude to Yom Kippur. The reason is that the Talmud
prohibits the asking for absolution of vows on a Sabbath or
festival unless the vows directly concern these holy days. Thus,
by virtue of a minor point of law, *Kol Nidre* received the prominent position it holds at the very inauguration of the most
sacred day of the Jewish year.

This happy accident entailed yet another which served to
enhance the power of the ritual—the wearing of the *tallit*. The
fringed prayer shawl is not worn at night and would ordinarily
play no role at the evening service which ushers in the Day of

Atonement. Since, however, the service on this occasion begins before sunset, it is permissible—and customary in nearly all communities—for men to wrap themselves in the full regalia of prayer.

In practically all communities, the *Kol Nidre* ceremonial begins with a dramatic opening of the *Aron ha-Kodesh*, the holy ark. The white *parokhet* (curtain) is drawn, revealing the massed scrolls of the Torah, which are likewise vested in white —the traditional color for the Days of Awe, symbolizing the themes of purity and atonement as well as the confidence of the penitent. One or, more commonly, a number of scrolls is removed; tradition requires that at least one scroll must be left in the ark at all times. In many congregations, the scrolls are carried by the communal elders, led by the *hazzan* and rabbi, in solemn procession through the crowded synagogue—often to the accompaniment of chants deriving from the Kabbalistic tradition. The scrolls are usually kissed (and embraced) by the worshipers; pious Jews ask forgiveness for their neglect of the Torah throughout the year past and resolve to show greater devotion in the future. When the procession returns to the *bimah*, some communities restore the scrolls to the ark immediately but most retain two of them to be held by distinguished members of the congregation who stand at either side of the *hazzan* until the *Kol Nidre* rite is completed.

The climax of the entire ceremonial is reached with the chanting of the *Kol Nidre* formula proper. In all but a few obsolete rites, the ancient words (for reasons already mentioned) are recited three times. The melody is begun almost in a whisper, gradually increasing in volume until it reaches a crescendo of clear, resonant tones, as prescribed in the thirteenth century *Mahzor Vitry*: "The first time he [the reader] must utter it very softly, like one who hesitates to enter the palace of the King to ask a gift of Him whom he fears to approach; the second time he may speak somewhat louder; and the third time more loudly still, as one who is accustomed to dwell at court and to approach his Sovereign as a friend."

Will *Kol Nidre* continue to retain its force in the generations

6. *Mahzor*. Germany. Circa 1320. University Library, Leipzig. See Chapter XI.

to come? It is hard to imagine otherwise. The psychoanalyst Theodor Reik contends that even Jews totally removed from any formal ties with Judaism are susceptible to *Kol Nidre* which, he believes, speaks to the collective Jewish unconscious of its deepest tribal memories. Such, at any rate, seems to have been the case with lapsed Jews like Heinrich Heine, Edmond Fleg, Theodor Herzl, and Franz Rosenzweig (who was dissuaded from converting to Christianity by an exposure to the Yom Kippur service). It also seems to be the case today with many antireligious Israelis—not to mention American and Russian Jews of similar bent. And this too is one of the many paradoxes surrounding the long and curious history of the *Kol Nidre* rite.[2]

VIII

THE MUSIC OF THE
YOM KIPPUR LITURGY

Max Wohlberg

The Yom Kippur liturgy offers both an unparalleled challenge and an unequaled opportunity for the composer and for
the *hazzan*. It incorporates the moods of reflection, self-examination, penitence, awe, devotion, prayer, and hope. Having been
spiritually alerted throughout the month of Elul by the sounds
of the *shofar*, on Rosh Hashanah the Jew acknowledges and
accepts God's sovereignty with all its concomitant implications.

During the Ten Days of Repentance he purges himself of
all moral and ethical impurities. On Yom Kippur he makes a
final confession of his sins and, confident of God's never-failing
acceptance of the sincerely repentant sinner, firmly resolves to
live a virtuous life.

The insertion of the *Viddui* in the afternoon service which
precedes the *Kol Nidre*, the donning of the *tallit* for the evening
service, the white robes worn by the officiants, the removal of
the Torah scrolls from the ark—all contribute to an atmosphere
of profound solemnity. In hushed expectancy and in a re-

strained manner the cantor utters the six words *Or zarua la-tzaddik ul-yishre lev simhah* (Psalms 97.11) (example 1*). He then leads a Torah procession in the sanctuary, intoning the significant six words[1] at deliberate intervals.

After the procession the cantor solemnly invokes (three times) the authority of both the heavenly and the terrestrial tribunals "to pray together with sinners" (example 2).

The cantor then proceeds to chant the *Kol Nidre*. Much has been written about this best-known and much loved synagogue melody.[2] A popular myth attributed its composition to a Spanish Marrano who was worshiping clandestinely in a concealed chamber during the oppressive period of the Inquisition. With considerable acumen and scientific skill Abraham Z. Idelsohn[3] has analyzed the melody, classified its elements, and traced most of them to cantillation motifs and to a medieval minne-song tune. He localized its source—southwest Germany—and attributed its arrangement to an unknown cantor functioning between 1450 and 1550.

Johanna Spector, in an article significantly titled "The *Kol Nidre*—At Least 1,200 Years Old,"[4] maintains that the intro-ductory motif, which together with the concluding formula Idelsohn considered a foreign element, is reminiscent of the Babylonian chant of *Bereshit bara* (partly so, in my opinion). Citing historic evidences linking Babylonia to Spain and France, Spector presents convincing information that it was customary in Babylonia to chant *Bereshit* before the Yom Kippur eve service. The anomaly still remains, however, that our *Kol Nidre* melody is totally unknown to all but Ashkenazic Jewry. During the past century[5] some of its early embellishments have been eliminated and its melodic elements have been more or less standardized (example 3).

The *Kol Nidre* is followed by several short biblical verses stressing heavenly forgiveness. A festive setting of the *Shehehe-yanu* benediction (example 4) concludes this impressive pro-logue to the evening service.

Following the *Amidah* a number of beautiful *piyyutim* are

* The musical examples follow this article.

recited (example 5). However, in most cases their musical settings did not gain general acceptance. An inspiring miscellany of biblical verses commencing with the words *Shomea tefillah* (example 6) is followed by several short paragraphs sung to oft-repeated *Misinai* tunes (example 7).[6] Exodus 34.6–7, containing the Thirteen Attributes of God, which serves here as a recurring theme, is introduced by a motif characteristic of the *Selihah* service (example 8).

Many of the *piyyutim* employ the form of the alphabetical acrostic. Some, like *Amnam Ken*, utilize one word—in this case *Salahti* (I have forgiven)—as a concluding refrain. A Germanic tune associated with this text became popular throughout Western Europe (example 9).

A captivating seven-strophic hymn *Ki Hinneh ka-Homer* received numerous settings. One of the oldest contains the *Ba'agala* motif associated with the *Kaddish* of the Sabbath eve service (example 10).

Composers have given special attention to texts appropriate for congregational singing. Among the best-known melodies for one of these poems, *Ki Anu Amekha* is that by Louis Lewandowski (example 11).

The *Viddui* (Confession), appearing as it does in each of the five Yom Kippur services, has its own mode, one of major quality set in a narrow range of six notes (example 12). In the exhaustive list of sins enumerated in the long confession (*Al Het*) the verse *Ve-al Kulam* is interposed. The melody for it by Yoshe Slonimer (example 13), an East European cantor functioning at the turn of the century, achieved wide favor.

Aside from the *Viddui* there are, musically speaking, only two elements that distinguish the Yom Kippur day service from that of Rosh Hashanah. They include a number of *piyyutim* with their own *Misinai* tunes, and the *Avodah* (description of the Temple service) with its traditional melodies. Among the former are *Kadosh*, *Adir* (example 14), *Ha-Aderet* (example 15), *Mi El Kamokha* (example 16), and *Mareh Khohen* (example 17). These appear in antiphonal form and with congregational refrain.

The paragraphs of the *Avodah* section beginning with *Amitz*

Koah have their distinct ending motif (example 18). Three times the cantor chants *Ve-Khach Hayah Omer*, with the congregation repeating the significant words. He confesses his own sins, the sins of his household, and those of the people (example 19). The compositions for cantor and choir of Hirsch Weintraub, Nisi Belzer, and Salomon Sulzer are among the finest for this text.

In the paragraph that follows, *Veha-kohanim* (example 20), the momentous utterance of the Ineffable Name by the high priest is recounted and the awed response of the tremulous multitude is conveyed. This impressive recollection and simulation of the ancient rite culminates in the majestic promulgation: *Barukh Shem Kevod Malkhuto le-Olam va-Ed.*

The *Kaddish* of the afternoon service has its own melody (example 21). In a number of congregations the hymn *El Nora Alilah* (example 22) from the Sephardic ritual is sung before *Neilah*. The motifs of the *Neilah Kaddish* (example 23) are repeated for the introductory paragraph of the *Amidah*.

This service contains some of the loftiest liturgical passages. A number of composers, particularly David Nowakowsky, have succeeded in fashioning appropriate ‧musical expression for these poignant prayers uttered "before the closing of the [heavenly] gates." The *Neilah Misinai* tunes (example 24) reflect a spirit of calm dignity and boundless confidence befitting this fateful pretwilight hour. Among the characteristic tunes associated exclusively with this service are those for *Zekhor Berit Avraham* (example 25), *Enkat Mesaldekha* (example 26), and *Yakhbienu* (example 27).

The *Neilah* ends with the cantor's dramatic intonation of the *Shema*,[7] followed by a rendition three times of *Barukh Shem*[8] and concluded by a recitation seven times of *Adonai Hu ha-Elohim*. The congregation's repetition of each of these verses is followed by a *tekiah gedolah*, a prolonged *shofar* blast, and a spirited exclamation in unison of *La-shanah ha-baah birushalaim* (Next year in Jerusalem).

Example 1   M. WOHLBERG

Or za-ru-a la-tza-dik, ul'-yish-re lev sim-ḥa.

Example 2   M. WOHLBERG

Bi-shi-va shel ma-la u-vi-shi-va shel

ma-ta, al da-at ha-Ma-kom v'-al da-at ha-ka-

hal, a-nu ma-ti-rin l'-hit-pa-lel im ha-a-var-ya-nim.

Example 3   L. LEWANDOWSKI

OPENING

darga tebir-Prophets

darga tebir-Esther   *Opening repeated*

Example 4   After S. SULZER & A. BAER

Ba - rukh A-ta_____ A-do-nai— E-lo-

he - nu_ Me-lekh ha-o - lam   she-he-he-ya-nu   v'ki-y'-

ma-nu   v'hi-gi-a - nu la-z'-man___ ha-ze.

Example 5   L. LEWANDOWSKI

Ya - a - le ta - ḥa - nu - ne - nu me - e - rev, v'yo - vo_ shav - a -

te - nu_ mi - bo - ker, v'ye - ra - e_ ri - nu - ne - nu

CANTOR   CHOIR

ad _ a - rev, v'ye - ra - e ri - nu - ne - nu ad a - rev.

Example 6   A. BAER

Sho - me - a t'- fi - la a - de - kha kol ba - sar ya - vo - u.

Example 7   After A. BAER

Dar - k'- kha E - lo - he - nu l' ha - a - rikh a - pe - kha la - ra -

im v' la - to - vim v' - hi - t'- hi - la - te - kha.

Example 8   M. WOHLBERG

Va - ye - red A - do - nai be - a - nan va - yit - ya -

tzev i - mo _ sham, va - yik - ra v' - shem _ A - do - nai. _

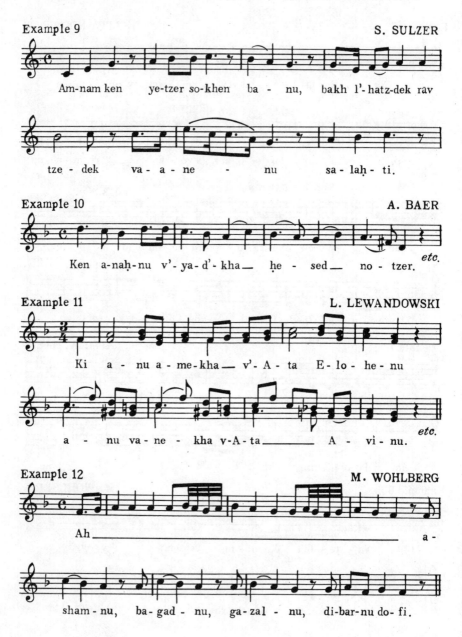

Example 9 — S. SULZER

Am-nam ken ye-tzer so-khen ba - nu, bakh l'-hatz-dek rav

tze - dek va - a - ne - nu sa - lah - ti.

Example 10 — A. BAER

Ken a-nah-nu v'- ya-d'-kha— he - sed— no - tzer. etc.

Example 11 — L. LEWANDOWSKI

Ki a - nu a - me-kha— v'-A - ta E - lo - he - nu

a - nu va - ne - kha v-A - ta——— A - vi - nu. etc.

Example 12 — M. WOHLBERG

Ah—————————————————— a -

sham - nu, ba - gad - nu, ga - zal - nu, di-bar-nu do- fi.

Example 13   YOSHE SLONIMER

V'- al ____ ku - lam_ E - lo-ha s'li - ḥot s'laḥ_

la - nu, m'ḥal_ la - nu, ka - per_ la - nu.

Example 14   A. BAER

CANTOR   CHOIR

Ka - dosh a - dir ba-a-li-ya-to.   Ba-rukh Shem k'vod mal-khu-to.

CANTOR   CHOIR

Ka - dosh bit-shu - va shat s'li-ḥa - to.   Ba-rukh Shem k'-vod mal-khu-to.

CANTOR   CHOIR

Ka - dosh gi - la l'a-mo sod da-to.   Ba-rukh Shem k'-vod mal-khu-to.

Example 15   A. BAER

CANTOR   CHOIR   CANTOR

Ha-a - de-ret v'ha-e - mu - na, l'- hai ___ o - la-mim. Ha-

CHOIR

bi - na v'hab - ra - kha, l'- hai ___ o - la-mim.

Example 16

A. BAER

Mi El ka-mo-kha. A-ha-lel-kha b' kol— ram ma-gen av-ra -
ham, mi El ka-mo-kha. B'- ya-d'- kha mim - tim m' ha-
ye ha-me - tim. Mi El—ka-mo-kha. God-l' - kha— ed -
rosh. Ha-Me-lekh ha- ka - dosh, mi El ka-mo - kha.

Example 17

I. & S.E. GOLDFARB

K' - o-hel ha-nim-tah b'- da-re ma-la, mar- e— kho - hen.— Kiv-
ra-kim ha-yotz - im mi-ziv ha - ha - yot mar - e— kho-hen.— etc.

Example 18

M. WOHLBERG

Ma-zim a - lav me-ha-tat_____ l'- ta - ha-ro zo-
rek mak-tir u - me-tiv— l'- hit - ra-gel_____ ba- a - vo-dah.

Example 19   M. DEUTSCH

V'khakh ha-ya — o - mer: A-na ha-Shem ḥa-ta - ti, a-vi-

ti, pa-sha - ti l'-fa-ne-kha a-ni — u-ve - ti *etc.*

Example 20   E. GEROVITSCH

V'ha - ko ——————— ha-nim v'ha —————

————— am ha-om-dim ba-a-za - ra k'she-ha-yu

shom-im et ha - Shem ha-nikh-bad v'ha-no ——— ra m' fo-

rash —— yo - tze — mi-pi — kho - hen — ga-

dol bi —— k'-du - sha —— u-v'-ta - ha - rah,

ha - yu ____ ko - r' - im   u - mish-ta

- ḥa-vim v'nof - lim ___ al   pne - hem,   v' - om - - rim'. ___

Ba - rukh Shem k'vod ___ mal - khu - to ___ l'o-lam va - ed.

Example 21   M. WOHLBERG

Yit - ga - dal ____   v' yit - ka - dash ___ sh' - me ra - ba,   b' ol-

ma di - v'ra _____ khir - u - te   v' - yam - likh ___ mal - khu - te
                                                              etc.

Example 22   *Fine*

El no-ra a - li - la ham-tze la-nu m'-ḥi-lah bi-sh'-at ha-n' - i-lah. M'-

                                                        D.C. al Fine

te mis-par k' - ru - im l' kha a - yin no-s' - im
um-sal-dim b' - ḥi - lah bi - sh' - at ha - n' - i - lah

Example 23   B. SCHORR

Yit-ga-dal v'yit-ka-dash sh'-me ra-ba, a - men, b'-
ol - ma - di-v'- ra khir-u - te v'yam-likh mal-khu - te *etc.*

Example 24   B. SCHORR

P' tah la - nu sha - ar b' et n'- i - lat
sha - ar ki fa - na yom.

Example 25   After A. BAER

Z' khor b' rit av-ra-ham va-a-ke-dat yitz-hak v' ha-shev sh'vut a-ha-
le ya - a-kov v'-ho-shi- e - nu l'-ma-an sh'- me-kha. Go-
el ha-zak l'-ma-an-kha p'-de - nu, r' - e ki az-lat ya-de - nu,

shur ki av-du ḥa-si-de-nu maf-gi-a en ba-a-de-nu v'shuv b'-ra-ḥamim al sh'-e-

rit Yis - ra-el   v'-ho-shi - e - nu l'-ma-an sh'-me-kha.

Example 26   M. WOHLBERG

En-kat m'-sal - de - kha   ta- al lif- ne khi - se kh'-vo-

de - kha. Ma - le mish - a - lot am m'-ya-ḥa- de - kha, sho-

me-a   t-fi - lat ___   ba - e___ a - de - kha.

Example 27   S. SULZER

Yaḥ-bi-e-nu tzel ya-do   ta-ḥat kan-fe hash-khi-na ḥon ya-ḥon ___

ki yiv-ḥon lev a-kov l'-ha-khi - na,   ku-ma naElo - he - nu u-

za u- zi ___ na, A - do-nai l'shav-a - te - nu ha-a - zi - na.

IX

HASIDIC TALES AND TEACHINGS[1]

Numberless are the tales of the hasidic rabbis that have been told and retold for generations since the days of Rabbi Israel Baal Shem Tov (1700–1760), founder of the movement. He and his disciples employed the story or anecdote to inspire their followers with the love of God and man. They succeeded in implanting faith and confidence, righteousness and hope, joy and gaiety in the hearts of despondent and poverty-stricken Jews throughout Eastern Europe. The hasidim cultivated an intimate relationship to God. During the High Holy Days they not only prayed to Him for atonement but actually demanded that He remit their sins; they even brought their complaints before Him. The compassionate hasidic master Rabbi Levi Isaac of Berditchev (1740–1809) was known as the eloquent defender of his people who saw only the good in man and evinced deep empathy for the widow, the orphan, the rejected, and the downtrodden. On Rosh Hashanah and Yom Kippur, the Berditchever composed original invocations and intercessions

which reflect his saintly character and reveal his ecstatic devo-
tion to God. Many of his tales and teachings, as well as those
of other hasidic rabbis, teem with profound insight into the
spiritual significance of these Days of Awe.

PROVIDING FOR BODY AND FOR SOUL

Rabbi Abraham Joshua Heschel of Apta once said: "The Holy
One, blessed be He, wanted to provide both for the soul and
body of Israel. Therefore, He assigned them different festivals
to sate their spiritual and bodily needs. Thus, the most sacred
and awe-inspiring day of the year, Yom Kippur, regarding which
the Torah states: 'And ye shall afflict your souls' (Leviticus
23.27), is preceded by the two days of Rosh Hashanah, concerning which it is written: 'Eat the fat and drink sweets, for
the joy of the Lord is your strength' (Nehemiah 8.10). Moreover, on the eve of Yom Kippur it is a duty to eat and drink,
as it is written: 'Whosoever eats and drinks on the ninth [of
Tishri], the Torah considers it as if he had fasted both on the
ninth and tenth' (*Berakhot* 8b)."

THE CORRECT MOTIVE

Rabbi Israel Salanter said: "It is as difficult to feast with the
right motive on the eve of Yom Kippur as it is to fast with the
right motive on Yom Kippur day."

LENIENT DECISIONS

Many women came to a hasidic rabbi on the eve of Yom
Kippur with questions relating to *kashrut*. He replied to each
one, without exception, that the food was kosher and could be
eaten. When approached by a rabbi colleague who suggested

that it might be more proper to be stricter in rendering decisions on the eve of the Day of Atonement, the hasidic rabbi responded: "On the contrary. If I should declare a chicken of doubtful *kashrut* unfit for eating, I may be guilty of sinning against my brethren who may not have anything else to eat before the fast, and a sin against man will not be expiated on Yom Kippur. However, if I declare the chicken to be kosher even though there may be some doubt, I am sinning only against God, and as you know, the Day of Atonement brings pardon for sins against Him."

THE MISSING RABBI

The congregation, assembled in the synagogue for the *Kol Nidre* service scheduled to begin before sunset, waited impatiently for the arrival of their rabbi, Israel Lipkin Salanter. The sun had already set over the treetops. The Jews were bewildered, for their saintly rabbi always came to the synagogue very early on the eve of the holiest night in the year.

Fearing that some tragedy might have befallen the rabbi, the congregants left the house of worship and sought to locate him.

Rabbi Israel was not found in his home. The streets and alleys were searched in vain. About to give up hope of locating the rabbi, the sexton noticed a light in the window of a shack, and he peered inside. To his amazement, he saw the saintly sage seated by the side of a cradle, rocking it gently.

Entering the shack, the sexton angrily exclaimed:

"Rabbi, the entire congregation is looking for you. The time for beginning the *Kol Nidre* service is already past. What are you doing here?"

Motioning silence from the sexton, the rabbi softly rejoined:

"On my way to the synagogue long before sunset, I passed this house and heard a baby crying. Receiving no reply when I knocked, I entered and saw the baby was alone. Since the infant's mother had evidently gone to the synagogue I remained here to rock the baby to sleep and watch over him."

WORTHY JEWS

As the recital of the awe-inspiring *Kol Nidre* ushering in Yom Kippur was about to begin, Rabbi Levi Isaac of Berditchev took a lighted candle in one hand, knelt down, and looked under the benches. Asked what he was seeking, the rabbi replied: "Jews." Drawing himself erect, he lifted his eyes to heaven, saying:

"Master of the Universe! See what a wonderful people the Jews are! Today, the eve of the Day of Atonement, when it is considered meritorious for a Jew to eat and drink more than usual, not a single drunkard, nor anyone sick or stuporous from overeating is under the benches. Are not Your children truly worthy? Is there any nation comparable to them? Are they not deserving of being inscribed and sealed for a year of good health, happiness, and prosperity?"

SINS BETWEEN MAN AND MAN

As the hour for *Kol Nidre* approached, Rabbi Meier of Premishlan, who was expected to chant this service, addressed the congregation of scholars and substantial businessmen:

"You are waiting for me to recite *Kol Nidre*, but I must tell you that even if you wait until morning, I will not do so. We have learned that the Day of Atonement brings forgiveness for sins committed against God but not for sins committed against a fellow man unless he is appeased. Therefore I demand that you pardon one another."

Immediately the congregants cried out that they forgave one another. But Rabbi Meier was still not satisfied.

"Do you think I am lacking in understanding? You forgive each other *now*, but after the Day of Atonement, whoever has a debt due him will insist on collecting it even if he takes the debtor's bedding. I demand that whoever is able to repay his debt but requires more time to do so shall be granted an extension of time. And if it is impossible for one to pay, what will you take from him—his soul?"

There were some merchants in the congregation who understood that the saintly rabbi was addressing them. They approached him and pledged: "Rabbi, we will heed your words."

Rabbi Meier turned to the holy ark and exclaimed: "Master of the Universe, the Jews admit they have sinned and will not sin again and You believe and pardon them. Therefore I, Meier, must also believe them." Turning to the congregation, he added: "Remember that if you take heed of my admonition, you will be blessed with a good and sweet year." Then he began to chant *Kol Nidre*.

REDEMPTION OF THE IMPRISONED

On the eve of the Day of Atonement Rabbi Hayyim Soloveitchik of Brisk was told that a wealthy congregant was bankrupt and was being held in the debtors' prison until he could pay five thousand rubles he owed his creditors. That evening when the *Kol Nidre* was to be said, Rabbi Hayyim addressed the congregation:

"Jews, compassionate children of compassionate sires, I have decided that *Kol Nidre* will not be recited until our affluent brethren will promise to provide five thousand rubles at the conclusion of Yom Kippur so that we may liberate our brother from prison."

An immediate response of pledges guaranteed the entire sum necessary. Only then did Rabbi Hayyim permit the chanting of *Kol Nidre*.

OPENING THE GATES OF REPENTANCE

A young illiterate herdsman who lived alone during the year came on the Day of Atonement to the synagogue of the Baal Shem Tov. Although the lad was unable to join the congregation in prayer, he grasped the significance and spirit of the occasion as the day wore on. He experienced a strong, overwhelming emotion to participate with the congregation in pleading for atonement. As the *Neilah* service was drawing to a close, the herdsman took from his pocket a reed whistle he used while tending his flock and blew on it lustily.

Hearing the solemn sanctity of the *Neilah* thus disturbed, the *hasidim* angrily upbraided the lad. However, the Baal Shem Tov, in a calm, decisive voice, took his followers to task:

"Despite all your prayers, your learning and piety, you have not learned to repent, nor have you been able to prevail upon God to grant you pardon. This illiterate young herdsman, possessed with a sincere desire to serve the Almighty, has opened the gates of repentance for all of us."

A LENIENT ILLITERATE

Levi Isaac of Berditchev asked an illiterate tailor what he did on Yom Kippur since he could not read the prescribed prayers.

The Jew reluctantly replied:

"I spoke to God and told Him that the sins for which I am expected to repent are minor ones. I also said to Him: 'My sins are inconsequential; I may have kept leftover cloth or occasionally forgotten to recite some prayers. But You have committed really grave sins. You have removed mothers from their children and children from their mothers. So let's reach an agreement. If You'll pardon me, I'm ready to pardon You.'"

The Berditchever rabbi angrily rebuked the unlettered Jew:

"You are not only illiterate but also foolish. You were too lenient with God. You should have insisted that He bring redemption to the entire Jewish people."

FORGIVENESS FOR TRUTH TELLING

Appealing to God for forgiveness, Rabbi Levi Isaac prayed as follows:

"Once Jews lied to You when on the Day of Atonement they intoned: 'We have sinned, we have dealt treacherously, we have robbed, we have uttered slander. . . .' In truth, they never sinned, nor did they deal treacherously, nor did they rob, nor did they speak slander. Actually, the Jews dealt honestly in business—their word was binding and a measure was a full measure. We, however, have committed all these sins and we are now telling You the truth. For our truthfulness, You must forgive us."

REDEMPTION FOR THE WORLD

The Berditchever rabbi ascended the pulpit before *Neilah* and addressed these words to God:

"Our sages have taught that whoever quotes a passage in the name of him who said it, brings redemption to the world. Therefore, since I quote: *'And God said:* I have pardoned according to your words,' You must pardon us and bring redemption to the world."

A VALID REASON TO SIN

Rabbi Zusya of Hanipol, enthralled by the cantor's beautiful and stirring singing of the prayer "O pardon us," raised his eyes heavenward and asked:

"Master of the Universe, answer me: If the children of Israel were not to sin, who would chant so beautifully for You 'O pardon us'?"

HEART BEATS

Rabbi Israel Meir, famed as the author of *Hafetz Hayyim*, was expounding the customs of Yom Kippur. Referring to the practice of beating one's heart when reciting the Confession of Sins, he explained:

"God does not forgive the sins of one who smites his heart but He pardons those whose hearts smite them for the sins they committed."

SPEAK FOR YOURSELF

On the eve of Yom Kippur a Jew came to Rabbi Naphtali Tzvi Horowitz of Ropshitz to confess and atone for his sins in accordance with the penance the rabbi might impose. Ashamed of his many transgressions, he said to the rabbi:

"A friend of mine who is guilty of many sins requested me to ask you for the proper method of atoning before Yom Kippur. He failed to attend the synagogue regularly. He even missed his private devotions occasionally. Once he violated the Sabbath by transacting business."

Rabbi Naphtali, undeceived, replied:

"Your friend is most foolish. He could have come to me and pretended that he was sent by a friend who was ashamed to come himself."

A FEARFUL CANTOR

Although he had no experience as a cantor, a pious *hasid* was invited by his rabbi to lead the services on Yom Kippur. He approached the rabbi as the *Kol Nidre* service was about to start and said:

"Rabbi, I am fearful."

The rabbi reassured him:

"Precisely for the reason that you have the fear of God I want you to lead the services."

A UNIQUE PRAYER

During the Yom Kippur services Rabbi Tzvi Elimelech Dinover was absorbed in a Kabbalistic prayer book, without turning a single page. Asked why it seemed he was not praying, he narrated the following story:

"An orphaned Jewish boy reared by a Christian family never had an opportunity to learn the ways of his forebears, although he knew he was Jewish. He had inherited from his father a Hebrew prayer book which he cherished dearly. When the lad was about seven years old, he was invited by the sexton of the synagogue of the Baal Shem Tov to attend the services on the Day of Atonement. The youngster cheerfully accepted the invitation and came to the synagogue with his prayer book.

"The Baal Shem Tov, noticing that the boy felt very uncomfortable because he was unable to join the congregation in prayer, prayed that the lad might be inspired to act in a suitable manner. Suddenly, in desperation, the boy shouted:

"'Lord! Listen to me also. I was never taught how to pray and I don't know what to tell You; however, I have my father's prayer book with me. Take it—I give You the entire book!' This caused the Baal Shem Tov to rejoice.

"I am like this boy," concluded Rabbi Tzvi Elimelech. "I am keeping this prayer book open and I have said to the Lord, 'Accept my prayers as if they were recited with all the hidden meanings found in the book itself.'"

THE ROAD TO ATONEMENT

Rabbi Israel, the Koznitzer *maggid*, said: "One who is guilty of many sins and is prepared to repent should start to perform good deeds, pray devoutly, and be careful to avoid other sins. When he is secure in the righteous way he has undertaken, only then should he seek atonement for his former transgressions. If he fails to heed this advice and fasts and mortifies himself, his determination to atone for his sins may weaken and he may give up his attempt at reformation. However, once he has embarked on the path of righteousness, it will be easier for him to continue."

A BLESSING IN VAIN

Rabbi Israel of Rizhyn raised the question: Why do Jews recite on Yom Kippur the blessing: "The King who pardons and forgives our sins"? Conceivably the Almighty may not forgive our sins, and if so we will have pronounced a blessing in vain, which is forbidden.

Then he continued: This is comparable to a clever child who wants the luscious apple in his father's hand and quickly recites the blessing for fruit which obligates him to eat it. The father will certainly not now attempt to withhold the apple, for then his son will have pronounced a benediction in vain.

So it is when we recite the benediction "The King who pardons and forgives our sins," the Almighty will not cause us to recite a blessing in vain.

A SOLDIER'S DUTY

After the evening service of Yom Kippur, Rabbi Joseph Dov Ber Soloveitchik of Brisk observed that a wealthy member of his congregation remained in the synagogue to recite psalms. The sage said to him reproachfully:

"Every soldier in an army is assigned to a division—artillery, cavalry, or infantry. Naturally, he has no authority to change from one division to another. If he does change without permission of the proper authorities, he is considered a deserter and he has to face a court-martial.

"Every Jew is a soldier in the army of the Lord and is given an assignment which he cannot change without authorization. The recital of psalms is the assignment given to the poor for repentance on the Day of Atonement. However, to you, as one blessed with riches, has been assigned the duty of giving charity to fulfill your responsibility for repentance. If you don't want to be court-martialed by the Celestial Court, you had better fulfill your own assignment."

LENIENCY IN SEVERITY

Rabbi Hayyim Soloveitchik of Brisk of the past century was asked why he was so lenient in permitting sick people to eat on the Day of Atonement. He replied subtly:

"I am not lenient. On the contrary, I am very severe when it comes to saving lives."

A QUICK THIRST QUENCHER

During the Day of Atonement the sexton told Rabbi Hayyim Sandzer that a congregant, who was both wealthy and miserly, had fainted due to the fast and asked if he could give him some water.

"According to the law, you can give him a spoonful of water," the rabbi said.

A few minutes later the sexton reported to the rabbi that the man was revived but had fainted again and asked for more water.

This time the sage decreed differently:

"Tell him that he can drink as much water as he requires provided he donates one hundred gilden to charity for each spoonful of water."

As soon as the rabbi's ruling was told to the revived congregant, his thirst disappeared and he felt sufficiently refreshed to continue with the Yom Kippur prayers.

MASQUERADING

The Kelemer *maggid* asked: Why is the Day of Atonement called in Hebrew *Yom ki-Purim* (a day like Purim)?

And he gave this answer: The similarity between the two days is based on the fact that on both days it is customary to masquerade. On Purim Jews masquerade and don the costumes of non-Jews. On the Day of Atonement, they masquerade as pious Jews.

X

YOM KIPPUR IN MODERN PROSE

▲▲▲

EVERY DAY IS A DAY OF ATONEMENT
(from Reb Azrielke's discourse in The Dybbuk*)*

S. ANSKI

God's world is great and holy. The holiest land in the
world is the Land of Israel. In the Land of Israel the holiest city
is Jerusalem. In Jerusalem the holiest place was the Temple,
and in the Temple the holiest spot was the holy of holies. (Brief
pause.) There are seventy peoples in the world. The holiest
among these is the people of Israel. The holiest of the people
of Israel is the tribe of Levi. In the tribe of Levi the holiest are
the priests. Among the priests the holiest was the high priest.
(Brief pause.) There are 354 days in the year. Among these the
holidays are holy. Higher than these is the holiness of the
Sabbath. Among the Sabbaths, the holiest is the Day of Atonement, the Sabbath of Sabbaths. (Brief pause.) There are
seventy languages in the world. The holiest is Hebrew. Holier

than all else in this language is the holy Torah, and in the Torah the holiest part is the Ten Commandments. In the Ten Commandments the holiest of all words is the Name of God. (Brief pause.) And once during the year, at a certain hour, these four supreme sanctities of the world were joined with one another. That was on the Day of Atonement, when the high priest would enter the holy of holies and there utter the Name of God. And because this hour was beyond measure holy and awesome, it was the time of utmost peril not only for the high priest, but for the whole of Israel. For if in this hour there had, God forbid, entered the mind of the high priest a false or sinful thought, the entire world would have been destroyed. (Pause.) Every spot where a man raises his eyes to heaven is a holy of holies. Every man, having been created by God in His own image and likeness, is a high priest. Every day of a man's life is a Day of Atonement, and every word that a man speaks with sincerity is the Name of the Lord. Therefore it is that every sin and every wrong that a man commits brings the destruction of the world.

Translated by Joseph C. Landis[1]

A DAY OF FESTIVITY

ARON BARTH

Judaism enjoins joy in life, and not undue affliction. We usher in our holy festivals with wine and we part from them with wine. "And wine that maketh glad the heart of man" is found among the blessings with which God has filled the world. One cannot trace in the whole of the Torah any precept requiring sorrow, and until our iniquities brought about the destruction of the Temple and the fasts connected therewith, there was no such law in Judaism. Yom Kippur, for example, is a day of affliction of the soul but is not a day of mourning. The Day of Atonement is a festival which we greet with the *Sheheheyanu* blessing. It is the greatest and most holy day of the year. "For on this day shall atonement be made for you to cleanse you; from all your sins shall you be clean before the Lord" (Leviticus

16.30). The high priest would make a celebration for his friends
when he entered the holy of holies in peace and left it in peace,
without hindrance. It was an exalted day of festivity and a day
of rejoicing in atonement and forgiveness.

Translated by Haim Shachter[2]

THE IMPORT OF THE *KAPPAROT* CEREMONY

JULIUS H. GREENSTONE

The persistence of a custom which appeals to the masses,
even though many of the best minds oppose it, is best illustrated
by the ceremony of *Kapparot* performed on the evening preceding Yom Kippur. The custom consists in taking a fowl,
usually a cock for males and a hen for females, and reciting
certain prescribed passages while the following formula is
pronounced:

> This is a substitute for me; this is in exchange for me; this is
> my atonement. This cock (or hen) shall be consigned to death,
> while I shall have a long and pleasant life and peace.

The fowl is then slaughtered and given to the poor, or eaten
by the one performing the ceremony and its value distributed
among the poor. It is preferable to use a white fowl for this
purpose, in accordance with the simile in Isaiah (1.18):
"Though your sins be as scarlet, they shall be as white as snow;
though they be red like crimson, they shall be as wool." White,
symbolizing purity, is taken as an assurance of atonement for
sins committed.

This custom had its origin some time during the geonic
period and met with great favor among the people, especially
through the influence of Kabbalists who elaborated it and surrounded it with many mystical ideas. Its primary purpose, of
course, was to serve as a sacrifice in place of the sacrifices
offered in the Temple. It is a sort of vicarious sacrifice, substituted for the prescribed offerings of the day which could no
longer be practiced after the destruction of the Temple. And it

is for this very reason that many of the older legal authorities strenuously opposed it. Joseph Karo, the compiler of the *Shulhan Arukh*, following some of the most prominent of the earlier authorities, said expressly that this custom should be abolished on the ground that it appears very much like a sacrifice, which must not be offered outside of the Temple precincts. Other authorities, however, especially those who followed the mystical lore of the Kabbalah, upheld the custom but endeavored to eliminate from it any element that might in the least make it resemble the old sacrificial rite. Thus only chickens or geese may be used for this purpose, or even fishes or plants, but not pigeons or doves, since the former were never offered on the altar whereas the latter were. While a white fowl is to be preferred, one should not look for it, since this is a heathen superstition.

No matter what the origin of this ceremony was, as it was developed in Jewish history it has a very definite ethical and religious value. It was early associated with the distribution of charity, always regarded as one of the most important elements in obtaining divine mercy and forgiveness. In fact, very often the entire ceremony is performed with money, usually a multiple of eighteen, the numerical value of the word *hai*, meaning life or living, and the money given to charity. The *kapparah*, whether in the form of fowl or of money, was made by every member of the household, including small children, even unborn babes. The day preceding Yom Kippur has always been a busy time for the poor of the community and for the various charitable organizations. In the vestibules of the synagogues, at the *Minhah* service, long tables would be set, on which were placed plates bearing inscriptions of the various philanthropic institutions of the community, and every person was expected to place his contribution there. On the streets where there were synagogues, hundreds of destitute persons stood in rows, ready to receive the gifts distributed to them by the people going to and from the houses of worship. From a household containing a large number of members, and most Jewish families were quite large, considerable sums would be obtained as a result of the *Kapparot* ceremony. Chastened by the awe of the approaching great day, humbled in spirit and weighted down by the consciousness of sin, every individual sought means to establish friendly relations with his fellow men and in this way obtain approval and consequent forgiveness from God.[3]

WHY FAST?

LOUIS JACOBS

Four main reasons are given for the command to fast on Yom Kippur.

Fasting as a penance: The most obvious reason for fasting on Yom Kippur is that by this means we show contrition for the wrongs we have done and the good we have failed to do. The man who "punishes himself" may be morbidly masochistic. But most people feel the need to give of themselves, to make some sacrifice, in order to demonstrate that their protestations of remorse mean something and are more than lip service. Self-affliction (Judaism does not encourage the excess of this) in moderation is an act affirming a man's sincerity. The man who fasts for his sins is saying in so many words, I do not want to be let off lightly; I deserve to be punished.

Fasting as self-discipline: Self-indulgence and lack of self-control frequently lead to sin. It is natural that repentance be preceded by an attempt at self-discipline. Disciplining oneself is never easy but all religious teachers have insisted on its value. It is true that history and literature abound in examples of the harm done by an overactive Puritan conscience, especially when it seeks to interfere with the behavior of others. Macaulay said that the Puritans objected to bear-baiting not because it gave pain to the bear but because it gave pleasure to the spectators! But the value of self-discipline must not be judged by its aberrations. The traditional Jewish character ideal is for a person to be harsh with himself but indulgent toward others. Fasting on Yom Kippur serves as a potent reminder for the need of self-discipline which leads to self-improvement.

Fasting as a means of focusing the mind on the spiritual: It has been noted frequently that Judaism frankly recognizes the bodily instincts and the need for their legitimate gratification. This is best illustrated in the rabbinic comment on the verse in the Book of Genesis that God saw all that He had created and behold it was very good—not simply *good*, remark the rabbis, but *very good.* Good refers to the good inclination; very good, to the evil inclination. For, the rabbis go on to say, were it not for the bodily instincts life would be good but it would be a colorless, unvarying good. A man would have no ambitions, he would not build a house or marry, the world would be left desolate. And yet with all its recognition of the bodily needs, religion seeks to encourage and foster the spiritual side of man's life. By fasting on Yom Kippur the needs of the body are left unattended for twenty-four hours and the Jew gives all his concentration to the things of the spirit. This is the meaning of the references in Jewish tradition that Jews are compared to the angels on Yom Kippur when, clothed in white, they spend the whole day in prayer, contemplation, and worship.

We must, of course, live in this world. "One world at a time" is sound Jewish doctrine. But unless our faith is to be denuded of its spirituality we must, from time to time, direct our thoughts to the nonphysical side of existence. Scripture says that "no man shall be in the Tent of Meeting" (Leviticus 16.17) when the high priest enters to make atonement there on Yom Kippur. This is taken by the Midrash to mean that at that awful hour the high priest was "no man," his body become ethereal like that of the angels. This is what happens to every Jew who observes the day as it should be observed.

Fasting as a means of awakening compassion: By knowing what it means to go hungry, albeit for a day, our hearts are moved for those who suffer. By fasting we are moved to think of the needs of others and to alleviate their suffering. In the Yom Kippur morning *haftarah* this idea is given its classic expression. The prophet castigates his people for their neglect of the poor. Their fasting and their pretence of piety is not acceptable to God if it serves merely as a cloak for inhumanity.[4]

WHY DO YOU FAST ON YOM KIPPUR?

EDMOND FLEG

"Why do I fast on Yom Kippur?" my doctor said. "That is very simple. I fast on Yom Kippur out of respect for the memory of my late father."

"That is your only reason?"

"The only one."

"Think again. You cannot think of any other reason?"

"Not one."

"My dear friend, will you allow me to ask you a few short questions in the Socratic manner? Your answers may lead us to some interesting discoveries."

"Go ahead."

"Do you contribute to charities?"

"My heart is not made of stone."

"And your father was a generous man?"

"Very."

"Are you charitable out of respect for his memory?"

"I don't think so. I give to charities because . . . because . . ."

"Because what?"

"For my own satisfaction."

"All right. Did your father tell lies?"

"Never."

"And you—do you lie, do you murder?"

"As little as possible."

"Out of respect for the memory of your father? Surely not. You don't tell lies and you don't murder . . ."

"For my own satisfaction."

"In short, you observe the Ten Commandments."

"Not all ten of them . . . perhaps three or four at the most."

"Right. Let's say five commandments. You observe five commandments for your personal satisfaction. But you fast on Yom Kippur."

"Out of respect for the memory of my father."

"Perfect. Now, be so kind as to tell me whether your father, while praying, used to put those leather straps which one calls *tefillin* on his forehead and arm?"

"Every morning."

"And you? Do you do this?"

"Never."

"Did he celebrate the *seder*, on the evening of Pesah?"

"Every year."

"Do you do the same?"

"I would not be able to."

"Did he eat kosher?"

"Of course."

"You did away with it?"

"Certainly."

"Summing up, he practiced all the customs of Judaism. Out of respect for his memory, you should not have abandoned any of those customs, whereas you only keep one: the fast of Yom Kippur. Why?"

"My father considered Yom Kippur to be more important than all the rest. When he came home at the end of the fast, I still see him, his face radiant."

"How do you explain that preference?"

"Yom Kippur was as dear to him as Israel itself. This fast, in his eyes, contained all that Judaism contains."

"If I understand rightly, you fast on Yom Kippur, in order to preserve within you something of Judaism."

"Certainly not! I care about Judaism as little as about Christianity, Mohammedanism, Buddhism, and Confucianism."

"Just a moment. Let me finish my sentence. You fast on Yom Kippur in order to preserve in yourself some aspect of Judaism . . ."

"Not at all."

". . . something of Judaism, out of respect for the memory of your father."

"All right, yes. If you want to put it that way."

"You see we agree on that. And may I ask you whether you believe in the immortality of the soul?"

"I don't even believe in the soul."

"Then, according to you, your father is no more. He does not

know you. He does not see you. You cannot please him anymore nor can you displease him. Your respect for his memory
cannot mean anything to him."

"His memory lives within me."

"Your father therefore is nothing else but a part of your
conscious self."

"A part of my conscious self which I value more than anything else."

"Therefore, you fast on Yom Kippur out of respect for a part
of yourself—which again means that you fast on Yom Kippur
for your personal satisfaction."

"Excuse me, excuse me . . ."

"In the same way as you observe half of the Ten Commandments for your own satisfaction."

"Oh, but . . ."

"But what?"

"Let us distinguish between . . ."

"Distinguish between what? You want to preserve within
yourself something of Judaism out of respect for the memory
of your father, but, as the memory of your father is nothing but
a part of yourself, this does not mean anything else than that
for yourself you want to preserve in you something of Judaism.
Now contradict this if you can."

"And so what? What does this prove?"

"I don't know. We shall see. Do you like to fast?"

"I prefer to have a good meal."

"And you deprive yourself of a good meal for your personal
satisfaction?"

"That I did not say."

"You said it by implication. Isn't it rather a strange satisfaction to deprive yourself of a pleasure? But perhaps, after all,
it is not strange that for your personal satisfaction you abstain
from lying, stealing, killing? Suppose you had to attend profes-
sionally to an enemy of yours. As a doctor it would be easy for
you to put him out of the way, without any danger to yourself.
Would you do this? No, of course not! But why not?"

"My duty as a doctor."

"There is therefore such a thing as duty."

"Professional duty, yes."

"But fasting on Yom Kippur is perhaps also a duty?"

"A duty to whom?"

"To yourself, for instance, because on that day you do not eat."

"You're too quick for me."

"I'm only following you, old chap. I don't do anything else but follow you. This duty, what is its origin? Who prohibited eating on Yom Kippur? Moses did. You obey Moses."

"Do I?"

"And from whom did Moses get this commandment? From God. God alone could give to this commandment the authority with which Moses has passed it on to us."

"So you maintain that I, a medical man, I who believe in materialism . . ."

"I know, you call yourself an atheist."

"I call myself an atheist, and I am one."

"You think you are. But since you fast on Yom Kippur, I am very sorry to say, my friend: you believe in God."[5]

THE DISTINGUISHING CHARACTERISTIC
OF THE DAYS OF AWE

FRANZ ROSENZWEIG

The Days of Awe are festivals of a special character, celebrated in the month of that feast which, among the feasts of the community, has as its content: arriving at rest. What distinguishes the Days of Awe from all other festivals is that here and only here does the Jew kneel. Here he does what he refused to do before the king of Persia, what no power on earth can compel him to do, and what he need not do before God on any other day of the year, or in any other situation he may face during his lifetime. And he does not kneel to confess a fault or to pray for forgiveness of sins, acts to which this festival is primarily dedicated. He kneels only in beholding the immediate nearness of God, hence on an occasion which transcends the earthly needs of today. For the same reason, the Prayer of

Benedictions said on every Sabbath omits the request for for-giveness of sins. The Day of Atonement, which climaxes the ten-day period of redemption, is quite properly called the Sab-bath of Sabbaths. The congregation now rises to the feeling of God's nearness as it sees in memory the Temple service of old, and visualizes especially the moment when the priest, this once in all the year, pronounced the Ineffable Name of God that was expressed by a circumlocution on all other occasions, and the assembled people fell on their knees. And the congregation participates directly in the feeling of God's nearness when it says the prayer that is bound up with the promise of a future time, "when every knee shall bow before God, when the idols will be utterly cut off, when the world will be perfected under the kingdom of the Almighty, and all the children of flesh will call upon His Name, when He will turn unto Himself all the wicked of the earth, and all will accept the yoke of His king-dom." On the Days of Awe, this prayer mounts beyond the version of the concluding prayer of the everyday service. On these Days of Awe the plea for bringing about such a future is already part of the central prayer, which—in solemn words—calls for the day when all creatures will prostrate themselves that "they may all form a single band to do God's will with a whole heart." But the concluding prayer, which utters this cry day after day, silences it on the Days of Awe, and, in complete awareness that this congregation is not yet the "single band" of all that is created, anticipates the moment of eternal redemp-tion by seizing on it now, in the present. And what the con-gregation merely expresses in words in the course of the year, it here expresses in action: it prostrates itself before the King of kings.

Translated by Francis C. Golffing[6]

REPENTANCE IN JUDAISM

Bernard J. Bamberger

Judaism teaches that man's duty is to obey and fulfill the law of God, and thus win the divine favor. But man's moral limitations prevent him from discharging this obligation: "For there is not a righteous man upon earth, that doeth good, and sinneth not" (Ecclesiastes 7.20). Sin not only makes man liable to punishment, but separates him from God, depriving him of the bliss of God's presence (Isaiah 59.2). Therefore God, in His compassion for human weakness, provided a means whereby a man can find his way back to the divine source: the way of repentance.

The Bible has several words to express regret and remorse (*niham, harat*), but repentance in the religious sense is indicated chiefly by the verb *shuv*, "to turn" or "to return." From this is derived the noun *teshuvah*, the usual term in postbiblical Hebrew for repentance. Thus repentance means to turn back to God, by turning from the ways of wrongdoing to the ways of righteousness. The ethical and the religious are inseparable and complement one another: by renouncing sin, man is restored to God's presence, and the yearning after God helps him to forsake the evil and choose the good. . . .

The idea of repentance was immensely deepened and spiritualized by the prophets. They insisted that sacrifice is not adequate to obtain God's forgiveness, that He calls for a change of heart which issues in better and nobler action. "Return, O Israel, unto the Lord thy God; for thou hast stumbled in thine iniquity" (Hosea 14.2). The means of return to God, then, is to forsake iniquity. In adding "Take with you words, and return unto the Lord," Hosea does not mean that words alone are enough, but that sacrifice is unnecessary. Words are sufficient to affirm the inner regeneration, which will have to be demonstrated in conduct. Thus a later prophet says: "Let the wicked forsake his way, and the man of iniquity his thoughts; and let him return unto the Lord, and He will have compassion upon him" (Isaiah 55.7).

The rabbis of the Talmud stress the same spiritual, prophetic note. The external means of atonement, the sin-offering and the Yom Kippur ritual, continued in practice until the fall of the Temple; and even thereafter these still left some impress on the thinking of many Jews. But the rabbis emphasized the importance of spiritual and moral rebirth, insisting that repent-

ance and good deeds are at least as efficacious as the old sacra-
mental methods of obtaining God's favor. They denounce as
self-deceived one who sins deliberately with the expectation of
repenting later, or in the hope that the Day of Atonement will
bring him absolution. They insist likewise that Atonement Day
grants no remission for sins committed against a fellow man,
unless amends are first made to the person wronged. . . .

It is clear that Judaism cannot tolerate the pagan notion
that one shows himself unmanly and "loses face" by admitting
himself to be at fault. Likewise, Spinoza's view, that an emotional sense of guilt and contrition is undesirable, is alien to
Judaism. Equally foreign to Jewish thought is the Pauline belief
that man can do nothing to extricate himself from sin and must
rely on God's grace alone. Judaism indeed recognizes the need
of divine grace, but it also declares that man can and must
attempt his own moral regeneration: the doctrine of return is
an affirmation of human freedom.[7]

"I HAVE FORGIVEN"

Samson Raphael Hirsch

You may have grown old in sin, every thought, every word,
every action up to now may have been a defiance of your God,
the tablets of the Law of your God may long have lain shattered
in your house, you may in misguided frenzy have danced round
the golden calf of a deified sensuality, you may everywhere have
sown only curses for yourself and extinguished in yourself
every spark of purity and stainlessness of thought and feeling,
yet *Yom ha-Kippurim* is there! The God who once uttered the
word *Salahti*, "I have forgiven," speaks it again. He forgives,
He atones and purifies. Only do you do your part; repair what
can still be repaired, cast out of your house the unjust penny,
make peace with the injured brother, restore the man you have
wronged, remove what is unlawful and ungodly in your married
life, in your education, in your business and pleasures, and then
come to Him, the Father who never rejects, who proclaims

eternally "as I live, I desire not the death and the downfall of
the sinner, but that he should return and win new life," who is
as gracious as He is just, and as omnipotent as He is gracious.
He thus not only forgives in His grace, but when He has forgiven, He with His unrestricted power lays hold on the spokes
of the wheel of destiny, on the fabric of your being, and with
His forgiveness He uproots every seed of curse which you have
yourself sown in the field of your destiny, and with His purify-
ing and sanctifying force plucks out every poisonous grain of
sin with which you have defiled your soul and made it troubled,
sick, ill, and lifeless, calling "Be ye clean again" (Leviticus
16.30) to all who in His presence seek to be pure again with a
new spirit and a new life. The whole future is again yours; the
whole past has been taken over by God.

And if you have been awakened and roused and brought to
God by the sound of the *shofar*, if *Yom ha-Kippurim* has found
you in the bosom of your Father in heaven, then He will place
you once again for the second time on His earth and teach you
to build the tabernacle of your life calmly and courageously,
with purified will and renewed strength on a soil which has
been cleansed and freed of all trace of sin. He will teach you
to perform the task of your life in cheerfulness and gladness
with earthly goods and means, to rejoice upon earth in the
presence of your God.

Translated by I. Grunfeld[s]

COMMUNITY CONFESSION

Herman Wouk

There is no machinery in Judaism for confession to a human
being or for release from sin through an agency on earth.
Confession in Judaism is a whisper of the entire congregation
at once. It is confession in formal unison, not an outpouring of
one's own misdeeds. An alphabetical table of offenses, two for
each letter, with a summary by categories of all religious failures,
is a central prayer of the Atonement liturgy, recurring many

times. This is all the confessing anybody does. The confession
table seems almost to be a mask to keep a man's wrongdoings
a final secret between himself and his Maker.

That the confession is drawn up as a prayer en masse is un-
mistakable. The wording throughout is plural: we . . . us . . .
our. . . . Such usage in a piece of liturgy at the heart of a holy
day cannot be an accident of rhetoric. It means something. A
man can acknowledge his own past sins in his heart when he
speaks the words that do describe things he has done; but he
utters no testimony against himself to any ear on earth. The
whole autonomy rests with the individual conscience.

But in a sweeping paradox, this same confession that seals
the individual in his privacy with God draws him into an
ancient communal bond. All the prophecy of Israel turns on one
simple but extremely difficult idea: namely, that all Israel,
living and dead, from Sinai to the present hour, stands in its
relation to God as a single immortal individual. The mass confession stamps that idea at the heart of Yom Kippur. . . .

In itself the idea is not so strange as it at first seems. We have
around us immortal compound individuals. General Motors is
one. Denmark is another. In principle, General Motors does not
die; it enters into contracts; it can commit crimes; it can be
punished. Denmark can owe debts though all the Danes who
borrowed and spent the money are dead. Were this not so, there
would be no selling of Danish bonds.

Immortal Israel, however, is something more. The Torah laws
do establish corporate Israel across space and time. In this they
resemble other national legislation, uniting many people under
a legal system. But the national idea undergoes a startling extension at the outset, at Sinai. Parallels break down.

The reader remembers the story. Moses ascends and descends
the mountain several times, acting as an intermediary between
the Lord and the elders of the people, renewing God's old
covenant (or testament) with Abraham. . . . The elders, speaking for themselves and their posterity—as founding fathers do
—solemnly declare themselves ready to undertake observance
of the Torah. The compact thus sealed, God reveals the Ten
Commandments and proceeds to unfold the rest of the Law. . . .

We Americans pay debts that dead congressmen contracted. We honor treaties that dead presidents signed, sometimes at the cost of our lives. We submit ourselves to a Constitution written by long-dead hands. It is the way of the world. But it is startling, for one not used to the color of Hebrew thought, to accept morality and worship of God as commitments of the same force.

What happened at Sinai was in its nature indescribable. Something happened there that the world has been unable either to fathom or to forget. The covenant that was proclaimed with blasts of the *shofar* still exists. The immortal individual who entered the covenant still lives. On days of annual judgment and atonement, this individual strikes the balance of his performance under the covenant and confesses his failures to blasts of the *shofar*. And so the compact between God and Israel carries forward into a new year, as it has already done several thousand times.[9]

THE JEWISH IDEA OF ATONEMENT

Leo Baeck

Just as Judaism emphasizes the closeness of God, so does it emphasize God's commandment and man's responsibility. It is in this dual emphasis that the Jewish idea of atonement finds its peculiar characteristic. Man is to return. "Let the wicked forsake his way, and the unrighteous man his thoughts: and let him return unto the Lord and He will have mercy upon him; to our God, for He will abundantly pardon" (Isaiah 55.7). In this concept atonement is no mere act of grace, or miracle of salvation, which befalls the chosen; it demands the free ethical choice and deed of the human being. Even in man's atonement, "Thou shalt" confronts him; in it are spoken the commanding words: "I, the Lord, am thy God." Man is not granted something unconditionally; he has rather to decide for something unconditionally. In his deed is the beginning of his atonement. As the Talmud expresses it: "To us who have sinned the commanding God speaks first, and only when we have listened to Him, does

He speak to us as the God of love; therefore it is said in the psalm, 'The Lord is just in all his ways, and loving in all his doings,' first just and then full of love." The first step is the return of man, for atonement is the work of a creative man.

The sinner himself is to turn to God, since it is he who turned away; it was his sin and it must be his conversion. No one can substitute for him in his return, no one can atone for him; no one stands between him and God, no mediator or past event, no redeemer and no sacrament. He must purify himself, he must attain his own freedom, for he was responsible for his loss of it. Faith and trust alone are therefore not sufficient; nor does confidence in God or a reliance upon an already acquired salvation suffice. Here again it is the deed which is paramount. Atonement is ours; it is our task and our way. This is the doctrine which, in contrast to Paul's gospel of redemption, has become the distinguishing characteristic of Judaism. This is the doctrine which gives ethical immediacy to the relation between man and God. This doctrine stands in sharpest contrast to the view of Paul and is especially underlined by the saying of Rabbi Akiba: It is before your Father in heaven that you purify yourselves.

All the elements of Jewish religiosity are most intimately combined in the experience of atonement: secret and commandment, source and path, the certainty of a granted divine love and the certainty of a commanding divine justice. In atonement, trust in God with its possession and reverence for God with its demand are welded into a single spiritual whole which gives to man his inner unity. Atonement is devoutness and duty joined into one. Here the two fundamental experiences of religion—that man is both created and a creator—find an encompassing harmony. Faith in God receives here its full expression and therewith does faith in man, which is ultimately faith in atonement—in the ethical redemption of ourselves, our fellow men, and all mankind.

Judaism is a religion of atonement. Two old rabbinic sayings express this thought: "The purpose and aim of all creation is atonement." "It was evening and it was morning—one day, that is, the Day of Atonement." The customs of Judaism also

give outward expression to this idea. Its most important holy
day and sacred center of the year is the Day of Atonement.
Joined with the New Year's Day, the "Day of Judgment," it
speaks to man at the beginning of the year of his responsibility
to God.[10]

THE SINNER AND HIS PENITENCE

SAMUEL BELKIN

Another of the concepts in Philo's work which clearly bears
the Jewish stamp and is unquestionably based upon the same
traditions as found in rabbinic literature, is the virtue of repentance. The Greek philosophers had nothing praiseworthy to
say about repentance. To their way of thinking, good men do
no wrong, and even a penitent is an evil person. In Judaism,
however, no man is so good that he can attain perfection, nor
is any sinner so bad that he cannot redeem himself through
penitence. Philo's understanding of repentance differs in no
way from the teaching of our sages. He formulates the essence
of repentance in the following words: "If shamed into wholehearted conversion, they reproach themselves for going thus
astray and make full confession and acknowledgment of their
sins, first, within themselves with a mind so purged that their
conscience is sincere and free from lurking taint; second, with
their tongues to bring their heart to a better way, then they will
find favor with God the Savior, the Merciful."

The elements of repentance listed by Philo are standards of
repentance formulated by our sages: genuine regret for the
sinful action of the past, a sincere resolve not to sin again, and
confession by word of mouth. In the case of sins committed
against a fellow man, Philo, like our sages, states that repentance avails not until the sinner rights the wrong he committed.
He must demonstrate "his repentance not only by a mere
promise but by his actions."

Sin, if repented, is not a stain on man. In Philo's view no man
can be entirely free of sin, "for absolute sinlessness belongs to

God alone or possibly to a divine man." But this fact gives man an opportunity to demonstrate his truth worth, for "conversion from sin to a blameless life shows a man of wisdom who has not been utterly ignorant of what is for his good." In fact, speaking of the penitence of the Day of Atonement Philo states that "the gracious God has given to repentance the same honor as to innocence from sin."

Despite this, it would appear that Philo accepted the view that in the scale of values the repentant holds second place to the one who is innocent from sin. In the Talmud, too, there is a dispute over whether the nonsinner or the penitent holds a higher rank in the eyes of God. It is clear, however, that both Philo and our sages were of the opinion that if a man genuinely repents and does not repeat his sins, he is forgiven by God and with good conscience may continue a normal life.[11]

THE JEWISH CONCEPT OF *TESHUVAH*

Joseph B. Soloveichik

The traditional view is that the *teshuvah* idea is penitence. For the Christian theologian *teshuvah* is a transcendent act dependent upon the grace of God who is all-merciful and benevolent. The erasure of man's sins is, from the rational standpoint, incomprehensible. Only the supernatural, miraculous intercession of God on behalf of the sinner may effectuate this cleansing. The task of the sinner is to repent, to mortify himself, to practice castigation, to cry and implore for divine mercy and pity. The convert, according to this concept, is a passive, pitiful creature who begs for and attains divine grace.

The halakhic interpretation of *teshuvah* differentiates between penitence and purification—*kapparah* and *taharah* (catharsis). *Kapparah*, penitence and absolution, is similar, in effect, to the universal concept of conversion, in toto. It is not a psychological phenomenon but a theological one, transcendent and nonrational. To alter the past is an act which denies the laws of causality and regulation in man's life.

But the halakhic concept of *teshuvah* contains yet another element: *taharah*, purification. This concept is not one that predicates the removal of sin but its exploitation. The *taharah* idea is, rather, to change the vectorial force of sin, its direction and destination. While the sinner of the first category attempts to forget his sin and beseeches God to erase it, the Jewish repentant strives to "remember" his sin. He strives to convert his sin into a spiritual springboard for increased inspiration and evaluation. This act is not supernatural but psychological. It conveys one law in mental causality; although a cause is given, the effect need not equal the cause. The effect need not be predetermined. Man himself may determine the vectorial character of the effect and give it direction and destination. . . .

The halakhic concept of *teshuvah* vouchsafes us the revelation that there are new values accessible to man from the springboard of sin, and that in attaining them the spirit of man can and does not only conquer sin but exploits it as a constructive creative force.

Taharah does not entail the act of reinstating man into a former status of repeating the past, in copying previous good deeds and performances. It must activate one, not alone to return to a former status of innocence and righteousness (for then the contamination itself serves no purpose, or *telos*, but is superfluous), but must convert and elevate one to a new stage. It must energize an ever-ascending spiral in man's spiritual state. . . .

In Jabneh, on the first Yom Kippur in exile, the Jews were left without the Temple and its ceremonial rites requisite for atonement, *kapparah*. The Jewish community was perplexed and disconsolate. They could not imagine that the beautiful ideals incarnated in the symbols of the day could be realized and effectuated without the performance of the high priest, without the ceremonial of the two kids, without the ceremony in the holy of holies, and without the public confession and sacrifices. They could not see how to dispense with all the glory and pomp which used to be displayed in the Temple on the Day of Atonement. The act of *teshuvah* and *kapparah* was closely associated in their minds with all these external and ceremonial acts. How can a Jew attain absolution and dispensation before God without the intercession and worship-forms of the high priest? It seemed as if, in the smoke of the destroyed Temple, the Jewish version of *teshuvah* and Yom Kippur had also disappeared.

Then rose Rabbi Akiva, the majestic, unswerving "optimist," and he said: There is no need for such mournfulness and helplessness. Indeed, we have been bereft of the Temple and its divine dispensation of grace for the atonement of sin. But we have lost only *kapparah*, atonement and penitence, but not *taharah*, purification. Besides *kapparah* we still possess a lofty idea, far superior to absolution. Indeed, we have been bereft of the ceremonies and sacrifices that are relevant to the transcendent act of the erasure of sin by supernatural grace and incomprehensible divine benevolence that alter the past and disrupt the causal chain. The attainment of *kapparah* will not be as complete and perfect now as it was when the cult worship acts of the high priest brought man into contact with transcendent and incomprehensible divinity. But we Jews have brought another message of *teshuvah* to man, that of *taharah*. There is nothing transcendent, miraculous, or nonrational about *taharah*. It rests, not without, but within causality. It is the discovery of a causal principle in spiritual and mental life— that the conflict created in a negative A may give birth to a positive B, by the rule of contrast.

The act of *taharah*, in which sin is not eradicated but, on the contrary, becomes part of my ego and is arrested and retained in its negative emergence and corruptive powers, awakens a creative force that shapes a new and loftier personality. There is no place here for worship or sacrifice. The performance of *taharah* is not directed at a transcendent divinity but at God, as our Father, Companion, and intimate Counselor who does not require any mysterious cult ceremonies or sacrifices. This *taharah* is based on an intimate relationship between man and God, creature and Creator, son and Father. And this communion of God-man has not been affected by the loss of outward ceremonial rites.

7. White tablecloth with gold brocade appliqué. Oberzell, Germany. 1781. Strauss-Rothschild Collection of the Cluny Museum, Paris. See Chapter XI.

When man stumbles and falls, becomes contaminated with sin, he should not despair nor resign himself; but he should cultivate hope, not only for regaining but "gaining" by his experience new visions and vistas. Our ideal is not repetition but re-creation on a higher level. And *teshuvah* contains hope and purification. Such an idea of *teshuvah* is not limited to any Temple or act of worship. All one requires is "before God," striving toward God.[12]

GO TO NINEVEH

HAYIM GREENBERG

The Book of Jonah, read in the synagogues every year on the Day of Atonement, has a lasting moral quality which overshadows the scholarly discussions as to when and by whom it was written. The Kabbalists and early Christians put a mystical interpretation on the book and connected it with their ideas on the immortality of the soul. But anyone approaching the book without any preconceived ideas can see that there are no mystic elements in it.

The style is simple, transparent, and not charged with any particular allusions. The story itself is straightforward and its moral is obvious. Once a man is endowed by God with a prophetic spirit, then he remains, willy-nilly, a servant of the Lord for the rest of his life. No rebellion on his part can change this.

Jonah, the son of Amittai, revolted against God. He wished to place his own will, his own prejudices, and his limited concept of justice above God's command. Should he "go to Nineveh, that great city, and proclaim against it," that it should be destroyed by God's wrath? Why should he? Nineveh was the capital city of Israel's mightiest enemy, a city rotten with sin and crime, for did not God Himself say, "their wickedness is come up before Me"? Then let the wicked perish without prophecy, without a warning. To be sure, God did not send him there merely as a bearer of evil tidings, to inform the inhabitants that the final sentence from which there is no appeal had been passed upon them. He suspected God of "weakness" and a desire to act not according to the strict letter of the law, of seeking to avert a punishment which He had already decreed upon the people of Nineveh: ". . . for I knew that Thou art a gracious God, and compassionate, long-suffering, and abundant in mercy, and repentest Thee of the evil." Jonah was afraid that perhaps the inhabitants of Nineveh might repent on hearing his prophecy and God would alter His decision. To use later terms, he considered himself the bearer of "the attribute of justice" and suspected God of being inclined toward the "attribute of mercy." What he forgot was that mercy and forgiveness were in themselves part of a righteous judgment.

Jonah had another motive for refusing to go to Nineveh. Nineveh lay outside of the land of Palestine, an alien city of pagan, unclean worship. But he was a prophet of Israel and for Israel. He believed that the spirit of prophecy was given to him with the understanding that he pour it out only upon Jewish soil for Jews to hear, that the Gentile had no part in it. . . . To bring to them the prophecy of destruction was risky. They might repent their sins: God might hearken to their prayers; and Nineveh might be saved.

"Jonah rose up to flee unto Tarshish from the presence of the Lord," rather than carry out his mission. . . . Jonah fled, but can one flee from God's command? A week later, legend tells us, the storm affected only that one ship, and all other ships proceeded on their way peacefully. Moreover, the fish which swallowed Jonah had been prepared for that task from the very first day of creation. "And the Lord prepared a great fish to swallow up Jonah"; the prophet was not to know of any limitations on the message he was to carry. He must carry it also to the lands of the uncircumcised. And if he wanted to narrow his horizon and narrow his heart, God would show him what narrowness was. He was not to reach Tarshish, and soon God was to hear his prayer "out of the fish's belly."

The rebellious prophet received his punishment by being incarcerated for days and nights in the dark dungeon of the fish's belly. A later commentary says that after the sailors on the ship had seen Jonah spewed out on dry land by the fish, they went to Jerusalem, had themselves circumcised, and devoted themselves and their wives and their children and their belongings to the service of the Lord. This showed that even these uncircumcised, sinful people were not beyond salvation, and what happened to them could also happen to the inhabitants of Nineveh. The God of Abraham, Isaac, and Jacob was also their God, and if they did not serve Him today they would be ready to serve Him tomorrow. "Go to Nineveh," He told Jonah.

But the story of Jonah is more than a protest against narrow nationalism. Its moral deals also with the very essence of Jewish prophecy. The prophet is not merely one who predicts events which will or which must occur in the future. If he were no more than that, there would be no difference between a prophet and a pagan oracle. For the oracle there is no "if." It only knows that thus it will be under all circumstances, no matter how man acts or fails to act. The decree which the pagan oracle knows is categorical and absolute and ultimate. Neither human will nor even the will of the gods can alter it. It is Fate, unchangeable and immutable. . . .

Jewish prophecy, in contrast to pagan prophecy, knows no fatalism. There is no Fate within the whole Jewish concept. There is no faith in blind decrees. But there is Providence watching and listening over the world. Providence may be appealed to, may be prayed to, may be moved to do man's desire, if that desire is just and pure. Jewish prophecy, therefore, is by its function and its character conditional rather than categorical. Jonah wanted to see an immutable decree in God's decision to destroy Nineveh. Had he been certain that God interpreted the decision in the same way, he would not have fled to Tarshish. Therein lay his transgression. Instead of being a prophet whose prophecy would bring warning and move the sinful to repent and to purge themselves of their sin, he preferred being an oracle, a *golem* through whom spoke the blind, brutal, fatal future. By this he lowered the prophetic calling; he destroyed the conditional nature of God's decrees. He confused

God's hatred of evil in man with God's hatred of the evil man, as if the evil man were evil in essence and beyond hope, and condemned forever to be wicked and with no road of repentance open to him. By his disbelief in repentance and in God's "duty" to accept it and to "rend the evil of His decrees" he became a blasphemer, closer to paganism than to the Jewish God. Still greater was his crime in not wanting to see the uncircumcised of Nineveh begin believing in his God and proclaim a day of fasting, clothing themselves in sackcloth, and the king of Nineveh shedding his mantle and covering himself with sackcloth and sitting in the ashes on the ground. He was unwilling to rejoice with God at the sight of the drama of human repentance and cleansing. It was for this narrow-minded, unprophet-like inability to rejoice with God that he was severely reprimanded. "Thou hast had pity on the gourd, for which thou hast not labored, neither madest it grew, which came up in a night, and perished in a night; and should not I have pity on Nineveh, that great city, wherein are more than six score thousand persons that cannot discern between their right hand and their left hand, and also much cattle."

That is why the Book of Jonah fits so well into the Yom Kippur service. The very sense of the Day of Atonement is faith in Providence and denial of Fate; faith in repentance and in its redeeming power; hatred of the evil in man and hope that man will ultimately overcome that evil. The moral horizon of Yom Kippur is wide and distant, limitlessly universal, in the perspective of which the barrier between one of the covenant and one of the uncircumcised is obliterated. "And all species may fear Thee, and all creatures may bow to Thee, and may they all become one community to do Thy will with a whole heart." And God is praised for his quality of forgiveness on Yom Kippur: "Thou extendest Thy hand to the sinners and Thy right hand is extended to receive those that return to Thee." For on that day prayers are offered also for the wicked. "For Thou wishest the repentance of the wicked and Thou dost not desire their death, for, as it is said, God said, 'As I live,' says the Lord God, 'I do not desire the death of the wicked, but the return of

the wicked from his ways.' " On Yom Kippur prayers are offered
for Nineveh, for all the Ninevehs of the world.[13]

YOM KIPPUR

Aaron David Gordon

I ask myself and I wonder whether I am alone in this question: What is the Day of Atonement to us, to those who do not
observe the forms of religion?

The nation set one special day aside devoted to meditating
upon itself as a nation; it set the day aside for its sons, a day for
the contemplation of the self, and as members of a definite
people, for weighing the values of life, for the complete devotion to the most lofty demands of the spirit of humanity. Private
affairs and accounts cease—prayers and supplications for a
livelihood are very few on Yom Kippur and Rosh Hashanah.
Important accounts and serious matters were the order of the
day—accounts of national, human, and universal significance.
Divisions existing among individuals were ended; the with-
drawal of each person within his own sphere of interest stopped.
All individuals felt themselves members of a single, sublime
organism, a single nation. As units of one exalted personality,
they came to take stock of themselves, with their lives, and with
their world. The individual personality, the unit, grew and rose
to higher levels with the growth of the exalted personality as
that in turn developed with the growth of the units. Herein is
the core of the matter: the individual as an individual is able
to take stock of himself every day or any day he feels so dis-
posed. But as in every national deed, especially of a religious,
national character, strength is important, the strength which is
increased when the individual personalities gather together. The
light that is poured on that personality because of the fullness
of the light in the exalted personality is also significant. So, too,
is the lofty melody important that is imparted to the individual
voice when it blends in a sea of voices composing the sublime,
human, cosmic choir.

I am not asking myself the origin of Yom Kippur or its ancient form. I do not ask whether the majority of the nation looked upon Yom Kippur from this point of view in preceding generations or whether it considers it in this light today.

Facing me are a fact and a possibility. It is a fact that for many generations it was a day which the entire people dedicated to repentance, prayer, and the service of the heart. It presented a possibility to spiritually sensitive people to make their inner reckoning on the loftiest plane.

I ask: Is this day for us merely a heritage from the past, a remnant of antiquity? Do we not really need such a day, especially as part of the national culture we are creating? If this day ceases to be what it has been—if it becomes an ordinary day like all others—will this not represent a great national and human loss, a spiritual disaster from which none of us, neither the people as a whole nor we, its individual children, can ever recover?

As long as we were penned within ghetto walls, ragged and cut off from the great life of the world, from man and from his broad and abundant life, we accepted what our ancestors had bequeathed to us. We believed in it and we gave our lives for it. When the walls of the ghetto fell—when we saw the world and all that is in it at close range, when we came to know man and his life, when we added cultural values from without to all this—we realized that the traditions of our ancestors were no longer in harmony with what was growing and developing in our own spirits. But did we deeply ponder this problem? Did we analyze and examine what had really become antiquated and unsuitable, utterly useless or decayed? In the final analysis, did we ask: What has become obscured or unacceptable in form only? What needs merely a more fitting and noble form, since it is alive and fresh? What is, in essence, sound, awaiting only a higher regeneration?

During our long exile we existed by the strength of our religion. It sustained us in our grave and prolonged suffering and inspired us to live—often to live heroically. Is it possible, can the mind entertain the possibility, that such a force is a mere figment of the imagination, of the rambling of an ignorant soul, and that it possesses no elemental and lasting core? Has the accepted idea been sufficiently examined and analyzed critically —is it sufficiently founded in logic and in the human spirit— that with the loss of the basis for the blind faith the basis for religion has also been destroyed?

Translated by Frances Burnce and Arthur Hertzberg[14]

FRANZ ROSENZWEIG'S SELF-DISCOVERY

NAHUM N. GLATZER

Franz Rosenzweig felt that a Jewish intellectual in Western Europe had only two choices: Zionism, if he wanted to affirm his Judaism, or baptism, if he turned to religion. There were other influences too, which led him to consider resolving his own intellectual and spiritual dilemmas by taking the latter step. His cousin Hans Ehrenberg had embraced Protestantism four years earlier. . . . As for himself, systematically minded and history-conscious, Rosenzweig made only one provision, a procedural one: he wished to enter Christianity as did its founders, as a Jew, not as a "pagan." He decided to attend synagogue services on the High Holy Days in preparation for this crucial event. He did not wish to "break off," but deliberately aimed to "go through" Judaism to Christianity.

When Rosenzweig entered the small Orthodox synagogue in Berlin on that fateful Yom Kippur in 1913, he joined a community of humble men, women, and children who had gathered to confess their sins and to pray for forgiveness. On the Day of Atonement, the Jew, though united with his brethren in prayer, stands utterly alone before his God. . . .

Rosenzweig left the service a changed person. What he had thought he could find only in the Church—faith that gives one an orientation in the world—he found on that day in the synagogue. What the day conveyed to him was that, essential as a mediator may be in the Christian experience, the Jew stands in no need of mediation. God is near to man and desires his unmediated devotion. Rosenzweig also realized for the first time in his life that Judaism is not a religion of bygone ages but a living faith. . . .

He wrote a friend: "After prolonged, and I believe thorough, self-examination, I have reversed my decision. It no longer seems necessary to me, and therefore, being what I am, no longer possible. I will remain a Jew." Rosenzweig, at the age of twenty-seven, was now sure of his ground.[15]

THE REVELATION OF *NEILAH*

AIMÉ PALLIÈRE

When I was seventeen years of age a strange incident occurred which came to exercise an influence over my whole life. On a certain Thursday in the autumn, when I was still on my vacation at Lyons, I was walking with a comrade on the Quai Tilsitt where the synagogue stands. We noticed that a number of shops had remained closed that day. My companion had heard that it was the great festival of the Jews and suggested to me that we enter the temple. I consented, not without hesitation. Alone I would never have done it, for the pious Catholic does not permit himself to enter any building belonging to another religion, and for strong reasons he must abstain from taking part in any ceremony. The synagogue was quite filled. All the votaries were standing and silent. I understood later that I had arrived at the moment of the prayer of *Neilah* on Yom Kippur. . . .

In order to discover in the traditional Jewish service the element of adoration, the non-Jew requires an acquaintance, a veritable initiation; perhaps even the knowledge of Hebrew, which makes it possible to penetrate to the meaning of the prayers. It is therefore all the more interesting to discover what could possibly strike a young Catholic, suddenly introduced, without any preparation, into a Jewish assembly on the Day of Atonement, that had so marked an effect on his spirit.

That which revealed itself to me at that moment was not at

all the Jewish religion. It was the Jewish people. The spectacle
of that large number of men assembled, their shoulders covered
by *talletim*, suddenly disclosed to my eyes a far-off past. The
Hebrews of the Doré Bible were there on their feet before me.
But two details struck me particularly as I noticed all about me
the faithful bent over their ritual. First, on seeing the prayer
shawls uniformly worn by all the participants in the service, I
thought that in a way they were all officiating. Several of them
robed in white shrouds were scattered about here and there in
the crowd, just like the priests who remained in the center of the
sanctuary. In the second place, it seemed to me that this silent
assembly was expectant of something about to happen. "What
are they waiting for?" I asked my companion. This double
aspect which Judaism disclosed to me held nothing that could
trouble the faith of a young Christian such as I then was. But
here was revealed to me at least very clearly, so that I could
understand what followed, two characteristic traits: the form
of collective priesthood of which the Judaism of the dispersion
consisted, and the spirit of expectancy and of faith in the future
which stamps its entire cult with a special seal.

In fact, in the synagogue service all Jews are equal, all are
priests, all may participate in the holy functions, even officiate
in the name of the entire community, when they have the required training. The dignity which distinguishes the *hakham*,
the doctor, the sage, is not a clerical degree but rather one of
learning and of piety quickened through knowledge. The *tallit*
would have given me the understanding of that peculiarity of
Judaism which would have escaped me, had my attention not
been captured from the first by this spectacle, so new to me, of a
multitude of men in white shawls at prayer. It is thus that rites
and symbols often constitute a more expressive language than
the best of discourses. The practices which have had the consecration of centuries come to us charged with the accumulated
thoughts of believing generations. They preserve the poetry,
the incomparable power of evocation. They may be suppressed,
but not replaced.

A precious legacy of antiquity, and yet Judaism's trend is not toward the past, but toward the future. An unconquerable faith in the final triumph of the good and the true has preserved it during the centuries and permeates it through and through. It awaits the messiah. Whenever the modern conscience busies itself with ideals of social regeneration, whenever it affirms its will to build the city of the future upon the ruins of wrongs and injustices, it is in communion with the soul of Judaism as it has not ceased to vibrate in the course of its long history.

Later I was to understand how the aspirations of national resurrection complete and define in Israel this attitude of expectancy, so different from the conceptions of other religions, but from my first contact this spirit revealed itself to me in the silent *Amidah* of the closing of Yom Kippur. . . .

And this it was that made another impression upon me, which was less confused and was to be more decisive. Fancy a young Christian, brought up in the naive conception that the Old Testament had no mission other than preparation for the New which was definitely to replace it, and that since the advent of Christianity the role of Israel had come to an end . . .

This was the revelation that came to me on that Thursday in October, in the synagogue of Lyons. And surely words are too inadequate to express anything so confused, so mysterious to me at that moment; and for some time I could not formulate that impression in my thoughts, still less interpret it to the outside world. But within me, like a germ implanted by the *Neilah*, this revelation was to affirm itself and grow stronger and stronger.

Near me, within reach of my hand, I noticed a book of prayer, left on a stall. I opened it. The unfamiliar characters had the effect upon me of notes of strange music, which I looked upon with curiosity. The next day I bought a Hebrew grammar on the Quai, and quite alone I set myself to study Hebrew.

Translated by Louise Waterman Wise[16]

XI

YOM KIPPUR IN ART

JOSEPH GUTMANN

No ancient illustration has survived of the dramatic cultic rite—performed by the high priest in the Jerusalem Temple and described in Leviticus 16—of casting lots over the two goats and sending the scapegoat forth into the desert to carry away the sins of Israel. In a fourteenth century medieval miniature, accompanying the *Avodah* service during *Musaf* of Yom Kippur, we find, however, a drawing of a Jew, dressed in medieval garb, standing on a cliff. He is about to cast the scapegoat to the waiting *Azazel*, which is depicted as a horned demon (fig. 1).

Kol Nidre ("All Vows"), the solemn opening prayer, is usually adorned in medieval German manuscripts. One such illustration in an early fourteenth century *mahzor* shows a fully arcaded page resting on two dragons. A stag is drawn next to the word *kol*, "all" (fig. 2).

During the morning service of the Day of Atonement, the Jew prays to "God, King of the Universe, who opens for us the gates of mercy and lightens the eyes of them that hope for Your forgiveness." In keeping with this pious yearning for those earnestly knocking at the gates of repentance, a fourteenth century *mahzor* depicts the open gates of mercy. The portal, to which two doors are attached, is adorned with five medallions— four representing the beasts of the vision of Ezekiel. The fifth, in the center of the portal, contains an empty chair: God's throne of divine justice and mercy—no doubt to illustrate the idea expressed in the morning service of Yom Kippur that "the Lord, above the holy beasts, is exalted. Above the heavenly chariot in radiance adorned, purity and justice stand before His throne." The figures in the medallions—the angel, winged lion, winged bull, and eagle—are taken from Christian art, where these four beasts of Ezekiel are symbols of the four Evangelists (fig. 3).[1]

A fifteenth century German *mahzor* has both doors of the Torah ark open, behind which a half-concealed curtain can be seen. The open doors, as in the previous miniature, symbolize the gates of heaven (fig. 4).

A miniature in an early fourteenth century *mahzor* has in the lower margin an illustration of Abraham saved from the fire of the Chaldeans—a legendary amplification of Genesis 15.7, where Ur is interpreted as fire of the Chaldees. The miniature accompanies a *piyyut* for the *Minhah* service praising Abraham as the first believer and recounting his trials ("Abraham, our steadfast forebear, discerned Your faithfulness in an age when man knew not Your will"). Abraham, in the legend, was condemned for having broken his father's idols. King Nimrod, in our miniature, sits in judgment. In front of him stand Terah, Abraham, and Haran. The prostrated man before Nimrod may be the jailer who pleaded with the king for Abraham's life. To the right we see Abraham saved by an angel's, or perhaps God's, hand from the midst of the fire (fig. 5).

It was very common to decorate the *piyyut* of the *Musaf* service in *mahzor* manuscripts, which begins with the word *shoshan*, "rose." In an early fourteenth century Rhenish manuscript we see a full-page decoration featuring four open flowers seen from above and such additional ornamentation as a dog, hare, and dragon (fig. 6).[2]

No specific ceremonial object is linked with the Yom Kippur holiday. Still, a few objects have survived which were used on the Day of Atonement both at home and the synagogue.

A very rare white tablecloth with gold brocade appliqué from Oberzell, Germany, dated 1781, is now in the Cluny Museum in Paris. It carries biblical inscriptions from Isaiah 1.18 ("although your sins be as scarlet, they shall be as white as snow") and Deuteronomy 32.29, as well as inscriptions from rabbinic sources (fig. 7).

In the synagogue services it was traditional to wear a white garment, called *kittel* or *sargenes*—the selfsame garment in which every orthodox Jew is to be buried. The *kittel* was usually tied or girdled with a rope—to divide symbolically the baser from the purer parts of the body. It also became customary in Eastern Europe, after about the eighteenth century, to substitute a belt secured by a silver buckle. The penitent worshiper is traditionally likened on that day to the ministering angels whose sinless record is as white as snow, and the cartouche on the belt buckle, which is frequently flanked by two lions or eagles, carries the Day of Atonement prayer which emphasizes this idea: "For on this day shall atonement be made for you, to cleanse you from all your sins, before the Lord you shall be clean" (Leviticus 16.30) (figs. 8 and 9).

Torah shields often carry a plate to indicate which Torah is to be read on Yom Kippur. A Torah shield made in Poland in the late eighteenth century reveals an open Torah ark with a Torah scroll within. It is flanked by two columns with two running stags below, and it is crested by two crowns, one of which is upheld by two lions (fig. 10).[3] Special white Torah curtains were also used in the synagogue for the occasion. In fact, this custom appears to go back to the fifteenth century, for Israel ben Pethahiah Isserlein tells us that at the time of the *Neilah* service, they would remove the Torah curtain and put a white one in its place.[4]

Books on Jewish customs and holiday observance written by

Jews and non-Jews from the fifteenth century on depict both the preparations for and the celebration of Yom Kippur. All the preparatory customs are shown in the small scenes surrounding the Yom Kippur service in the eighteenth century print found in Johann C. G. Bodenschatz's *Kirchliche Verfassung der heutigen Juden*. In the top center roundel we see a man, who has removed his shoes, seated before three witnesses. It was once customary to confess one's sins before Yom Kippur in front of witnesses, then to remove one's shoes, sit on the ground, and recite penitential prayers in order to be forgiven for sins and false oaths. In the next roundel we see Jews at a cemetery, wearing the prescribed Jewish cloaks, ruffs, and barrettes, since it was customary to beg for forgiveness of the dead and to pray that they intercede for the living so that God may inscribe and seal them in the Book of Life. In the lower left scene, Jews are again seen at the cemetery, this time depositing money in the alms plate (fig. 11).

A print in Friedrich Christiani's *Der Juden Glaube und Aberglaube* shows two men lying on the ground, supported on their knees, while two figures are about to beat them with a leather belt (fig. 12). This etching reveals the custom of Jews beating each other thirty-nine times on the back as a means of atonement. The man inflicting the punishment would recite the thirteen words of Psalms 78.38 three times to correspond with the necessary thirty-nine lashes—"But He, being full of compassion, forgives iniquity and destroyeth not;/Yea, many a time doth He turn his anger away/And doth not stir up all His wrath."

Perhaps the best-known custom preceding Yom Kippur is the *Kapparot* ceremony, which has been recorded in rabbinic literature since the early geonic period. The etching in the Christiani book and the illustrations in other books portray men and women swinging chickens over their heads (figs. 11 and 12). It was customary to use a white rooster for a man and a white hen for a woman. For a pregnant woman, two chickens were used (as in our illustration)—one rooster and one hen, since it was not known whether the child would be a boy or a girl. The chicken is swung over the head three times, while verses from Psalm 107 and Job 33.23–24 and the following prayer is recited during the ceremony: "This chicken shall be in my stead, shall be my atonement, it shall go to death, so that I can attain a good life and peace." In his powerful sculpture "The Prayer" Jacques Lipchitz has fashioned a tattered old figure swinging a rooster over his head. This work was done shortly after Lipchitz escaped the Nazi holocaust, and he wanted the *Kapparot* ritual to be a grim, symbolic reminder of the slaughter of his innocent fellow Jews in Europe (fig. 13).

In the etching in Kirchner's *Jüdisches Ceremoniel* we see eighteenth century Jews going to the synagogue in the late afternoon prior to Yom Kippur, to take big wax candles which were to burn in the synagogue. It was the custom to take two wax candles—one for themselves and one for deceased parents or friends (others say one candle for the body and one for the soul) (fig. 14).

Moritz Oppenheim (1800–1882) painted a sentimental picture of *Kol Nidre* night, reproductions of which once hung in many German-Jewish homes. It depicts husband and wife affectionately separating at the door of the synagogue. The husband enters the synagogue proper, while the wife will ascend the balcony leading to the women's section. In the right-hand corner of the painting, we see friends exchanging greetings, while on the left, a father blesses his son (fig. 15). Bernard Picart and other artists of the eighteenth century try to capture the solemnity of the Yom Kippur synagogue services in Ashkenazic synagogues. The dimly lit interior in the Picart etching shows the shrouded figures, wearing the prescribed *kittel* and sandals, huddled close together in various attitudes of introspective contemplation (fig. 16). Marc Chagall in *Burning Lights* simply sketches the large figure of the cantor anxiously peering into the lit candles as if to divine the future awaiting him and the congregation (fig. 17).

Maurycy Gottlieb (1856–1879) in his "Jews at Prayer on the Day of Atonement," done in 1878, departs from the sentimentality of the Oppenheim painting. His dignified, earnest figures, though appearing somewhat posed, are real. The stamp of suffer-

8. Belt buckle for Yom Kippur. Silver. Poland. 19th century. Harry G. Friedman Collection, The Jewish Museum, New York. See Chapter XI.

9. Belt buckle for Yom Kippur. Silver. Eastern Europe. 19th century. Museum of the Hebrew Union College–Jewish Institute of Religion, Cincinnati. See Chapter XI.

ing is on their faces—each appears absorbed in the task of self-examination. Gottlieb, who appears in the painting as the man shadowing his face with his hand, identifies himself with his people by posing next to the old Jew with the Torah scroll (fig. 18).[5]

The ceremonial objects and illustrations we have discussed allow us to relive and vividly recall sacred moments of Yom Kippur in our Jewish past.

XII

YOM KIPPUR IN MANY LANDS

YOM KIPPUR IN THE DAYS OF THE SECOND TEMPLE

SOLOMON IBN VERGA

This purported account of the entrance of the high priest into the sanctuary and his departure from it, by Marcus, Roman consul and justice of the Jews, who held office in Jerusalem during the days of the Second Temple, is found in Shevet Yehudah (c. *1550), which is attributed to Solomon ibn Verga, a Spanish historian.*

Seven days before the special day called Yom Kippur, the most important of their holidays, they would prepare a space and chairs to sit on in the house of the high priest, for the head of the court, the patriarch, the high priest, the prefect of the priests, and the king, besides seventy chairs of silver for the seventy members of the Sanhedrin. Then the eldest of the priests would stand up and address the high priest with these words of admonition and exhortation:

[163

"Look before whom you are about to enter, and know that if you fail to concentrate on what you are about to do, not only will you at once fall dead but the atonement of Israel will be lost as well. Lo, the eyes of all Israel are hanging upon you, so search your ways; perhaps you have committed a transgression, however slight, for one transgression may balance off many good deeds, and the scale is in the hands of the God of knowledge. Also search the ways of your brother priests and purify them; remember always that you are about to come before the King over all kings, who sits on a throne of justice and scatters all evil before Him with His eyes. Then how shall you come before Him, the enemy being with you?"

Then the high priest would say to them that he had already searched his deeds and repented for every transgression that was apparent to him, and that he had also called his brother priests together into the court of the Temple and had adjured them by Him who rested His Name there, that each of them was to reveal the evil which he was aware of in his fellow and the evil which he was aware of in himself, in order that the high priest might give them the correct penance for each transgression.

The king too would speak warmly to the high priest and assure him that he would honor him when he came out of the sanctuary in peace. After this, they would announce that the high priest was going out to his chamber in the sanctuary, and then the people would go out to accompany him, and go before him in perfect order. And this I have seen with my very eyes: first to go before him would be all those who were of the seed of the kings of Israel (for the more important a man, the nearer he stands to the high priest); after them went all those who were descended from the kings of the house of David, all in their proper order, one following another. A herald would go before them crying, "Give honor to the house of David!" After them came the house of Levi, and a herald crying, "Give honor to the house of Levi!" There were thirty and six thousand of them, and all the prefects wore clothing of blue silk, and the priests, of whom there were twenty-four thousand, clothing of white silk. After them came the singers, and after them those who played upon instruments, and after them the trumpeters, and after them the guards of the gate, and after them the incense-makers, and after them the curtain-makers, and after them the watchmen, and after them the treasurers, and after them a class called *kartofilos*, the chair-bearers, and after them all the workingmen who worked in the sanctuary, and after them the seventy of the Sanhedrin, and after them a hundred priests with silver rods in their hands to clear the way, and after them the high priest, and after him all the elders of the priesthood, two by two. And the heads of the academies stood at vantage points and cried, "Lord High Priest, may you come in peace! Pray to our Maker to grant us long life that we may engage in His Torah."

When the procession reached the foot of the mountain of the sanctuary, they would there pray for the continuance of the kingship of the house of David, and after that for the priests and for the sanctuary, and the noise was so great, because of the great number of the people crying Amen, that the birds flying overhead fell to the earth. Then the high priest would bow to all the people and turn aside in tears and awe. And the two prefects of the priesthood would lead him to his chamber, and there he would separate from all his brother priests. So much for his entrance.

But when he came out the honor was doubled, for all the people that were in Jerusalem passed before him, most of them carrying torches of white wax, and all of them dressed in white clothing; and all the windows were garlanded with embroideries, and lit with candles. Priests have told me that often the high priest could not reach his home before midnight, because of the press of the people passing before him, and because of the great numbers, for although all the people were fasting, they did not go home until they had seen whether they could not reach the hand of the high priest and kiss it. The day afterward he would make a great feast and invite friends and relatives, and declare a holiday because he had come out of the sanctuary in peace.

Afterward the high priest would order a smith to make a gold tablet, and engrave upon it these words: "I [so and so] the high priest, son of [so and so], the high priest, have served in the high priesthood in the grand and holy house in the service of Him who rested His Name there, and it was such and such a year after the creation. May He who found me worthy of this service find my son after me worthy to serve before the Lord."[1]

MARRANOS AND THE DAY OF PURITY

CECIL ROTH

In the Inquisitional records the Day of Atonement is consistently referred to as being celebrated on the tenth day after the New Moon of September, and the Passover as coinciding with the Full Moon of March. What seems to have happened was that the Marranos made use of the current solar calendar as a basis for their lunar reckoning. Thus they celebrated the Day of Atonement on the tenth day after the New Moon which fell in the month of September. In most cases this reckoning would have been accurate, within a day or two; but sometimes it must have been nearly a month out. Thus in 1606, when the Day of Atonement actually fell on October 12, it was celebrated at Coimbra some time between the tenth and the fifteenth of the previous month.

Ultimately a further complication was introduced. At the time of the more solemn celebrations of the Jewish year, the Inquisition and its myrmidons became more vigilant. In order to evade their watchfulness it became customary to wait for a day or two, until their attention was relaxed. Then the customary rites could be observed with comparative impunity. Thus the Day of Atonement was kept on the eleventh day after the New Moon of September, instead of the tenth.

The Day of Atonement, in particular, retained all its solemnity among the Marranos, who braved all perils in order to celebrate it together. On the previous day they bathed, in accordance with the traditional practice. In the evening candles were lighted in abundance "for the living and for the dead," being placed upon clean white cloths. The entire day was spent in one another's company, in complete abstention from food. Meanwhile, all the prayers they knew were repeated, time after time, or the messianic prophecies of the Bible were discussed. Among the ancient traditions of the day preserved was that of having four services between sunrise and sundown, instead of the normal three. Though the practice of wearing no shoes was retained, they did not recognize it as one of the traditional deprivations, but considered it as a tribute to the sanctity of the place of prayer, finding biblical precedent in the conduct of Moses before the burning bush. The title given to the day was *Dia Pura*, or "Day of Purity"—an obvious corruption of the Hebrew *Kippur*, but giving nevertheless an impression of the special character with which it was invested in their eyes. The traditional Jewish characterization as the "Day of Pardon" (from heaven) seems to have been slightly misinterpreted, for an outstanding feature of the celebration was the formal forgiving of one another for offenses received. Thus, at the prayer meeting at Coimbra in 1616 all the congregation were urged to pardon one another, "for that was the Day of Pardon." It was natural for the dates of the various celebrations of the coming year to be publicly announced at the general assemblage on this occasion. Before and after the fast it was customary to make a meal of fish and vegetables: not meat, since none was available which had been prepared according to the prescribed fashion.[2]

THE DAY OF ATONEMENT OF THE FALASHAS

WOLF LESLAU

The Day of Atonement, called *astäsrĕyo*, is celebrated on the tenth day of the seventh moon. It is considered the most important fast day of all, and even if it falls on a Sabbath the fast is strictly observed. The fasting starts on the evening of the ninth. The priests bless the people and pray for the remission of their sins. The people thereupon kiss one another and say,

"Forgive me, forgive me." They pass the whole night of the
ninth in prayer as well as the whole day of the tenth. Before
the end of the prayers they perform the *emen*, a word of Cushitic
origin which seems to mean "reminder." The *emen* consists in
putting a handful of millet on stones and leaving it there for
the birds in order to commemorate the dead. . . . After the
prayers the people bring food and drink to the synagogue, have
it blessed by the priests, and then eat it. In former days they
blew the trumpet on the evening of the tenth day, but this is no
longer done.[3]

THE ATONEMENT DAY OF THE BENE-ISRAEL

HAEEM SAMUEL KEHIMKAR

The tenth of the month of Tishri was called *Darfalnicha San*,
or the "Holiday of the Closing of Doors." It was, of course, the
Day of Atonement. Eben Saphir in his book of travels says of
the Bene-Israel that on this day they fast and sit with closed
doors inside their houses. He says that he could not understand
the meaning of the vernacular name, neither could the Bene-
Israel explain it well to him; and he conjectures that as there
is an additional prayer of Yom Kippur called the *Neilat Shearim*,
or "Closing of the Gates," it may have come to pass that from
this the Bene-Israel have given this name to Yom Kippur.

There is a peculiar notion among the Bene-Israel that the
souls of the departed visit their habitation on the day known as
Erev Kippur, i.e., the day previous to Atonement Day, and leave
on the night of *Simhat Kohen*, i.e., the day immediately suc-
ceeding the Atonement Day. This notion is, it is believed, based
upon the Yom Kippur prayer for the souls of the departed. The
Jews "go a day previous to the Day of Atonement to their burial
ground to visit the dead, the object of which is to invoke their
intercession for the ensuing day. In passing along from grave
to grave, the most pious are deeply affected, especially entreat-
ing their relations and friends to pray for them the next day."

On the tenth of this month the Bene-Israel observe the great fast of the Day of Atonement, but on the morning of the previous day, i.e., on the ninth day, after the propitiatory prayers, when the morning service is over, the Bene-Israel recite the prayer of forgiveness, as it is done on the last day of the month of Elul, and return home, when some of the Bene-Israel perform the ceremony of *Kapparot*, or atoning sacrifice. Afterward they sit down to dinner at about 10 A.M.; first of all they offer a dish which contains some pieces of *gharies* (cakes of rice flour fried in oil), some pieces of *puries* (tarts) made of wheat flour and sugar, or coconut kernel scrapings and jaggery [sugar made from palm sap] and some pieces of liver and gizzards, fried in oil, different kinds of fruit, *subja*, and a cup of wine. Prayers are first offered over it, and then some wine is poured on the ground as a libation, while the rest is sipped by the adult members of the family. The ingredients in the dish, as well as other sweetmeats made at home, are then distributed among the family. In the afternoon they first bathe in hot and then in cold water, which bathing is called *tevilah* (purification), when some devout Bene-Israel subject themselves to the whip or twisted cloth correction. Before sunset all the Bene-Israel, whether male or female, take their supper and dress themselves with white apparel, and repair to the synagogue, which is beautifully lighted. Before the evening service is commenced, all the Law books are taken out of the ark. Only those who promise to offer very large sums of money are allowed to take the scrolls out of the ark. They take them out and hold them in their hands, standing in front of the *hakhal* when the reader (*hazzan*) formally rescinds previous vows. . . . Afterward a prayer is offered for the prosperity of the royal family, the viceroy and governor general of India, and the governor of Bombay. When this is over, the evening service commences; it lasts for three hours, and during that time the Confession of Sins, which is the most essential and characteristic element in the service of the day, is made, and pardon implored. It must be remarked here that on this day the Bene-Israel synagogues are more than crowded, as those who are so careless as not even to pay their visit to the synagogue at any other time of the year are careful to be present on that day. At the end of the service, a few remain in the synagogue reading "The Crown of Supreme Sovereignty," a poem by Rabbi Solomon ibn Gabirol, and psalms.

The next day early in the morning, i.e., on the morning of the tenth of this month, both males and females again attend the place of worship and remain there till sunset, confessing their sins and imploring pardon from God and praying for the continuance of His mercy and loving-kindness. At nightfall a sound of the *shofar* proclaims the termination of the fast and the conclusion of the day's sacred observances.

The next day was called *Shila San*, i.e., "Stale Holiday," which is, of course, *Simhat Kohen*, or the day of "Rejoicing for the High Priest," who after having performed all the services of the Day of Atonement, rejoiced and made a festival for his friends when he came out in peace from the holy place. In like manner the Bene-Israel visited one another and were entertained by their relatives and friends on this day, in token of the preservation of their lives in spite of their sins, and gave alms to the poor. This merrymaking day is only observed by the Bene-Israel of the Bombay Presidency, and perhaps indicates that their ancestors were of the tribe of Levi.[4]

WITH THE JEWS OF LIBYA

Devora and Menahem Hacohen

On Rosh Hashanah and Yom Kippur eves it was customary to eat special *kreplach*, called *spanz*, which were fried in the streets of the ghetto and sold in huge numbers, like doughnuts.

For the *Kapparot* preceding Yom Kippur, Libyan Jews insisted on white fowl. On Yom Kippur eve, morning prayers at the synagogue were followed with a community meal, rich and poor eating together and wishing one another a good year. This was also the time for the people to pay all the pledges they had made in the synagogue during the preceding year. The trustees of the synagogue sat in the courtyard, at tables covered with flowers and decorative plants. The members of the community passed by them and made their payments, not forgetting the *hazzan*, the *shammash*, and the welfare institutions. Boys from the ages of nine to eleven, dressed in their best, gathered in the yard to sing wedding songs (Yom Kippur, according to the sages, was likened to the wedding day).

At *Neilah* time all the youngsters, even the infants, were present in the synagogue for the priestly blessing. The father lifted his hands, holding his *tallit* above the heads of his married sons, who in turn placed their own hands on the heads of their sons, as the blessing was pronounced—a moving sight which the women in the gallery accompanied with whispered prayer. The *kohanim* treated the day after Yom Kippur as a holiday, engaging in no work, in commemoration of the priesthood in the days of the Temple.

Translated by Israel I. Taslitt[5]

ATONEMENT DAY AMONG PERSIAN JEWS

Devora and Menahem Hacohen

Among Persian Jews the spirit of the High Holy Days was intensified by frequent fasting during the days of *Selihot*, preceding Rosh Hashanah, and the Ten Days of Penitence between Rosh Hashanah and Yom Kippur.

The *kapparah* (atonement offering) on Yom Kippur eve was a custom observed scrupulously. Each member of the family presented his individual offering: a rooster for the male, a hen for the female, and, for the pregnant woman, a hen for herself and a rooster and a hen for whatever sex the fruit of her womb would be. After the recitation of the *Kapparot* prayer, the fowl was turned over to the *shohet*; the women plucked the feathers for bedding, and the meat was given partly to the poor and part was eaten prior to the fast.

The men went to the bathhouse for the seven ritual dips, and then proceeded to the synagogue for the penitential flagellations: the *mula* (religious functionary) passed a thong over their bare backs, as he recited penitential prayers for himself and his flock. After the very moving and impressive *Kol Nidre* service, many men remained in the synagogue all night, reciting psalms and the "Crown of Sovereignty" of ibn Gabirol, in Persian. On Yom Kippur day everyone, even suckling infants, came to services. At nightfall the congregation went out to the yard for *Kiddush Levanah* (blessing of the moon, symbol of renewal of creation), and good wishes for the new year were exchanged.

Translated by Israel I. Taslitt[6]

YOM KIPPUR IN PERSIA, 1944

H. Z. HIRSCHBERG

The eve of Yom Kippur came. . . . The hour of *Minhah* approached, according to our custom. But the Persian synagogue was empty. When we had returned to the Ashkenazim, after the last repast before the fast, to prepare ourselves for *Kol Nidre*, the Persian Jews assembled to pray *Minhah*, after which they returned to their homes for the final meal. I expressed my surprise, but the Ashkenazim, who had grown accustomed to the usages of their Persians, assured me that still greater wonders were in store for me. The sun was setting and we assembled for *Kol Nidre*. It was already evening when the Persians gathered, but they were in no hurry. They observe an ancient custom that at this hour they purchase roses and other flowers in the synagogue, which they send to their relatives and friends as a mark of esteem and regard. We had already concluded the evening prayer and the psalms, when, while making our exit, we heard the strains of *Kol Nidre* rising from the neighboring synagogue.

The next morning, I went to the synagogue of the Iraqi Jews. In the spacious courtyard of the Alliance Israélite Universelle school, by the pool, the merchants had made their place of prayer for the festivals. Carpets were spread on the terrace, armchairs had been set out, an ark had been brought, while tarpaulins stretched overhead protected the congregation from

the fierce rays of the sun. To enable the womenfolk to participate in the prayers, seats had been arranged on the balconies.
I must confess that the service in this place made a peculiar
impression upon me. There was nothing of the atmosphere that
envelopes our houses of prayer on these "Days of Awe," nothing
of that solemnity which so characterizes our prayers. The men,
clad in light white suits, sat in their easy chairs in a semicircle
by the fish pond, as if at some festivity at a summer club. The
cool air, the tranquil pools with the goldfish darting hither and
thither, and the tentlike covering overhead strengthened this
impression. A large number of small children, some of them
without hats, had come with their parents to the service and
were playing in the courtyard, though they did not raise their
voices nor disturb the prayers in any way. I sat lost in thought
at the sight. Perhaps these Baghdadi Jews had preserved the
ancient traditional atmosphere of Yom Kippur in its pristine
purity, for "There were no more festive occasions for Israel than
the fifteenth of Ab and Yom Kippur," we learn in tractate *Taanit*.
Perhaps precisely this solemn day should be observed in a joyful
spirit and marked by flowers, and we should conduct ourselves
rather as sons asking the forgiveness of a Father and not as
servants fearful of their Master's rebuke.[7]

YOM KIPPUR IN AN EAST EUROPEAN TOWN

HAYYIM SCHAUSS

The first ten days of Tishri, which include both Rosh
Hashanah and Yom Kippur, are known as "The Ten Days of
Repentance." The days between the two holidays are already
colored by the solemnity of Yom Kippur. The very pious fast
till midday every day of this period, with the exception of the
Sabbath and the day before Yom Kippur, days on which it is
forbidden to fast.

The Saturday between the two holidays is called *Shabbat
Shuvah* (Sabbath of Penitence), from the first word of the
portion of the Prophets which is read on that day. This Sabbath

is observed much more strictly than are ordinary Sabbaths, and the rabbi delivers a long sermon before the afternoon prayers, in which he endeavors to arouse the congregation to whole-hearted penitence.

The second day before Yom Kippur has special significance in that it is the day of *Kapparot*. There is no specified time for this ceremony; some observe it in the afternoon, some early in the evening, some late at night, and others the following morn-ing. The men use roosters for the ceremony and the women, hens. When the family is large it is rather expensive to supply a fowl for each member of the family, so money is used instead. Those who use money for the ceremony generally perform it the morning before Yom Kippur.

The homes are unusually noisy. The fowls, their legs tied, cluck and crow at the tops of their voices. It generally happens, too, that a rooster gets excited and begins to run and fly all over the house, despite his bound feet, and there follows a long struggle to subdue him.

First the fowl, or the money, is held in the hand and everyone reads selections from certain psalms, beginning with the words *Sons of Adam*. Then the fowl is circled about the head nine times, the following being recited at the same time: "This is instead of me, this is an offering on my account, this is in expiation for me; this rooster (or hen) shall go to his (or her) death (or, this money shall go to charity), and may I enter a long and healthy life."

The day before Yom Kippur has a double character. It is the day on which Jews prepare for Yom Kippur, and it is also a holiday in its own right. Exactly as it is a religious command-ment to fast on Yom Kippur, so is it a religious requirement to eat heartily the day before.

The Jewish population is busy all day. Immediately after the morning services the ceremony for the release from vows is observed. Any personal vow, affecting only the vower himself, that he regrets, can be declared void by one ordained teacher or by three laymen. Some have already attended to the release the day before Rosh Hashanah, but many wait for this day. The ceremony is performed in groups, for, as said before, a

court of at least three must be present. The pleader stands and
recites the text relating to the release from vows, and the other
three sit and listen, answering him according to the text. When
he is finished he sits down and becomes one of the court,
another rising and reciting from the text, and so on, till the
entire group is finished.

Some Jews perform the *Kapparot* ceremony on the morning
of this day. There are also some who make it an occasion for
visiting the cemetery. The pious go to the bathhouse to bathe in
the ritual pool, some even making a confessional in the water.
The holiday feast is eaten about eleven or twelve o'clock; it
consists of soup, *kreplach* (a three-cornered pastry filled with
meat), and carrot pudding. The meal is served early, to allow
time for the next meal, the final one before the fast.

At about two in the afternoon people begin to go to the synagogue for *Minhah*, afternoon services. Not all pray together.
When a group of ten assembles a service begins. This occurs
several times during the afternoon.

The older and more pious Jews of the town go through
malkot, the symbolic ceremony of being flogged for sins committed. There is one flogger for the entire town, a certain poor
man who does it regularly, year after year; he gets coins from
each one he flogs, and this augments his yearly income. It is
said that in former days there were more pious people so that
many Jews acted as floggers on the day before Yom Kippur and
barely had time to finish their work.

The flogger appears in the synagogue at the beginning of the
afternoon service, a leather lash in his hand. He spreads some
hay on the floor near the door. The elders, wearing their over-
coats, stretch out on the hay face down and make a confession,
while the flogger strikes the coat lightly with his lash, reciting a
prescribed sentence three times (Psalms 78.38). The sentence
consists of thirteen words which, repeated three times, makes
thirty-nine, the number of lashes inflicted upon sentenced crim-
inals in olden days. The flogger races through his ritual so fast
that the pious Jew receiving the lashes barely has time to finish
his confession.

Long tables are set up in the corridor of the synagogue, bearing alms plates for the various institutions and charities of the community. Each member of the community pays his congregational dues after the afternoon services and distributes coins in the various plates. At the door are many paupers, townspeople, and strangers, and all who pass give them alms.

The sun falls lower and lower in the heavens. It is time for the evening meal, the last one before the fast, at which the rooster of the *Kapparot* ceremony and soup made from it is eaten. After the meal the blessing is repeated accompanied by tears and sighs. Then wishes for the coming year are expressed, and all rush off to the synagogue, the men in prayer shawls and white robes, the women in white dresses.

All is quiet and peaceful in the town. Not a living soul is visible in the streets. All are in the synagogue. Only the older girls and younger children have been left at home. The older girls stand with prayer books in their hands and beat their breasts in prayer, and watch the huge, twenty-four-hour candle burning on the table. Each family has at least two of them, one for the dead, which is taken to the synagogue, and one for the living, which burns at home.

The synagogue is crowded. Candles glow everywhere, wherever there is room to put one. Lamps and pendant candelabra gleam overhead, casting additional light on the crowded congregation, which stands praying and shaking in white robes and white prayer shawls; the worshipers beat their breasts and weep, shouting their prayers over the sobs and screams which come from the women's section.

The most solemn and exalted moment of the Yom Kippur eve service comes when the cantor sings *Kol Nidre*. As soon as he begins the well-known chant, an air of solemn and exalted absorption falls on the congregation. A deep sadness pervades the melody, but it imparts, at the same time, warmth and tenderness, and arouses all the hidden religious feelings and longings of man.

A second tense moment in the Yom Kippur service comes in the prayers of the next day when the order of the Temple service

10. Torah shield. Silver. Poland. Late 18th century. Museum of the Hebrew Union College–Jewish Institute of Religion, Cincinnati. See Chapter XI.

is recited and sung; through poetic descriptions and beautiful melodies, sung by the cantor and congregation in unison, the Temple service is dramatically relived.

There is life and stir in the synagogue when the time comes for this prayer. The cantor sings, but not alone; the worshipers join in a wordless, exalted melody. And when he mentions the prostration in the court of the Temple, all throw themselves to the ground and bury their faces, exactly as did their ancestors in the Temple of Jerusalem when they heard the high priest call out the Ineffable Name of God.

A third exalted moment comes at the *Neilah*, or concluding prayers, of Yom Kippur. The word means closing, and it originally meant the closing of the gates of the Temple. But it was interpreted to mean the closing of the gates of heaven, when one has the final opportunity to do penance wholeheartedly and to plead for a successful year.

It is an extraordinary moment. The sun is already setting, and shadows begin to fall. The great Yom Kippur candles are almost burned down. The congregation stands, weakened from the long fast and arduous prayers. This is the end. In a moment, a man's fate will be sealed.

Pale stars begin to appear in the sky. The *shofar* is blown, one long, resounding *tekiah*. And the trumpet call is answered with the cry and hope that next year will find them all in Jerusalem. With lightened spirits they recite the evening prayers. Yom Kippur is over. If it is a clear evening, the people do not rush home to eat. First they recite the appropriate blessing for the appearance of the New Moon.

Pious Jews partake of the barest amount of food necessary and then begin preparations for the building of the *sukkah*, the booth for the Sukkot holiday. Only after they have observed this religious precept do they really sit down to the feast that breaks their fast.

Worshipers arise earlier than usual on the morning after Yom Kippur. They do this so that Satan will have no cause to argue before God that, once Yom Kippur is over, Jews become lax and are too lazy to get up for the morning services.

Translated by Samuel Jaffe[8]

DAY OF ATONEMENT IN VITEBSK, RUSSIA

BELLA CHAGALL

A quite different air, heavy and thick, pervades the night of Yom Kippur.

All the shops are long closed. Their black shutters are locked as though forever. The sky too is black, as if God himself—heaven forbid—had deserted it. It is terrifying to walk in the streets. Perhaps God metes out punishment instantly, and one will sprain an ankle. I shudder at hearing laughter somewhere in the distance. The *goyim* are not afraid at all. They laugh even on the Day of Atonement.

My head is still throbbing with the clamor that came from father's white *kapparah* rooster.

A black-garbed, scrawny-looking *shohet* slunk into our court-yard late in the evening. From the folds of his coat a long knife flashed. He chased Father's cock; the cock shrieked, shaking the courtyard with his din. Other cocks ran after him with excited cries.

The cook seized a cock by the leg, but the cock wrenched himself free. The courtyard was littered with feathers.

It sounded like a thousand gongs clanging for a fire: the courtyard reechoed with the crowing of the cocks, with their embattled uproar. But gradually they spent their strength. The yard grew quieter and quieter.

Mother's and my own white chicken hid in a hole in their fear. One could only hear them clucking low and crying.

The cook caught both chickens at the same time and put them at the *shohet*'s feet. Blood poured over the whole balcony. When I came to myself, all the cocks and hens lay on the ground. From their necks ran threads of blood. Blood had spattered their white feathers. They were left to cool off in the dark night.

I remember how my little chicken quivered in my hands when I held it upraised for the rite. I too was quivering. My finger recoiled at once when I touched the chicken's warm belly. The chicken uttered a shriek and tried to fly over my head, like a little white angel.

I raised my eyes from the prayer book, I wanted to look at the chicken. It cried and clucked as though begging for mercy of me. I did not hear the passages that I was to repeat. And I was suddenly seized by fear that the chicken, as I held it up high, might befoul my head.

Mother is calling me. From a distance I see her eyes gleaming, her hands moving quietly as though preparing to embrace someone. She tells me to hold the skeins of thread before the large wax candles that will burn in the *shul* at the cantor's reading stand. She pulls out the first thread.

"For my beloved husband, for Shmul Noah—may he be healthy and live to his hundred-and-twentieth year." She draws out the thread, slowly weaves a benediction into it, sprinkles it with her tears, and passes a big piece of wax over it, as though trying to rub it full of good wishes.

"Hold fast to the end of the thread, Bashke," Mother says to me.

"For my son, for Itchke—may he be healthy and live in happiness and joy till his hundred-and-twentieth year!" She draws out the second thread and rubs it too with wax.

"For my oldest daughter, for Hannah."

Names are slowly intoned, threads are drawn, now yellow with wax and tears. I can hardly hold all the ends that remain free of wax. They slip from the tips of my fingers. I hold them with all my strength.

Mother prays a long time for each child, each relative. I no longer know what she is saying. With every name a tear drops on the thread and at once is imbedded in the wax like a little pearl. One heavy candle is now ready. Mother tackles the others.

"May all of us live long. For my deceased father, Barukh Aaron Raishkes—may he rest forever in paradise. My father, pray well for us, for me and my husband and my little children. Entreat from God good health and good fortune for all of us." Now mother weeps aloud. She almost cannot see the threads shaking in her hands.

"May all of us live long. For my deceased mother, Aige—may she pray well for us. My mother, do not forsake your only daughter, Alta," Mother prays over the thread she has drawn out. Apparently she would like to linger with her mother as long as possible; she moves the wax slowly and does not let the thread go from her hands.

"May all of us live long. For my deceased little son, Benjamin." Mother begins to weep again.

At this point I can check myself no longer. I weep too over my little brother who was one year old when he died and whom I never saw.

Mother glances at me through her tears, catches her breath, and blows her nose. The skein of threads grows thicker and thicker. Dead relatives, members of closely and distantly connected families, come as on a visit to us. For each one Mother sheds a tear; it is like sending a greeting to every one of them. I no longer hear their names; I might be walking around an unfamiliar graveyard. I see only stones, I see only threads. I am even filled with fear at the thought of how many dead relatives have been drawn forth and entwined among Mother's threads. Will we, the living, burn in the same way, like the souls of the dead?

I am glad when at last the *shammash*, who is waiting for the candles, carries them to the *shul*. Exhausted, I go to bed.

Next day we are prompted from early morning on. We are given a special snack, in order to fortify us before the fast, and to give us opportunity to say another prayer. We are trying to do good deeds. My brothers apologize to one another.

"Abrashke, you're not angry with me?" I rush to my brother— I recall that I have not always done things he wanted me to do.

Mother goes down to the courtyard. There is a neighbor with whom she has quarreled. She begs him earnestly to forgive her.

My brothers change clothes, make ready to go to *shul*. They almost do not speak. They do not even jostle one another. They seem to have been seized with awe.

They wait at some distance while Mother slowly blesses her candles. Then they come first to Father, next to Mother, wishing them both a good year. My parents place their hands on each of them and speak a blessing upon each head. Even the grown sons and daughters look like little children under the outspread hands of their parents. I, the youngest, go to them last. Father, with lowered eyes, touches my head, and I immediately choke with the tears that mount to my eyes. I can hardly hear the benedictions that he pronounces over me. His voice is already hoarse.

I fancy that I am already burning on the big twisted candle that mother has prepared. Sanctified, I leave the circle of its light—to me it is like white warm hands shining behind the benedictions and tears—and stand under my mother's shaking hands.

When I am near her, I quiet down a little. I feel more at ease when I see her tears. I hear her simple, heartfelt prayers. I do not want at all to come out from under her hands. And actually I begin to feel cold as soon as the murmur of the benedictions ceases over my head.

Everyone is in haste to go to *shul.*

"*Gut yom tov!*" Father quietly approaches Mother and shakes hands with her.

"*Gut yom tov!*" Mother answers with lowered eyes.

I remain alone at home. The candles burn on, holy and warm. I take my place at the wall to say the Silent Prayer at once.

The benedictions that father has spoken over my head still sound in my ears. I beat my chest while reciting the Confession of Sins. I am afraid, for I probably have committed more sins than are enumerated in the prayer book.

My head grows hot. The letters of the sacred writing begin to spread in height and width. Jerusalem sways before my eyes. I should like to hold up the Holy City with the thick prayer book that I clutch tightly with both hands.

Alone I cry to God and do not leave the wall until I can no longer think of anything to pray for.

The children now return from *shul.* The house is deserted, the table empty. Only the white tablecloth gleams dimly under the stumps of the half-burnt candles. They smoke. We do not know what to do with ourselves. So we go to sleep.

Next morning when I wake up, everyone has long since gone to *shul*. Again I am alone in the house. I remember everything that I am supposed to do. I only pour water over my fingers, I do not even brush my teeth, and with parched mouth I begin to pray. Gentile schoolmates come in; they want to do their homework with me. I do not move from the spot until I have finished praying.

I run to see my grandfather. He is old and sick and he too has remained alone at home. The rabbi of Bobruisk (Grandfather is a follower of his) has ordered Grandfather not to fast. He must take a spoonful of milk every hour. So I go to my grandfather to give him his milk.

Grandfather is praying. He does not even glance at me and bursts into soft weeping. The spoon with the milk shakes in my hand, my fingers are splashed. Grandfather's tears drop into the spoon, mingle with the milk. He barely wets his pale lips and weeps more copiously under my tending. Heavy-hearted, I return home.

"Bashutke, come and have a bite!" Our Sasha begs me to come to the kitchen and eat a piece of cold chicken with her. "You must surely be starved!"

I am angry at myself because I am not yet fasting through the whole day. Every year I beg Mother to permit me to fast. I cannot eat after witnessing Grandfather's tears, and after seeing Father come home with his pale, drawn face. He comes from *shul* to rest a little. With his white lips, his white *kittel*, and his white socks he looks—God forbid—as though he were not alive at all. I fancy that his soul has already become very pure and that it shines through his white garments. I begin to pray more fervently. I want to be at least in some small measure as pious as Father.

Mother stays at the *shul* through the whole day. Before *Musaf* I go to see her to ask how she is. The cantor can no longer be heard. The men's section is half empty. Some have gone home

to rest, others sit on benches, their eyes on their prayer books.
Boys play in the *shul* courtyard; some have apples to eat, some
have pieces of *hallah* with honey. But the women's section is
full of stifled weeping. In every corner a woman sighs and
laments.

"Lord of the Universe, Lord of the Universe!" The chant re-
sounds on all sides.

Mother is weeping quietly. She can scarcely any longer see the
little letters of her prayer book through her clouded spectacles.

I stand at some distance and wait. Mother catches her breath,
raises her weeping face, and nods to me to tell me that she is
feeling well, although she resumes her weeping at once. I come
closer to her. I do not know what to do among all these weeping
mothers. I look down into the men's section. The cantor's white
kittel and white skullcap are still. I look among the rows of tall
candles for our two. They are burning among all the other
candles, burning high into the air at either side of the holy ark.

Suddenly a humming and a clamor rise over the *shul*. It becomes full of men. There is a bustle, the air grows hot. Men
throng around the cantor. The heavy curtain of the holy ark is
drawn aside. Now there is silence, the air has become motionless. Only the rustle of prayer shawls can be heard. The men
hurry toward the holy ark. The shining scrolls of the Torah,
like princesses awakened from sleep, are carried out from the
ark. On their white and dark red mantles great stars gleam—
the shield of David embroidered in silver and gold. The handles
are mounted with silver, encrusted with mother-of-pearl, and
crowns and little bells hang from them.

Light glows around the scrolls of the Torah. All the men in
the *shul* are drawn toward them. The scrolls are surrounded,
escorted. The men crowd after the scrolls of the Torah, trying
at least to catch a glimpse of them, send a kiss to them from
a distance. And they, the beautiful scrolls of the Torah, tower
high above the heads of the worshipers, above all the out-
stretched hands, and move slowly through the *shul*.

I can hardly keep myself behind the handrail of the women's

section. I should like so much to jump down, to fall straight into the embrace of the holy Torahs, or at least move closer to them, to their quivering light, at least touch them, kiss their bright glory. But the scrolls are already being carried back, back to the holy ark. From both sides of it the tall candles twinkle at them. The velvet curtain is drawn, darkness comes to my eyes.

As though to drown the sadness, the men begin at once to pray aloud.

I remain standing at the window. I am attracted by the men's section, its clamorous air, filled with white *tallitim*, like up-raised wings surging through the *shul*, covering every dark spot. Only here and there a nose or an eye peeps out. The *tallit* stripes sway like stairs above the covered heads.

One *tallit* billows up, emits a groan, and smothers the sound within itself. The *shul* grows dark. I am seized by fear. The *tallitim* bend, shake, move upward, turn to all sides. *Tallitim* sigh, pray, moan. Suddenly my legs give way. *Tallitim* quiver, drop to the ground like heavy sacks. Here and there a white woolen sock sticks out. Voices erupt as from underground. *Tallitim* begin to roll, as on a ship that is sinking and going down amid the heaving waves.

I do not hear the cantor at all. Hoarse voices outshout one another. They pray, they implore, asking that the ceiling open for them. Hands stretch upward. The cries set the lamps shaking. At any moment now the walls will crumble and let Elijah the Prophet fly in.

Grown-up men are crying like children. I cannot stand it any longer. I myself am crying more and more. I recover only when I perceive at last a living, weeping eye behind a crouching *tallit*, when I hear trembling voices saying to one another: "*Gut yom tov! Gut yom tov!*"

I run home, for soon everyone will be back from *shul*, and I must set the table. "Sasha, hurry, hurry, prepare the samovar!" I cry to the maid.

I drag the tin box of pastry from the cupboard. I empty it all out on the table—cakes, cookies, gingerbread, wafers, all sorts of buns. There is no room left even for a glass of tea.

Sasha lights the lamp and carries in the cheerfully humming samovar. Even the samovar seems glad that it has survived, that it has been remembered. Now the voices of my brothers can be heard. They rush in like hungry animals, one after the other.

Mother, looking worn, enters with a soft smile on her face and says to everyone: "*Gut yom tov!*"

"*Gut yom tov!*" says the cook. She runs in from the kitchen and smiles a pale smile.

We are waiting for Father. As always, he is the last to come from *shul*. In high spirits we fall upon the food. Glasses of tea are poured and drunk.

We have saved ourselves. We are no longer hungry. May God give His seal upon a good year for all of us. So be it, amen!

Translated by Norbert Guterman[9]

YOM KIPPUR IN KASRIELEVKY

MAURICE SAMUEL

Now, if the Kasrielevkites could put so much emotion into remote memories and expectations and give them such burning immediacy, how much more were they stirred by the festivals of the New Year and the Day of Atonement, which touched their quickest interests! For the period of nearly two weeks enclosing these festivals was the period of heavenly decision on all human destinies. "The Days of Awe" were filled with repentance, mutual forgiveness, and supplication. The grandeur of the New Year and Yom Kippur services owed nothing to external circumstances, everything to the imagination. How much the Kasrielevkites did, with how little! Their place of worship was a tumbledown wooden chapel which could not hold more than three or four hundred persons; but no Notre Dame of Paris or Saint Peter's of Rome, with vast spaces, forests of pillars, great colored windows, and thunderous organs was ever filled with a more impressive inner magnificence than a Kasrielevky synagogue on the Day of Atonement. Consider, for instance, the *shofar*, or ram's horn, which is sounded in the synagogue in the Days of Awe, when the heavens are open. The *shofar* is, as a musical instrument, an unfortunate invention. It has less volume than a saxophone and less dignity than a trombone. The original users of the *shofar* on the hills of ancient Judea may have imparted to it a certain primitive ferocity; but when the *baal tekiah* of Kasrielevky blew into it, the *shofar* yielded, at best, a tremulous staccato fading into a bronchitic wheeze. And yet in the ears of the Kasrielevkites it was the trumpet of doom pealing from end to end of the universe, and their hearts contracted with fear. A modern Jew acquainted with nothing more than the respectabilities of Western synagogues has not the remotest notion of the glory and terror which filled the little tabernacles of Sholom Aleichem's world on Yom Kippur. . . .

Israel Zangwill somewhere makes a sarcastic comment on the custom of Western Jews who send one another greeting cards for the High Holy Days, on which the words appear: "Wishing you a happy New Year *and well over the fast.*" Kasrielevkites certainly wished themselves and one another a happy New Year, but the twenty-four-hour fast was nothing to make a fuss about. They did make a genuine fuss, however, about repentance and mutual forgiveness.

Noah Wolf, the butcher, for instance: a hard, rough man, who from one year's end to the other is the terror of his customers. A woman comes in and says, quite innocently: "Reb Noah Wolf, have you any fresh meat this morning?" And Reb Noah answers: "Fresh meat? Certainly not. Rotten meat, stinking meat, crawling meat is all I deal in." "Reb Noah Wolf, give me a good portion." "I'll give you exactly the portion you've earned." Why does Noah Wolf talk like that? He does not know. It simply comes out of him. But in the days of repentance Reb Noah Wolf is as meek as one of his own slaughtered lambs; and on the day before Yom Kippur, Noah Wolf, burly, clumsy, heavy of speech, makes the rounds of his neighbors and customers, saying to each one: "If I've offended you with a harsh word, forgive me, and may you have a happy year." To which they answer: "You too, Reb Noah Wolf. May God forgive." And they offer him cake.

Or Ezriel the fisherman, whose tongue is as sharp as Noah

Wolf's, and who adds to this virtue a universal suspiciousness
that every customer is trying to steal something. And if you
should happen to poke a finger into one of his fish, just to try
it out, he's liable to pick up the fish and slap you across the face
with it. And nothing to be done either; Ezriel is the only fish-
dealer in town; you must buy from him or do without fish for
the Sabbath. The day before Yom Kippur he makes the rounds
and however hard he finds it, he says: "If I've offended you
with a harsh word, forgive me, and may you have a happy New
Year." To which they answer: "You too, Reb Ezriel. May God
forgive." And they offer him cake.

And so with Gonte the Hebrew teacher, and Moses Velvel the
drayman, and Sanne the water-carrier, and Getzi the beadle, and
all the others. "If I've offended you with a harsh word, forgive
me." "You too, you too. May God forgive."

Noah Wolf and Ezriel and Gonte and Moses Velvel and Sanne
and Getzi remained what they were, of course. What, then, was
the good of Yom Kippur, if it did not make them better? Well,
perhaps it prevented them from becoming worse.[10]

YOM KIPPUR IN FRANKFORT

HERMANN SCHWAB

It was on Yom Kippur, 1888, a few minutes before nightfall.
Over a thousand men and women were standing in silence. The
majesty of the departing day filled the synagogue, and from the
gas candelabra rose waves of dim light to the ceiling, veiled in
shadow. From my father's seat in the middle of the synagogue
I could see that the pulpit was being set up, and there was a
whisper that the rabbi [Samson Raphael Hirsch] would preach.
I hastened to the foot of the pulpit. The rabbi stood in his *kittel*
and *tallit*. I saw his shining white hair under his white cap and
his eyes wandering silently through the synagogue. Then he
spoke. He spoke of the last Amen of the last *Kaddish*. He asked
his *kehillah* not to forget it. "Whenever there may be an hour of
fear and sorrow, when good intentions and faithful promises

might fade in the coming year, then say 'Amen,' my brothers
and sisters, and Yom Kippur will return to you with all its
blessings." "Say 'Amen,' my brothers and sisters." Once again
his voice came with deep emotion from the pulpit and, helped
by the *shammash*, he descended the steps and went to his seat.
The sound of the *shofar* rang through the synagogue. It was
the rabbi's last sermon.[11]

THE GREAT WHITE FAST IN THE LONDON GHETTO

Israel Zangwill

The morning of the Great White Fast broke bleak and gray.
Esther, alone in the house save for the servant, wandered from
room to room in dull misery. The day before had been almost a
feast day in the ghetto—everybody providing for the morrow.
Esther had scarcely eaten anything. Nevertheless she was fasting, and would fast for over twenty-four hours, till the night
fell. She knew not why. Her record was unbroken, and instinct
resented a breach now. She had always fasted—even the Henry
Goldsmiths fasted, and greater than the Henry Goldsmiths!
Q.C.'s fasted, and peers, and prize-fighters and actors. And yet
Esther, like many far more pious persons, did not think of her
sins for a moment. . . .

About noon her restlessness carried her into the streets.
There was a festal solemnity about the air. Women and children,
not at synagogue, showed themselves at the doors, pranked in
their best. Indifferently pious young men sought relief from the
ennui of the day-long service in lounging about for a breath of
fresh air; some even strolled toward the Strand, and turned into
the National Gallery, satisfied to reappear for the twilight
service. On all sides came the fervent roar of prayer which
indicated a synagogue or a *hevrah*, the number of places of
worship having been indefinitely increased to accommodate
those who made their appearance for this occasion only.

Everywhere friends and neighbors were asking one another
how they were bearing the fast, exhibiting their white tongues

and generally comparing symptoms, the physical aspects of the
Day of Atonement more or less completely diverting attention
from the spiritual. Smelling salts passed from hand to hand,
and men explained to one another that, but for the deprivation
of their cigars, they could endure Yom Kippur with complacency.

Esther passed the ghetto school, within which free services
were going on even in the playground, poor Russians and Poles,
fanatically observant, forgathering with lax fishmongers and
welshers; and without which hulking young men hovered un-
easily, feeling too out of tune with religion to go in, too conscious of the terrors of the day to stay entirely away. From the
interior came from sunrise to nightfall a throbbing thunder of
supplication, now pealing in passionate outcry, now subsiding
to a low rumble. The sounds of prayer that pervaded the ghetto,
and burst upon her at every turn, wrought upon Esther
strangely; all her soul went out in sympathy with these yearning
outbursts; she stopped every now and then to listen, as in those
far-off days when the Sons of the Covenant drew her with their
melancholy cadences.

At last, moved by an irresistible instinct, she crossed the
threshold of a large *hevrah* she had known in her girlhood,
mounted the stairs, and entered the female compartment without hostile challenge. The reek of many breaths and candles
nearly drove her back, but she pressed forward toward a remembered window, through a crowd of bewigged women, shaking their bodies fervently to and fro. . . .

Here, lost in a sweet melancholy, Esther dreamed away the
long gray day, only vaguely conscious of the stages of the service
—morning dovetailing into afternoon service, and afternoon
into evening; of the heavy-jowled woman behind her reciting a
jargon version of the Atonement liturgy to a devout coterie; of
the prostrations full-length on the floor, and the series of im-
passioned sermons; of the interminably rhyming poems, and
the acrostics with their recurring burdens shouted in devotional
frenzy, voice rising above voice as in emulation, with special
staccato phrases flung heavenwards; of the wailing confessions
of communal sin, with their accompaniment of sobs and tears

and howls and grimaces and clenchings of palms and beatings of the breast. She was lapped in a great ocean of sound that broke upon her consciousness like the waves upon a beach, now with a cooing murmur, now with a majestic crash, followed by a long receding moan. She lost herself in the roar, in its barren sensuousness, while the leaden sky grew duskier and the twilight crept on, and the awful hour drew nigh when God would seal what He had written, and the annual scrolls of destiny would be closed, immutable. She saw them looming mystically through the skylight, the swaying forms below, in their white graveclothes, oscillating weirdly backwards and forwards, bowed as by a mighty wind.

Suddenly there fell a vast silence; even from without no sound came to break the awful stillness. It was as if all creation paused to hear a pregnant word.

"Hear, O Israel, the Lord our God, the Lord is One!" sang the cantor frenziedly.

And all the ghostly congregation answered with a great cry, closing their eyes and rocking frantically to and fro:

"Hear, O Israel, the Lord our God, the Lord is One!"

They seemed like a great army of the sheeted dead risen to testify to the Unity. The magnetic tremor that ran through the synagogue thrilled the lonely girl to the core; once again her dead self woke, her dead ancestors that would not be shaken off lived and moved in her. She was sucked up into the great wave of passionate faith, and from her lips came, in rapturous surrender to an overmastering impulse, the half-hysterical protestation:

"Hear, O Israel, the Lord our God, the Lord is One!"

And then in the brief instant while the congregation, with ever-ascending rhapsody, blessed God till the climax came with the sevenfold declaration, "The Lord, He is God," the whole history of her strange, unhappy race flashed through her mind in a whirl of resistless emotion. She was overwhelmed by the thought of its sons in every corner of the earth proclaiming to the somber twilight sky the belief for which its generations had lived and died—the Jews of Russia sobbing it forth in their pale

of enclosure, the Jews of Morocco in their *mellah* and of South
Africa in their tents by the diamond mines; the Jews of the
New World in great free cities, in Canadian backwoods, in
South American savannahs; the Australian Jews on the sheep
farms and the gold fields and in the mushrooming cities; the
Jews of Asia in their reeking quarters begirt by barbarian popu-
lations. The shadow of a large mysterious destiny seemed to
hang over these poor superstitious zealots, whose lives she knew
so well in all their everyday prose, and to invest the unconscious
shuffling sons of the ghetto with something of tragic grandeur.
The gray dusk palpitated with floating shapes of prophets and
martyrs, scholars and sages and poets, full of a yearning love
and pity, lifting hands of benediction. By what great high roads
and queer byways of history had they traveled hither, these
wandering Jews, "sated with contempt," these shrewd eager
fanatics, these sensual ascetics, these human paradoxes, adap-
tive to every environment, energizing in every field of activity,
omnipresent like some great natural force, indestructible and
almost inconvertible, surviving—with the incurable optimism
that overlay all their poetic sadness—Babylon and Carthage,
Greece, and Rome; involuntarily financing the Crusades, out-
living the Inquisition, elusive of all baits, unshaken by all persecutions—at once the greatest and meanest of races? Had the
Jew come so far only to break down at last, sinking in morasses
of modern doubt, and irresistibly dragging down with him the
Christian and the Moslem; or was he yet fated to outlast them
both in continuous testimony to a hand molding incompre-
hensibly the life of humanity?[12]

YOM KIPPUR IN OLD SAN FRANCISCO

HARRIET LANE LEVY

On the morning of Yom Kippur, the sacred day of days,
Father, Mother, and I went to the synagogue at an early hour.
We owned two seats in the second row on the center aisle. As
the pews were not ordinarily filled except on holidays, the

11. Yom Kippur scenes. From *Kirchliche Verfassung der heutigen Juden*, by Johann C.G. Bodenschatz, Erlang, 1748. See Chapter XI.

ownership of two seats might be largely interpreted, might be
made to include a third member of the family, slender or submissive to compression, the understanding being that any
strain beyond two would be held excessive on the Sabbath and
inadmissible on holidays.

This morning, as we stopped at our pew, we saw that our
neighbors, the Goldsmiths, were already established there—
father, mother, daughter, and the redheaded bar mitzvah son
spread out like a cultivated vineyard. At our approach they
contracted as a unit, whispering to one another without moving
their lips, their eyes glued to their books in an excess of devotion. No shrinkage, however, could reduce the amplitude of four
bodies to the measure of two. Well enough did Mr. Goldsmith
see Mother standing erect, the jet of her bonnet tinkling, making
no movement to enter the pew. He looked up, as if discovering
us, his shrewd eyes calling an invitation to a humorous interpretation of his dilemma. But Mother turned away and looked
toward the entrance door of the synagogue until the sexton
approached and trained an eye upon the occupants of the pew.
He pointed an index finger, jerking it upward in admonition,
as if to say, "Arise," and the redheaded son of Mr. Goldsmith
arose, fingering his new gold watch chain, his freckled face
flushing as he disappeared into an empty pew close against the
wall. Only then did we take our places, three of us occupying
two seats in unquestioned privilege.

With deliberation Mother opened her stiff black leather, gold-
tooled prayer book and, having found the place in the service,
retreated into her devotion. She read the text in Hebrew, and I,
leaning against her, read the translated page: "From everlasting to everlasting is the existence of the one true God. Thou
rulest the whole universe with kindness and fillest Thy creatures
with love, O Eternal Being, unto whom alone our praises are
due." Into the text percolated an alien note: "Hutzpah [cheek],"
Mother was muttering, and again, "Hutzpah." Through her
lowered lids, I intercepted the fierce, oblique glance directed
at our neighbor.

The old sexton shuffled down the aisle looking to the right

and to the left, seeking; now he touched the shoulder of a man sitting close to the end of the pew, bending to whisper; now he nodded to another beyond the reach of his finger, his lips moving, naming a name. I hoped that he would pass by our pew, that he would not touch Father, whispering to him. But no, he stopped and communicated the word which would be the signal for Father to go up to the altar and say a prayer during the reading from the scroll of the Law, or at the close of the reading to fit the scroll into the white satin cover, crested with tinkling bells, and return it to the ark behind the white velvet curtain, a participation for which Father would have to wear his prayer shawl. To bend, to abstract the prayer shawl from the little wooden box beneath his seat, to drop it over the shoulders and ascend to the altar was but a succession of simple movements to any other man. Father alone made of it an occasion for struggle and confusion. Repeated failure should have hinted the futility of the strain, but still hoping to pierce the keyhole of his box without rising from his seat, he bent far forward, his hand frantically jabbing in the direction of his box. Only when his top hat suffered displacement by collision with a neck in the front pew did he yield, turn about, and drop upon his knees. To the sensitive ear of the family, each fresh effort to penetrate the slot magnified the tinkle of his keys until it grew to a volume that reached to the choir.

"*Wilst du noch aufstehen* [Are you ever going to get up]?" Mother demanded of the strained breadth of broadcloth arched beneath her, and when Father finally raised a moist roll of neck and arose, it was as if he were returning from a long journey. Hardly had he seated himself and adjusted his white silk shawl when the reader called, "*Yaamod Levi*," and Father arose, walked up the side steps to the altar, and approached the reading desk. He raised the fringe of his shawl to his lips, offered a prayer, and listened to a reading from a portion of the Law selected for the day. Again he prayed, received a blessing for himself, another for his family, whispered a donation for the synagogue, and returned to our pew, crowding us against our neighbors as he relaxed. . . .

The rabbi stood at the higher reading desk, his white satin gown a shroud against the white velvet curtains. He waited until the last tardy member was seated, the last muscle commanded, until every recreant eye had converged toward his own. Then he began in a low voice which presently rose and later swelled to a volume of accusation, darkened to prophetic gloom, and finally emerged again into hope and promise. My interest lived in the manipulation of the text which would be lost and recovered and lost again like a trail, until at the very end of the hour, after we had traveled far, far away on foreign highways, it reappeared with comforting familiarity recovered by some unpredictable ingenuity. The thunder against moral laxity exposed and vilified was welcome to my ear which received enjoyment from the inundation of the volume of sound, and from experience I knew of the ointment that would be applied to the bruises of flagellation.

We found pleasure in rebuke as well as in solace; we wore our rabbi like an ornament and thrilled in our ownership of his eloquence. Under denunciation of our shortcomings the sense of sin voluptuously melted into appreciation of the art that had awakened it, and when the rabbi, paled by the vehemence of accusation and appeal, regained his seat, the congregation regarded with tender approval how he wiped the perspiration from his forehead with his soft white silk handkerchief.

After the tumult of the sermon was over, I welcomed the empty spaces of the pulpit, the vertical fall of the white velvet curtains, the president and vice-president motionless in the high-backed chairs, the rabbi spent, slanted in his flowing white robe, his white velvet cap touchingly awry. Except for the flickering lights of the seven-branched candlesticks and the everlasting red light above the ark, the altar rested in quiet. The picture dispensed repose and comfort under which tense muscles relaxed and a neighbor whispered the question, "*Eine schoene drosche* [A fine sermon]?" to which another answered, "*Und wie* [And how]!"

After interest in the sermon ebbed, the younger members sought relaxation in the foyer where the strain of enforced silence was released into sudden excited chatter. Boys and girls met by appointment to trip gaily away for a promenade up and down the block, or a visit to a distant synagogue. Some stopped to dive into a candy shop furtively and secure provision for the hour of sundown when the fast would be over, hastening back to their synagogue for the vesper when all the members of the family regathered so as to return home in unbroken formation.

The lull that followed the morning sermon ushered in the memorial service for the dead—the long, long hour devoted to remembrance and offering. A few mourners sat dry-eyed, more wiped away a tear, and occasionally a sob, exposing fresh grief, broke from behind a heavy crepe veil. At that sound the heart contracted and the congregation turned toward the mourner. Faces sobered at the reminder of death, twisting into quick sympathy and common fear. Following one another in a long train, a father or son took his place on the altar between cantor and president, read a chapter from the Bible, and whispered a donation in memory of someone, perhaps long dead. The officers of the synagogue incorporated into the service the amount in uninterrupted chant. An old forgotten name popped from the past like a ghost from a midnight grave. Sometimes whole families reappeared, crowding the altar with familiar shapes which came and vanished like figures upon a screen.

We had no dead and I experienced regret, quickly smothered, at my exclusion from the full measure of the excitement of an intimate resurrection. I regretted, too, that my lack of understanding of Hebrew denied me knowledge of the amount of the whispered donation. I should have liked to have been able to measure the grief by its offering, instead of being obliged to make my deduction from the grunt of a neighbor. I envied Father, who greeted Greenberg's impressive donation (Greenberg whose recent failure had been so disastrous to Father) with "*Fur mein Geld* [For my money]." How soothing to an anxious ghost to be valued generously, I reflected. How surprising and humiliating the revelation of a niggardly appraisal! I anticipated my own death and the lavish benefaction that would divulge to the congregation an incurable anguish.

It was difficult to fill the long hours of the afternoon, given to confession and repentance. As the unbroken presence of my family excluded me from entering into the memorial service, so poverty in sin denied me purification. Among the long list of transgressors I sought a place; I should have liked to have joined the congregation in a private trespass, but any sin that I was able to muster was too frail to mingle with the flood of lamentation rolling to the throne of God. I had not scoffed nor been stiff-necked, rather erring toward weak conciliations and shyness. I had not committed iniquity nor wrought unrighteousness; nor, lacking the robustness of opposition, had I manifested a rebellious spirit. A questioning mind edged with intolerable curiosity gave me no opportunity to counsel evil, nor should I have found an audience to such an inclination; and so I was obliged to leave contrition to my parents and to the other older people who had lived long enough to have known what it was to scoff and be proud, to corrupt themselves and "commit abominations." Without reluctance, therefore, when the memorial service was over, I yielded my place to Addie, who arrived with heavy wraps and a lemon pierced with cloves for my parents to smell, and revive their strength diminished by the rigors of the fast. I would return for *Neilah*, the closing service of the day.

The *Neilah* service passed before my eyes like a dream. Senses blurred by the heat and rhythmic, spatial repetition of a verse lowered me into deep lassitude. Behind a curtain of trembling light and heat on the higher platform the white figure of the rabbi stood elongated, his face paled to the whiteness of his robe, his dusky hair and beard blackened against the white velvet of the ark. "Open unto us, O God, the gates of mercy, before the closing of the gates, ere the day is done." The voice came down from a height above the altar which floated before me like a vision. Upon the mists before it, high white gates, widespread, slowly approached each other. "The day vanishes, the sun is setting, let us enter Thy gates."

A wave of sound came from the congregation. It rose and washed over me on its way to the altar, ebbing again into a broken murmur. Then another and another, bending me beneath the undulating weight of rich sensation. I looked up and saw the stained glass of the western windows stir and glow under the rays of the sinking sun. The sun *was* sinking, the day *was* departing, just as it was being said. Then it was true. Suddenly it was all true. In a moment what had been a dream became actuality and the service of the day—sin, confession, forgiveness—was charged with meaning, concerned me. I was frightened; I who had confessed no sin, who *had* hardened my head, who *had* been stiff-necked and scoffing. About me the congregation sat as one unit, heads bowed, lips moving under a common feeling. I sat without, a stranger, alone. In a panic I sought a sin, a remorse, even the smallest one indicative of a contrite heart, but before I could seize upon one the gates had closed and the *Neilah* service was over. . . .

With the blowing of the ram's horn and the benediction the fast was over, and the congregation, dazed by the heavy air and the long fast, slowly moved toward the door, stopping to make inquiry for the well-being of one another. Father and Eph Newman remained seated, chanting aloud. Mother protested, "*Chapt Gott bei den füssen* [Grabs God by His feet]," and she tapped Father on the shoulder until he returned his prayer shawl to the box and came out with us. Polly and Addie were at the door to greet us. We labored to the street, step by step. Three closed carriages, hired from Michelson's stables, drove up to the sidewalk and groups of Friedenthals and Greens and Meyerfelds disappeared within them. The drivers slammed the doors behind them, jumped into their seats, and drove away on a double curve.

Better than us!

The cold air cut between our shoulder blades. We drew our coats and capes closer about our necks and followed the crowd down the street to the cable car that would take us to our home.[13]

YOM KIPPUR IN BROWNSVILLE

CHAVER PAVER (GERSHON EINBINDER)

Yom Kippur morning no one in Brownsville went to work. Yom Kippur morning there was not a single home in Brownsville where an alarm clock was allowed to scream. Yom Kippur morning it was so quiet in Brownsville that Gershon couldn't sleep. It was even quieter than on Sunday mornings. Sunday mornings you might hear an occasional car or truck riding by. Yom Kippur morning—not a truck, not a car, as though the street had gone into hiding, afraid to utter a sound. Even on *Kol Nidre* night, cars were rare in Brownsville. The Brownsville taxis, which usually cruise on Pitkin Avenue, disappeared. Pitkin Avenue itself, where even on a *Shabbos* you could find stores and restaurants open, had been dark since the previous evening.

Gershon had gone to the Thatford Avenue Synagogue for *Kol Nidre*. He had felt homesick for the *Kol Nidre* evenings of Bershad, but when he entered the synagogue he grew even more so. Here in the Thatford Avenue *shul* there were also big candles burning on the reader's platform, and many of the men were dressed in white *kittels*. Missing, however, was Hirshke Redhead, the *hazzan* of the old synagogue in Bershad. When Hirshke Redhead used to begin *Kol Nidre* in his pious powerful voice, the gates of heaven opened, and a sacred tremor went through the synagogue. Himself a complete pauper, Hirshke had had plenty of complaints to the Almighty, not only those of the congregation, but his own personal ones. . . .

Here in the Thatford Avenue Synagogue there was a famous cantor who demanded a big fee and who sang the *Kol Nidre* with his choir as though he were giving a concert. Missing here, too, was Gershon's father, tall in his white *kittel*, with his old heirloom *tallit* covering his head. On *Kol Nidre* night and all the next day of Yom Kippur his father rarely sat down; all day he stood on his feet, absorbed in his prayers and his thoughts.

But Gershon loved Brownsville on that clear, autumn Yom Kippur day as he strolled along the streets which the golden autumn sun had painted with magic colors. They were deserted, these Brownsville streets. The entire adult population was inside the synagogues. Only one man was not in *shul*—Moishe der Meshugener. Dirty-faced, slovenly, he walked on Pitkin Avenue all alone with his sack of rags over his shoulder. Nor did he even stop to cry out, as was his practice: "May America burn up! I'd rather go to Philadelphia!" What was the use of crying and complaining when there was not another living soul on the street to hear?

And there were so many synagogues in Brownsville—one for perhaps every two blocks. Of course, many of them were only temporary synagogues, in a store, or a private house, and after the holidays they would "adjourn" for another year. But there were also a great many permanent synagogues, and near one of these, on Herzl Street, Gershon saw signs of a commotion. A congregant in the women's section had fainted, probably from fasting, and they had brought her outside, and a doctor was immediately found among the worshipers, and with his *tallit* still on his shoulders he bent over her and felt her pulse. . . .

Gershon's mother, too, had been in the habit of fainting, almost every Yom Kippur. . . .

Translated by Max Rosenfeld[14]

THE TWO-DAY YOM KIPPUR IN JAPAN

DAVID KRANZLER

During World War II a situation developed wherein a group of refugees in Kobe, Japan, observed the Sabbath for *two* days (i.e., on Saturday and Sunday in Japan) and fasted a full forty-eight hours on Yom Kippur. The unusual circumstances occurred when two thousand Jews from Nazi-occupied Poland found a temporary haven in Kobe, after having traversed Siberia. Among these Polish refugees was a group of about five hundred rabbinic students and teachers, more than half from the famous talmudic college of Mir, Poland. Here questions were raised about the proper day for observing the Sabbath, Yom Kippur, and other Jewish holy days. These doubts were due to the problem of the location of the "Jewish Date Line."

What is presently the universally accepted position of the International Date Line is the arbitrary, almost uninterrupted

hypothetical line measuring 180 degrees longitude from Green-
wich, England, passing along most of its length through the
Pacific. This line was found to be the most convenient place for
mariners to change dates, since the farther eastward one travels
without adjusting his watch, the shorter the length of the day—
one hour per 15 degrees—as measured from noon to noon.
Traveling westward one will find a corresponding increase in
the length of the day—traveling twenty-four hours for 360
degrees. Thus, for example, a traveler going west from San
Francisco to China loses one day when crossing this date line,
while gaining a day going in the opposite direction.

As early as the medieval period differences arose as to the
location of the "Jewish Date Line." This issue achieved prom-
inence during the early months of 1941 as the rabbinical
students and scholars poured into Kobe, and it became crucial
with the approach of Yom Kippur that year. For the purpose of
resolving the doubts raised by the rabbinic students concerning
this holiest of Jewish days, an assembly of rabbis was convened
in Jerusalem in September 1941 under the leadership of Chief
Rabbi Isaac Halevy Herzog. After much learned discussion, the
assembly concluded that neither the Sabbath nor Yom Kippur
should be changed from the calendar observed in Kobe, although
the reasoning for this decision differed among the authorities.
A telegram was sent by Rabbi Herzog to the refugees in Kobe
on behalf of the rabbinical assembly, advising them not to
make any change from Wednesday for the local observance of
Yom Kippur.

Indeed, along similar lines, the old-time Jewish community of
Kobe, comprised of about fifty families of Sephardic as well as
Russian Ashkenazic origin, relied upon the decision of Aaron
Moshe Kisseloff of Harbin, Manchuria, chief rabbi of the Far
Eastern Jewish communities, who also advised that they re-
frain from making any change in the locally established days.

One lone voice of dissent reached Kobe, stating categorically
that the refugees were "to eat on Wednesday"—the local Yom
Kippur—and "fast on Thursday." So wrote Rabbi Avraham
Yeshayahu Karelitz (better known as the Hazon Ish), considered

one of the greatest Torah authorities of the past generation, who disagreed with the conclusions of the rabbinical assembly. His views were based primarily upon the interpretation of a talmudic discourse on the intercalation of the "New Moon," by Judah Halevi in his *Kuzari*, and Rabbi Zerachia Halevi (*Baal Hamoar*) who placed the change of a day six hours (i.e., 90 degrees) east of Jerusalem. Since Japan was located beyond this "Date Line," Hazon Ish ruled that the refugees change the day for both the Sabbath as well as Yom Kippur.

It was due to the deference on the part of most of the yeshiva scholars and students to the authority of the Hazon Ish that the unique situation of a dual Sabbath and a forty-eight-hour Yom Kippur was observed. In practice, most of the yeshiva students observed the normal local Saturday as the Sabbath in full detail. For the second day (i.e., Sunday) they observed all the biblical injunctions and were more lenient with respect to the rabbinic ordinances. Thus, on Sunday while they performed no work they wore phylacteries during prayers (normally worn only on weekdays), though omitting the usual benedictions.

Though the problem of Yom Kippur was the more pressing issue—one for which the above-mentioned assembly gathered in Jerusalem—it affected a much smaller number of refugees than did the related issue of the Sabbath. This was because by Yom Kippur a majority of the refugees, who had been unable to secure visas to any other country, had been sent to Shanghai on the orders of the Japanese authorities who were already preparing for war. The relatively small group of yeshiva students still in Kobe during Yom Kippur observed the fast in the following manner: those physically able fasted on Thursday as well as Wednesday and the others who were unable to fast two days fasted on Wednesday and ate on Thursday only in piecemeal quantities of less than the minimum measure (slightly less than an average-sized egg) for which one was culpable on Yom Kippur. The usual Yom Kippur prayers, however, were omitted on the second day as well as the *Yaale ve-Yavo* in the Grace after Meals recited by those unable to fast for two days.[15]

YOM KIPPUR IN THE WARSAW GHETTO

MICHAEL ZYLBERBERG

As soon as war started in 1939, we Jews in Warsaw realized that besides the general Nazi attack, we had to face another war specially directed by the Germans against the Jews. From the very first day of the invasion, the Germans concentrated their bombing attacks on the Jewish streets of Warsaw and other towns in Poland. They tried to wipe us out. Thousands of Jews were killed on the first day of the war.

Rosh Hashanah 1939 will always remain in my memory. All day long the planes bombarded the two Warsaw Jewish districts —Nalewki and Grzybow. Whole streets went up in flames, and thousands of Jews died.

On Yom Kippur, Warsaw was still held by the Poles. All synagogues and houses of study were closed. Jews gathered for *Kol Nidre* in private houses and in cellars, and prayed to the accompaniment of falling bombs.

On Yom Kippur morning I was asked to go to the high school at 18 Bielanska Street, in order to hand the building over to the military authorities. While I was on my way, the Germans started a new attack. Throughout the day and night bombs rained down on the Jewish district. Thousands of Jews perished and large numbers of families were left homeless. I did not reach my destination. It did not really matter, as the school was hit and destroyed. I had to take refuge. All that day I lay hiding in a cellar among strangers. Next day, when we came out of our hiding places, we stepped over corpses lying in the streets. Many of them were our relatives and friends.

That was our first Yom Kippur of the war. A few days later, the Nazis, after heavy fighting, occupied Warsaw. The Nuremburg Laws were introduced, and Jews were required to wear special distinguishing markings. All Jewish banking accounts were seized, and Jewish property, factories, and shops confiscated. Day after day, cars and carts poured into Warsaw from the provinces, bringing more Jewish families to the capital. We

did not lose hope. We were determined to live, and to defeat
the enemy.

On Yom Kippur 1940 there was no question of assembling
for services. The Germans had ordered all synagogues and
houses of study to be closed. But on that Yom Kippur day the
Jews of Poland recited their prayers more devoutly than ever.
Minyanim were organized in almost every Jewish house in
Warsaw. There is no doubt that the Nazis knew of these
gatherings.

Precisely at noon, between *Shahrit* and *Musaf,* loudspeakers
announced that a Jewish ghetto was to be set up. All Jews in
Warsaw had to leave their dwellings within eight days, and
move into that part of the city which had been marked off as
the ghetto.

Yom Kippur became Tishah be-Av. Within a few days,
500,000 Jews had to congregate in the small ghetto. Non-
Jewish householders in the ghetto area were given wonderful
flats, with all modern conveniences, in exchange for their small,
dirty rooms. And, in addition, the Jews had to pay large sums in
key money to get in.

Yet the Jews somehow managed to adapt themselves to the
terrible conditions. A new chapter in Jewish persecution began.
Homelessness, hunger, and disease; these were the three pillars
of the New Year. Five hundred Jews died daily of hunger,
dysentery, and typhus. A wall nearly ten feet high was put up
around the ghetto area.

That year I lived and worked with the well-known Jewish
pedagogue Dr. Janusz Korczak (Goldschmidt). A few days
before Rosh Hashanah 1941 Dr. Korczak asked me whether I
could help him organize Rosh Hashanah and Yom Kippur services for 150 orphan children. He wanted the services to be
properly organized, in order to impress the children. "In these
terrible times," he said, "religion is our only positive force, our
only safeguard." I was surprised. Dr. Korczak had not been a
religious Jew. He was an assimilationist who had been out of
touch with religious Jewish life.

We found a young *hazzan*. The children prepared the large

hall in the Children's Home, at 33 Chlodna Street, for the services, laid carpets, and arranged flowers. Rosh Hashanah and Yom Kippur 1941 in the Children's Home was a great experience. Dr. Korczak, wearing a black silk skullcap, stood in his corner throughout the day, with his Polish prayer book. His sermons were most moving. He spoke of life and death, of Jewish faith, of the Torah, of Israel. "Who knows," he said in his last address at *Neilah*, "whether we shall live to assemble again next Yom Kippur." Next Rosh Hashanah the children were no longer there. And Dr. Korczak was dead.

Weeks and months passed. Life in the Warsaw ghetto became more difficult, more unbearable. Night after night, people were dragged out of their beds, and shot in the streets. On Tishah be-Av 1942 the deportation of Jews to Treblinka started. By Yom Kippur 1942 there were only about sixty thousand Jews left in the Warsaw ghetto. They were slaves of the Germans, working all day in the Nazi factories. There were still children and old people among us who had managed to hide with the working members of their families. They did not survive Yom Kippur 1942.

The day before Yom Kippur, at noon, all factories were surrounded, and the Nazis carried out a search to find all nonworking elements. There were heartrending scenes in every Jewish home. Children were torn from their parents, fathers and mothers from their children. Sick people were shot on the spot.

That is how we began Yom Kippur 1942. The Nazis issued further instructions, ordering the directors of the factories to make another search on Yom Kippur night to find the rest of the "nonproductive" Jewish elements. Most of the directors of the factories were Jews, and they tried to save their brethren still in the ghetto.

That night was one of the most terrible in the whole of our stay in the ghetto. The day passed "normally." We worked in the factories, as on every other day. When they served our midday meal, the Jews got together, placed a guard at the doors, and prayed. We did not know which of us had to say the memorial prayer for the dead; so we all said it, even the youngest among us.

By Yom Kippur 1943 Warsaw was *Judenrein*. Only a few Jews were still alive, and these lived outside the ghetto, posing as non-Jews. It was only by chance that I learned it was Yom Kippur. Even non-Jews were in great danger in Warsaw. Every day people were stopped in the streets, and shot as "reprisal" for acts of terrorism committed against the Germans. The safest place to hide at that time was in a church. I spent the whole of that Yom Kippur in the church of the Plac Zbawiciela —one of Warsaw's largest churches.

This church was always open and crowded with worshipers, and a Jew could enter without attracting attention. At eight o'clock in the morning, I took my place among the hundreds of worshipers assembled in the church for High Mass. As I sat, my thoughts were far away. I could see our old *baal shahrit* crying, with a trembling voice, "*Hammelekh*," as he approached the pulpit.

Three hours later High Mass ended, and most of the worshipers left. I stayed on, and, looking around, saw a number of other Jews. Many were women, heads bowed in prayer, preparing to spend the day in the church—to make their *heshbon ha-nefesh*. Some were former pupils of mine, who had graduated from the high school. We did not make any sign of recognition. We were all strangers.

The silence in the church was broken by a priest in a white gown, who stood before the altar praying for those in need of help. The melody of the prayer sounded so Jewish, so near to our own unhappiness. It reminded me of the pain and suffering of Jewry throughout the ages.

We stayed in church all day, sharing the same thoughts and sentiments. Every time we looked up, we saw our own pain reflected in the faces of Jesus and Mary over the altar. As dusk fell, I saw the unfortunate Jews stealing out one by one. I, too, left, with my heart full of pain and desperation, the sad melody of the prayer accompanying me.

I often heard this melody in other churches, and, when I came to London last year and attended the Sabbath morning

service at the Sephardic synagogue off Maida Vale, I heard the
very same melody. The same mournful melody which reminded
me of our two thousand years of wandering and suffering in
the Diaspora.

Yom Kippur 1944 followed immediately after the Warsaw
rising under Bor Komorowski. The Nazis took possession of the
whole city, and the entire non-Jewish population was driven
out, and with them those few Jews who had still remained. They
were all interned in the Prushkov camp, near Warsaw, and a
special effort was made to root out all Jews living there as non-
Jews. Very few survived to tell the story. I am one of them.[16]

KOL NIDRE IN THE DACHAU CONCENTRATION CAMP

LEVI SHALIT

How did they, the eight thousand Jews in that particular
Dachau camp, get to know that the next day would be Yom
Kippur?

Cut off from the flowing of time, insulated from the living
world, not knowing even the place where they found themselves,
caught up in a mad macabre dance of death, having long ago
lost count of days—yet here, to the eight thousand men and
women walled up behind electrified wires, came the quiet
whisper carried from lip to lip: "Yom Kippur!"

The sun sets on the blood-red horizon, on the distant snow-
covered mountain tops. Emaciated faces, staring eyes, look far
into the sunset. Now one would be in the synagogue. . . . Bygone
Yom Kippur days leap to the memory. Torturing thoughts tire
the enfeebled brain.

Are we really "more guilty than other peoples?" Worse than
all the other peoples on earth? Why such a decree last year?
What decree this year? Will a happier year be inscribed—a year
of life? But all around is death. How many have, even today,
breathed their last? How many will be brought back dead from
work today? And the mind flares up in rebellious heresy: No!
There is no judge and no justice! But the heart is so desperately

12. Yom Kippur scenes. From *Der Juden Glaube und Aberglaube*, by Friedrich A. Christiani, Leipzig, 1705. See Chapter XI.

eager to believe; no good philosophizing, when the thought aches to lean on something—on God.

Someone wipes a tear from his eyes. The thud of feet drowns the weak groan. Now they pass the bean field where ripe fascicles of beans stand ready. Every day, passing here, dozens of men jump out of the line to try and snatch a few beans. The warders know this and wait for it in order to divert themselves with floggings and the setting on of the dogs. Today no one runs toward the field, and the warders remark to each other, "Their fast today." They also grow quieter. The oppressive silence of the captive always overwhelms the guard. The mute forbearance of a prisoner is often the best weapon against his keeper.

Eight thousand lie or stand, scattered over the large camp area, preparing for the fast with moldy bread crumbs and watery soup. And when the sirens shriek and the dogs begin to bark they run, with the last mouthful hardly swallowed, to the place of roll call. From here, the day workers go to their barracks, the night workers to their work. . . .

At our place of work the overseers are waiting. They look at the gang and wonder. Somehow today the Jews allow themselves, with constrained indifference, to be pushed into every kind of work wherever they are taken. Always there is a stampede from the lines; everyone struggles to get to "his" work, makes an effort to be among those who work under a roof, runs to "his" master, claims to be an artisan. Today they all stand as if frozen, letting themselves be taken like sheep.

There is the usual hum among the laborers. The German firm MAL is building an underground refuge here in the forest for the bombed Messerschmidt airplane factory. Thousands of skeleton figures are ministering night and day to hundreds of concrete mixing machines. Locomotive whistles pierce the air. Trains rush from the whole of Europe to bring building material. Everything moves at a feverish pace to save the near-toppling Germany. Night falls—cold, murky, inky black. In the midst of the brightly lit forest thousands of workers go to and fro, linking one job with the other, bringing iron, timber, machine parts— and also covert messages. Yes, there will be divine service soon during the meal break in the middle of the night. And when the sirens signal the rest pause, shadows glide stealthily to pre-arranged spots, right in the forest.

Someone takes his stand near a tree, leans as if at the holy ark, and in the midst of fear and silence begins: "In the heavenly court. . . . *Kol Nidre.* . . ."

We gather closer to the *hazzan*, a young Hungarian lad. Here stands Warsaw's last rabbi, his face yellow, hairless, wrinkled, his aged body bent; his hands are rocking like reeds in the wind; only the eyes, sparkling stars, look out toward the cold sky above, and his lips, half-open, murmur softly.

What does he say now, how does he pray, this last of the rabbis of Warsaw? Does he lovingly accept for himself and for all Israel the pain and suffering, or does he, through the medium of his prayer, conduct a dispute with the Almighty, asking him the ancient question: Is this the reward for the Torah?

Huddling to the *hazzan* stands Alter—the Kovno cab driver. His broad shoulders lean against a young tree and his mouth emits staccato sounds as if they were hummed out of his insides. No, he does not beg; he does not pray; he demands! He demands his rights, he calls for justice: Why were his children burnt by the Nazis, why was his wife reduced to ashes? He hums mutely, without words. He does not know the words because he is not capable of saying all the prayers by heart. Does the Lord require words? He requires the heart. Where, then, is His hearty, divine mercy? Since Alter the cab driver can't find this mercy, he hums in revolt against the Almighty. It is probably the strongest prayer that was ever heard since the days of Levi Yitzhak of Berditchev.

Here stands Consul Naftel, of Memel, his face drawn and worn. With his bowed head his figure reminds you of a bent thorn. Why does he cling so closely to the *hazzan*? Why doesn't he want to miss a single word? Has he become so pious?

I remembered a remark made by the Lubavitcher Rebbe when he passed through Kovno. He said: "Jews are believers, always; under the hail of bullets in the besieged Warsaw I saw it even more clearly. In the air raid shelters I heard Jews crying, *Shema Yisrael.*"

Is it really so? Have the Jews of Warsaw or of Dachau—has Consul Naftel called unto God out of piety, or . . . ?

This question is of no importance. What difference does it make why and how Jews called out unto God near the crematorium of Dachau? The prayer was in any case the greatest and the deepest, even though Consul Naftel took poison on the day after Yom Kippur. . . .

Lips murmur after him—quiet, quiet, muffled words hardly manage to pass, remain sticking in the throat.

Then—a stream of tears and sobs burst from the throat, the heart eases. There is sudden relief as if one has rolled something heavy away. What was it that brought this relief? Faith? If so, then of this—of faith at such a time—even the Baal Shem Tov could have boasted. To how many of those worshipers at the little tree in the darkness of the Bavarian forest was it vouchsafed to live another year?[17]

YOM KIPPUR IN KOREA

BILLY ROSE

When Eleanor and I were in Tokyo a little over a year ago, we got to know Col. Anthony Story, Gen. MacArthur's pilot. This morning I got a letter from Tony with a Korea dateline, and it contained a story which I think is worth passing along.

In one of the Marine Corps regiments which recently slogged into Inchon, there was a corporal named Abraham Geller, who had been brought up a nickel phone call away from Delancey Street. Abe is the son of a rabbi, and even at the front where sleep is the most important thing in the world, he never failed to wake a half hour before his buddies and go through the ritual of the Orthodox morning prayers.

On September 20, 1950, Abe's regiment crossed the Han and cut the Seoul-Kaesong road and, what with snipers in every rice paddy, by dusk the men were glad to dig in and catch a few hours of clammy sleep—especially since they knew that the drive for the Korean capital itself was scheduled for sunup.

An hour before dawn, aside from the sentries, only two men in the company were awake: Cpl. Geller, bent over his prayer book, and Capt. George O'Connor, surveying the terrain and figuring out how best to deploy his troops in the coming action.

When Abe was finished, the captain said, "Go back to the chow truck and get yourself a cup of coffee."

"Thanks, Captain," said Geller, "but today's Yom Kippur, and I'm not supposed to eat until sundown."

"You mean to say you're going to fast the day we bust into Seoul?" said the Captain.

The East Sider grinned. "I figure I've got enough calories packed away for twenty-four hours," he said.

Well, as the papers have told you, the marines ran into plenty of trouble the first day of the drive, and along about sundown Capt. O'Connor's men were inching their way across a field littered with dead North Koreans. One of the Commies, however, though badly wounded, was only playing dead, and as the officer came within range he rolled over on his side and aimed his pistol.

Abe, was only a few feet from his commanding officer, saw the body move. He jerked his bayonet out of his belt and made a dive for the enemy soldier, but in finishing him off he got the three bullets which had been intended for O'Connor.

The captain did the best he could for Abe, but at this stage the situation was what military commentators called "fluid" and it was almost three hours before the corporal got a shot of penicillin and was carried to a hospital tent.

The operation lasted over an hour, and when the surgeon finally came out Capt. O'Connor was waiting for him.

"How does it look?" he asked.

"The kid's doing fine," said the surgeon.

"I figured he was done for," said O'Connor.

"So did I," said the surgeon. "The bullets went through his abdomen and several loops of intestine, and wounds like that are generally fatal if penicillin isn't administered pretty fast. The spillage almost always causes peritonitis."

"I don't get all the words," said the captain, "but his pulling through seems like something of a miracle."

"In a manner of speaking, it is," said the surgeon. "Geller owes his life to the fact that when he was shot there was hardly any food in his stomach."[18]

YOM KIPPUR AT THE VIET FRONT

BARRY CUNNINGHAM

TAN SON NHUT, VIET NAM, Sept. 24, 1966—The destinies of more than two thousand Jewish soldiers were sealed in the Book of Life tonight as twilight over Viet Nam ushered in the holiest day of the Jewish year.

Yom Kippur, the Day of Atonement, was celebrated here by over five hundred soldiers arriving from jungle war zones by helicopter, by truck convoy, by hook or crook. Other services were held in Da Nang and Pleikuo.

The men's faces were somber as they stacked their M-16 rifles in the pews of Tan Son Nhut chapel and donned prayer shawls. They came in sweat-soaked fatigues and mud-splattered boots. Many brought their war wounds with them and had trouble fitting their skullcaps on heads already covered with gauze.

Capt. Alan Greenspan, one of three Jewish chaplains in Viet Nam, cradled in his arms a photostatic-copy Torah, part of a collapsible Army-issue synagogue kit which he regularly carries to the field for frontline Sabbaths.

He is everywhere where they need him, it seems, in battles, in hospitals. And on this day their lives were made poignant by the prayer: "On Rosh Hashanah their destiny is inscribed and on Yom Kippur it is sealed. How many shall pass away and how many shall be brought into existence, who shall live and who shall die."

The white skullcaps were in short supply because of the unexpected number of worshipers arriving earlier in the day, and local seamstresses were hastily summoned to sew together new ones.

"The first Viet Namese yarmulkes in history," announced Rabbi Greenspan. Before services began at dusk he stood outside chatting with the first handful of GIs to be greeted from the field.

Two men were killed by sniper fire in the cargo plane that brought Sp/4 Robert Freshman to this "Sabbath of Sabbaths." It took ten hours for PFC Yoram Stein to make his way down from Cu Chi on a minesweeper convoy.

Some of the men, like PFC Mark Scott and PFC Rubin Fidler, brought with them their religious anxieties over the war. "Biblically," Greenspan told them, "men of God fought wars. Moses was not only a man of peace, he had to fight battles."

"Why are we here?" asked Stein.

"A Jew in Viet Nam is what he has always been," said the rabbi, "a fighter and a champion of the rights of man."

"Whose side is God on?"

"God judges all mankind," said Greenspan. "We feel that God's on our side and I believe it."

The men went inside and bowed their heads for the *Kol Nidre* supplication by Cantor Nathaniel Berman, a twenty-one-year-old PFC.

"Hear, O Israel," he intoned in Hebrew. He hesitated until the ear-splitting roar of a fighter jet droned over the horizon, "the Lord our God, the Lord is One."

The men began their fast. It will end at sundown tomorrow with bagels and salami provided by the National Jewish Welfare Board. In the morning they will weep at *Yizkor*, the memorial prayer for the souls of Jewish soldiers who have fallen in the war. They will beat their chests as a sign of confession and tomorrow at sundown, as a ram's horn sounds a solitary note over the bleak runways and quonset huts of Tan Son Nhut, the celestial book of accounts will close.

The men will return to the war.[19]

YOM KIPPUR IN MOSCOW

Elie Wiesel

It was Yom Kippur eve, and as I stood in the Great Synagogue of Moscow, I thought I had come to pray in the company of

Marranos, Jews who once each year decided to leave their places of hiding and worship their Creator in public. I felt like a stranger, a Gentile among them.

Yet, on the surface at least, I might have been in any prewar synagogue in Europe or America, not in the very heart of the Russian capital, ten minutes away from the golden domes of the Kremlin and from the infamous Lublianka, headquarters of the secret service, its darkened cellars once the final home of many who were tortured and condemned to die simply because they were Jews.

The sanctuary was brightly lit and crowded. Many were wearing white holiday robes and prayer shawls. As usual the number of older people was large, but there were also many of middle age and quite a few between the ages of twenty and thirty. Three generations had come together—grandfather, who still remembered the edicts of the tsar; his son, who had spent years in a labor camp in Siberia; and his grandson . . . but what was he doing here? Someone, a comrade at school or at work, must have reminded him that after all he, too, was a Jew, only a Jew—by force if not by choice.

The old people prayed with all their hearts, the younger generation sat listening in silence. They seemed thoughtful, worried, distracted. But this was only natural; it was Yom Kippur, the Day of Judgment. Who shall live and who shall die, who shall be banished and who set free, who shall be afflicted and who shall be at rest? Thoughts like these occupy the mind of every Jew on this night, wherever he may be. But here they are of immediate moment.

The prayers went on in an orderly fashion, with traditional melodies sung by a cantor and choir. The scrolls of the Torah were removed from the ark, and as the procession wound around the pulpit the elderly rabbi, Yehuda Leib Levin, declared in a trembling voice, "*Or zarua la-tzaddik* . . . Light is sown for the righteous, and gladness for the pure of heart." What light? What gladness? The cantor sang *Kol Nidre*. Here and there one heard a quiet sigh. A woman sobbed. And as the final blessing was intoned, "Blessed art Thou who hast kept us alive, and hast sustained us, and enabled us to reach this day," a shudder passed through the congregation. Another year.

Suddenly I sensed my neighbors eyeing me peculiarly. Their look was unfriendly, insulting. They were examining me, trying to tear an imaginary mask from my face and thus reveal the true purpose of my presence among them. I heard whispers. "Does anyone know him?" No one. "Does anyone know where he's from or why he's here?" No one knew. No one could possibly know. I had spoken to no one, had in fact just arrived, almost directly from the airport. Barely seven hours before I had been in Paris.

Their suspicion did not surprise me, although it did trouble me somewhat. I tried to start a conversation; they pretended not to hear. The fact that I had deliberately chosen to sit in the main part of the synagogue instead of in the visitors' section only increased their mistrust. When I spoke, they pretended not to understand Yiddish. Despite the crowding and the close quarters, a kind of distance opened between us.

It was only when I began to pray aloud, in witless desperation, that the barriers fell. The Prince of Prayer had come to my aid. They listened closely, then drew nearer; their hearts opened. They crowded around me. The crush was unbearable, but I loved it. And the questions poured out. Are there Jews in America? In Western Europe? Are they well off? Any news from Israel? Can it resist its enemies? All they wanted was to hear me talk. They refused to answer my questions. "Better not ask," said one. Another said the same. "We can't say, we can't talk," said a third. Why not? "Because. It's dangerous." They turned to me with hunted looks. I could never be one of them, because I would never be in their place. The wall of fear had risen to cut us off.

"Don't talk," one said to me. "Just pray. That is enough. How good it is to know there are young Jews in the world who still know how to pray." I felt like an outsider, a sinner. . . .

I forgot the rabbi and the cantor and the choir. Even God receded from my mind. I closed my eyes and raised my voice in prayer. Never in my life have I prayed with such a sense of devotion. . . .

Outside it was already dark. The last prayer was almost over. Old men wept as the gates of heaven began to close; the Book of Judgment was being sealed—who shall live and who shall die, who shall be set free and who shall be afflicted. Their tears were a last effort to rend the skies and avert some terrible decree.

The hall was tense and crowded; the worshipers perspired heavily, suffocating from the heat and the effects of their day-long fast. No one complained. Outside, a large crowd was trying to push its way in. There was no room, but somehow they would manage. If there were places for two thousand, there would be places for three. An air of expectancy swept over the congregation.

Something was about to happen. They seemed nervous, serious, as if preparing for a dire and momentous act, a collective act that would be remembered forever.

The cantor finished the last prayer for forgiveness. He quickened his pace, as if rushing toward some critical event. Our Father our King, seal us in the Book of Life. Our Father our King, do it for the sake of the little children. Everyone seemed to be standing on tiptoe. *Kaddish.* Another minute. They counted the seconds. The cantor proclaimed, "God is the Lord!" Seven times, with the congregation responding after him. The old sexton brought the *shofar. Tekiah!* The congregation held its breath. And then it happened. As if in response to a mysterious command from an unknown source, three thousand Jews turned as one body toward the visitors' section, stood up straight and tall, facing the representatives of Israel, looking directly into their eyes, as if trying to read in them their past and their future, the secret of their existence. Then in the awful mounting silence they suddenly burst into a wild spontaneous cry which seemed to issue from a single throat, a single heart: "Next year in Jerusalem! Next year in Jerusalem! Next year in Jerusalem!"

Translated by Neal Kozodoy[20]

XIII

YOM KIPPUR IN POETRY

EREV YOM KIPPUR

Mollie R. Golomb

I lay my pain upon Your altar, loving God;
This is my lamb, my ram, my sacrifice,

My plea for pardon, plea for forgiveness
For all my sins of doing and not doing,

Prayers that blossom like flowers out of pain
Above the earth-pull.

My people's pains have flamed in sacrifice
Upon Your altar through slow-moving time.

Pain for all evil, hatred, cruelty,
For the sick of body and the sick of heart,
For all the loneliness, the lovelessness of men,

The unmeasurable loss of those that know not You—
The pain of all the world, dear God, I place
Before Your shrine.

Look down in pity and forgiveness,
*Cause Your countenance to shine upon us
And give us peace.*[1]

THE *TZADDIK*'S DEFENSE

RUFUS LEARSI

Oh may the soul of Moses Leib
    All mortal sinners fair bestead!
For he shall dwell with the blessed tribe,
    The verdict high hath now been read:
With Abraham, Isaac, Jacob he
Shall dwell in heaven by His decree.

Then up the high accuser rose
    And bowed him low before the throne.
All soft and fair his language flows,
    Yet maketh all sweet angels moan.
The *tzaddik*'s soul, for all God's grace,
A trembling fear doth now embrace.

"They rate me harsh," the accuser spake,
    "But fame hath ever been unjust.
I've held my peace for his merit's sake,
    Yet now at length demur I must.
For who shall with the patriarchs bide,
Save those who stainless lived and died?

"It was the dread Atonement Eve,
    Holiest night, *Kol Nidre* night!
And greater sin who may conceive
    Than holiness so great to slight?
Yet stainless else, this heavy stain
Upon this soul on earth hath lain.

"That night within the house of prayer
  The people whisper low and moan.
In fear they bide, nor do they dare
  The loud *Kol Nidre* chant intone.
For empty still beside the Ark
The place of Moses Leib they mark!

"For him they look to whom alone
  By grace divine hath power been given
To lift their prayer before this throne,
  To ope for them the gates of heaven.
Their holy shepherd him they deem:
Yet where is he this hour supreme?

"And long they wait till mortal sin
  They had incurred to tarry more,
And when at length he entered in
  The dread *Kol Nidre* chant was o'er.
I say no more, yet is it well
That soul so stained with Abraham dwell?"

Low droops each gleaming angel wing,
  Each shining angel head droops low;
And tears like sudden fountains spring,
  On heaven's crystal floor they glow,
Alas for the soul of Moses Leib,
Unworthy of the patriarch tribe!

But hark! a voice deep-toned and calm
  Like music mounts through heaven's hall!
And on each angel heart like balm,
  Hope distilling, the accents fall.
The High Defender 'tis, and may
His gracious words all pains allay:

"What deed of man would grace allow
  But for the Eye that seeth all?
Metatron, angel sweet, O thou
  Who bearest prayers, thee I call!

For thou didst hover by his side
That night; so tell what did betide."

To glorious crowns of majesty
    He wreathes for God the prayers of men:
Metatron, gentle angel, he
    His golden voice uplifted then.
His brow serene a tent of light,
His eyes two suns with blessings bright!

Metatron, angel good and great,
    Whose wings the prayers of men upbear!
How shall my song thy tale relate,
    O angel sweet beyond compare?
The tale that oped for Moses Leib
The gleaming gates of the patriarch tribe.

"My happy charge it was to bear
    His prayers before the awful throne,"
He quoth, "and so, with eager care
    Above his roof right early flown,
I hovered close to see him leave
For house of prayer that holy eve.

"He issued forth while yet the sun
    Stood high above the western rim;
I gleaned the silent prayers he spun
    As flying close I followed him.
For oft of prayers that men scarce breathe
For God the brightest crown I wreathe.

"Anon we wound our way through lanes
    Where dwell the poor, the anguished poor,
Whose broken roofs proclaim long pains,
    And wasted walls dark griefs immure:
'Dear God,' he prayed, 'Thy people bless,
Look down and heal their great distress!'

"We hear a sudden cry of dole
    From out a lowly hut arise,

So keen the sound it wrings the soul
    Of Moses Leib who stops and sighs.
Then swift he turns and enters in
To see whence comes the grievous din.

"One taper tall in the chamber's gloom
    A web of ghostly rays did weave.
'God bless,' he prayed, 'the soul for whom
    This candle burns on Atonement eve.
'Tis the widow Rachel's poor abode:
Make light, dear Lord, her bitter load!'

"Breaks on his orison again
    The helpless wail, more plaintive-loud,
A human voice, yet fraught with pain
    As for a creature dumb and cowed.
From a little cradle comes the cry,
Where left alone a babe doth lie.

"Above the crib the *tzaddik* stood
    And gazed perplexed upon the child,
Whose infant tears its rags bedewed,
    Whose wailing rose more shrill and wild.
'Sweet wight,' he sighed, 'must I essay
They bitter anguish to allay?

" 'Within the house of prayer doth weep
    Thy mother now for thee and moan.
In sooth she cradled thee to sleep
    Or e'er she left thee here alone;
For thee her tears this holy night;
For thee, her care, her sweet delight.'

"Over the crib the *tzaddik* bent,
    He lifted up the weeping child;
And straight was hushed its loud lament,
    It nestled to his heart and smiled.
He held it in a close embrace:
'God shed,' he prayed, 'on thee His grace!'

"That prayer in virtue of my art
  I did not a star exalt;
It flared aloft, a brilliant dart,
  Up to the seventh heaven's vault,
Where lo! it shines a lovely gem
In God's resplendent diadem!

"And joy was mine to see the saint
  The tiny timid mite cajole
With crooning strange and gestures quaint,
  Demeanor whimsical and droll.
How come to him this mother art,
But from the love that filled his heart?

"He rocked the bantling in his arms
  And sang to it a lullaby;
So sweet the song, all dread alarms
  From out the infant soul did fly.
For oh, what love impelled the sound!
What folds of love the babe enwound!

"And long the *tzaddik* sang and crooned
  And rocked within his arms the child,
Until the lullaby he tuned
  To peaceful sleep the babe beguiled:
He gave the infant kisses twain
And laid it in its crib again.

"Meanwhile had set the autumn sun
  And night was come upon the earth.
Kol Nidre chant, he knew, was done,
  Yet was there in his heart great mirth:
'O Lord,' he sighed, 'do Thou receive
Thy people's prayers, this sacred eve!'

"The stars they danced that hallowed night
  As to the house of prayer he ran
Where every glance with joy alight
  Beamed welcome to the holy man.

Now ends my tale, save that each prayer
I swiftly bore to heaven's stair."

Loud praise the angel choirs declare
   Who see the gates of gold swing wide,
The gates that ope on splendors where
   The blessèd patriarchs abide!
For Moses Leib hath reached his goal:
Bestead us, Lord, his stainless soul![2]

KOL NIDRE

ZEEV FALK

All the vows on our lips,
The burdens in our hearts,
The pent-up regrets
About which we brooded and spoke
Through prayers without end
On last Atonement Day
Did not change our way of life,
Did not bring deliverance
In the year that has gone.
From mountain peaks of fervor
We fell to common ways
At the close of the fast.

Will You hear our regret?
Will You open our prison,
Release us from shackles of habit?
Will You answer our prayers,
Forgive our wrongs,
Though we sin again and again?
In moments of weakness
We do not remember
Promises of Atonement Day.
Look past forgetfulness,
Take only from our hearts;
Forgive us, pardon us.

Translated by Stanley Schachter[3]

YOM KIPPUR

Israel Zangwill

I saw a people rise before the sun,
A noble people scattered through the lands,
To be a blessing to the nations, spread
Wherever mortals make their home; without
A common soil and air, 'neath alien skies,
But One in blood and thought and life and law,
And One in righteousness and love, a race
That, permeating, purified the world—
A pure fresh current in a brackish sea,
A cooling wind across the fevered sand,
A music in the wrangling marketplace;
For wheresoe'er a Jew dwelt, there dwelt truth,
And wheresoe'er a Jew was, there was light,
And wheresoe'er a Jew went, there went love.
This people saw I shake off sleep, ere flamed
The sunrise of Atonement Day, and haste,
The rich and poor alike, the old and young,
Each from his house unto the house of God,
The whole race closelier knit that day by one
Electric thought that flashed through all the world.
And there from dawn to sunset, and beyond,
They prayed, and wept, and fasted for their few
Backslidings from the perfect way; for they
Did justice and loved mercy, and with God
Walked humbly; pride and scorn they knew not; lust
Of gold or power darkened not their souls;
The faces of the poor they did not grind,
But lived as man with man; yet all the day
In self-abasement did they pray and fast.
The ancient tongue of patriarchs and seers,
A golden link that bound them to the past,
Was theirs; as woven by their saints
And rabbis into wondrous songs of praise
And sorrow; sad, remorseful strains, and sweet,

Soft, magic words of comfort. As they prayed,
They meditated on the words they spake,
And thought of those who wrote them—royal souls
In whom the love of Zion flamed; poets clad
Not in the purple, sages scorning not
The cobbler's bench; and then they mused on all
The petty yet not unheroic lives
Of those who, spite of daily scorn, in face
Of sensual baits, kept fast the marriage vows
Which they in youth had pledged their bride, the Law,
Whom they had taken to their hearths; no spirit
Austere and mystic, cold and far away,
But human-eyed, for mortal needs create,
Who linked her glory with their daily lives,
Bringing a dowry not unblent with tears—
A marriage made in heaven to hallow earth.
They thought of countless martyrs scorning life
Weighed 'gainst their creed; poor, simple workmen made
Imperial by their empery of pain;
Who clomb the throne of fire and draped themselves
In majesty of flame, and haughtily
As king for king awaited death's approach.
The inspiration of such lives as these
Was on the worshipers; the stormy passion
Of their old, rugged prophets filled their hearts
With yearning, aspiration infinite,
Submerging puny fears about themselves,
Their individual fates in either world,
In one vast consciousness of destiny.
For other faiths, like glowworms glittering,
Had come to lift the darkness; and were dark.
And other races, splendid in their might,
Had flashed upon the darkness and were gone.
But they had stood; a tower all the waves
Of all the seas confederate could not shake;
And in the tower a perpetual light
Burned, an eternal witness to the hand
That lit it. So all day they prayed and wept

And fasted. And the sun went down, and night
Came on; and twilight filled the house of God,
And the gray dusk seemed filled with floating shapes
Of prophets and of martyrs lifting hands
Of benediction. Then a mighty voice
Arose and swelled, and all the bent forms swayed,
As when a wind roars, shaking all the trees
In some dim forest, and from every throat
Went up with iteration passionate
The watchword of the host of Israel,
"The Lord our God is One! The Lord is God!
The Lord is God!" And suddenly there came
An awful silence. Then the trumpet's sound
Thrilled. . . .
And I awoke, for lo! it was a dream.[4]

YOM KIPPUR

JESSIE E. SAMPTER

With you, my people, you, my precious ones
I pleaded and I cried a night and day.
I did afflict my soul, I made confession.

I said, Lord has chosen—He will keep!
I said, the Lord created—will He blast?
Mine own, to whom the letters of the Law
Like burning angels leaped and seized upon you,
Mine own, that rose possessed with God and truth,
Mine own, that drunk with holy wine, aroused
The world from sluggishness to thought and deed,
Where are you now? Awake, and plead your cause!

We met Thee, face to face, O Lord of hosts.

As one that wandered long, through bogs and briers,
Within a mountain spring in horror sees
His haggard face, his rags and his defilement,
We saw ourselves in Thee, Thy chosen ones!

We stood before Thee, we, a driven remnant.

And for the rest, we made confession, Lord;
The rest are in the marketplace, at ease,
In schools and theaters and academies;
With skillful tricks they wipe away the mark
That Thou hast burned to mark Thy chosen sheep.

The servant of the Lord, Israel, a people!
How can a people serve without a land?
How long, O Lord, without a tongue to praise Thee?
How long can martyrs live and rear their children?
And when, O Lord, shall nations turn to Thee
If we, the nation of the Lord, are dumb?

Our children run to fashion's wares and choose
The shadow of a virtue, and are proud,
And cry: "We know the Lord. His name is Man."
And good and wise are they, in their own eyes.

But, Lord, we are not proud, we know our folly,
We have no vanity of clothes or manners,
We long are burned to plain and fearful steel,
We have the hearts that die in flame and massacre,
We have the hands that work, the coarsened hands,
We sin, we fall, but, oh, we do not scorn,
We are the remnant—we, the common remnant.

O come, my people, come and cry for life,
For wisdom and for strength to dream and do.
The Lord has spoken it: to build and do.
So day-long, O my people, I was with you,
And when the evening came I drank and ate
And turned again to God and cried to Him.

As there I lay upon my bed and sought Him,
Behold, He heard, He answered all my cries;
From depths beyond the stars, from depths within,
He spoke—from everywhere—He filled the world.

I stretched my arms—they could not reach to Him;
I stretched my throat for breath too big to pass;
I stretched my heart—I could not hold Him there.
My heart was beating loud as one who knocks.
So wide a stream of life was thundering through me,
It seemed that I must die with too much living.
His awe and wonder crushed me like a hand.

And then He said: Be still. And I was still.
He said: Be comforted. And I was comforted.
He said: Before the Law, I am. He said:
Before the mountains cried aloud in birth,
Before the seas conceived the worm of life,
Was I your refuge, I your comforter.

When histories are dim, forgotten paths,
When flesh has ceased to throb and rock to fall,
When stars are dark and planets whirl no more,
Beyond the Law am I, and I shall be
Your light, your refuge, and your comforter.

Again He said: Be still. And I was still.
For what is man, and what his histories?
Yet God has chosen one to be His lot,
And he that once seen the face of God
Cannot forget, his seed cannot forget.
Upon the mountain in the midst of peoples
His seed is sown at last—upon the rock
His wheat shall grow to feed the sons of men.

When earth in travail bled with ice and flame
And cried with seething rock and reeled in swoon,
One comforted, He covered her with leaves.
And He will cover us with leaves at last,
And He will plant us there, whence vision came,
For He will sow again our scattered seed,
And water us with knowledge and with faith,
And all the sons of men shall pasture there.

Lord, we have sinned! The Lord will comfort us.[5]

13. "The Prayer." Sculpture. By Jacques Lipchitz. 1943. Philadelphia Museum of Art. See Chapter XI.

ATONEMENT

RUTH F. BRIN

In the fall, in the fall,
When the leaves are red as blood,
When the butterflies are dust,
We repent us of our sins.
And our sins are very great,
Greater than the sins of our fathers.

We had six million brothers and sisters
Who perished in the night.
In that long and shrieking night
We had six million brothers and sisters
Who summoned no angels, witnessed no miracles,
Who suffered and died.

We reached out our hands to our brothers and sisters
But our hands were feeble and saved only a few.
We Jews lost the war.
We mourn our dead, our twice dead:
Dead once in the gas chambers,
Dead again in the dripping chambers of our hearts.

We repent the weakness of our hands,
We resolve to strengthen them.
O our brothers and our sisters,
Mourning you, we have no rest,
Mourning you, we cannot be dumb.
Mourning you, we are forced
Into the claws of politics.

And after the gas chambers
There was this small, man-made, amateur miracle:
No angels carried the children from the fiery furnace,
This stubborn sturdy wonder
Growing on a harsh, dry foreign coast,

Two million brothers and sisters
Speaking an old harsh tongue,
Living in this half-born state of Israel,
Practicing miracles, learning to cope with history.

We make ourselves responsible for history,
For our six million dead brothers and sisters
And for every living, sweating brother and sister
Anywhere on this whole unpredictable planet.

Come, let us consider and examine,
Recognize our sins and vanities,
Forgo weeping and sackcloth and ashes, for those
Are the privileges of other days,
And start anew our struggle to master history,
For the kingdom of God is to be the doing of man
And we know that after the mushroom-cloud bang
There would be no single whimper.

In the recesses of our souls
Knowing full well the vast measure of the unknown,
The treachery of the human heart, even ours,
And the finality of death,
In the fall, in the time of blood and dust,
Of penitence and remembrance,
We urgently pray for the gifts of God,
Which are courage and love,
Order in the world,
Grace in ourselves
And wisdom to worship Him.[6]

CONFESSION

SOLOMON IBN GABIROL

Shame-stricken, bending low,
My God, I come before Thee, for I know
That even as Thou on high
Exalted art in power and majesty,

So weak and frail am I,
That perfect as Thou art,
So I deficient am in every part.

Thou art all-wise, all-good, all-great, divine
Yea, Thou art God: eternity is Thine,
While I, a thing of clay,
The creature of a day,
Pass shadowlike, a breath, that comes and flees away. . . .

My God, I know my sins are numberless,
More than I can recall to memory
Or tell their tale: yet some will I confess,
Even a few, though as a drop it be
　　In all the sea.

I will declare my trespasses and sin
And peradventure silence then may fall
Upon their waves and billows' raging din,
And Thou wilt hear from heaven, when I call,
　And pardon all. . . .

My God, if mine iniquity
Too great for all endurance be,
Yet for Thy Name's sake pardon me.
For if in Thee I may not dare
To hope, who else will hear my prayer?
Therefore, although Thou slay me, yet
In Thee my faith and trust is set:
And though Thou seekest out my sin,
From Thee to Thee I fly to win
A place of refuge, and within
Thy shadow from Thy anger hide,
Until Thy wrath be turned aside.
Unto Thy mercy I will cling,
Until Thou hearken pitying:
Nor will I quit my hold of Thee
Until Thy blessing light on me.

Remember, O my God, I pray,
How Thou hast formed me out of clay,
What troubles set upon my way.
Do Thou not, then, my deeds requite
According to my sins aright,
But with Thy mercy infinite.
For well I know, through good and ill
That Thou in love has chastened still,
Afflicting me in faithfulness,
That Thou my latter end may'st bless.

Translated by Alice Lucas[7]

DAY OF ATONEMENT

GUSTAV GOTTHEIL

To Thee we give ourselves today,
Forgetful of the world outside;
We tarry in Thy house, O Lord,
From eventide to eventide.

From Thy all-searching, righteous eye
Our deepest heart can nothing hide;
It crieth up to Thee for peace
From eventide to eventide.

Who could endure, shouldst Thou, O Lord,
As we deserve, forever chide?
We therefore seek Thy pardoning grace
From eventide to eventide.

O may we lay to heart how swift
The years of life do onward glide;
So learn to live that we may see
Thy light at our life's eventide.[8]

DAY OF ATONEMENT

ABRAHAM VIEVIORKA

O God of mercy, of repentance,
Your people stands with sobs and moan,
And prays forgiveness for its sins,
And beats its breast. But I alone
My lips are shut and will not pray.
My eye is hard, as hard as stone.
Yet God, me too forgive, I am Your child,
And in my heart I also sob and moan.

Translated by Joseph Leftwich[9]

COMPASSIONATE FATHER

ALEXANDER ALAN STEINBACH

All-merciful Father, ever-living Lord,
Creator of our life and destiny,
Hearken to these supplications poured
From out my deepest spirit unto Thee.

Thou art enthroned above our mortal days,
Thou art exalted, Father, over all;
Help me, Lord, to mend my errant ways,
Accept my heart's petition when I call.

Too often I have listened to the blare
Of trumpets heralding their transient pleasures,
Too often I've been blinded by the glare
Of shining tinsel masked as lasting treasures.

Compassionate Father, upraise me when I falter,
Direct my yearning soul toward Thy shrine;
I bring my prayers like garlands to Thy altar,
My soul repines for Thee, O Lord divine.[10]

DAY OF ATONEMENT

CHARLES REZNIKOFF

The great Giver has ended His disposing;
the long day
is over and the gates are closing.
How badly all that has been read
was read by us,
how poorly all that should be said.

All wickedness shall go in smoke.
It must, it must!
The just shall see and be glad.
The sentence is sweet and sustaining;
for we, I suppose, are the just;
and we, the remaining.

If only I could write with four pens between five fingers
and with each pen a different sentence at the same time—
but the rabbis say it is a lost art, a lost art.
I well believe it. And at that of the first twenty sins that
        we confess,
five are by speech alone;
little wonder that I must ask the Lord to bless
the words of my mouth and the meditations of my heart.

Now, as from the dead, I revisit the earth and delight
in the sky, and hear again
the noise of the city and see
earth's marvelous creatures—men.
Out of nothing I became a being,
and from a being I shall be
nothing—but until then
I rejoice, a mote in Your world,
a spark in Your seeing.[11]

YOM KIPPUR

HOWARD HARRISON

Night and day, and somberly I dress
In dark attire and consciously confess
According to the printed words, for sins
Suddenly remembered, all the ins
And outs, tricks, deals, and necessary lies
Regretted now, but then quite right and wise.

The benches in the *shul* are new. So this
Is what my ticket bought last year; I miss
My easy chair, this wood is hard, and I
Have changed my mind, refuse to stand and lie
About repentance. No regrets at all.
Why chain myself to a dead branch, I fall
In estimation of my neighbors who
Would have me be a liberated Jew
Ridiculing medieval ways
Keep up with them in each swift modern craze
To dedicate our souls to modern taste
To concentrate our minds on endless waste.

"Medieval" must be too new a term
For deeper, longer, truer, something firm
Within me used the word "waste." Despite years
Assimilating lack of faith, the fears
My father felt of God, their will to know
That vanity and greed were far below
The final aim of life will help me, too,
Atone, and be a Jew, and be a Jew.[12]

14. Yom Kippur scenes. From *Juedishes Ceremoniel,* by Paul C. Kirchner, Nuremberg, 1726. See Chapter XI.

YOM KIPPUR

BEN A. SOCHACHEVSKY

Fear not!
Softly on tiptoe come.
Break not the solemn silences
In which our breath is hushed.
Hark!
Earth shudders,
Worlds tremble.
Something is born and dies,
And again is born.
Fear-stricken sounds arise,
And breaking hearts pray,
My soul weeps,
Would rise to heaven,
To the mercy seat of God.
The sun radiates burning fire.
Does she mean to show all her light to men?

Ah, this road is long,
And I am full of sins and weary,
Did I not rejoice when I heard the cry of the weak?
What shall I pray?
Can my prayer ascend if God will not hear?
I ran away from Him!
I wanted to forget even myself!
And now—
Look!
On the bowed neck of the earth
A light is burning.
The flame is red as if it had been soaked in blood.
The light beckons,

Calls me,
Clasp me to your breast!
Let me not remain alone!
I am afraid!
Hark!
Sounds of strange men approaching.
They come nearer, nearer,
From far-off ways,
From erring ways,
They seek their homes,
Seek them with bowed heads.
Do they repent?
Look!
The sun is smiling down
Through gleaming fire.
Does she mean to kiss our earth?
But why tremble these living corpses?
Are they afraid because of the presence of God?

Look!
The sun goes down, grows dark.
Shadows creep upon the earth.
They fear to show their sins in the light.
In the darkness they pray,
In hidden hollows.
Will their prayers reach up to God?

Translated by Joseph Leftwich[13]

NEILAH

FANIA KRUGER

With gaze fixed on the scarlet *bimah* table,
Symbol of Cain who killed his brother Abel,
An old man sits in *shul* imploring grace,
Wrapped in a *kittel* and a praying shawl,
Pogrom and slaughter graven on his face:
"Humble the mighty, lift up those who fall."

His words are reaching through the dusk, the dark,
Perpetual flame beside the holy ark;
He summons strength to chant the closing prayer:
"Open the gates," (he beats his breast and cries,
His pleas resounding through the shadowy air)
"Succor the starving, dry the tear-wet eyes."

And still he chants beside the *bimah* table,
Symbol of Cain who killed his brother Abel.
"Let all men come into Thy grace at last!
Dear Lord, the hour is growing late, so late!"
The *shofar*'s note proclaims the end of fast,
The opening of mercy's gate.[14]

XIV

YOM KIPPUR IN
THE SHORT STORY

THE PRAYER BOOK

MARTIN BUBER

It was the custom of the rabbi of Dynow, when he stood up to pray before the ark of the covenant on the two High Holy Days known as the Awful Days, that is, the Feast of New Year and the Day of Atonement, to open the large prayer book of Master Luria and to put it on his lectern. It lay open before him all the while he prayed, though he neither looked into it nor touched its pages, but let it lie before the ark and the eyes of the people, large and open, so that its strong unblurred black letters glared forth from its wide yellowish background while he stood over it in his sacred office like the high priest celebrating before the altar. Such was his habit and the eyes of the people saw this time after time, but no one of the *hasidim* ever dared to speak thereof. Once, however, a few took heart and asked the rabbi: "Master and teacher, if you pray from the

book of the Master Luria why do you not look into its pages and
follow the order of its prayers? But if you do not, why does it
lie open before you all the time?" And the rabbi said to them: "I
will tell you something that happened in the days of the holy
Baal Shem, blessed his memory.

"In a certain village there lived a Jewish landholder with his
wife and little son. The lord of the manor was fond of him, for
he was a quiet man, and granted him many favors. Evil days,
however, came on him. Summer after summer bad crops
followed, and want grew and swelled in his house till the gray
waves of misery dashed over his head. He had held his own
against hard work and poverty, but beggary he could not face.
He felt that his life was ebbing away, and when his heart
stopped at last it was like the dying of a pendulum swing whose
steady slowing passes unnoticed, until its final lull seems to
take one by surprise. His wife, who had passed with him
through the good and evil days of his fortune, soon followed
him. When he was buried she could no longer restrain herself;
she looked at her young son and not even then could she
smother her longing for her dead husband. So she lay down,
saying to herself all the time that she was not going to die—till
she was dead.

"Little Nahum was three years old when his parents died.
They had come from a faraway country, and no one knew their
kinsmen. So the lord of the manor took him into his house, for
the boy with his small face shimmering blossom-white out of
his golden locks found grace in his eyes. He soon came to love
more and more this delicate, dreamy child, and brought him
up as his own. And thus the boy grew in light and joy, and was
taught in all the arts and sciences. Of the faith and nation of
his parents he knew nothing. Not that his foster father kept
from him the knowledge that his father and mother had been
Jews, but when speaking of this he would always add: 'But I
have taken you and you are now my son and all that is mine
shall be yours.' This Nahum could well understand, but what
was said of his parents seemed to him to be one of those fairy
tales told by the servants, stories of wood spirits, mermaids,

and gay elfin folk. That he himself should be involved in such a story was dark and wonderful to his mind, and he felt wrapped in a strange twilight, and fear and longing arose in him, a yearning which seemed at times to bathe his soul in light dreamy waves, which was always weird and marvelous to him.

"One day he suddenly came upon a deserted room of the house where there lay a heap of things which his parents had left behind. Strange and unknown these were to him. He saw a curious loose white tunic with long black stripes; a woven kerchief of fine yet simple workmanship; a large many-branched candelabrum of faded splendor; a richly chased, crown-shaped spice box about which there still seemed to linger a faint aroma. And there was finally a large thick book bound in dark brown faded velvet with silver-trimmed edges and silver clasps. These were things which his parents could not part from even in the extreme of poverty. And little Nahum stood and looked at them, and the messengers of dusk seemed nearer than ever around him. Then he took the book shyly and carefully, and clasping it with both arms he carried it to his room. There he unfastened the clasps and opened it wide. The large black letters stared at him, strange and yet familiar, winked at him like a group of young friends, beckoned to him like a cluster of dancing play-mates, whirled around him, twined through the pages, flew up and down, swam before his eyes—and lo! the letters vanished, the book was like a dark sea, and two eyes gazed at him from its depth, tearless yet full of eternal sadness. And Nahum knew that this was the book from which his mother had prayed. From that day on he kept it hidden in the daytime but every night would take it out from its hiding place and, by the light of the lamp or, better, by the living light of the moon, he would look at the strange letters which danced before him and flowed into a sea whence the eyes of his mother gazed at him.

"And thus came the days of judgment, the days of grace, the Awful Days. From many villages Jews traveled to the city to stand before God with the clamor of the multitude, to bring Him their sins together with the sins of thousands and burn them on the fire of His mercy. Nahum was standing by the door of his house and saw numberless wagons hurry by, saw men and women in festive garments and a spirit of expectancy over all. And he thought that these were messengers to him, no longer envoys of darkness but of light now and peace of soul, and that they passed him by because he failed to hail them. And he stopped one of them and asked him: 'Where are you going, and what day is this for you?' And the man answered and said: 'We are going to the Day of Rebirth, the Day of Beginning when our deeds and their forgiveness are recorded in the Book of Heaven. And now we journey to plead to God in great multitude and to join our voices into one prayer.' The boy heard these words, but stronger than these another Word flew to him, a greater Call that came to him out of Eternity. From this hour forth the Call was always with him, roaring in the silence like a mighty storm-wind, silent amidst the noise like the winging of a silent bird. And the Call lit up the darkness which had surrounded his world for so long a time, and his fear lost itself in his longing, and his yearning was like to a young green blade in the sun. So passed by the Ten Days of Repentance, and the Day of Atonement was on hand. And the boy saw again the Jews of the villages going on the road to the city. Still and hushed they sat on their carts, and their faces were paler than before. And again Nahum asked one of them: 'Where and why are you going?' And the man said to him: 'This is the day we hoped and waited for, the Day of Atonement, when our sins melt away in the light of the Lord and He welcomes His children in the house of grace.'

"Then the boy rushed into his room and took the silver-trimmed book in his arms and ran out from the house and ran and ran till he came to the city. There he directed his steps to the house of worship which he entered. When he came in it was the hour of *Kol Nidre*, the prayer of absolution and holy freedom. And he saw the people standing in their long white shrouds, kneeling and rising before the Lord. And he heard them crying to God, crying from the depth of their hearts to the Light, crying from the hidden places of their souls to the Truth. And the spirit of God touched the boy, and he bowed and rose before Him and cried unto Him. Then he heard around him the sound of words in a foreign tongue, and he felt that he could not pray like the others. And he took his mother's book and laying it on the lectern before him he cried out: 'Lord of the Universe! I do not know what to pray, I do not know what to say. Here lies before you the whole prayer book, Lord of the Universe!' And he put his head on the open book and wept and spoke with God.

"It happened on that night that the prayers of the people fluttered on the ground like birds maimed of wing, and could not soar heavenwards. And the house was full of them, the air was close; dark and gloomy the thoughts of the Jews. And then came the Word of the boy and taking all the prayers on its pinions rose with them to the bosom of God.

"The Baal Shem saw and understood all that happened, and he prayed with great rapture. And when the Atonement Day was over he took the boy along with him and taught him the meaning of life and all open and secret wisdom."

Such was the tale the rabbi of Dynow told his pious followers. And then he added: "I too do not know what to do, and how much to do, and how to achieve the purpose of the holy men who first uttered these prayers. That is why I take the book of our blessed Master Luria and keep it open before me while I pray, that I may offer it to God with all its fervor, ecstasy, and secret meaning."

Translated by Simon Chasen[1]

THE BOY'S SONG

MEYER LEVIN

The enemy did not forswear the battle, but came out openly and spread his iron wings between the earth and heaven. The wings were as thick as a mountain is high, and all through they were made of heavy iron. He wrapped his wings around the earth as he would enclose it within the two cups of his hand.

On earth, all was darkness. The wings of the enemy pressed forever closer to the earth, and crushed the spirits of men.

When Rabbi Israel was about to enter into a synagogue, he stopped outside the door and said, "I cannot go in there. There is no room for me to enter."

But the *hasidim* said, "There are not many people in the synagogue."

"The house is filled from the ground to the roof with prayers!" said the master.

But as he saw the *hasidim* taking pride because of his words, he said, "Those prayers are all dead prayers. They have no strength to fly to heaven. They are crushed, they lie on top of the other, the house is filled with them."

And he returned to Medziboz.

He felt the weight of the wings of the enemy pressing ever closer upon him. He sought for a way to pierce that iron cloud, and make a path to heaven.

Not far from Medziboz there lived a Jewish herdsman. This man had an only son, the boy was twelve years old but so slow-witted that he could not remember the alphabet. For several years the Jew had sent his son to the *heder*, but as the boy could not remember anything, the father ceased to send him to the school, and instead sent him into the fields to mind the cows.

The boy took a reed and made himself a flute, and sat all day long in the grass, playing upon his flute.

But when the boy reached his thirteenth birthday, his father said, "After all, he must be taught some shred of Jewishness." So he said to the lad, "Come, we will go to the synagogue for the holidays."

He got in his wagon, and drove his son to Medziboz, and bought him a cap and new shoes. And all that time, David carried his flute in his pocket.

His father took him to the synagogue of Rabbi Israel.

They sat together among the other men. The boy was very still.

Then the moment came for the prayer of *Musaf* to be said. David saw the men all about him raise their little books, and read out of them in praying, singing voices. He saw his father do as the other men did. Then David pulled at his father's arm.

"Father," he said, "I too want to sing. I have my flute in my pocket. I'll take it out, and sing."

But his father caught his hand. "Be still!" he whispered. "Do you want to make the rabbi angry? Be still!"

David sat quietly on the bench.

Until the prayer of *Minhah*, he did not move. But when the men arose to repeat the *Minhah* prayer, the boy also arose. "Father," he said, "I too want to sing!"

His father whispered quickly, "Where have you got your fife?"

"Here in my pocket."

"Let me see it."

David drew out his fife, and showed it to his father. His father seized it out of his hand. "Let me hold it for you," he said.

David wanted to cry, but was afraid, and remained still.

At last came the prayer of *Neilah*. The candles burned trembling in the evening wind, and the hearts of the worshipers trembled as the flames of the candles. All through the house was the warmth of holiness, and the stillness as before the Presence.

The boy could hold back his desire no longer. He seized the flute from his father's hand, set it to his mouth, and began to play his music.

A silence of terror fell upon the congregation. Aghast, they looked upon the boy; their backs cringed, as if they waited instantly for the walls to fall upon them.

But a flood of joy came over the countenance of Rabbi Israel. He raised his spread palms over the boy David.

"The cloud is pierced and broken!" cried the master of the Name, "and evil is scattered from over the face of the earth!"[2]

OUT OF THE DEPTHS

Shmuel Yosef Agnon

Asonovki is a large village in the district of Podolia. It used to be a place where the Gentiles grew wheat and tended flocks and the Jews lived peacefully by their side. The sons of Jacob did not covet the worldly goods of the sons of Esau, and the sons of Esau, busy since time immemorial with working their fields, let the sons of Jacob go their way unharmed.

The village belonged to the fief of the baron of Buczatz, and all the Jews in it belonged to the congregation of Buczatz, from whence they received not only the exact dates on which the feasts fell each year, but also the palm branches, the citrus fruit and the myrtle for the Feast of Tabernacles, and all the various things a Jewish soul needs to keep up his Jewishness.

And yet when the *Yamim Noraim*, the Solemn Days, came round, they all went into town to pray. For it was the law of Israel and ancient custom that on New Year's Day and on the Day of Atonement people from the villages came to pray in the house of the Lord for three whole days. As this was before the time of the *hasidim*, before there were any divisions in the Jewish camp, the villagers looked up to the heads of the congregation, whose word was law unto them.

And so, each year, on the eve of the New Year, the Jews of Asonovki got up before dawn, saddled the horses, loaded their carts, and, having said their penitential prayers, set out to converse in God's mystery in the town of Buczatz. So they traveled, leaving their homes and worldly goods at the mercy of the Gentiles, but the Lord kept watch over their belongings, as He had done in the land of Israel, when the people made their pilgrimage to Jerusalem three times a year.

When the villagers arrived in the town for the holy feasts, they made their way to the houses of their relatives bearing presents, the best fruit, butter and cheese, healthy fowl, as heavy as fattened calves, to be eaten as a *kapparah*, an atonement for sins. They brought sweet-smelling honey, in which the piece of bread eaten after the blessing over the bread was dipped. Indeed, they brought enough honey for all bread to be smeared with it from that day until the Feast of Lights in winter, when the fat of slaughtered geese was melted down.

As they emptied their sacks, out rolled some of the wonders of the earth—roots and herbs and tree barks used in cures, and sweet-smelling beeswax to make candles with, candles for the house of the Lord and candles in remembrance of the dead. All these gifts were safely packed away in the hay which filled the carts; this hay was afterwards spread on the floor of the house of prayer. Such was the offering of the villager when he came to town, there, in the midst of his brethren, to glory in the nearness of the Lord.

And the synagogue was crowded with worshipers on feast days. There was hardly room for all the townspeople, and so all the villagers had to pray in the anteroom; they sat when others sat, and when all the others got to their feet to say Amen, so did they, although they could barely hear the blessings and the prayers.

But after the morning prayer, when the Torah was read, it was customary to read slowly and in a loud and clear voice. Books were heaped in front of them, so that they, too, should follow the readings and be uplifted to the light of the holy books, instead of wasting away their lives in the darkness of the villages.

Such was the custom of these simple people for many years; each year they came into Buczatz meeting people from other surrounding villages, because on these days they all came into town to pray.

Such, then, had been the custom of the people of Asonovki. So, one day, on the eve of the New Year, as they set out for Buczatz as usual, the baron was leaning over the parapet, and, seeing the travelers, he said to his servants: "People are coming down the mountain." And his servants answered: "They are Jews, coming to pray before their God."

Then the baron said to his servants: "I tremble with sudden fear for these poor people, for if the bridge collapses under their weight they must surely fall into the deep river and drown." And as he talked, he smiled.

And his servants understood.

"Yes," they said, "the bridge will certainly give way under their weight and they will all be drowned in the raging currents. Indeed, they are not thin and light-boned like the Jews of the town, they are heavy with fat and bursting with health."

And the baron said: "Why do you stand around doing nothing;

why don't you go forth and attack the Jews as they arrive at the crossing, and by shoving their carts into the water save the bridge from destruction."

And his servants said to him: "We are your obedient servants, your honor, and we shall do as you wish." And they left the baron to prepare an ambush for the people of God.

The bridge over the gorge was made of strong and heavy iron, because the currents of the river flowing underneath were swift and terribly dangerous. And there were two tollhouses at the foot of the bridge, because everyone passing over the bridge either in a cart or riding a horse had to pay a toll. That was where the baron's servants lay in wait for the people of God.

As the crowded carts approached the river the baron's servants left their hiding places and surrounded them. When the Jews of Asonovki saw that the Gentiles were intent on taking their lives a great fear seized them. Quickly they unwrapped their prayer shawls and put them on, saying: "We shall not meet our Maker in everyday clothes." And so they made themselves ready to die.

And the Gentiles heaved the carts and their occupants into the deep river. Those that stayed in the carts were buried under them, and those who tried to jump out were crushed beneath the wheels. And the horses, blind with rage flaring up in their blood, lashed out with their hooves, lacerating in their crazed fury the breasts of their erstwhile masters, whose lifeblood poured away into the river. And the people of God drowned in the dark waters.

This happened at a spot where they used to say: "Let us pause here and say the *tashlikh* prayer in honor of our merciful God." The waters parted to receive their bodies and closed over them, leaving no trace of a hint that the serene flow of the river had ever been disturbed.

It happened shortly after this that the commander of Demisov decided to give a big banquet, and to entertain his guests with the best fare in the land. So he commanded his servants to go to the river and bring him the best of the huge fat fish to be found there. And he sent fishermen to fish in the bays and inlets of the neighboring rivers, as the fish in one river tasted different from the fish in another. And many fishermen went out to fish, each with his own net, and they stood fishing on the banks of the river in the middle of the night.

The sharp wind which blew during the month of Tishri ruffled the river, and the fish trembled in the water, and the moon had not yet arisen, and darkness clung to the reeds and the rushes. The fishermen cast their nets on the water and hauled them in empty, without a single fish. So they lowered the nets again, and this time brought to the surface the carcasses of a few dead chickens, the skull of a horse, and a cartwheel.

Suddenly an apprentice boy said to his masters: "It seems God has sent us a very big fish today because the net in my hand feels most heavy." And indeed the net was so heavy that, try as he might, he could not draw it out of the water by himself. So his masters ran to help him. And they drew up the net, and there was a dead body in it. They saw the dead body and were afraid and crossed themselves. Then they brought it to the village to give it a decent burial.

But when they came to the priest, he said to them: "Don't make such haste to bury the dead. Can you not see that this is the body of a Christian boy who was slaughtered by the Jews, so that they could mix his blood in their Passover bread?"

When they heard these words the villagers trembled with rage and wanted to go out and avenge the gruesome crime there and then. But the priest quieted them down and said: "Have no fear, brothers, this deed shall be fittingly punished, as there is justice in the land. Be patient until the Day of Atonement arrives, when the watchman of the synagogue, who is one of us, shall hide the body there and the judges shall see for themselves the proof of the crime of which we accuse the Jews."

And they said to him: "That is the right thing to do, Father." And so saying they went back to their homes and to their work. And the priest started a rumor all over the countryside that the son of a Christian was missing from his home, that they had searched for him in all the villages, and that he could not be found. And to the people the priest said: "Do not lift up your hand in anger until I give you the sign."

And when the Jews heard what was happening and of what they were falsely accused, they trembled with fear. And they said: "The Day of Atonement is near, let us take courage. Perhaps the Lord will help."

Many simple folk living in those parts, on hearing the rumors that were put about, armed themselves with hatchets and sticks and set forth to attack the Jews that night. And the people of Israel were filled with fear, and they all put on their festive garments and their prayer shawls and went to God's house, there to wait for His will to be done. And their brothers living in the surrounding villages came, too, as they had done in the past, saying: "If God has cast us off and delivered His people to the slaughter, then let us die near Him, in saintly company."

And the synagogue was filled to overflowing. And although the air was festive, hearts were sick. They opened the ark and brought out the scrolls of the Torah, and each and everyone in the congregation kissed them and they all wept bitterly. And the cantor intoned: "Light is sown for the righteous, and gladness for the upright in heart."

And two old men from among the elders of the congregation stood by his side, one to the left of him and one to the right of him, and the cantor chanted the *Kol Nidre* first softly, then somewhat louder and the third time loud and clear, followed by the blessing *Sheheheyanu vekyemanu*, Blessed be the One who has preserved our lives.

And there was a great crowd of people in the synagogue, greater than any that had been seen there since the day the house was built. The air in the hall was heavy and hot, and the people became weary of their prayer shawls and removed them from their heads. And when they had done so they noticed that there were strangers among them who looked like villagers. And the strangers stood in their midst, silent and still, covering their features with their prayer shawls.

Suddenly the strangers turned toward the door, got up from

their places and walked, one behind the other, into the *genizah*, the store chamber for disused books, and brought out of there the dead body of a child. They carried him in front of the ark, swung him around like a sacrificial offering, and then walked silently out of the building carrying the body with them. And the people in the synagogue glanced at them and saw them descending the slope toward the river bed, and their hearts grew faint at the sight.

While they were wondering what to do, a huge crowd surrounded the synagogue, and called out: "Bring forth the child that you have slaughtered." And so saying they rushed in and opened the ark and all other places where a body could have been hidden, but search as they would they could find no dead body. And the priest went up to the memorial stones and monuments in the courtyard, saying: "I tell you that this is surely the place these God-cursed people have buried the slaughtered child." And they searched the memorials and found nothing, and the people who had come with the priest were filled with amazement. Thus they only devastated the house of prayer, without harming anybody who was in it.

While the fishermen were fishing at the command of their lord and master, he himself, accompanied by his followers, was hunting in the forest, bringing terror to the birds and animals within his reach. Finally, sated with hunting, the company returned home by a route passing the river; there the fishermen were standing along both banks, casting their nets. And as they made ready to draw them forth again, the net became taut until they were ready to burst with the weight of the catch.

Laughing gleefully, the fishermen drew in their nets with all their might; and the first net that was drawn ashore had a dead man caught in it who was shielding the small boy he had in his arms with his prayer shawl.

And the fisherman screamed, and the nobleman and his retinue shouted to each other that there was not a single net that did not have its dead. And they were filled with horror and amazement at having caught nothing but dead bodies in their nets, and they knew that these were the remains of the Jews whom the baron of Buczatz had drowned in the waters of the Strifa.

And the thing became known in Demisov; and the gladness the Jews felt at their own salvation was turned to mourning. And next day they all set out to ransom the bodies from the hands of the fishermen. And they paid the ransom money in full and brought the dead back with them and gave them a burial in hallowed ground. And they buried them not in shrouds but wearing their clothes and their shoes, so as not to provoke God's anger and vengeance.

Ever since that day the Jews of Demisov have come to pray on the Day of Atonement without covering themselves with their prayers shawls, in memory of the slaughtered who came to pray in the house of the Lord that night.

Translated by Yoram Matmor[3]

THREE WHO ATE

DAVID FRISHMAN

This is a story of three who ate. Not on an ordinary day did these three eat, but on the Day of Atonement; not hidden where no one could see them, but openly, in the great synagogue before the entire congregation, did they eat. Nor were they strangers whom no one knew and nobody cared about, but the most honored citizens of the community: the *rav* and his two *dayyanim*. And yet they remained, even after having eaten in public on the Day of Atonement, the most honored citizens of the community. That Day of Atonement I shall never forget!

I was but a child then, understanding little of the significance of the thing they did, yet I vaguely realized that a stirring event had taken place in those bitter days.

Yes, those were bitter days! A great calamity had befallen us from heaven—cholera! From far away, from the depths of Asia, it had come to our little town. It spread pestilence in the streets; and in the houses it heaped up horror a hundredfold. Silent

15. "*Kol Nidre* Eve." Painting. By Moritz Oppenheim (1800–1882).
From *The Jewish Year . . . Paintings by Professor Moritz Oppen-heim*, Philadelphia, 1895. See Chapter XI.

through the nights and invisible through the days it reaped its harvest. Who could enumerate the names of all who died during those days? Who could count the fresh mounds of earth of the graves?

And the worst of its grim work the plague did in the Jewish ghetto. Like flies people fell, young and old. There was no house but had its dead.

Above us, on the second floor, nine had died in one day; below us, in the cellar, a mother and her four children. In the house opposite we heard, one night, the loud lamentations of the sick, but in the morning there was not a sound.

They who buried the dead grew weary. The corpses lay upon the ground, body against body, yet people no longer cared.

Thus the summer passed. And there came the Holy Days. And the holiest of all—the Day of Atonement. That day I shall not forget!

Evening in the synagogue. Before the ark stood, not the cantor and two honored citizens, as is the custom, but the *rav* and his two *dayyanim*. Around and around immense wax candles burned. The worshipers stood facing the east wall, wrapped in their white prayer shawls, swaying to and fro in silence. And the shadows on the walls swayed with them. Were they really shadows? Or were they the shadows of the dead swaying to and fro upon the walls? Shadows of the dead who, finding no peace in their graves, had come to hear *Kol Nidre*?

Silence! The *rav*'s voice rose suddenly, accompanied by his two *dayyanim*, with a great sigh that penetrated the congregation. And then the words were heard:

"With the grace of God and the forbearance of the assembled, we permit you to pray together with the transgressors."

I listened. . . . What did the *rav* mean? Who were now the sinners? And did he not fear that Satan might overhear him now, in such a time, such a bitter time?

A looming dark fear swooped down upon me, and it seemed to me that the same fear fell upon the entire congregation, young and old.

Then I saw the *rav* mounting the almemar. Did he mean to deliver a sermon to console the mourners and strengthen their faith?

But the *rav* did not begin a sermon. Despite custom and ritual, he intoned a prayer for the recent dead. How long the list of names! The minutes passed one after another, and there seemed to be no end to his enumeration of the victims of the plague.

Those prayers will ever be vivid in my memory. They were not prayers but a painful moan—a long moan that rose from the hearts of the congregation to pierce the heavy skies. And when the prayers were over no one left the synagogue.

I stood there through the night and felt as if a fog rested on my eyes. I heard the men chanting: "And the angels flutter through the air, and fear and trembling embraces all." Fear and trembling! It seemed to me I could see the clouds through the fog, and the angels fluttering up and down, up and down. And among them I discerned in the darkness the Black Angel with his multitudinous eyes—from head to foot eyes—everywhere eyes—and what eyes!

No one left the synagogue that night, yet in the morning two were gone. Two who died in their prayer shawls—ready to be taken from the house of prayer to the house of the dead. From the streets reports filtered in. But no one spoke of them or asked questions, so afraid were they to know what might be in their homes. That Yom Kippur eve I shall not forget.

And yet even more frightful was the day that followed. Even now, if I close my eyes for a second, I can see the scene!

Noon of the Day of Atonement. On the almemar stood the *rav* with his head high and proud. The *rav* was old, eighty or more years old, his beard was white with a silver whiteness, and the hair on his head was as newly fallen snow. His face, too, was white; but his eyes, unlike the eyes of old men, were black and glowing. I had known the *rav* from my earliest childhood. I knew him as a holy man whose wisdom was respected afar, and whose word and judgment were as the word of Moses.

I stood in my corner looking at him, at the glowing black eyes that shone from his white face with its white hair. The congregation was silent, waiting for their leader to speak.

At first his voice was low and weak, but it gradually gained in strength and volume. He spoke of the holiness of *yom tov*, and what the Giver of the Torah had meant to convey thereby; he spoke of living and dying, of the living and the dead. He spoke then of the dreadful plague, of the horror of its pains and of the trail of woe it left behind it. And worst of all—he said—no end to its devastations seemed in sight. His voice rose. The pale cheeks flushed, and the blue lips turned red. Then I heard him say: "And when a man sees that great sorrows have befallen him, then it is that he should search his deeds in his relation to his God, but also in his relation to himself, his own body, his very flesh, his daily needs."

I was but a child then, but I remember that I suddenly turned cold.

And then the *rav* spoke of the cleanliness that kept us alive, and the uncleanliness that bereaves us of life; of thirst and of hunger; branding thirst and hunger as evil powers that come, in time of a plague, to kill and destroy mercilessly. Then I heard him say: "In the holy *Gemara* it is said: 'And he shall live by his virtues and not die through them.' And again the wise men said: 'There comes a time when it is considered a virtue to trespass a law of the Torah. There is even a time when it is better that a man destroy all of the Torah if thereby he saves a life for the world!' "

What did the *rav* mean? At what did his words aim? Of what did he want to persuade his congregation on that day of days?

Then I saw that the *rav* was weeping. And, as I stood there in my corner, I too began to cry, the tears running to the corners of my mouth.

Even now, as I close my eyes, I can see the *rav* stretch out his hand and beckon to his *dayyanim*. They approach and rise on the almemar. Now the three are standing there, the *rav*, the tallest of them, in the center, with one *dayyan* to the right of him and one *dayyan* to the left of him. What does he whisper in their ears that they suddenly turn pale? Why do they lower their heads? A sigh passes through the congregation and is hushed by the voices of the three on the almemar chanting in unison:

"With the grace of God and the forbearance of the assembled, that you may not grow faint in this time of plague—we permit —you—to eat—and to drink—today!"

A deadly silence settled on the synagogue. No one stirred. I remained in my corner and heard my heart beating: one; one-two, one . . . And an inexplicable dark fear seized me. Shadows swam about the walls and among them I seemed to recognize the recent dead—passing in endless procession. Like a rushing tide the realization of what the *rav* asked of us swept over me. He wanted us to eat! He wanted Jews to eat on the Day of Atonement! Because of the plague! The plague!

I began to cry loudly, but I was not heard. For I was not alone. Many wept. And the three on the almemar wept, too. And the tallest of the three wept like a child. And like a small child he pleaded: "Eat! Go and eat! The time is such! There comes a time when it is a virtue to trespass a law of the Torah! We must live by them, our virtues, and not die on account of them! Go! Go and eat!" . . .

But no one in the synagogue stirred. He stood there pleading, assuring them that he would take upon himself their sin of eating and drinking on this fearful day; that they would appear innocent before God.

No one stirred.

Suddenly the *rav*'s voice changed. He no longer pleaded, but commanded: "I order you to eat! I! I! I!" His words darted forth like arrows.

The congregation listened with bent heads.

Again the *rav* pleads tearfully: "Why have you all united against me? Must you drive me to the last extremity? Have I not suffered enough this day of days?"

And the *dayyanim* plead along with him. But no one moves. The *rav* pauses. His face turns ash white, his head sinks upon his breast, and a heartrending sigh escapes his throat. "It is the will of God!" he murmurs. And with a dry, submissive voice he adds: "Eighty-two years have I lived and not been brought to such a trial. It seems God's will that I should not die before I have fulfilled this too!"

The silence of a graveyard!

And the *rav* calls: "*Shammash!*"

The beadle approaches. The *rav* whispers in his ear, and the beadle leaves the synagogue. Then the *rav* turns to his *dayyanim*, whispers to them, and they nod their heads in assent. In a little while the beadle returns from the *rav*'s home with wine and cake.

That scene will remain with me to my dying day! The scene of the three who ate, of the three heroic holy men who ate in the synagogue on the Day of Atonement before the entire congregation.

For heroes they were. Who can measure the struggle that must have torn their hearts? Who can weigh their pain and suffering?

"You wanted me to do it—and I did it!" The *rav* now spoke with a firm clear voice, then added: "Blessed be the Name of the Lord!"

And the congregation ate—ate and wept. . . .[4]

THE MIRACLE ON THE SEA

Isaac Loeb Peretz

In a little cottage, half sunk in the mud of a little fishing village on the coast of Holland, there lived a dumb soul, a Jewish fisherman named Satya. He may have been named after some ancestor of his who had been named Sadyah. But of this he knew nothing; he knew little of anything Jewish.

As far back as was known, from father to son, his family had been fishermen, had spent their days and nights upon the sea, and had lived, one isolated Jewish family, among non-Jews. What could he have known of Jewishness?

Satya caught fish; his wife repaired his nets and looked after the house; the children played in the sand, and searched for shells. And when Satya went fishing, and a storm arose, and the lives of those that were on the seas were in peril, neither Satya in his boat, nor his wife and children at home, could say even *"Shema Yisrael!"* Satya gazed silently up to heaven, his wife tore her hair and looked angrily at the black skies, and the children threw themselves upon the sand, and like all the other children, they cried aloud: "Sancta Maria! Sancta Maria!"

And how should they have known better? The nearest Jewish community was far away, in the town; it was impossible to go there often on foot, and the poverty-stricken family, who had hardly enough to eat, could not afford to spend money in traveling. Besides, the sea would not let them go.

Satya's father, Satya's grandfather, and Satya's great-grand-father had all died at sea; but the sea has a wonderful power of attraction. It is man's greatest enemy, very often a false enemy, and yet men love the sea, they are drawn to it as by magic. It is impossible to tear ourselves away from the sea; it fascinates us, and we are content to live upon it, we are content to die in it.

One Jewish observance this fisher family retained—Yom Kippur. On the day before, they all rose very early, and taking with them the largest fish of the previous day's catch, the whole family walked to the town. There the fish was handed to the *shohet,* in whose house they stayed over the fast. All day they sat in the synagogue, listening to the singing of the choir, to the rumbling of the organ, and to the cantor's recital of the Hebrew prayers. They did not understand one word of it all; they just looked at the ark of the Law, and they watched the rabbi in his gold embroidered cap. When the gold embroidered cap stood up they also stood up, and when the gold embroidered cap sat down, they also sat down. Sometimes Satya fell asleep, and then someone sitting near him nudged him till he awoke.

And this was the whole of Satya's Yom Kippur. That it was the Great Judgment Day, the Great Day of Atonement, that even the fishes trembled in the waters, of all that took place in heaven on this dread day, Satya knew nothing. He knew that it was a custom to go to synagogue on Yom Kippur, to listen to the choir and to the organ, without tasting food all day; and after *Neilah* (he did not even know that it was called *Neilah*), he knew that he had to go to the *shohet*'s house for supper.

Probably the *shohet* himself knew little more. Holland! . . . Immediately after supper Satya and his wife and the children got up, and they said good-bye to the *shohet* and his wife, and they walked all through the night, back to the sea.

Not "home"; back to the sea! They consistently refused to stay overnight. "Think," argued the *shohet* and his wife, "you have not even seen the town." Satya's face clouded. He spoke little; the sea had taught him silence. He hated the town, it was crowded; there was no air in it and no heaven, except a little strip of it that showed between the houses. And he was accustomed to the free life of the sea, where there is a vast expanse of sky, and where it is possible for a man to breathe. "But," people argued with him, "the sea is your enemy, it is your death." "A kindly death," he replied. Satya wanted to die as his father and his grandfather had died, in full health, upon the sea; he did not want to lie on a bed and suffer God knows how long, and then be buried in the hard earth—ugh! He felt cold all over, when he thought of such a burial.

So they walked all through the night, back to the sea.

And when the dawn broke, and they saw the golden shimmer of the sandheaps, and the reflection of the rising sun in the waters of the sea, they were overwhelmed with joy, and they clapped their hands. A bridegroom could not greet his bride more joyfully.

And so it went on from year to year . . . custom remained custom. And the custom is a mix-up of a fast, a choir, and an organ, together with a huge fish, and a supper after *Neilah* in the *shohet*'s house, the parting and the good wishes, all rolled into one. And this mix-up, all of it together, is the single thread which binds Satya to all Israel.

And it came to pass about dawn, when the east was beginning to redden, that the sea awoke silently, breathing softly, so that one could scarcely hear its murmuring, and it stretched itself lazily, half dreamily, and then drew back. . . . Somewhere, white wings flapped in the air, a bird cried out, and again it was still. Silent shapes flew across the sea, golden shadows glided over the yellow sands. The fishermen's huts on the shore are shut. One door opens, and Satya comes out.

It is the day before Yom Kippur. Satya's face is earnest and composed, and his eyes are gleaming. He is going to perform a holy duty, he is going out to find a fish for Yom Kippur. He takes hold of the chain, by which his boat is fastened to the shore, and the chain falls and clangs. The fishermen thrust their heads through the little windows of their homes, and they warn Satya not to go. Don't! . . .

Quietly, calmly, the sea spreads far and wide and is lost in the fresh, laughing morning skies. There is scarce a breath of air, there is not a ripple upon the surface, save near the shore; and there, even in the face of a good, kindhearted mother, silvery dimpled smiles are dancing among the ripples. And the sea murmurs softly, and it tells a wonderful story to the scattered rocks, all overgrown with great weeds and water plants, that look like hair growing upon their heads. And the sea strokes their hair, smilingly, playfully. . . . But the fishermen know the sea well, and they will not trust it. And they warn Satya not to venture out upon it. Don't. . . . The sea rocks gently, and so it will continue to rock, faster and faster, and then its playfulness will fall away, and it will change to earnest, and the soft murmuring will grow into clamorings and thunder, and the ripples will rise up as waves, and will swallow boats and ships, even as the Leviathan swallows little fishes.

Don't! . . .

A barefooted old fisherman, with a head of uncovered, shaggy gray hair, with a face wrinkled like the sea but without its false sweet smile, approaches Satya, and taking him by the arm, he points up at the sky: "Look!" And upon the edge of the horizon, he shows him a tiny speck which only a fisherman's eye can discern. "That grows into a cloud," he remarks quietly. "I shall be back long before then," answers Satya, "I am going to catch

only one fish." The old man's face grows hard and grave. "You
have a wife and children, Satya." "And a God in heaven," Satya
answers, pushing off his boat and jumping into it. Lightly as a
feather Satya's boat travels across the sea, and the ripples rock
it murmuring softly, lovingly, and enfold it with their most
beautiful froth pearls. And the old fisherman stands on the
shore, and mutters: "Sancta Maria! Sancta Maria!"

The boat glides easily across the sea. Satya throws his net
skillfully, and at once it grows heavy. Exerting all his strength,
Satya slowly raises the net, and it is full of weeds and star-
fish . . . there is not even a single small fish entangled in the
meshes. The old fisherman upon the shore has lost sight of the
boat. And Satya pulls up his net for the third and the fourth
time; it is not easy to pull the net up, for it is heavy, and it is
filled with seaweed, and with all manner of water plants; but
there is not a single fish among it all. The sea is now rocking
more violently. The sun is high in the heavens, but it is pale,
moist and weeping. And the black speck upon the edge of the
horizon spreads out like a long snake, and it grows darker and
darker, and it moves rapidly toward the sun.
    It is noon, and Satya is still on the sea, searching for his fish.
    "God does not wish me to observe the custom this year," he
mutters sadly, and his heart grows heavy. "I must have sinned
against Him, and He will not accept my offering." He grips his
oars and turns the boat toward home; but immediately the
spray dashes into his face, and looking round, he sees a huge,
marvelous golden fish, sporting quite close to him, playfully
throwing the water up with its tail. "There!" shouts Satya ex-
citedly, "there is my fish!" Surely God had answered him out of
his anguish of heart, out of his longing, that he might fulfill his
holy duty. And he is off after that fish! The sea grows agitated
and enraged; the waves rise higher and higher. The sun is now
almost hidden by clouds, but its rays force themselves through
and beat down upon Satya. The fish is breasting the waves, and
Satya's boat flies after it, quickly. Suddenly the fish is lost to
sight; a wave has rolled up between them, and the boat is being

tossed high upon the crest of a huge wave, whipped up and swollen by the storm: "I am befooled; my eyes are deceiving me," Satya mutters to himself; and he is about to turn the boat toward home, when suddenly the wave subsides as if it had been sucked into the sea, the fish comes up, and looks at him imploringly with its great eyes, as if appealing to be taken . . . so that Satya might fulfill in him his holy duty. Satya turns, and immediately the fish has vanished; a huge wave rolls once more between them, and the sea begins its song again. It is no soft, pleasing melody the sea is singing; it is an angry outburst against the rash human who has dared it in its wrath. As if afraid of its anger, the sun hides behind a mass of cloud, and the wind breaks loose with a savage roar. It rages wildly, and it swirls and beats upon the sea, but the sea becomes more angry, and it shouts and thunders as if a thousand drums were being beaten within its bosom.

Satya determines to return, and he gathers his nets into the boat. He grips his oars, and he rows back with all his strength. The veins swell and stand out upon his hands, as if about to burst. Huge waves, high as mountains, toss his boat, up and down like an empty nutshell; the heavens are black, the sea rages tempestuously, and Satya rows back toward his home, his heart beating like the wild flood about him. Suddenly there is something drifting alongside his boat; it is a human form—the body of a woman, drowned or drowning. Her black raven hair is spread out like a net before her. His wife's hair is black like that. And her hands are white, just like the hands of his wife! And a voice calls "Help!" It is she, the mother of his children. She must have followed him, and she is drowning, she is calling for help! Satya turns his boat toward her, but the sea thrusts him back, huge waves roll over her, and the storm shouts and shrieks. And above it all he hears her voice, "Help, Satya! Help!" Satya exerts all his strength in one mighty effort. He is near her, her hair has already gone under, and her form is sinking; with his oars he pulls her toward him, and he is reaching over to pull her into the boat when suddenly a huge wave pushes him away, and the form has disappeared.

"An illusion!" he mutters, remembering his experience with
the marvelous golden fish. He looks toward the shore, and he
sees the lights gleaming through the windows of the little
fisher huts.

"Yom Kippur!" he cries, and drops his oars.

"Do with me what You will!" he calls up to heaven. "I will
not row on Yom Kippur!" The wind rages madly, the waves toss
his boat up and down, and Satya is sitting quietly, his hands
resting on his knees; his eyes are wide open, and he looks calmly
up to the frowning heavens, then down to the boiling, seething
seas. "Do with me what You will!" he repeats aloud. "Your will
be done, O God!" He seems to hear the choir, accompanied by
the organ, singing in the synagogue, and he joins in—this dumb,
silent soul, who has only this solemn melody with which to
communicate with his God! And as he sings, the heavens grow
blacker and blacker, the waves rise higher and higher, the storm
rages more fiercely, and his boat is tossed from one mountain
wave to another. One wave carries away his oars, another comes
up from behind, and follows him with mouth gaping, ready to
swallow him. The wind shrieks like a thousand wolves, and
amid all this clamor, Satya calmly sings *"Mi Yenuah, u-Mi
Yenua,"* and the choir of the synagogue, accompanied by the
organ, is singing with him. The waves break against his boat,
and Satya determines that he will die like this, singing.

Suddenly his boat is overturned; but Satya is not yet destined
to die. Two forms, nebulous as if woven out of the mist, are
walking barefoot on the sea, their hair streams behind them,
and their eyes gleam like fire. And as Satya's boat is overturned,
they hold him up, between them, and they walk with him across
the waves, as over mountains, through storm and tumult.
Satya tries to speak to them, but they stop him, saying: "Sing,
Satya! Sing! Your song will calm the fury of the seas!"

And turning round, Satya sees his boat following them, and
the golden fish is in the meshes of the net. They left him on the
shore, and when he came home, he found the *shohet* and his
wife in his hut. There had been a fire in the town, so they had

come to spend Yom Kippur with him, to be his guests over the fast.

And the golden fish was killed, and custom remained custom.

Translated by Joseph Leftwich[5]

NEILAH IN GEHENNA

ISAAC LOEB PERETZ

The town square . . . an ordinary day, neither a market day nor a day of the fair, a day of drowsy small activity. . . . Suddenly there is heard, coming from just outside the town, approaching nearer and nearer, a wild impetuous clatter, a splutter and splashing of mud, a racket of furious wheels! In-ter-est-ing, think the merchants, wonder who it is? At their booths, at their storefronts, they peer out, curious.

As the galloping horse, the thundering wagon, turn into and career through the square, they are recognized! The townsfolk recoil, revulsion and fear and anger upon their faces. The informer of the neighboring town is at it again! Posthaste to the capital! God alone knows on whom he is going to do a job now.

Suddenly a stillness falls upon the marketplace. Reluctantly, with loathing, the townsfolk look around. The wagon has come to a halt. The horse is lazily nuzzling in the mire of the wheel ruts. And the informer, fallen from his seat, lies stretched out on the ground!

Well, even an informer has a soul; they can't just let him lie there, so the townsfolk rush forward to the body, motionless in the mud. Dead—like every other corpse! Finished! The members of the Burial Society make ready to do the last rites for the deceased.

Horse and wagon are sold to pay for the funeral expenses; the informer is duly interred: and those little imps of dispatch, who crop up just there where you won't see them, snatch up his soul and bear it off to the watchers of the gates of Gehenna.

There, at the gates, the informer is detained while the fiend of reception, he who keeps hell's register of admission and discharge, wearily puts the questionnaire to him and as wearily, with his leaking pen, enters the answers: Who, When, How.

The informer—in hell he feels cut down to size—respectfully answers: Born in such and such a place; became a son-in-law in such and such a place; was supported by father-in-law for such and such a number of years; abandoned wife and children; pursued, in such and such places, his chosen profession, until, his time having come, as he was passing with horse and wagon through the marketplace of Ladam—

At the mention of this name the fiend of reception, in the middle of a yawn, pricks up his ears. "How do you say it? La-ha—"

"Ladam!"*

The fiend goes red in the face, little lights of puzzlement twinkle in his eyes, and he turns to his assistants. "Ever hear of such a town?"

The assistant imps shrug their shoulders. Their tongues stuck between their teeth, they shake their heads. "Never heard of it!"

"*Is* there such a town?"

Now in the records of Gehenna every community has its own file, and these files are all alphabetically arranged, and every letter has its own filing cabinet. So a careful search is made through L—Lublin, Lemberg, Leipzig, they're all there—but no Ladam!

"Still, it's there," the informer persists, "a town in Poland."

"Contemporary or historical?"

"Founded twenty years ago. The baron built it up. It boasts, in fact, two fairs a year. Has a synagogue, a house of study, a bathhouse. Also two gentile taverns."

Again the registrar addresses himself to his assistants. "Any of you remember—did we ever get anybody here from Ladam?"

"Never!"

Impatiently they turn to the informer. "Don't they ever die in this Ladam of yours?"

---

* The original Hebrew has LHDM, which are the initial letters of the phrase "*lo hayu devarim me-olam,*" meaning "these things never were," "a pure fiction."

"And why shouldn't they?" he answers Jewish-wise, by returning a question. "Close, congested hovels that stifle you. A bathhouse where you can't catch your breath. The whole town—a morass!"

The informer is now in his element.

"Never die!" he continues. "Why, they have a completely laid out cemetery! It's true that the Burial Society will flay you for the costs of burial before they bring you to eternal rest, but still they do have a cemetery. And not so long ago they had an epidemic too."

The interrogation at an end, due judgment is rendered concerning the informer, and concerning the town of Ladam due investigation is instituted. A town twenty years old, a town with an epidemic in its history—and not one soul landed in Gehenna! This was a matter one couldn't let drop.

The imps of inquiry are sent forth diligently to search the thing out.

They return.

True!

And they report as follows: That in the realm of Poland there is indeed a town called Ladam; that it is still extant; that it boasts its tally of good deeds and admits to a quantum (greater) of misdeeds; that its economy presents the usual occupations and the usual struggle; and that the spirit of evil representing hell's interest in the said place, he too is not unemployed.

Why, then, have there never been any candidates for Gehenna from Ladam?

Because Ladam has a cantor! There lies the explanation! And what a cantor! Himself he's nothing! But his voice! A voice for singing, so sweet, so poignant-sweet, that when it weeps it penetrates right into hearts of iron, through and through; it melts them to wax! He has but to ascend the prayer stand, this cantor, and lift his voice in prayer, and behold, the entire congregation of Ladam is made one mass of repentance, wholehearted repentance, all its officers and members reduced, as if one person, to singlehearted contrition! With what result? With the result that Up There Ladam's sins are nullified, voided, made of no effect! With the result that for Ladam the gates of paradise—because of this cantor—are forthwith flung apart! When somebody comes before those gates and says he's from Ladam—no further questions asked!

It was easy to see that, with such a cantor in the vicinity, Gehenna would have to operate in Ladam at a loss. Accordingly the matter was taken over by That Certain Party himself! Head of hell, he would deal with the cantor personally.

So he orders that there be brought to him alive from the regions mundane a crowing Calcutta rooster, with comb of fiery red.

Done.

The Calcutta cock, frightened and bewildered in its new roost, lies motionless on the satanic altar, while he—may his name be blotted out!—circles around and around it, squats down before it, never taking his eye off it, his evil eye upon that bright red crest; winds around it, encircles it, until, the spell having worked, the red crest blenches and pales and grows white as chalk. But suddenly, in the midst of this sorcery, an ominous rumbling is heard from Up There. The Holy One, blessed be He, waxes wrathful! So he—may his name be blotted out!—in alarm desists, but not before he spits out a farewell curse:

"Cockcrow, begone! Begone his singing voice! Until the hour of his death!"

Against whom he really launched this curse, you, of course, have already surmised, and indeed even before the blood returned to the crest of the comb of the Calcutta rooster, the cantor of Ladam was minus his voice. Smitten in the throat. Couldn't bring out a note.

The source and origin of this affliction was known, but known, naturally, only to truly holy Jews, and even of these perhaps not to all. But what could one do? One couldn't, of course, explain it; the cantor just wouldn't understand. It was one of those things. Now, had the cantor himself been a man of good deeds, worth, and piety, one might perhaps have interceded for him, hammered at the gates of heaven, clamored

16.   Yom Kippur in a synagogue in Amsterdam. From *Cérémonies et coutumes religieuses*, by Bernard Picart, Amsterdam, 1723. See Chapter XI.

against injustice, but when the cantor was, as all knew, a man of insignificant merit, a trifle in the scales, a nothing, why, then . . .

So the cantor himself went knocking at the doors of the great rabbis, soliciting their help, imploring their intervention before the heavenly throne.

To no avail. It couldn't be done.

At last, winning his way into the court of the *tzaddik* of Apt, he clings to the *tzaddik*, won't be sundered from him, weeps, begs, and, unless and until he is helped, won't budge a step from the court. It is a most pitiable thing to see. Not being able to suffer the poor cantor's plight any longer, the *tzaddik* of Apt reluctantly decides to tell the cantor the irrevocable, but not without mixing in it some measure of consolation. "Know, cantor," he says, "that your hoarseness will persist until your death, but know also that when, at the hour of your death, you come to say the Prayer of Repentance, you will say it with a voice so clear, you will sing it with a voice so musical, that it will resound through all the corridors of heaven!"

"And until then?"

"Lost!"

The cantor still refuses to depart. "But, rabbi, why? Rabbi, what for?"

He persists so long that at last the *tzaddik* tells him the whole story—informer, rooster, and curse.

"If that's the case," the cantor cries out in all his hoarseness, "if that's the case, I—will—have—my—revenge!" And he dashes out.

"Revenge? How and from whom?" the *tzaddik* calls after him. But the cantor is gone.

This was on a Tuesday, some say Wednesday; and that Thursday, in the evening, when the fishermen of Apt, out on the river to catch their fish for the Sabbath, drew up their nets, they drew forth the drowned body of the cantor of Ladam!

A suicide! From the little bridge over the river! For the saying of the Prayer of Repentance his singing voice had indeed come back to him, even as the *tzaddik* of Apt had promised, the learned *tzaddik* interpreting the words of That Certain Party and stressing them, *"until* the hour of his death"—but not *the* hour of his death.

Yet despite this assurance the cantor—and this was his revenge, as you will soon see—purposely, in that last hour, both on the bridge and in the water, refrained from saying the Prayer of Repentance!

No sooner is the cantor buried, according to the rite of suicides, than the imps are at his soul and to Gehenna he is brought. At the gates the questions are put to him, but he refuses to answer. He is prodded with a pitchfork, stimulated with glowing coals—still he keeps silent, won't answer.

"Take him as is!"

For these questionings in hell are but a matter of form; hell's own agents have all these years lain in wait for the unsuspecting cantor; hell knows in advance the answers to Who, When, What for. The cantor is led to his proper place. A caldron seethes and boils before him.

But here, here the cantor at last permits himself the privilege of his voice. Clear and ringing he sings it forth: *"Yit-ga-da-al . . ."*

The *Kaddish* of *Neilah!*

He intones it, he sings it, and in singing his voice grows bolder, stronger . . . melts away . . . revives . . . is rapturous . . . glorious as in the world aforetime . . . no, better . . . sweeter . . . in the heart, deeper . . . from the depths . . . clamorous . . . resurgent. . . .

Hushed are all the boiling caldrons from which up to now there had issued a continual sound of weeping and wailing; hushed, until, after a while, from these same caldrons, an answering hum is heard. The caldron lids are lifted, heads peer out, burned lips murmur accompaniment.

The fiends of calefaction stationed at the caldrons, refuse, of course, to make the responses. Bewildered, abashed, they stand there as if lost, one with his faggots for the fire, another with his steaming ladle, a third with his glowing rake. Faces twisted . . . mouths agape . . . tongues lolling . . . eyes bulging from the sockets. . . . Some fall into epileptic fits and roll, convulsed and thrashing, on the ground.

But the cantor continues with his *Neilah.*

The cantor continues, and the fires under the caldrons diminish and fade and go out. The dead begin to crawl forth from their caldrons.

The cantor sings on, and the congregation of hell in undertone accompanies him, prays with him; and passage by passage, as the prayer is rendered, hurt bodies are healed, become whole, torn flesh unites, skin is renewed, the condemned dead grow pure.

Yes, when the cantor comes to the verse where he cries out, "Who quickeneth the dead," and hell's poor souls respond, "Amen, Amen," it is as if a resurrection, there and then, is taking place!

For such a clamor arises at this Amen that the heavens above are opened, and the repentance of the wicked reaches to the heaven of heavens, to the seventh heaven, and comes before The Throne itself! And, it being a moment of grace and favor, the sinners, now saints, suddenly grow wings! One after the other out of Gehenna they fly . . . to the very gates of paradise.

Thereafter there remained in Gehenna only the fiends, rolling in their convulsions, and the cantor, stock still at his stand. He did not leave. True, here in hell he had brought, as he had brought on earth, his congregation to repentance, but he himself had not known a true repentance. That unsaid Prayer of Repentance . . . that matter of suicide. . . .

In the course of time Gehenna was filled again, and although additional suburbs were built, it still remains crowded.

Translated by A. M. Klein[6]

A SAVIOR OF THE PEOPLE

Karl Emil Franzos

When we were in danger of losing our lives, who was it that saved us? A timid little man whom no one could have imagined capable of a courageous action, and whose name I have only to mention to send you into a fit of laughter. It was little Mendele. . . . Ah, see now how you are chuckling! Well, well, I can't blame

you, for he is a very queer little man. He knows many a merry
tale, and tells them very amusingly. And then it is certainly a
very strange thing to see a gray-haired man no taller than a
child, and with the ways and heart of a child. He used to dance
and sing all day long. I don't think that anyone ever saw him
quiet. Even now he does not walk down a street, but trots instead; he does not talk, but sings, and his hands seem to have
been given for no other use but to beat time. But—what of
that? It is better to keep a cheerful heart than to wear a look of
hypocritical solemnity. Mendele Abenstern is a great singer,
and we may well be proud of having him for our *hazzan* (cantor). It is true that he sometimes rattles off a touching prayer
as if it were a waltz, and that when reading the Torah he fidgets
about from one leg to the other as if he were a dancer at a
theater. But these little peculiarities of his never interfere with
our devotions, for we have been accustomed to Mendele and his
ways for the last forty years, and if anyone happens to get
irritated with him now and then, he takes care not to vent it on
the manikin. He cannot help remembering, you see, that little
Mendele can be grave enough at times, and that the poor *hazzan*
once did the town greater service by his gift of song than all the
wise and rich could accomplish by their wisdom or their wealth.

I will tell you how that came to pass.

You know that a Jew is looked upon nowadays as a man like
everyone else; and that if any noble or peasant dares to strike or
oppress a Jew, the latter can at once bring his assailant before
the Austrian district judge at the court hall, and Herr von
Negrusz punishes the offender for his injustice. But before the
great year when the emperor proclaimed that all men had equal
rights, it was not so. In those old days, the lord of the manor
exercised justice within the bounds of his territory by means of
his agent; but what was called justice by these men was generally great injustice. Ah, my friends, those were hard times! The
land belonged to the lord of the manor, and so did all the people
who lived on it; and the very air and water were his also. It was
not only in the villages that this was the case, but in the towns
too, especially when they belonged to a noble, and when their

inhabitants were Jews. The noble was lord of all, and ruled over his subjects through his agent, or *mandatar*.

At least it was so with us in Barnow. Our master, Graf Bortynski, lived in Paris all the year round, and gave himself no trouble about his estates or their management. His agent was supreme in Barnow, and was to all intents and purposes our master. So we always used to pray that the *mandatar* might be a good man, who would allow us to live in peace and quietness. And at first God answered our prayers, for stout old Herr Stephan Grudza was as easy-tempered a man as we Jews could have desired. It's true that he used to drink from morning till night, but he was always good-natured in his cups, and would not for the world have made any one miserable when he was merry. But one day, after making a particularly good dinner, he was seized with apoplexy and died. The whole district mourned for him, and so did we Jews of Barnow. For, in the first place, Herr Grudza had been kind to everyone; and in the second— who knew what his successor would be like!

Our fears were well grounded.

The new *mandatar*, Friedrich Wollmann, was a German. Now the Germans had hitherto treated us less harshly than the Poles. The new agent, however, was an exception to this rule. He was a tall, thin man, with black hair and bright black eyes. His expression was stern and sad—always, always—no one ever saw him smile. He was a good manager, and soon got the estate in order; he also insisted on the laws being obeyed; taught evil-doers that he was not a man to be trifled with; and I am quite sure that no one with whom he had any dealings defrauded him of a halfpenny. But he hated us Jews with a deadly hatred, and did us all as much harm as he could. He increased our taxes threefold—sent our sons away to be soldiers—disturbed our feasts—and whenever we had a lawsuit with a Christian, the Christian's word was always taken, while ours was disbelieved. He was very hard upon the peasants too—in fact, they said that no other agent at Barnow had ever been known to exact the *robota* [compulsory servitude] due from the villein to his lord with so much severity, and yet in that matter he acted within the letter of the law; and so there was a sort of justice in his mode of procedure. But as soon as he had anything to do with a Jew, he forgot both reason and justice.

Why did he persecute us so vehemently? No one knew for certain, but we all guessed. It was said that he used to be called Troim Wollmann, and that he was a Christianized Jew from Posen; that he had forsworn his religion for the love of a Christian girl, and that the Jews of his native place had persecuted and calumniated him so terribly in consequence of his apostasy that the girl's parents had broken off their daughter's engagement to him. I do not know who told us this, but no one could deny the probability of the story who ever had looked him in the face or had watched the mode of treating us.

So our days were sad and full of foreboding for the future. Wollmann oppressed and squeezed us whether we owed him money or not, and none that displeased him had a chance of escape. Thus matters stood in the autumn before the Great Year.

It isn't the pleasantest thing in the world for a Jew to be an Austrian soldier, but if one of our race is sent into the Russian service his fate is worse than death. He is thenceforward lost to God, to his parents, and to himself. Is it, then, a matter for surprise that the Russian Jews should gladly spend their last penny to buy their children's freedom from military service, or that any youth whose people are too poor to ransom him should fly over the border to escape his fate? Many such cases are known: some of the fugitives are caught before they have crossed the frontiers of Russia, and it would have been better for them if they had never been born; but some make good their escape into Moldavia, or into our part of Austrian Poland. Well, it happened that about that time a Jewish conscript—born at Berditchev—escaped over the frontier near Hussintyn and was sent on to Barnow from there. The community did what they could for him, and a rich, kind-hearted man, Hayyim Grünstein, father-in-law of Moses Freudenthal, took him into his service as groom.

The Russian government of course wanted to get the fugitive back into their hands, and our officials received orders to look for him.

Our *mandatar* got the same order as the others. He at once

sent for the elders of our congregation and questioned them on
the subject. They were inwardly much afraid, but outwardly
they made no sign, and denied all knowledge of the stranger.
It was on the eve of the Day of Atonement that this took place—
and how could they have entered the presence of God that
evening if they had betrayed their brother in the faith? So they
remained firm in spite of the agent's threats and rage. When he
perceived that they either knew nothing or would confess nothing, he let them go with these dark words of warning: "It will
be the worse for you if I find the youth in Barnow. You do not
know me yet, but—I swear that you shall know me then!"

The elders went home, and I need hardly tell you that the
hearts of the whole community sank on hearing Wollmann's
threat. The young man they were protecting was a hardworking
honest fellow, but even if he had been different, it wouldn't
have mattered—he was a Jew, and none of them would have
forsaken him in his adversity. If he remained in Barnow, the
danger to him and to all of them was great, for the *mandatar*
would find him out sooner or later—nothing could be kept from
him for long. But if they sent him away without a passport or
naturalization papers, he would of course be arrested very soon.
After a long consultation, Hayyim Grünstein had a happy inspiration. One of his relations was a tenant farmer in Marmaros,
in Hungary. The young man should be sent to him on the night
following the Day of Atonement, and should be told to make
the whole journey by night for fear of discovery. In this manner
he could best escape from his enemies.

They all agreed that the idea was a good one, and then par-
took with lightened hearts of the feast which was to strengthen
them for their fast on the Day of Atonement. Dusk began to fall.
The synagogue was lighted up with numerous wax candles and
the whole community hastened there with a broken and a
contrite heart to confess their sins before God; for at that
solemn fast we meet to pray to the Judge of all men to be
gracious to us, and of His mercy to forgive us our trespasses.
The women were all dressed in white, and the men in white
graveclothes. Hayyim Grünstein and his household were there

to humble themselves before the Lord, and among them was the poor fugitive, who was trembling in every limb with fear lest he should fall into the hands of his enemies.

All were assembled, and divine services was about to begin. Little Mendele had placed the flat of his hand upon his throat in order to bring out the first notes of the *Kol Nidre* with fitting tremulousness, when he was interrupted by a disturbance at the door. The entrance of the synagogue was beset by the Graf's men-at-arms, and Herr Wollmann was seen walking up the aisle between the rows of seats. The intruder advanced until he stood beside the ark of the covenant and quite close to little Mendele, who drew back in terror, but the elders of the congregation came forward with quiet humility.

"I know that the young man is here," said Wollmann; "will you give him up now?"

The men were silent.

"Very well," continued the *mandatar*, "I see that kindness has no effect upon you. I will arrest him after service when you leave the synagogue. And I warn you that both he and you shall have cause to remember this evening. But now, don't let me disturb you; go on with your prayers. I have time to wait."

A silence as of death reigned in the synagogue. It was at length broken by a shrill cry from the women's gallery. The whole congregation was at first stupefied with fear. But after a time everyone began to regain his self-command, and to raise his eyes to God for help. Without a word each went back to his seat.

Little Mendele trembled in every limb; but all at once he drew himself up and began to sing the *Kol Nidre*, that ancient simple melody, which no one who has ever heard can forget. His voice at first sounded weak and quavering but it gradually gained strength and volume, filled the edifice, thrilled the hearts of all the worshipers, and rose up to the throne of God. Little Mendele never again sang as he did that evening. He seemed as though he were inspired. When he was singing in that marvelous way, he ceased to be the absurd little man he had always hitherto been, and became a priest pleading with God for his people.

He reminded us of the former glories of our race, and then of the many, many centuries of ignominy and persecution that had followed. In the sound of his voice we could hear the story of the way in which we had been chased from place to place— never suffered to rest long anywhere; of how we were the poorest of the poor, the most wretched among the miserable of the earth; and how the days of our persecution were not yet ended, but ever-new oppressors rose against us and ground us down with an iron hand. The tale of our woes might be heard in his voice—of our unspeakable woes and our innumerable tears. But there was something else to be heard in it too. It told us in triumphant tones of our pride in our nation, and of our confidence and *trust in God.* Ah me! I can never describe the way little Mendele sang that evening; he made us weep for our desolation, and yet restored our courage and our trust. . . .

The women were sobbing aloud when he ceased; even the men were weeping; but little Mendele hid his face in his hands and fainted.

At the beginning of the service Wollmann had kept his eyes fixed on the ark of the covenant, but as it went on he had to turn away. He was very pale, and his knees shook so that, strong man as he was, he could hardly stand. His eyes shone as though through tears. With trembling steps and bowed head he slowly passed Mendele, and walked down the aisle to the entrance door. Then he gave the soldiers a sign to follow him.

Everyone guessed what had happened, but no one spoke of it.

He sent for Hayyim Grünstein on the day after the fast, and, giving him a blank passport, said, "It will perhaps be useful to you."

From that time forward he treated us with greater toleration; but his power did not last long. The peasants, whom he had formerly oppressed, rose against him in the spring of the Great Year, and put him to death. . . .

Now my friends, this is the story of the savior of the Jews of Barnow. Let it teach you to think twice before saying who is great and who is small, who is weak and who is mighty!

Translated by M. W. Macdowall[7]

YOM KIPPUR

ELIEZER DAVID ROSENTHAL

Erev Yom Kippur, *Minhah* time!

The eve of the Day of Atonement, at afternoon prayer time.

A solemn and sacred hour for every Jew.

Everyone feels as though he were born again.

All the weekday worries, the two-penny-half-penny interests, seem far, far away; or else they have hidden themselves in some corner. Every Jew feels a noble pride, an inward peace mingled with fear and awe. He knows that the yearly Judgment Day is approaching, when God Almighty will hold the scales in His hand and weigh every man's merits against his transgressions. The sentence given on that day is one of life or death. No trifle! But the Jew is not so terrified as you might think—he has broad shoulders. Besides, he has a certain footing behind the "upper windows," he has good advocates and plenty of them; he has the "binding of Isaac" and a long chain of ancestors and ancestresses who were put to death for the sanctification of the holy Name, who allowed themselves to be burnt and roasted for the sake of God's Torah. *Nishkoshe!* Things are not so bad. The Lord of all may just remember that, and look aside a little. Is He not the compassionate, the merciful?

The shadows lengthen and lengthen.

Jews are everywhere in commotion.

Some hurry home straight from the bath, drops of bath water dripping from beard and earlocks. They have not even dried their hair properly in their haste.

It is time to prepare for synagogue. Some are already on their way, robed in white. Nearly every Jew carries in one hand a large, well-packed *tallit* bag, which today, besides the prayer scarf, holds the whole Jewish outfit: a bulky prayer book, a book of psalms, and so on; and in the other hand, two wax candles, one a large one that is the "light of life," and the other a small one, a shrunken-looking thing, which is the "soul-light."

The Tamschevate house of study presents at this moment the

following picture: the floor is covered with fresh hay, and the
dust and the smell of the hay fill the whole building. Some of
the men are standing at their prayers, beating their breasts in
all seriousness. "We have trespassed, we have been faithless, we
have robbed," with an occasional sob of contrition. Others are
very busy setting up their wax lights in boxes filled with sand;
one of them, a young man who cannot live without it, betakes
himself to the platform and repeats a "Bless ye the Lord."
Meantime another comes slyly, and takes out two of the candles
standing before the platform, planting his own in their place.
Not far from the ark stands the beadle with a strap in his hand,
and all the foremost householders go up to him, lay themselves
down with their faces to the ground, and the beadle deals them
out thirty-nine blows apiece, and not one of them bears him any
grudge. Even Reb Groinom, from whom the beadle never hears
anything from one Yom Kippur to another but "may you be . . ."
and "rascal," "impudence," "brazen face," "spendthrift," "car-
rion," "dog of all dogs"—and not infrequently Reb Groinom
allows himself to apply his right hand to the beadle's cheek, and
the latter has to take it all in a spirit of love—this same Reb
Groinom now humbly approaches the same beadle, lies quietly
down with his face to the ground, stretches himself out, and
the beadle deliberately counts the strokes up to thirty-nine.
Covered with hay, Reb Groinom rises slowly, a piteous expression on his face just as if he had been well thrashed, and he
pushes a coin into the *shammash*'s hand. This is evidently the
beadle's day! Today he can take his revenge on his householders
for the insults and injuries of a whole year!

But if you want to be in the thick of it all, you must stand
in the anteroom by the door, where people are crowding round
the plates for collections. The treasurer sits beside a little table
with the directors of the congregation; the largest plate lies
before them. To one side of them sits the cantor with his plate,
and beside the cantor, several house of study youths with theirs.
On every plate lies a paper with a written notice: "Visiting the
Sick," "Supporting the Fallen," "Clothing the Naked," "Talmud
Torah," "Refuge for the Poor," and so forth. Over one plate,

marked "The Return to the Land of Israel," presides a modern
young man, a Zionist. Everyone wishing to enter the house of
study must first go to the plates marked "Call to the Torah" and
"Seat in the Synagogue," put in what is his due, and then throw
a few kopeks into the other plates.

Berel Tzop bustled up to the plate "Seat in the Synagogue,"
gave what was expected of him, popped a few coppers into the
other plates, and prepared to recite the afternoon prayer. He
wanted to pause a little between the words of his prayer, to
attend to their meaning, to impress upon himself that this was
the eve of the Day of Atonement! But idle thoughts kept coming
into his head, as though on purpose to annoy him, and his mind
was all over the place at once! The words of the prayers got
mixed up with the idea of oats, straw, wheat, and barley, and
however much trouble he took to drive these idle thoughts away,
he did not succeed. "Blow the great trumpet of our deliverance!"
shouted Berel, and remembered the while that Ivan owed him
ten measures of wheat; ". . . lift up the ensign to gather our
exiles! . . ."—and I made a mistake in Stephen's account by
thirty kopeks. . . . Berel saw that it was impossible for him to
pray with attention, and he began to reel off the Eighteen Benedictions, but not till he reached the Confession could he collect
his scattered thoughts, and realize what he was saying. When
he raised his hands to beat his breast at "We have trespassed,
we have robbed," the hand remained hanging in the air, half-
way. A shudder went through his limbs, the letters of the words
we have robbed began to grow before his eyes, they became
gigantic, they turned strange colors—red, blue, green, and
yellow—now they took the form of large frogs—they got bigger
and bigger, crawled into his eyes, croaked in his ears: You are
a thief, a robber, you have stolen and plundered! You think nobody saw, that it would all run quite smoothly, but you are
wrong! We shall stand before the throne of glory and cry: You
are a thief, a robber!
Berel stood some time with his hand raised midway in the air.
The whole affair of the hundred rubles rose before his eyes.

A couple of months ago he had gone into the house of Reb Mosheh Halfon. The latter had just gone out, there was nobody else in the room, nobody had even seen him come in.

The key was in the desk—Berel had looked at it, had hardly touched it—the drawer had opened as though of itself—several hundred-ruble notes had lain glistening before his eyes! Just that day, Berel had received a very unpleasant letter from the father of his daughter's bridegroom, and to make matters worse, the author of the letter was in the right. Berel had been putting off the marriage for two years, and the *mehutan* wrote quite plainly that unless the wedding took place after Tabernacles, he should return him the contract.

"Return the contract!" the fiery letters burnt into Berel's brain. He knew his *mehutan* well. The *mitnagged*! He wouldn't hesitate to tear up a marriage contract, either! And when it's a question of a by no means pretty girl of twenty-odd years! And the kind of bridegroom anybody might be glad to have secured for his daughter! And then to think that only one of those hundred-ruble notes lying tossed together in that drawer would help him out of all his troubles. And the Evil Inclination whispers in his ear: "Berel, now or never! There will be an end to all your worry! Don't you see, it's a godsend." He, Berel, wrestled with him hard. He remembers it all distinctly, and he can hear now the faint little voice of the Good Inclination: "Berel, to become a thief in one's latter years! You who so carefully avoided even the smallest deceit! Fie, for shame! If God will, He can help you by honest means too." But the voice of the Good Inclination was so feeble, so husky, and the Evil Inclination suggested in his other ear: "Do you know what? *Borrow* one hundred rubles! Who talks of stealing? You will earn some money before long, and then you can pay him back— it's a charitable loan on his part, only that he doesn't happen to know of it. Isn't it plain to be seen that it's a godsend? If you don't call this providence, what is? Are you going to take more than you really need? You know your *mehutan*? Have you taken a good look at that old maid of yours? You recollect the bridegroom? Well, the *mehutan* will be kind and mild as milk.

The bridegroom will be a 'silken son-in-law,' the ugly old maid, a young wife—fool! God and men will envy you. . . ." And he, Berel, lost his head, his thoughts flew hither and thither, like frightened birds, and—he no longer knew which of the two voices was that of the Good Inclination, and—

No one saw him leave Mosheh Halfon's house.

And still his hand remains suspended in midair, still it does not fall against his breast and there is a cold perspiration on his brow.

Berel started, as though out of his sleep. He had noticed that people were beginning to eye him as he stood with his hand held at a distance from his person. He hastily rattled through "For the sin . . . ," concluded the Eighteen Benedictions, and went home.

At home, he didn't dawdle, he only washed his hands, recited "Who bringest forth bread," and that was all. The food stuck in his throat, he said grace, returned to the synagogue, put on the *tallit*, and started to intone tunefully the Prayer of Expiation.

The lighted wax candles, the last rays of the sun stealing in through the windows of the house of study, the congregation entirely robed in white and enfolded in the prayer scarfs, the intense seriousness depicted on all faces, the hum of voices, and the bitter weeping that penetrated from the women's gallery, all this suited Berel's mood, his contrite heart. Berel had recited the Prayer of Expiation with deep feeling; tears poured from his eyes, his own broken voice went right through his heart, every word found an echo there, and he felt it in every limb. Berel stood before God like a little child before its parents: he wept and told God all that was in his heavily laden heart, the full tale of his cares and troubles. Berel was pleased with himself, he felt that he was not saying the words anyhow, just rolling them off his tongue, but he was really performing an act of penitence with his whole heart. He felt remorse for his sins, and God is a God of compassion and mercy, who will certainly pardon him.

"Therefore is my heart sad," began Berel, "that the sin which

a man commits against his neighbor cannot be atoned for even
on the Day of Atonement, unless he asks his neighbor's forgiveness . . . therefore is my heart broken and my limbs
tremble, because even the day of my death cannot atone for
this sin."

Berel began to recite this in pleasing, artistic fashion, weeping and whimpering like a spoiled child, and drawling out the
words, when it grew dark before his eyes. Berel had suddenly
become aware that he was in the position of one about to go
in through an open door. He advances, he must enter, it is a
question of life and death. And without any warning, just as
he is stepping across the threshold, the door is shut from
within with a terrible bang, and he remains standing outside.

And he has read this in the Prayer of Expiation? With fear
and fluttering he reads it over again, looking narrowly at every
word—a cold sweat covers him—the words prick him like pins.
Are these two verses his pitiless judges, are they the expression
of his sentence? Is he already condemned? "Aye, aye, you are
guilty," flicker the two verses on the page before him, and
prayer and tears are no longer of any avail. His heart cried to
God: "Have pity, merciful Father! A grown-up girl—what am I
to do with her? And his father wanted to break off the engagement. As soon as I have earned the money, I will give it
back. . . ." But he knew all the time that these were useless
subterfuges; the Lord of the Universe can only pardon the sin
committed against Himself, the sin committed against man
cannot be atoned for even on the Day of Atonement!

Berel took another look at the Prayer of Expiation. The words
"unless he asks his neighbor's forgiveness" danced before his
eyes. A ray of hope crept into his despairing heart. One way is
left open to him: he can confess to Mosheh Halfon! But the
hope was quickly extinguished. Is that a small matter? What
of my honor, my good name? And what of the match? "Mercy,
O Father," he cried, "have mercy!"

Berel proceeded no further with the Prayer of Expiation. He
stood lost in his melancholy thoughts, his whole life passed
before his eyes. He, Berel, had never licked honey, trouble had

17. "The Cantor." By Marc Chagall. From *Burning Lights*, by Bella Chagall, New York, 1946. See Chapter XI.

been his in plenty, he had known cares and worries, but God had never abandoned him. It had frequently happened to him in the course of his life to think he was lost, to give up all his hope. But each time God had extricated him unexpectedly from his difficulty, and not only that, but lawfully, honestly, Jewishly. And now—he had suddenly lost his trust in the providence of His dear Name! "Donkey!" thus Berel abused himself, "went to look for trouble, did you? Now you've got it! Sold yourself body and soul for one hundred rubles! Thief! thief! thief!" It did Berel good to abuse himself like this; it gave him a sort of pleasure to aggravate his wounds.

Berel, sunk in his sad reflections, has forgotten where he is in the world. The congregation has finished the Prayer of Expiation, and is ready for *Kol Nidre*. The cantor is at his post at the reading desk on the platform, two of the principal, well-to-do Jews, with Torahs in their hands, on each side of him. One of them is Mosheh Halfon. There is a deep silence in the building. The very last rays of the sun are slanting in through the window, and mingling with the flames of wax candles. . . .

"With the consent of the All-Present and with the consent of this congregation, we give leave to pray with them that have transgressed," startled Berel's ears. It was Mosheh Halfon's voice. The voice was low, sweet and sad. Berel gave a side glance at where Mosheh Halfon was standing, and it seemed to him that Mosheh Halfon was doing the same to him, only Mosheh Halfon was looking not into his eyes, but deep into his heart, and there reading the word *thief*! And Mosheh Halfon is permitting the people to pray together with him, Berel the thief!

"Mercy, mercy, compassionate God!" cried Berel's heart in its despair.

They had concluded *Maariv*, recited the first four chapters of Psalms and the Song of Unity, and the people went home, to lay in new strength for the morrow.

There remained only a few, who spent the greater part of the night repeating psalms, intoning the Mishnah, and so on; they snatched an occasional doze on the bare floor overlaid with a wisp of hay, an old cloak under their heads. Berel also stayed the night in the house of study. He sat down in a corner, in robe and *tallit*, and began reciting psalms with a pleasing pathos, and he went on until overtaken by sleep. At first he resisted, he took a nice pinch of snuff, rubbed his eyes, collected his thoughts, but it was no good. The covers of the Book of Psalms seemed to have been greased, for they continually slipped from his grasp, the printed lines had grown crooked and twisted, his head felt dreadfully heavy, and his eyelids clung together; his nose was forever drooping toward the Book of Psalms. He made every effort to keep awake, started up every time as though he had burnt himself, but sleep was the stronger of the two. Gradually he slid from the bench onto the floor; the Psalter slipped finally from between his fingers, his head dropped onto the hay, and he fell sweetly asleep. . . .

And Berel had a dream . . .

He was watching a peasant with a horse, and he liked the look of the horse so much that he bought it and mounted it. And he looked at it from where he sat astride, and saw the horse was a horse, but at the selfsame time it was Mosheh Halfon as well. Berel wondered: how is it possible for it to be at once a horse and a man? But his own eyes told him it was so. He wanted to dismount, but the horse bore him to a shop. Here he climbed down and asked for a pound of sugar. Berel kept his eyes on the scales, and—a fresh surprise! Where they should have been weighing sugar, they were weighing his good and bad deeds. And the two scales were nearly equally laden, and oscillated up and down in the air. . . .

Suddenly they threw a sheet of paper into the scale that held his bad deeds. Berel looked to see—it was the hundred-ruble note which he had appropriated at Mosheh Halfon's! But it was now much larger, bordered with black, and the letters and numbers were red as fire. The piece of paper was frightfully heavy, it was all two men could do to carry it to the weighing machine, and when they had thrown it with all their might onto the scale something snapped, and the scale went down, down, down.

At that moment a man sleeping at Berel's head stretched out a foot, and gave Berel a kick in the head. Berel awoke.

Not far from him sat a gray-haired old Jew, huddled together, enfolded in a *tallit* robe, repeating psalms with a melancholy chant and a broken, quivering voice.

Berel caught the words:

> Mark the perfect man, and behold the upright:
> For the end of that man is peace.
> But the transgressors shall be destroyed together:
> The latter end of the wicked shall be cut off. . . .

Berel looked round in a fright: Where was he? He had quite forgotten that he had remained for the night in the house of study. He gazed round with sleepy eyes, and they fell on some white heaps wrapped in robes and prayer scarfs, while from their midst came the low, hoarse, tearful voices of two or three men who had not gone to sleep and were repeating psalms. Many of the candles were already sputtering, the wax melting into the sand, the flames rose and fell, and rose again, flaring brightly.

And the pale moon looked in at the windows, and poured her silvery light over the fantastic scene.

Berel grew icy cold, and a dreadful shuddering went through his limbs.

He had not yet remembered that he was spending the night in the house of study.

He imagined that he was dead, and astray in limbo. The white heaps which he sees are graves, actual graves, and there among the graves sit a few, sinful souls, and bewail and lament their transgressions. And he, Berel, cannot even weep, he is a fallen one, lost forever—he is condemned to wander, to roam everlastingly among the graves.

By degrees, however, he called to mind where he was and collected his wits.

Only then he remembered his fearful dream.

"No," he decided within himself, "I have lived till now without the hundred rubles, and I will continue to live without them. If the Lord of the Universe wishes to help me, he will do

so without them too. My soul and my portion of the world to
come are dearer to me. Only let Mosheh Halfon come in to pray,
I will tell him the whole truth and avert misfortune."

· This decision gave him courage, he washed his hands, and sat
down again to the psalms. Every few minutes he glanced at the
window, to see if it were not beginning to dawn, and if Reb
Mosheh Halfon were not coming along to the synagogue.

· The day broke.

With the first sunbeams Berel's fears and terrors began little
by little to dissipate and diminish. His resolve to restore the
hundred rubles weakened considerably.

"If I don't confess," thought Berel, wrestling in spirit with
temptation, "I risk my world to come. . . . If I do confess, what
will my Chantzeh-Leah say to it. *He* writes, either the wedding
takes place, or the contract is dissolved! And what shall I do
when his father gets to hear about it? There will be a stain on
my character, the marriage contract will be annulled, and I
shall be left . . . without my good name and . . . with my ugly
old maid. . . .

"What is to be done? Help! What is to be done?"

The people began to gather in the synagogue. The reader of
the morning service intoned "He is Lord of the Universe" to the
special Yom Kippur tune, a few householders and young men
supported him, and Berel heard through it all only, Help! What
is to be done?

And suddenly he beheld Mosheh Halfon.

Berel quickly rose from his place, he wanted to make a rush
at Mosheh Halfon. But after all he remained where he was,
and sat down again.

"I must first think it over, and discuss it with my Chantzeh-
Leah," was Berel's decision.

Berel stood up to pray with the congregation. He was again
wishful to pray with fervor, to collect his thoughts, and attend
to the meaning of the words, but try as he would, he couldn't! . . .

Berel was very dissatisfied with himself. He finished the
morning prayer, stood through the additional service, and proceeded to devour the long *piyyutim*.

The question, What is to be done? left him no peace, and he was really reciting the *piyyutim* to try and stupefy himself, to dull his brain.

So it went on till *Unetanneh Tokef*.

The congregation began to prepare for *Unetanneh Tokef*, coughed to clear their throats, and pulled the *tallitim* over their heads. The cantor sat down for a minute to rest, and unbuttoned his shroud. His face was pale and perspiring, and his eyes betrayed a great weariness. From the women's gallery came a sound of weeping and wailing.

Berel had drawn his *tallit* over his head, and started reciting with earnestness and enthusiasm:

> We will express the mighty holiness of this day,
> For it is tremendous and awful!
> On which Thy kingdom is exalted,
> And Thy throne established in grace;
> Whereupon Thou art seated in truth.
> Verily, it is Thou who art judge and arbitrator,
> Who knowest all, and art witness, writer, sigillator, recorder
>   and teller;
> And Thou recallest all forgotten things,
> And openest the Book of Remembrance, and the book reads
>   itself,
> And every man's handwriting is there. . . .

These words opened the source of Berel's tears, and he sobbed unaffectedly. Every sentence cut him to the heart, like a sharp knife, and especially the passage:

"And Thou recallest all forgotten things, and openest the Book of Remembrance, and the book reads itself, and every man's handwriting is there. . . ." At that very moment the Book of Remembrance was lying open before the Lord of the Universe, with the handwritings of all men. It contains his own as well, the one which he wrote with his own hand that day when he took away the hundred-ruble note. He pictures how his soul flew up to heaven while he slept, and entered everything in the eternal book, and now the letters stood before the throne of glory, and cried, "Berel is a thief, Berel is a robber!" And he has the impudence to stand and pray before God? He, the offender, the transgressor—and the synagogue does not fall upon his head?

The congregation concluded *Unetanneh Tokef*, and the cantor began: "And the great trumpet of ram's horn shall be sounded . . ." and still Berel stood with the *tallit* over his head.

Suddenly he heard the words:

> And the angels are dismayed,
> Fear and trembling seize hold of them as they proclaim,
> As swiftly as birds, and say:
> This is the Day of Judgment!

The words penetrated into the marrow of Berel's bones, and he shuddered from head to foot. The words "This is the Day of Judgment" reverberated in his ears like a peal of thunder. He imagined the angels were hastening to him with one speed, with one swoop, to seize and drag him before the throne of glory, and the piteous wailing that came from the women's court was for him, for his wretched soul, for his endless misfortune.

"No! no! no!" he resolved, "come what may, let him annul the contract, let them point at me with their fingers as at a thief, if they choose, let my Chantzeh-Leah lose her chance! I will take it all in good part, if I may only save my unhappy soul! The minute the *Kedushah* is over I shall go to Mosheh Halfon, tell him the whole story, and beg him to forgive me."

The cantor came to the end of *Unetanneh Tokef*, the congregation resumed their seats; Berel also returned to his place and did not go up to Mosheh Halfon.

"Help, what shall I do, what shall I do?" he thought as he struggled with his conscience. "Chantzeh-Leah will lay me on the fire . . . she will cry her life out . . . the *mehutan* . . . the bridegroom . . ."

The additional service and the afternoon service were over, people were making ready for the concluding service, *Neilah*. The shadows were once more lengthening, the sun was once more sinking in the west. The *shul goy* began to light candles

and lamps, and placed them on the tables and the window
ledges. Jews with faces white from exhaustion sat in the anteroom resting and refreshing themselves with a pinch of snuff,
or a drop of hartshorn, and a few words of conversation.
Everyone feels more cheerful and in better humor. What had
to be done, has been done and well done. The Lord of the Universe has received His due. They have mortified themselves a
whole day, fasted continuously, recited prayers, and begged
forgiveness!

Now surely the Almighty will do His part, accept the Jewish
prayers and have compassion on His people Israel.

Only Berel sits in a corner by himself. He also is wearied and
exhausted. He also has fasted, prayed, wept, mortified himself,
like the rest. But he knows that the whole of his toil and trouble
has been thrown away. He sits troubled, gloomy, and depressed.
He knows that they have now reached *Neilah*, that he has still
time to repent, that the door of heaven will stand open a little
while longer, his repentance may yet pass through . . . otherwise,
yet a little while, and the gates of mercy will be shut and . . .
too late!

"Oh, open the gate to us, even while it is closing," sounded
in Berel's ears and heart . . . yet a little while, and it will be too
late!

"No, no!" shrieked Berel to himself, "I will not lose my soul,
my world to come! Let Chantzeh-Leah burn me and roast me, I
will take it all in good part, so that I don't lose my world to
come!"

Berel rose from his seat, and went up to Mosheh Halfon.

"Reb Mosheh, a word with you," he whispered into his ear.

"Afterwards, when the prayers are done."

"No, no, no!" shrieked Berel, below his breath, "now, at once!"

Mosheh Halfon stood up.

Berel led him out of the house of study, and aside.

"Reb Mosheh, kind soul, have pity on me and forgive me!"
cried Berel, and burst into sobs.

"God be with you, Berel, what has come over you all at once?"
asked Reb Mosheh, in astonishment.

"Listen to me, Reb Mosheh!" said Berel, still sobbing. "The

hundred rubles you lost a few weeks ago are in my house! . . .
God knows the truth, I didn't take them out of wickedness. I
came into your house, the key was in the drawer . . . there was
no one in the room. . . . That day I'd had a letter from my
mehutan that he'd break off his son's engagement if the wedding
didn't take place in time. . . . My girl is ugly and old . . . the
bridegroom is a fine man . . . a precious stone. . . . I opened
the drawer in spite of myself . . . and saw the bank notes. . . .
You see how it was? . . . My *mehutan* is a *mitnagged* . . . a
flint-hearted screw. . . . I took out the note . . . but it is shorten-
ing my years! . . . God knows what I bore and suffered at the
time. . . . Tonight I will bring you the note back. . . . Forgive
me! . . . Let the *mehutan* break off the match if he chooses, let
the woman fret away her years, so long as I am rid of the
serpent that is gnawing at my heart and gives me no peace! I
never before touched a ruble belonging to anyone else, and
become a thief in my latter years I won't!"

Mosheh Halfon did not answer him for a little while. He took
out his snuff and had a pinch; then he took out of the bosom of
his robe a great red handkerchief, wiped his nose, and reflected
a minute or two. Then he said quietly:

"If a match were broken off through me, I should be sorry.
You certainly behaved as you should not have, in taking the
money without leave, but it is written: Judge not thy neighbor
till thou hast stood in his place. You shall keep the hundred
rubles. Come tonight and bring me an IOU, and begin to repay
me little by little."

"What are you, an angel?" exclaimed Berel, weeping.

"God forbid," replied Mosheh Halfon, quietly, "I am what
you are. You are a Jew, and I also am a Jew."

Translated by Helena Frank[8]

THE DAY WITHOUT FORGIVENESS

ELIE WIESEL

With a lifeless look, a painful smile on his face, while digging
a hole in the ground, Pinhas moved his lips in silence. He

appeared to be arguing with someone within himself and, judging from his expression, seemed close to admitting defeat.

I had never seen him so downhearted. I knew that his body would not hold out much longer. His strength was already abandoning him, his movements were becoming more heavy, more chaotic. No doubt he knew it too. But death figured only rarely in our conversations. We preferred to deny its presence, to reduce it, as in the past, to a simple allusion, something abstract, inoffensive, a word like any other.

"What are you thinking about? What's wrong?"

Pinhas lowered his head, as if to conceal his embarrassment, or his sadness, or both, and let a long time go by before he answered, in a voice scarcely audible: "Tomorrow is Yom Kippur."

Then I too felt depressed. My first Yom Kippur in the camp. Perhaps my last. The day of judgment, of atonement. Tomorrow the heavenly tribunal would sit and pass sentence: "And like unto a flock, the creatures of this world shall pass before Thee." Once upon a time—last year—the approach of this day of tears, of penitence and fear, had made me tremble. Tomorrow we would present ourselves before God, who sees everything and who knows everything, and we would say: "Father, have pity on your children." Would I be capable of praying with fervor again? Pinhas shook himself abruptly. His glance plunged into mine.

"Tomorrow is the Day of Atonement and I have just made a decision: I am not going to fast. Do you hear? I am not going to fast."

I asked for no explanation. I knew he was going to die and suddenly I was afraid that by way of justification he might declare: "It is simple, I have decided not to comply with the Law anymore and not to fast because in the eyes of man and of God I am already dead, and the dead can disobey the commandments of the Torah." I lowered my head and made believe I was not thinking about anything but the earth I was digging up under a sky more dark than the earth itself.

We belonged to the same Kommando. We always managed to work side by side. Our age difference did not stop him from treating me like a friend. He must have been past forty. I was fifteen. Before the war, he had been *rosh yeshivah*, director of a rabbinical school somewhere in Galicia. Often, to outwit our hunger or to forget our reasons for despair, we would study a page of the Talmud from memory. I relived my childhood by forcing myself not to think about those who were gone. If one of my arguments pleased Pinhas, if I quoted a commentary without distorting its meaning, he would smile at me and say: "I should have liked to have you among my disciples."

And I would answer: "But I am your disciple; where we are matters little."

That was false, the place was of capital importance. According to the law of the camp I was his equal; I used the familiar form when I addressed him. Any other form of address was inconceivable.

"Do you hear?" Pinhas shouted defiantly. "I will not fast."

"I understand. You are right. One must not fast. Not at Auschwitz. Here we live outside time, outside sin. Yom Kippur does not apply to Auschwitz."

Ever since Rosh Hashanah, the New Year, the question had been bitterly debated all over camp. Fasting meant a quicker death. Here everybody fasted all year round. Every day was Yom Kippur. And the book of life and death was no longer in God's hands, but in the hands of the executioner. The words *Mi yihye u-mi yamut*, who shall live and who shall die, had a terrible real meaning here, an immediate bearing. And all the prayers in the world could not alter the *gezar din*, the inexorable movement of fate. Here, in order to live, one had to eat, not pray.

"You are right, Pinhas," I said forcing myself to withstand his gaze. "You *must* eat tomorrow. You've been here longer than I have, longer than many of us. You need your strength. You have to save your strength, watch over it, protect it. You should not go beyond your limits. Or tempt misfortune. That would be a sin."

Me, his disciple? I gave him lessons, I gave him advice, as if I were his elder, his guide.

"That is not it," said Pinhas, getting irritated. "I could hold out for one day without food. It would not be the first time."

"Then what is it?"

"A decision. Until now, I've accepted everything. Without bitterness, without reservation. I have told myself: 'God knows what He is doing.' I have submitted to His will. Now I have had enough, I have reached my limit. If He knows what He is doing, then it is serious; and it is not any less serious if He does not. Therefore, I have decided to tell Him: 'It is enough.' "

I said nothing. How could I argue with him? I was going through the same crisis. Every day I was moving a little further away from the God of my childhood. He had become a stranger to me; sometimes, I even thought He was my enemy.

The appearance of Edek put an end to our conversation. He was our master, our king. The *kapo*. This young Pole with rosy cheeks, with the movements of a wild animal, enjoyed catching his slaves by surprise and making them shout with fear. Still an adolescent, he enjoyed possessing such power over so many adults. We dreaded his changeable moods, his sudden fits of anger: without unclenching his teeth, his eyes half closed, he would beat his victims long after they had lost consciousness and had ceased to moan.

"Well?" he said, planting himself in front of us, his arms folded. "Taking a little nap? Talking over old times? You think you are at a resort? Or in the synagogue?"

A cruel flame lit his blue eyes, but it went out just as quickly. An aborted rage. We began to shovel furiously, not thinking about anything but the ground which opened up menacingly before us. Edek insulted us a few more times and then walked off.

Pinhas did not feel like talking anymore, neither did I. For him the die had been cast. The break with God appeared complete.

Meanwhile, the pit under our legs was becoming wider and deeper. Soon our heads would hardly be visible above the ground. I had the weird sensation that I was digging a grave. For whom? For Pinhas? For myself? Perhaps for our memories.

On my return to camp, I found it plunged into feverish antici-pation. They were preparing to welcome the holiest and longest day of the year. My barracks neighbors, a father and son, were talking in low voices. One was saying: "Let us hope the roll call does not last too long." The other added: "Let us hope that the soup is distributed before the sun sets, otherwise we will not have the right to touch it."

Their prayers were answered. The roll call unfolded without incident, without delay, without public hanging. The section chief hurriedly distributed the soup; I hurriedly gulped it down. I ran to wash, to purify myself. By the time the day was drawing to a close, I was ready.

Some days before, on the eve of Rosh Hashanah, all the Jews in camp—*kapo*s included—had congregated at the square where roll was taken, and we had implored the God of Abraham, Isaac, and Jacob to end our humiliation, to change sides, to break his pact with the enemy. In unison we had said *Kaddish* for the dead and for the living as well. Officers and soldiers, machine guns in hand, had stood by, amused spectators, on the other side of the barbed wire.

Now, we did not go back there for *Kol Nidre*. We were afraid of a selection: in preceding years, the Day of Atonement had been turned into a day of mourning. Yom Kippur had become Tishah be-Av, the day the Temple was destroyed.

Thus, each barracks housed its own synagogue. It was more prudent. I was sorry, because Pinhas was in another block.

A Hungarian rabbi officiated as our cantor. His voice stirred my memories and evoked that legend according to which, on the night of Yom Kippur, the dead rise from their graves and come to pray with the living. I thought: "Then it is true; that is what really happens. The legend is confirmed at Auschwitz."

For weeks, several learned Jews had gathered every night in our block to transcribe from memory—by hand, on toilet paper —the prayers for the High Holy Days. Each cantor received a copy. Ours read in a loud voice and we repeated each verse after him. The *Kol Nidre*, which releases us from all vows made under constraint, now seemed to me anachronistic, absurd, even though it had been composed in similar circumstances, in Spain, right near the Inquisition stakes. Once a year the converts would assemble and cry out to God: "Know this, all that

we said is unsaid, all that we have done is undone." *Kol Nidre?*
A sad joke. Here and now we no longer had any secret vows to
make or to deny: everything was clear, irrevocable.

Then came the *Viddui*, the great Confession. There again,
everything rang false, none of it concerned us anymore.
Ashamnu, we have sinned. *Bagadnu*, we have betrayed. *Gazalnu*,
we have stolen. What? Us? *We* have sinned? Against whom?
By doing what? We have betrayed? Whom? Undoubtedly this
was the first time since God judged His creation that victims
beat their breast accusing themselves of the crimes of their
executioners.

Why did we take responsibility for sins and offenses which
not one of us could ever have had the desire or the possibility of
committing? Perhaps we felt guilty despite everything. Things
were simpler that way. It was better to believe our punishments
had meaning, that we had deserved them; to believe in a cruel
but just God was better than not to believe at all. It was in order
not to provoke an open war between God and His people that
we had chosen to spare Him, and we cried out: "You are our
God, blessed be Your name. You smite us without pity, You shed
our blood, we give thanks to You for it, O Eternal One, for You
are determined to show us that You are just and that Your
name is justice!"

I admit having joined my voice to the others and implored the
heavens to grant me mercy and forgiveness. At variance with
everything my lips were saying, I indicted myself only to turn
everything into derision, into farce. At any moment I expected
the Master of the Universe to strike me dumb and to say: "That
is enough—you have gone too far." And I like to think I would
have replied: "You, also, blessed be Your name, You also."

Our services were dispersed by the camp bell. The section
chiefs began to yell: "Okay, go to sleep! If God hasn't heard
you, it's because He is incapable of hearing."

The next day, at work, Pinhas joined another group. I
thought: "He wants to eat without being embarrassed by my
presence." A day later, he returned. His face even more pale,
even more gaunt than before. Death was gnawing at him. I

caught myself thinking: "He will die because he did not observe Yom Kippur."

We dug for several hours without looking at each other. From far off, the shouting of the *kapo* reached us. He walked around hitting people relentlessly.

Toward the end of the afternoon, Pinhas spoke to me: "I have a confession to make."

I shuddered, but went on digging. A strange, almost childlike smile appeared on his lips when he spoke again: "You know, I fasted."

I remained motionless. My stupor amused him.

"Yes, I fasted. Like the others. But not for the same reason. Not out of obedience, but out of defiance. Before the war, you see, some Jews rebelled against the divine will by going to restaurants on the Day of Atonement; here, it is by observing the fast that we can make our indignation heard. Yes, my disciple and teacher, know that I fasted. Not for love of God, but against God."

He left me a few weeks later, victim of the first selection.

He shook my hand: "I would have liked to die some other way and elsewhere. I had always hoped to make of my death, as of my life, an act of faith. It is a pity. God prevents me from realizing my dream. He no longer likes dreams."

Nonetheless, he asked me to say *Kaddish* for him after his death, which, according to his calculations, would take place three days after his departure from camp.

"But why?" I asked. "Since you are no longer a believer?"

He took the tone he always used when he explained a passage in the Talmud to me: "You do not see the heart of the matter. Here and now, the only way to accuse Him is by praising Him."

And he went, laughing, to his death.[9]

THE CALL

Victor Barwin

The mighty magnate of the stock exchange got out of his bed as soon as the morning sun entered the bedroom window of his palatial Parktown mansion. His face was drawn and pale, his eyes were dim and dream-haunted—the effects on him of a sleepless, restless night. He had had a very busy time on the stock exchange the day before; excitement must have unstrung his nerves and disturbed the usual equanimity of his mind. Had he been able to turn his sleeplessness to account, to lie awake in bed and think over his affairs as clearly and as intelligently as he did at his desk, he would not have minded at all. But his trouble was that he could not get any benefit from sleeplessness—he was not awake enough to have control over his mind and regulate his thoughts at will. In his semisomnolent state his thoughts flitted and tumbled in most confused disorder. The unfinished transactions of the previous day seemed to finish themselves of their own accord in an unpractical, unbusinesslike manner; deeds and documents which still required careful consideration seemed to get themselves correctly and properly signed by the mysterious hand of some invisible forger; valuable scrip and vouchers got out of their bundles, tore themselves up into countless little scraps, and were wafted about like worthless flakes of snow; small precious samples of gold and diamonds, which he had thought were securely locked up in his safe, were strewn about the room; moneybags he had carefully and tightly tied up unloosed themselves so that the money fell out and was scattered all over the place; and as if to increase his torment, little street urchins gathered round and picked up every coin of it.

And there in the distant background he could discern strings of ghastly specters—ghostly shadows of phthisis-stricken miners; crushed, distorted workmen, writhing and shivering as though still in agony, grinning and growling and shaking their clenched fists at him with deadly threats.

No wonder the mighty magnate was glad to get out of his bed. He felt the reality of his life again as he stamped his foot on the carpeted floor. In a short time he would be back in his office, again the mighty magnate of yesterday, with his scrip and documents neatly tied up and filed, and those hideous

18. "Jews at Prayer on the Day of Atonement." Oil painting on canvas. By Maurycy Gottlieb (1856–1879). See Chapter XI.

victims of disease and accident dead and buried, and unable to
do him any harm.

He touched the bell on his table to summon his servant, who
soon appeared—a big, burly fellow, well groomed, well liveried,
and evidently well contented with himself.

"I want you to have the car ready at once," ordered the magnate. "Very important business on 'Change today, and I must
be there early."

The servant looked at his master in surprise, "To the Exchange, sir? The Exchange is closed today, sir."

"Closed?" repeated the magnate, as much startled as though
he had been told that all the gold in his mines had turned to
copper. "Why, what's on today?"

"Well, sir," explained the servant, "I can't make out myself
exactly what's on today, but I think it is the Jewish Christmas,
the day of dethron—"

"The Day of Atonement, you mean," said the master, correct-
ing him. "Does it fall today?"

"I don't know much about it falling due nor the Day of
Atonement neither," answered the servant, "I only tell you, sir,
what I saw in the papers this morning."

"I think you are right. Strange I did not think of it myself—
I won't require the car, then. You can go."

The servant turned on his heels and disappeared, wondering
why his master did not look overpleased with the prospect of
having a day off.

The magnate remained in the room reflecting.

The Day of Atonement—and it was left to his gentile servant
to remind him—a Jew—of its occurrence. He could not help
smiling at the bitter irony of it; while he felt that the mention
of the day had touched some dormant spot in his heart. It had
stirred a hidden chord in his nature and had sent his mind
wandering away—away back to the almost forgotten past—to a
Day of Atonement of many years ago in the home of his poor
parents, in the little ghetto village, when his sweet mother, with
tears in her eyes, spread her trembling hands—like angel's
wings—on his head and prayed and blessed him to be for ever

"a good and pious Jew"; when his good father, patriarchlike, in a snow-white gown, took him by the hand and led him to the synagogue, where he stood frightened and fascinated by the awe-inspiring day and the fantastic spectacle of a weeping congregation. And he saw himself bow his head in humility, and with his small fist smite his childish heart, as he confessed his sins and made the solemn promise "to sin no more."

How was his mother's blessing fulfilled, and how had he kept his solemn vow?

What was the Day of Atonement for him now? How often on that day had he rushed by in his stately motor car, past the synagogue and the strings of Jews flocking to it without the least look of concern? He had married out of his faith a Christian woman, who did not bless his children on that day as his mother blessed him. Neither did *he* lead them to the synagogue in the manner his father had led him. His soul, his heart, had become hardened, metallic, and was now locked up with his gold and diamonds. Mammon was his god, the 'Change his synagogue, and his prayers there had been answered sooner than all his tearful prayers and earnest devotions in the synagogue of his childhood—for was he not now the great man he had always striven to become, the possessor of millions, the mighty magnate?

And his dim eyes brightened with the luster of the rich man's vanity and self-glorification as his thoughts brought him back to his actual position, to the happy materialism of his life, and he wondered why those absurd memories of the past should come back to trouble his mind. He longed now to fly back to the city, to throw himself into the turmoil of his business, to wrap himself up in his scrip and documents, designing and contriving new schemes and projects. Once in his natural element and all would be well again. But 'Change was closed on account of some stupid Jewish brokers who were not rich enough to keep away from the synagogue.

He washed and dressed, rather carelessly and shabbily—he did not need to show off his riches—and went down the stairs to his early breakfast. His wife and children were round the table, sipping their morning coffee peacefully. He greeted his wife indifferently, she answered him with a slight nod of her head. She was a prepossessing, full-breasted Dutch woman, and looked in her new dress, her rings, bracelets, and brooches more the magnate's wife than her husband looked the magnate.

The children were pretty, with their father's dark eyes and their mother's fair hair—perfect blends of Teuton and Semite. But their love and affections were entirely one-sided, Teutonic only; they were attached and devoted to their mother, and only knew their father as a stranger in the home. They saw so little of him. At all times and at all hours they enjoyed their mother's kisses and caresses, and it was therefore her influence and authority which formed their character and held sway over their sentiments and beliefs.

"What made you and the children get up so early?" asked the husband. "You are all dressed as though for driving out."

"And so we are," answered the wife, putting down her coffee cup and taking up her husband's question. "I received a letter from Father inviting us to his *dorp* for the *Nachmaal*. There is going to be a grand ceremony at the consecration of the new church. Will you join us?"

"To church!" he faltered, and as he uttered these words the shape of his old village synagogue once again appeared before his eyes. "Join you for the *Nachmaal*? No, I cannot; not today; it is the Day of Atone—"

"The day of what?" interrupted his wife. "It is always the wrong day when I ask you to go with us. You don't go to your church yourself, neither will you join us; but I don't want you; I'll go with the children," she finished defiantly.

He dropped his head dejectedly, not finding courage to answer her. He felt the cowardice of conscience.

"Why don't you come with us, Daddy?" said his eldest son. "We shall have such a nice time with Grandpapa. Why don't you come?"

The father shrank under the naive, coaxing words of his son. He lifted the boy in his arms and kissed him affectionately.

"I cannot go to that church, my child," he told him; "I do not

belong to it; my church is a different one. If you like I'll take
you there, to my church—in the synagogue."

The Christian mother jumped up from her chair and rushed
to her son as if to save him from the peril of his life. She tore
him away from his father's arms and pressed the boy to her side.

"Come away," she exclaimed. "Your father is a Jew!"

That his father was a Jew was quite a revelation to the boy,
who had never been told, just as he had never been told the true
dignity of the religion. The only man he knew as a Jew was a
bearded, shabby-looking man who occasionally came to the
back door shouting for old clothes, whom the housemaids
addressed in an insolent manner and upon whom he considered
it great sport to set the dogs barking and biting. That his
father should be like that man almost terrified the simple child,
and he pressed close to his mother as though seeking her
maternal protection.

And the father saw and understood. He saw and understood
the hateful look which his wife threw at him as she led the
children out of the room.

He was left alone—an outcast in his own home. Not the respected magnate of the 'Change and club, but the despised
Jew: hated by his gentile wife, feared by his un-Jewish children.

He loved his children dearly, though he did not manifest his
love for them in such a manner that they would perceive it. In
his more reflective moments he always thought of his children
first and of his money only as the means of making them happy
in life. He remembered the misfortunes of poverty—when as a
poor alien he came to South Africa, scorned and disdained,
trampled on and downtrodden, until he made money enough to
command recognition and respect—and he wanted to spare his
children those misfortunes. But in his struggle for the means
he too often forgot the end; his moments of reflection were few
and far between and most of his time was taken up, absorbed
and consumed by the fervent, feverish hunt after gold. In his
endeavor to give to his children he stole from them what was
morally theirs—the few hours he should have devoted to them
to teach them to understand and respect their father and the

illustrious race from which he had sprung. He only realized his
guilt now that he felt the punishment; he had no time to spare
for them, and they had no love to give him. They went to their
mother and they followed her way—to her father, to the Church.

And what remained for him to do now? He wondered de-
spondently as he stood at the parting of the ways; should he
take the final step and join his children at the *Nachmaal*, go
over to the Church, to the other and stronger side, assimilate
and be absorbed by them; or go back to the synagogue, to the
broken vows of his childhood, to his God and his people whom
he had so long forsaken?

His servant's entry into the room roused him from his reverie.
"Here are your letters, sir," he said. "They were sent over from
the office as they don't expect you there today."

There were many letters, and they looked important with
their big envelopes and printed headlines on them. At another
time he would have pounced on them impetuously and devoured
their contents, but he had no interest in them now. He was just
putting them aside indifferently when a square, blue, foreign-
looking envelope attracted his attention. He felt a shudder pass
through his body as he recognized the Russian postmark with
the name of his little ghetto village stamped on it. His fingers
trembled as he broke open the envelope and drew forth a
crumpled sheet of notepaper, covered with scribbled and
scrawled lines, dotted and stained with dried tears; he read:

My dear and only son,

From my death bed I write this letter to you. Read it. Don't
throw it away, for I shall trouble you no more; there will be no
more blood left in my veins after this with which to write another
line. Little have I asked from you in this world, much less have
you given me. You reveled in affluence and luxury while I was
pining with want and starvation. But I forgive you, I bear you no
grudge, my dear son! I die with love for you in my heart, a prayer
and a blessing for you on my lips—only grant me this request,
my last will and favor—be forever a Jew! It was my prayer as I
rocked your cradle; I repeat it now with my dying groans as I am

to be taken to my grave—remain a Jew! Do not give up your Judaism as lightly as you have given up your mother, for I can forgive you, but who will forgive you if your forsake your God and people? Be truer to your God than you have been to me, and stand by your people. Help them if there is help needed, and suffer with them if there is only suffering—there is bravery in suffering and only cowards give in. Let your conscience awake, and let these words move your heart. Let my dying cry not be lost in the jingle of your gold, and amidst all your riches, remember your mother! This letter will reach you about our great Day of Atonement when all who are good in Jewry will go to the synagogue. Go with them, and pray for my soul; say *Kaddish* for me, and make amends for your living self. Turn and go to the synagogue; to your people—say *Kaddish*—your mother . . .

The sentences here were broken and snapped, just as the life-thread of the writer was snapped. A few strokes of the pen followed underneath; a mother's dying attempt to pen her signature to her last letter to her son—and the son deciphered it, his mother's name.

He flung his arms forward on the table and buried his head between them; he uttered a frenzied cry of affliction and a storm of tears filled his eyes, which had not wept for many a year.

He could see his mother's dead, shrunken face shaping itself out of the scrawled lines. He kissed the letter passionately, devotedly, as he would have kissed his mother's cheeks, had they been near his lips.

Her words had, indeed, moved his heart. "Remain a Jew!" The Jewish part, which, like the gold in his mines, had been always hidden, deep, deep within him, at last flared up. Hardened as he had become through the years, he felt himself softening, melting under the weight of grief and regret, through the warmth of a Jewish consciousness and a mother's tenderness. He felt himself being transformed from an unfeeling automaton into an emotional, passionate human being, into the father of his children, into the son of his mother.

After a while he lifted up his head and dried his tears. He

looked different. His material worries were subdued by spiritual peace, upon his face smiled the consolation of repentance, and in his eyes shone the light of good resolution. He went back to his room, and from a lower drawer, from among many useless odds and ends, he took out an old faded velvet bag containing his prayer book and shawl. He put it under his arm and walked to where his mother implored him to go, to where his own conscience now moved him to go—to his people, to his synagogue.[10]

THE SEARCH

SHOLOM ALEICHEM

"Now, listen to *me*," said a man with round bovine eyes, who had been sitting in a corner by the window, smoking and taking in stories of thefts, holdups, and expropriations. "I'll tell you a good one, also about a theft, which happened in my town, in the synagogue of all places, and on Yom Kippur too! You'll like it.

"Our Kasrielevky—that's where I come from—is a small town and a poor one. We have no thieves and no stealing, for there is nobody to steal from and nothing to steal. And aside from all that, a Jew just isn't a thief. I mean to say, even if a Jew is a thief, he is not the kind of thief who sneaks in through a window or goes at you with a knife. He may twist you and turn you, outtalk you and outsmart you—granted; but he won't crawl into your pockets, he won't be caught red-handed and led down the street in disgrace. That may happen to a thieving Ivan but not to a Jew. Imagine, then, someone stealing in Kasrielevky, and quite a bit of money too—eighteen hundred rubles at one stroke!

"One day a stranger arrived in our town, a Jew, some sort of contractor from Lithuania. He appeared on the evening of Yom Kippur, just before the time for prayer. He left his bundle at the inn and hurried out to look for a place to pray and found the old synagogue. He arrived in time to attend the evening prayer and ran into the trustees with their collection box.

" 'Sholom aleichem!' 'Aleichem sholom!' 'Where are you from?' 'From Lithuania.' 'And what's your name?' 'What difference does that make to your grandmother?' 'Well, after all, you've come to our synagogue!' 'Where else do you want me to go?' 'You surely want to pray here?' 'Have I any choice?' 'Then put something in the box.' 'Of course. Did you think I was going to pray for nothing?'

"Our stranger took three silver rubles out of his pocket and put them in the box. Then he put a ruble in the cantor's plate, gave a ruble for the rabbi, another for the school, and threw half a ruble into the poor box; in addition, he handed out coins to the beggars standing at the door—we have so many poor people in our town, God bless them, that if you really went at it you could distribute Rothschild's fortune among them.

"When we saw the kind of stranger he was we gave him a place right at the east wall. You will ask how one could be found for him when all the places were occupied. Some question! Where does one find a place at a celebration—a wedding, say, or a circumcision feast—after all the guests have been seated at the table and suddenly there is a commotion—the rich guest has arrived! Well, all the others squeeze together until a place is made for the rich man. Jews have a habit of squeezing— when no one else squeezes us, we squeeze one another."

The round-eyed man paused for a moment, looked at the audience to see what impression his quip had made, and resumed his tale.

"In short, the stranger occupied a place of honor. He asked the *shammash* for a prayer stand and, donning his cloak and prayer shawl, began to pray. Bending over his stand, he prayed and prayed, always on his feet, never sitting down, let alone lying down. He did not leave his stand for a minute, that Litvak, except when the Eighteen Blessings were recited and everyone had to face the ark, and during the kneeling period. To stand on one's feet on a day of fasting without ever sitting down— only a Litvak can do that.

"After the *shofar* was blown for the last time, and Haim-Hune the teacher, who always conducted the first night prayer after the holiday, began to chant '*Ha-ma-a-riv a-a-arovim*,' we suddenly heard a cry, 'Help, help, help!' We looked around and saw the stranger lying on the floor in a faint. We poured water on him to bring him to, but he fainted again.

"What happened? A fine thing! He had on him—the Litvak, that is—eighteen hundred rubles; and he had been afraid, so he said, to leave his money at the inn. You think it's a trifle, eighteen hundred rubles? To whom could he entrust such a sum in a strange town? Nor did it seem right to keep it in his pocket on Yom Kippur. So, after thinking the matter over, he decided quietly to slip the money into his stand—yes, a Litvak is quite capable of such a thing! Now do you understand why he did not leave his stand for a minute? Someone had apparently snatched his money during the Eighteen Blessings or one of the kneeling periods.

"In short, he screamed, he wept, he lamented—what would he do now without the money? It was, he said, someone else's, not his, he was only an employee in some office, a poor man, burdened with many children. All he could do now, he said, was to jump into the river or hang himself right here in the synagogue in front of everybody.

"On hearing such talk the whole congregation stood paralyzed, forgetting that they had been fasting for twenty-four hours and were about to go home to eat. It was a disgrace before a stranger, a shameful thing to witness. Eighteen hundred rubles stolen, and where? In a place of worship, in the old synagogue of Kasrielevky! And when? On Yom Kippur! Such a thing was unheard of.

" 'Shammash, lock the door!' our rabbi ordered. We have our rabbi—his name is Reb Yosefel—a true and pious Jew, not over-subtle but a kindly soul, a man without gall, and sometimes he had brilliant ideas, such as wouldn't occur even to a man with eighteen heads! When the door was locked the rabbi addressed the congregation. His face was white as the wall, his hands were trembling and his eyes burning.

" 'Listen carefully, my friends,' he said. 'This is an ugly business, an outrage, unheard of since the creation of the world, that in our town, in Kasrielevky, there should be such an offender, such a renegade from Israel, who would have the

impudence to take from a stranger, from a poor man, a sup-
porter of a family, such a large sum of money. And when? On
a holy day, Yom Kippur, and perhaps even during the closing
prayer! Such a thing has been truly unheard of since the
creation of the world! I can't believe such a thing is possible, it
just can't be! Nevertheless—who can tell?—some wretched man
was perhaps tempted by this money, particularly since it
amounted to such a fortune. The temptation, God have mercy
on us, was great enough. So if it was decreed that one of us
succumb to the temptation—if one of us has had the misfortune
to commit such a sin on a day like this—we must investigate
the matter, get to the bottom of it. Heaven and earth have sworn
that truth must come to the top like oil on water, so we must
search each other, go through each other's garments, shake out
the pockets of everyone here—from the most respectable member of the congregation to the *shammash*, sparing no one. Begin
with me: here, my friends, go through my pockets!'

"Thus spoke our rabbi, Reb Yosefel, and he was the first to
open his caftan and turn all his pockets inside out. After him,
all the members of the congregation loosened their girdles and
turned out their pockets, and each of them in turn was searched,
and felt all over, and shaken out. But when they came to Laizer
Yosl he turned all colors and began to argue. The stranger, he
said, was a swindler; the whole thing was a Litvak's trick, no
one had stolen any money from him. 'Can't you see,' he said,
'that the whole thing is a lie, a fraud?'

"The congregation broke out in loud protests. 'What do you
mean?' they said. 'Respectable citizens have submitted to a
search—why should you be excepted?' The whole crowd clamored, 'Search him, search him!'

"Laizer Yosl saw that things were going badly for him, and he
began to plead with tears in his eyes, begging that he be spared.
He swore by every oath: may he be as pure of all evil as he was
innocent of stealing. And on what grounds was he to be spared?
He couldn't bear the disgrace of being searched, he said, and
implored the others to have pity on his youth, not to subject
him to such an indignity. Do anything you want, he said, but

do not go through my pockets. How do you like such a scoundrel? Do you think anyone listened to him?

"But wait a minute, I have forgotten to tell you who this Laizer Yosl was. He was not a native of Kasrielevky; he came from the devil knows where to marry a Kasrielevky girl. Her father, the rich man of our town, had unearthed him somewhere and bragged that he had found a rare gem, a real genius, for his daughter, a man who knew by rote a thousand pages of the Talmud, who was an expert in Scriptures, a Hebraist, and a mathematician who could handle fractions and algebra, and who wielded the pen like nobody's business—in short, a man with all seventeen talents. When his father-in-law brought him, everyone went to look at this gem, to see what kind of rare bargain the rich man had acquired. Well, if you just looked at him he was nothing special, a young man like many others, fairly good-looking, only the nose a little too long, and a pair of eyes like two glowing coals, and a mouth with a sharp tongue in it. He was examined; they made him explain a page of the Talmud, a chapter from the Bible, a passage from Rambam, this and that, and he passed the test with flying colors—the dog was at home everywhere, he knew all the answers! Reb Yosefel himself said that he could be a rabbi in any Jewish community —not to mention his vast knowledge of worldly things. Just to give you an idea, there is in our town a subtle scholar, Zeidel Reb Shaye's son, a crazy fellow, and he doesn't even compare with Laizer Yosl. Moreover no one in the world could equal him as a chess player. Talk about cleverness!

"Needless to say, the whole town envied the rich man such a genius, although people said that the gem was not without flaws. To begin with, he was criticized for being too clever (and what there's too much of isn't good), and too modest, too familiar with everyone, mingling too easily with the smallest among the smallest, whether it be a boy or a girl or even a married woman. Then he was disliked because of the way he walked around, always absorbed in thought. He would come to the synagogue after everyone else, put on his prayer shawl, and page the *Well of Life* or *Ibn Ezra*, with his skullcap on askew—never saying a word of prayer. No one ever saw him doing anything wrong; nevertheless it was whispered that he was not a pious man— after all, no one can have all the virtues!

"And so when his turn came to be searched his refusal was at once interpreted as a sign that he had the money on him. 'Make me swear an oath on the Bible,' he said. 'Cut me, chop me to pieces, roast me, burn me alive, anything, but don't go through my pockets!'

"At this point our Rabbi Yosefel, though the gentlest of men, lost his temper and began to scold. 'You so-and-so,' he cried, 'you deserve I don't know what! What do you think you are? You see what all these men have gone through—all of them have accepted the indignity of a search, and you want to be an exception! One of the two—either confess and give back the money, or show your pockets! Are you playing games with an entire Jewish community? I don't know what we'll do to you!'

"In short, they took this nice young man, laid him on the floor by sheer force, and began to feel him all over and shake out his pockets. And when they shook out—guess what?— chicken bones and a dozen plum pits; everything was still fresh, the bones had recently been gnawed, and the pits were moist. Can you imagine what a pretty sight it was, all this treasure shaken out of our genius's pockets? You can picture for yourself the look on their faces, he and his father-in-law, the rich man, and our poor rabbi too. Our Reb Yosefel turned away in shame; he could look no one in the face. And later, when the worshipers were on their way home to eat after the fast, they did not stop talking about the treasure they had discovered in the young man's pockets, and they shook with laughter. Only Reb Yosefel walked alone, with bowed head, unable to look anyone in the eyes, as though the remains of food had been shaken out of his own pockets."

The narrator stopped and resumed his smoking. The story was over.

"And what about the money?" we all asked in one voice.

"What money?" the man said, with an uncomprehending look as he blew out the smoke.

"What do you mean, what money? The eighteen hundred—"

"O-o-o-oh," he drawled. "The eighteen hundred? Vanished without a trace."

"Vanished?"

"Without a t-r-a-c-e."

Translated by Norbert Guterman[11]

XV

PRE-YOM KIPPUR FEASTING

The festive pre-Yom Kippur meal goes back many centuries. In Galilee and Babylonia elaborate banquets were held on the eve of the Day of Atonement.[1] The Talmud states: "If a man eats and drinks on the ninth [day of Tishri], Scripture considers it as if he fasted on both the ninth and tenth day [Yom Kippur]."[2] The feasting symbolizes rejoicing and spiritual exaltation evoked by the imminent approach of the day on which atonement is attained. The heart of the Jew glories in the knowledge that the following day will provide an opportunity for genuine repentance, thereby leading to self-regeneration and to removing whatever chasm may intervene between him and his Maker. In light of this anticipated spiritual boon that will be showered upon him on Yom Kippur, eating and drinking on the eve of its arrival is considered a *mitzvah*.[3]

There is yet another consideration. On all other festivals it is customary to partake of a *seudat mitzvah* (a meal in fulfillment of a commandment). But Yom Kippur, being a fast day, does not come within the purview of this practice; therefore the festive meal was introduced on the eve of the Day of Atonement. Indubitably, humanitarian considerations also prompted the institution of special meals. The welfare of the individual was always a precious component in Jewish law; he must be provided with vitality to endure the fast and to concentrate on the day-long prayers and communion with God. In their zeal to approach the Day of Awe adequately prepared, Persian Jews established the custom of eating seven meals before the eve of Yom Kippur.[4]

It is regarded as meritorious to offer hospitality to the poor when preparing for the Day of Atonement. In the days of the Temple in Jerusalem the sacrifice on the altar made atonement for man's sins; at present "a man's table makes atonement for him," according to the Talmud.[5] Rashi interprets "table" as "hospitality," implying that one should invite the needy to partake of the pre-Yom Kippur meal.

In Eastern Europe there prevailed a custom that, after the morning services on the eve of the Day of Atonement, the sexton or the *gabbai* of the synagogue would distribute candy or slices of honey cake to all the worshipers. Before eating each would say, "If, God forbid, it is the celestial decree that in the coming year I will be condemned to accept charity, may I fulfill the decree with this morsel I took from you."[6]

The *hallot* for the eve of Yom Kippur are usually round and braided.[7] In Lithuania they were decorated with dough in the shape of a ladder, as a metaphorical allusion to the *piyyut* "May our entreaty rise to Thee . . ." recited on the night of Yom Kippur. *Hallot* were also baked in the shape of wings, in keeping with the tradition that on the Day of Atonement Jews are considered pure as angels. A piece of *hallah* dipped in honey is eaten when the benediction on bread is recited.

The favorite dish on this day is *kreplach*, dough filled with meat. The meat symbolizes inflexible justice; the soft dough which covers it denotes compassion. Like the *hallot*, the *kreplach* are a metaphorical allusion, suggesting that the attribute of God's strict justice (*midat ha-din*) will be mellowed on the

19. *Kapparot*. Ministry for Foreign Affairs, State of Israel.

side of mercy (*midat ha-rahamim*). *Kreplach* are eaten three times a year: Yom Kippur eve, Hoshanna Rabbah, and Purim—days reckoned as festivals with regard to eating and drinking, but not as regards forbidding work.

The main dish of the meal is generally poultry. In communities like those in North Africa, chicken was "such a luxury that it was almost never eaten by any but the very rich except once a year at the last meal before the annual fast day of Yom Kippur."[8] A noted Jewish world traveler has stated that poultry and rice are "fasting foods all the world over."[9]

Fish and spicy foods which may create thirst are generally avoided.

After the final meal a white cloth is spread over the dining table, on which a Bible, a *siddur*, and other sacred books are placed in lieu of the traditional Sabbath and festival loaves. The books are covered with a cloth until the break-the-fast meal as symbolic testimony that this holy day is being honored, not with food and drink, but with study and prayer. A lamp in memory of departed members of the family is lit and placed on the table.

One is expected to eat and rejoice on the night following Yom Kippur, which is considered somewhat of a festival.[10] According to the Midrash, at the conclusion of the long day of fasting a heavenly voice proclaims:

> Go thy way, eat thy bread with joy
> And drink thy wine with a merry heart;
> For God hath already accepted thy works.[11]

In the Sephardic Day of Atonement rite, this verse from Ecclesiastes is quoted immediately following the *shofar* blast which concludes the *Neilah* service.

XVI

YOM KIPPUR MISCELLANY

NAMES

Yom ha-Kippurim (literally, "Day of Atonements") is the biblical version (Leviticus 23.27) of the vernacular singular term *Yom Kippur*. The Bible also denominates this day *Shabbat Shabbaton*—"Sabbath of solemn rest" (Leviticus 16.31).

The Talmud refers to the Day of Atonement as *Yoma*, "the day," the name also applied to the tractate dealing with this holy day. In Babylon it was called *Yoma Rabbah*, "Great Day,"[1] while in Palestine it was designated *Tzoma Rabbah*, "Great Fast."[2]

Yom ha-Asor—"The Tenth Day"—is another name by which Yom Kippur was known.[3]

More recently Yom Kippur became known as the White Fast, in contradistinction to Tishah be-Av which is called the Black Fast, as many tragic events in Jewish history occurred on this day. Furthermore, white is the symbol of purity, in accordance with the prophecy: "Though your sins be as scarlet, they shall be as white as snow" (Isaiah 1.18). Too, on Yom Kippur a white robe (*kittel*) is worn, the synagogue ark is draped in white, and the Torah scrolls are adorned with white mantles.

Sephardic Jews designated this day merely as "*Kippur*." The Palestinian Arabs used the odd appellation "Festival of Chickens," for on the days preceding Yom Kippur they sold white chickens to the Jews for the *Kapparot* ceremony.[4]

TWO DAYS OF YOM KIPPUR

The Jewish calendar arrangement provides that the Day of Atonement, which is the *Shabbat Shabbaton* (Sabbath of solemn rest), can never fall on a Friday or a Sunday, to avoid the hardships that would be entailed in the preparation of food for two consecutive Sabbaths. Nevertheless, some God-fearing Jews in the Middle Ages observed Yom Kippur for two consecutive days, fasting on both and repeating the liturgy on the second. It is said that the Kabbalah of Isaac Luria introduced a second Day of Atonement,[5] but the Talmud records an earlier instance of such observance. Rabba, uncertain as to the exact day fixed by the court in Jerusalem, fasted for two days.[6] Most of the rabbis opposed this practice primarily because of the burdens and pressures it would impose and also because it would raise these questions of law: If the day after Yom Kippur is also Yom Kippur, how can the laws pertaining to eating on the previous day be observed? Is one obligated to don phylacteries on the second Yom Kippur? What prayers should be recited? Because of these difficulties the second day of Yom Kippur has long since been abolished.[7]

THE MINOR YOM KIPPUR

In addition to the regular Day of Atonement, some devout Jews observe the day preceding every new month (*Rosh Hodesh*) as a minor Day of Atonement (*Yom Kippur Katan*), with fasting, repentance, and penitential prayers. The fasting is not obligatory, and the general character of the day is far less stringent than that of Yom Kippur. This monthly practice is said to have been instituted by Kabbalists of Safed in the sixteenth century. Rabbi Isaiah Horowitz (c. 1555–1630), referring to *Yom Kippur Katan*, said: "Following the custom of the very pious, one must repent and make restitution in monetary and in personal acts, in order that he may enter the new month as pure as a newborn infant."[8]

PARALLELS IN ISLAM

The Day of Atonement was a model for the Muslim *Ashurah* (tenth) day of fasting, originally instituted by Mohammed to coincide with the tenth day of Tishri. In the belief that Jews fasted on Yom Kippur to commemorate their victory over Pharaoh, Mohammed instituted this holy day to mark his own victories when he entered Medina.

According to Jewish tradition, the second tablets of the Law were given to Moses on Yom Kippur; the Muslim belief was that the Koran was sent from heaven on the *Ashurah* fast. Muslims considered *Ashurah* as a day of atonement and forgiveness of sins, stressing repentance as the means for achieving these ends. While all other Muslim fast days were observed from dawn to sunset, Mohammed decreed that *Ashurah* should extend from sunset to sunset. Later he abolished the fast of *Ashurah* and replaced it by fasting during the month of Ramadan.[9]

"NEXT YEAR IN JERUSALEM"

According to the Talmud[10] there are divergent opinions concerning the period of redemption. One maintains that inasmuch as the children of Israel were redeemed from Egypt in Nisan, they will be delivered in the future in the same month. Another opinion holds that because their slavery ceased in Tishri, Israel's future redemption will take place in that month. Accordingly, both the Passover *seder* and the Yom Kippur services are concluded with the prayer: "Next year in Jerusalem!"

THE *SHOFAR* AT THE WESTERN WALL

The Western Wall of the Temple in Jerusalem was the object of friction between Arabs and Jews for many years. In 1929, as a gesture of appeasement to the Arabs, the British Mandatory government forbade the sounding of the *shofar* at the Western Wall at the conclusion of Yom Kippur, but the Jewish underground decided to ignore this prohibition.

As the *Neilah* service was being concluded with the cantor chanting the *Avinu Malkenu*, he interpolated the Hebrew verse, "Our Father, our King, we have the *shofar*; draw a circle around us." There was a momentary deep hush when suddenly, from one end of the wall, a tremulous but clear *shofar* sound clarioned from a child's voice. As the British police converged upon the child, a *tekiah gedolah* reverberated from the other end of the wall. Whereupon the assembled worshipers united in a spontaneous cry "Next year in Jerusalem rebuilt," and then burst out in singing *Hatikvah*.[11]

The following year Moshe Segal, a watchman in the Galil, came to spend Yom Kippur in Jerusalem and to pray at the Western Wall. When the fast day ended he blew a *shofar* and was immediately arrested by the British. They held him at the police station without food until midnight, when he was released. Only then did he learn how his release was effected. The late chief rabbi of Palestine, Abraham Isaac Kook, when informed that Segal was arrested, phoned the secretary of the British administration and told him, "I have fasted all day but I will not eat until you will free the man who blew the *shofar*." "But the man violated a government order," the secretary replied. To which Rabbi Kook retorted, "He fulfilled a religious commandment." The rabbi's moral suasion prevailed, and the secretary promised to release Segal.[12]

Year after year, despite the arrest of Jews, many of whom were disciples of Segal, ways were devised to outwit the British police and to conclude Yom Kippur according to tradition. When the Old City of Jerusalem became part of Jordan in 1948, Jews ascended Mount Zion adjacent to the Old City, and facing the Western Wall, they sounded the *shofar* to conclude the ritual of the holiest day of the year.[13]

On June 7, 1967, when the Israel Defense Forces recaptured the Old City of Jerusalem and assembled at the Western Wall, the *shofar* was again sounded to proclaim the victory and to reassert the right of the Jews to worship in freedom at their most sacred site. At the end of Yom Kippur that year Moshe Segal, at the request of Minister Menahem Beigin, was given the distinction of being the first to sound the *shofar*.[14]

YOM KIPPUR LIKENED TO WEDDING DAY

There is a talmudic dictum that "when a man marries his sins are forgiven."[15] Hence a wedding day is equated with Yom Kippur. As Yom Kippur atones for sins, so matrimony is a bridge to forgiveness and atonement. To emphasize the nexus between Yom Kippur and their wedding day, the bridegroom and bride fast on that day. In the afternoon service, the bridegroom recites the *Viddui*, the solemn Yom Kippur Confession. As it is customary to wear white on the Day of Atonement as a symbol of purity, so it is traditional for the bride to wear a white gown and for the bridegroom to be clad in a *kittel* (white robe).[16]

CANDLES FOR YOM KIPPUR

In addition to the lighting of festival candles by the housewife before going to the synagogue on *Kol Nidre* evening, the custom of kindling many candles in the house of worship originated in the Middle Ages. All the householders would enter the synagogue bearing aloft lighted candles as they sang in unison the verse "Light is sown for the righteous and gladness for the upright in heart" (Psalms 97.11). This led to the practice of chanting this passage three times before reciting *Kol Nidre*. The custom may have arisen from the necessity to provide sufficient light for the pious Jews who spent the night in prayer and study in the synagogue. Furthermore, since the fast day could not be honored with festive meals, other means were sought to give it recognition, namely, candle-lighting. This was in consonance with the prophet's injunction, "Glorify the Lord with lights" (Isaiah 24.15). Others believed that light was an augury of a man's fate in the new year. Rabbi Ami in the Talmud stated, "When one desires to know whether or not he will survive the coming year, let him take a burning lamp during the ten days from Rosh Hashanah through Yom Kippur and place it in a house where there is no draft. If the flame continues to rise, he will know that he will survive the year."[17]

In this same period the custom originated to light a "soul candle" in memory of one's departed parents and thereby atone for them. In the Bible the glowing candle is equated with man's soul: "The spirit of man is the lamp of the Lord, searching all the inward parts" (Proverbs 20.27).

In Poland the "soul candles" were hand made by pious women. After visiting the cemetery to measure the graves of their parents and relatives with cords while reciting prayers and supplications, they used each cord for the wick of a candle.[18]

On the day before Yom Kippur Jews in Kurdistan brought to the synagogue a large wax candle called "the blessed candle"; it was approximately two yards in length. In the synagogue in Seneh every family bereft of a close relative in recent years kindles a thick, wax candle about a yard long, until the house of worship is suffused with a plethora of light from these memorial lamps. In Sacho the honor of carrying the candle, decorated with handkerchiefs and a wreath of roses, is auctioned at the *gabbai's* home, where refreshments are first served. The sale is conducted amid much gaiety and revelry. As the candle is borne to the house of prayer, the women shower the bearer with wheat and raisins. The candle is extinguished on the day after Yom Kippur and is used for the Sabbath *Havdalah* ceremony throughout the ensuing year.[19]

In some East European synagogues, the *shammashim* (beadles) would collect the wax that remained of the candles to make new ones to be used as *shammashim* (auxiliary candles) for kindling the Hanukkah lamps and as the lights employed in the search for leaven prior to Passover.

FORTY DAYS AND NIGHTS OF SILENCE

Rabbi Israel Salanter, founder of the *Musar* (moralist) movement in Lithuania, devoted the forty-day period from the first of Elul to Yom Kippur to contemplation and meditations in solitude and complete silence. His example of pious preparation for the High Holy Days was emulated by many of the early musarists.[20]

THE NUMBER TEN

The number ten symbolizes perfect holiness as the aim on the most sacred day of the year. The Ten Days of Repentance are concluded on the tenth of Tishri (Yom Kippur). The *Viddui* (Confession of Sins) is recited ten times on the Day of Atonement to coincide with the tradition that the Temple high priest pronounced the name of God ten times when he invoked divine pardon on Yom Kippur.[21] Yom Kippur also recalls the Ten Commandments, which serve as advocates before the Supreme Judge in behalf of the children of Israel, who accepted them with love after the nations of the world refused them.[22]

A DECEPTIVE APPEARANCE

During the seventeenth century the Jews in Mexico lived in fear of the inquisitors and observed Jewish traditions secretly, while outwardly appearing to practice Catholicism. There is a record of at least two Jews who would stroll on Yom Kippur in the Almeda, the public park in Mexico City, with toothpicks in their mouths to give the appearance of having eaten. Apparently the advent of Yom Kippur was known at least to some non-Jews.[23]

AN EMERGENCY DECREE

It was reported that Rabbi Samson Raphael Hirsch, the famous spiritual leader of German Orthodox Jewry, ruled while he was the rabbi in Oldenburg that *Kol Nidre* was not to be recited in the synagogue. He had learned that members of his congregation were not keeping their vows, relying on *Kol Nidre* to absolve them. Hence he did not hesitate to issue this *horaat shaah* (emergency decree) to halt the violation of the Torah's law of honesty.[24]

AN ORDER TO EAT

Rabbi Shlomoh Goren, chief of chaplains of the Israel Defense Forces, ordered that during a battle on Yom Kippur a soldier engaged in fighting is obligated to eat if he feels his military effectiveness is declining, so as not to jeopardize the outcome of the battle.[25]

NUT GAMES

In the Middle Ages it was customary for children to play with nuts on Yom Kippur afternoon.[26] This pastime continued for some time in Germany; young girls would play a variety of nut games and eat the winnings after nightfall.[27]

YOM KIPPUR BALLS

In 1886 a small group of Jewish radicals, atheists, and so-called anarchists on the Lower East Side of New York organized the Pioneers of Freedom, a club dedicated to the propagation of antireligious ideas. They distributed parodies of penitential prayers mocking the traditions of the sacred Day of Atonement.

One such Yiddish parody of *Tefilah Zakah*, the meditation for the eve of Yom Kippur, derided some of the fundamental beliefs of Judaism. These parodies provoked a furor in the Jewish community. Climaxing their efforts were the Yom Kippur Balls held on *Kol Nidre* evening.

In 1889 circulars were distributed inviting Jewish workingmen to spend *Kol Nidre* evening at the Clarendon Hall on Thirteenth Street. On the evening of the scheduled event the owner of the hall, in consequence of political pressure put on him, refused to open the doors. A near-riot ensued until the police dispersed the crowds.

The ticket of admission to this affair in 1890 read in part: "Grand Yom Zom Kippur Ball with theater. Arranged with the consent of all new rabbis of liberty. . . . The *Kol Nidre* will be offered by John Most. Music, dancing, buffet, Marseillaise, and other hymns against Satan."[28]

Yom Kippur Balls were not confined to New York. Philadelphia sponsors created such a disturbance that some were arrested and sentenced to thirty days in prison for disturbing the peace.[29] The Jubilee Street Club in the East End of London was also the scene of such frenetic affairs conducted by antireligious Jews.[30]

The anarchists determined to scandalize Orthodox Jews, particularly on Yom Kippur. One year they advertised on the eve of the Day of Atonement that a certain restaurant on Division Street in New York's Lower East Side would remain open on the following day to feed all freethinkers. Many outraged Jews came to protest and the ensuing battle between traditional Jews and the atheists brought out the police reserves.[31]

Not only Orthodox Jews but even the German uptown Jews were indignant at this gross public desecration of Jewish tradition.

A YOM KIPPUR BLOOD LIBEL IN NEW YORK

On September 22, 1928, in Massena, a small town in northern New York State, Barbara Griffith, a four-year-old girl, was reported missing. A rumor spread through the town that Jews had murdered the child in order to use her blood at the Day of Atonement services commencing the following evening. As the small congregation was preparing to assemble in their synagogue for the *Kol Nidre* service, a mob gathered around the local police station. Mayor Gilbert W. Hawes dispatched Cpl. H. M. McCann of the state police to bring Rabbi Berel Brenglass to police headquarters, where he was ruthlessly interrogated: "Is tomorrow a big holiday, a fast day?" "Can you give any information as to whether your people in the old country offer human sacrifice?" "Was there a time when the Jewish people used human blood?"

Outraged by the vicious slander, the rabbi indignantly denied the charges and explained carefully that not only the use of human blood but even of animal blood is forbidden by Jewish law.

Shortly thereafter Barbara, who had fallen asleep in the nearby woods, was found. Following the intervention of national Jewish agencies and Gov. Alfred E. Smith, the mayor and the state trooper made public apologies. Thus another savage blood libel—in 1928, in New York—was exposed as a cruel anti-Semitic canard.[32]

YOM KIPPUR IN THE *KIBBUTZ*

While the observance of Yom Kippur in the secular *kibbutzim* of Israel is still the subject of debate and it has not yet attained the same degree of acceptance as have other Jewish holidays, a goodly number of these collective settlements have established various patterns for marking this day.[33] This developing trend represents a radical departure from the time, not long ago, when Yom Kippur was officially ignored and not observed in any manner in most of these *kibbutzim*.[34]

In recent years *kibbutz* members, whatever their motivation may be, have been searching for a rationale to legitimize Yom Kippur within the framework of their ideology. A member of

Maoz Hayyim emphasized that while Yom Kippur—the holiest day of the year among the Jewish people—bears a religious stamp, it is unique in that it strengthens universal Jewish solidarity among all the scattered ones of Israel, including the believing Jew, the secularist, and the assimilationist. Pointing out that the day has been fixed in the Jewish consciousness for thousands of years and even in the present it still possesses a force that unites Jewry in their dispersion, he urged that it be infused with new content based on the ancient Yom Kippur symbols. He also commented that this day is set apart not only for a reckoning between man and God but also for a reconciliation between man and his fellow man, and for self-scrutiny—the latter concepts being acceptable to secularists.[35] A similar thought was expressed by a *kibbutz* member of Gaash that the "Yom Kippur Jew" is not a hypocrite but rather an individual in whom there still pulsates a Jewish heart.[36]

More than twenty years ago Nahum Benari urged the *kibbutz* movement to strive to capture some of the spirit of Yom Kippur —its great ideals of social morality. He proposed the preparation of a *mahzor*—"not necessarily with the prayers of Kalir"—taking from the rich Hebrew literature of all generations suitable selections for reading and singing calculated to elevate the community to an ennobling level.[37] The proposal to edit a *mahzor* found acceptance in a number of *kibbutzim* in recent years. Small booklets for Yom Kippur services, generally conducted on *Kol Nidre* evening, have been produced containing the following: selections from the traditional liturgy (*Kol Nidre, Yaaleh, Avinu Malkenu, Hashivenu, Uv-Khen Ten Pah-dekha*, among other prayers) and commentaries on them; also readings from the Bible, the Talmud, hasidic tales, the *haftarah* for Yom Kippur morning, a story by S. Y. Agnon, the legend of Rabbi Amnon, poetry from the *Selihot* and from modern Hebrew poets, and community singing (*Ve-Taher Libenu, Ani Maamin, Yibane ha-Mikdash*). Provision is also made for playing one or more recordings, such as *Kol Nidre* by Max Bruch or Jan Peerce, *Kaddish* by Maurice Ravel, *The Baal Shem Suite* by Ernest Bloch, *Yaaleh* by Yossele Rosenblatt, *Unetanneh Tokef* or *Hinneh ka-Homer* by Leib Glantz. Discourses or discussions may take place either at the *Kol Nidre* service or the following day on subjects like repentance, soul-searching, the relationship between man and man, personal relations in the *kibbutz*, the crisis in modern society, the deficiency of secular humanism, and the *kibbutz* as a way of life.

Memorial services for parents, members of the *kibbutz*, and war casualties has become an established practice in a goodly number of settlements, with a public roll call of the departed as part of the service. The dining hall is set up with a wreath of white flowers arranged on a black background and a memorial lamp to create the appropriate mood. A visit may also be made to the local cemetery.

Whether or not to fast on Yom Kippur has been a frequent subject of acrimonious debate in the secular collective settlements. Some members who fasted were called hypocrites, while others maintained that fasting on Yom Kippur is an act of solidarity with the Jewish masses throughout the world. In one *kibbutz* a proposal to advance the evening meal so as to avoid eating at *Kol Nidre* time was defeated by a majority vote of the members on the grounds that it would be considered religious coercion. Nevertheless, thirty members did fast, and other *kibbutzim* report that an increasing number are fasting on Yom Kippur.[38]

Several *kibbutzim* have introduced traditional, albeit abbreviated, prayer services on Yom Kippur with an increasing attendance from year to year. Kfar ha-Maccabi, a settlement near Haifa, decided to institute religious ceremonies when some of their members came to realize there is an inseparable link between the Jewish people and the Jewish religion. Among the practices they accepted were some for the Days of Awe. On Yom Kippur the majority of the adults fast, as do some of the youngsters. Congregational prayers are conducted on *Kol Nidre* evening, when the hall is filled to capacity, and on the following day for a smaller number of worshipers. For *Neilah* the hall is full again, especially with children waiting to hear the sound of the *shofar*. Most of the worshipers at the services, led by their own members, are of the older generation; the youth are nearly all absent.[39] When a synagogue was erected in Ain Harod in 1968 the new building was unable to accommodate all the *kibbutz* members who thronged to it on Yom Kippur. The children were brought to the services by their teachers; the young women who attended the *Yizkor* service wept bitter tears; many of the youth came to the *Neilah* service. More than 150 members of this "secular" settlement fasted throughout the day.[40]

There is ample evidence to suggest that the trend in non-religious *kibbutzim* is toward a more traditional observance of Yom Kippur. While as yet no set pattern has emerged, there are already certain elements that have been instituted which are recurring year after year and betoken a return to the Jewish sources of the most sacred day in the Jewish calendar.

XVII

CHILDREN'S STORIES
FOR YOM KIPPUR

HOW K'TONTON WAS FORGIVEN ON YOM KIPPUR

SADIE ROSE WEILERSTEIN

(Age level four to seven)

It all began the day after Rosh Hashanah. K'tonton [a little Jewish Tom Thumb] and his mother were in the kitchen. "Meow, meow!" came a faint sound.

A thin little gray and white kitten stood in the doorway. No one knew whose kitten it was or where it had come from. K'tonton didn't know. His father didn't know. His mother didn't know! It looked at K'tonton and mewed plaintively.

"It's hungry," said K'tonton. "Give it some milk, please, Mother."

But Mother shook her head.

"If I give it milk, it will be back every day."

Just the same, she filled a saucer with milk and set it down in the doorway.

Lap, lap, lap! In and out, in and out went the kitten's pink tongue until the saucer was empty.

Next day the kitten came back just as Mother had said it would. On the third day it came too. Mother was just making *teiglach*. She set a cup of honey at the edge of the table and fetched the kitten its dish of milk. Father called her at that moment.

In and out, in and out went the kitten's pink tongue. K'tonton watched her from his place on the table. Perhaps it made him hungry to see her lap the milk so greedily, but his eyes turned to a trickle of honey running down the side of the cup. He stuck his finger into the golden trickle and licked it off. M-m-m! It was good. And there was more honey around the rim of the cup. K'tonton leaned forward to reach it, when crash! Down went the cup from the table. The honey ran in a stream across the floor. The startled kitten sprang up and ran through the stream of honey to the door.

Just then in came Mother.

"Oh, oh!" she cried, "my honey! and it's all I have in the house. K'tonton, did you do this?"

K'tonton said nothing.

Mother's eyes fell on the kitten's sticky little footprints.

"It's that kitten," she said. "It must have sprung on the table and upset the cup. I told you I should never have begun giving it milk."

She looked sternly at K'tonton as if she suspected him of shielding the kitten.

K'tonton's heart beat wildly.

"Speak up, K'tonton," something was whispering inside him. "Tell Mother you upset the cup. Don't let the poor kitten be blamed."

But K'tonton did NOT speak up. He just stood there hanging his head.

Next day when the kitten came for its milk, Mother shooed it away.

"Scat!" she said. "Scat! I'll have no more mischief."

Oh, how guilty K'tonton felt! But by that time it was even harder to explain than the day before.

And now it was *Erev* Yom Kippur, the Day of Judgment, the Great White Fast, and K'tonton had this sin on his heart.

"Even the fish in the sea trembles on Yom Kippur," thought K'tonton. "How much more should I be trembling."

"I'll give all my pennies for charity," he said. "I won't keep even one. I'll fast all day and I'll pray. God will know I am sorry. No one could be more sorry than I."

He was thinking of the verse in the prayer book, "Charity, prayer, and penitence avert the evil decree."

But there was something else that the Torah taught, which K'tonton was trying hard to think about.

"If a man wrong his neighbor, let him go to his neighbor and make right the wrong. Otherwise Yom Kippur cannot atone for him."

K'tonton pushed the thought aside.

At *Minhah* he dropped a coin in every saucer that had been set out in the doorway of the synagogue; a coin for the land of Israel, one for the *yeshivot*, one for the aged, one for the orphans, one for the hungry.

"The kitten is hungry without its milk," the voice inside K'tonton whispered. "Maybe it's an orphan, too."

K'tonton put the thought aside.

Next morning he refused the milk which Mother offered him.

"I'm fasting," he said, and went off to the synagogue with his father.

All through the morning K'tonton stood on the arm of Father's bench and prayed with the congregation. He swayed, he joined in the responses; he beat his breast at each verse of the confession. When they came to the part, "For the sin which I have committed before Thee in wronging a neighbor," he beat it especially hard.

The morning service was over.

"Go home now and eat, K'tonton," Father said. "See, Sammy has eaten and he is older than you."

20. The meal before the Yom Kippur fast. Ministry for Foreign Affairs, State of Israel.

K'tonton shook his head.

The *Musaf* service was over. Mother sent down a message. "Send K'tonton home at once. The child will be ill if he fasts any longer. David will take him. I have left his dinner on the table."

"Come on, K'tonton," urged David.

K'tonton was tempted. He thought of the fresh *hallah*, of the little fish ball that Mother had made especially for him, of the good milk. But the thought of milk brought the kitten to mind. Because of his sin the poor kitten had no milk.

"Please, please, Father, let me fast. I must!" begged K'tonton.

He spoke so earnestly, Father had not the heart to insist.

On and on went the service. David had gone home to eat and had returned. K'tonton felt queer and shaky. So this was what it was like to be hungry! Maybe this was how the kitten felt.

Maybe it was standing in the doorway now all weak and empty. K'tonton could hear its plaintive mew. He raised his voice higher in prayer, but the voice inside whispered.

"Foolish K'tonton, what if you don't have your milk. That won't give the kitten ITS milk. Go and tell the truth to your mother."

K'tonton could stand it no longer. He clutched the fringe of Father's *tallit*.

"Father, Father," he called. "Take me to Mother. I must go to Mother at once."

Father looked down, startled: "K'tonton, little son, what is wrong? Are you sick?"

"No, no," said K'tonton and he sobbed out the whole story! . . .

In the shadows of the Yom Kippur afternoon K'tonton and David stood in the kitchen watching a thin gray and white kitten lapping up its milk. In and out, in and out went the little pink tongue.

"Kitten, will you forgive me?" asked K'tonton soberly.

"Mew, Mew!" said the kitten.

K'tonton knew he was forgiven.[1]

I'M SORRY

SADIE ROSE WEILERSTEIN

(Age level five to eight)

Rosh Hashanah was past and Yom Kippur was coming, but you wouldn't think it to look at Ruth and Debby. They went about like two little thunderclouds.

> Not a dimple.
> Not a smile!
> Pouts and frowns
> All the while.

They wouldn't play. They wouldn't even speak to each other. Now this was an astonishing thing, because usually Ruth and Debby chattered together all day long. You could hear them whispering when the lights were out and they lay next to each other in their little white beds. You could hear them chatter as soon as you opened your eyes in the morning.

> Chatter, chatter, chatter!
> Chatter, chatter, chatter!

"Where do you find so many things to talk about?" Mother would ask.

But now for two days Ruth and Debby hadn't said a word to each other, not a single word. It began when they were bouncing ball.

> One, two, three, O'Leary,
> Four, five, six, O'Leary,

sang Debby.

Bounce went the ball with each one, two, three. Over the ball went Debby's foot when she said "O'Leary."

"Seven, eight, nine, O'Leary," sang Debby. "Ten . . ." But that was as far as she got.

"You've missed," said Ruthie. "It's my turn. You put your foot over at the wrong place."

"I did not," said Debby.

"You did so."

"I didn't."

"You did."

"If you don't believe me, I'll do it over again," said Debby.

"Doing over isn't fair."

Ruthie reached out to grab the ball from Debby's hand. And then—I don't know how it happened or who began—but Ruth and Debby did something they had never done before. I'm almost ashamed to tell you about it. *They scratched each other like two naughty kittens.* After that Ruth wouldn't speak to Debby and Debby wouldn't speak to Ruth.

> They wouldn't laugh;
> They wouldn't play.
> They only sulked
> And frowned all day,

Now, it isn't pleasant to live with two little thunderclouds. "Where are your smiles?" Mother asked. "We've got to find your smiles."

So she stood Ruth and Debby opposite each other.

"Look straight into Debby'e eyes," she said to Ruthie.

"Look straight into Ruthie's eyes," she said to Debby.

Ruth and Debby looked into each other's eyes. They shut their lips tight. They kept their faces stiff and their eyes sober. "We won't smile," they thought. "We won't." But their eyes began to crinkle. Their lips opened. A little laugh came up, up into their throats. They COULDN'T keep it back. The first thing they knew they were laughing. After that Ruth and Debby found they weren't angry at each other anymore.

> The little storm clouds
> Blew away!
> A pleasant smile
> Had come to stay.

But still they didn't speak. They wanted to, but they didn't. Debby was waiting for Ruthie to speak first and Ruthie was waiting for Debby to speak first.

And the first thing they knew Yom Kippur was coming. It was coming that very night. Debby wished that she and Ruthie could be friends on Yom Kippur. Yom Kippur was such a solemn day. Mother and Daddy went to synagogue. They stayed all day long. They didn't eat a thing.

"What do you do in synagogue?" Debby asked Mother.

"We pray," said Mother, "and we think. Sometimes we do things that we wish we hadn't done. We think about those things on Yom Kippur. We tell God we are sorry."

"Do mothers say they are sorry?" asked Debby. She looked surprised.

"Of course," said Mother, "Fathers do too. All the grown-ups."

"Oh," said Ruth and Debby together.

The next minute—I don't know who began it or which spoke first—Ruth was saying, "I'm sorry, Debby," and Debby was saying, "I'm sorry, Ruth."

Then they kissed and made up. They felt MUCH better.

And they felt still better on Yom Kippur night, when it was time for Daddy and Mother to leave for synagogue. Mother was dressed all in white. The tall candles were shining. Daddy laid his hands on Ruth's and Debby's heads and blessed them. How glad they were that they were friends![2]

INNOCENT

LEVIN KIPNIS*

(Age level eight to eleven)

It was dusk on Yom Kippur eve. The family sat at the table eating the last meal before the fast of the Day of Atonement.

"Eat, children, eat," the mother urged her young ones. "You know, of course, that it is forbidden to touch food or drink between now and tomorrow night."

* All rights reserved by the author.

"I shall fast all day tomorrow as all grown-ups do," said Chanina, a boy with a pale face and gleaming eyes.

"You'll fast all day? You are only boasting," Chanina's younger sister, Esther, mocked him.

"Do not mock him, Esther," their father intervened. "Chanina is a big boy and can fast all day if he wishes."

To Chanina he said, "It is all right, my son . . . be brave and strong and grow up to be a man of courage."

Chanina was very happy. It is true, he had never fasted all day before. His mother had forbidden it because he was pale and weak. He had fasted only until noon last year because his father had scolded him and ordered him to eat. Now even his father had agreed to let him fast. Now it all depended upon him. . . . He would show everybody that he could do it.

The meal was over and Chanina picked up his *Mahzor* and started for the synagogue. He met his friends and at once announced his readiness to fast. His friends laughed at him.

"How can such a paleface, such a bag of bones fast a night and a day?" And his friend Menashe dared him, "Yes, you'll fast like you did last Yom Kippur. . . ."

Chanina was enraged by the insult, but he remembered the holiness of the day and forgave his friends. Seeing his father approaching, Chanina joined him and the two of them went into the synagogue.

Chanina prayed all evening that God would give him strength to fast. He awakened the following morning and ran to the synagogue. He was very happy because he felt neither hunger nor thirst.

Chanina went home during the reading of the Torah. His sister, Esther, met him with a chicken leg in one hand and a slice of *hallah* in the other. She had a mouthful of food and chewed it with great enjoyment. Chanina turned his head so as not to look at the food, but his sister jumped in front of him and tempted him. "Do you want some? . . . Do you?"

Chanina was angry but he controlled his feelings and only laughed. He ran out of the house.

Back in the synagogue he stood for the prayer of *Musaf*. He began to feel the pangs of hunger and thirst. His face became paler than usual. His father looked at him with pity, but Chanina assumed an air of bravado and attempted to pray in a loud, singing voice. However, he soon became aware that his voice was becoming weaker and sleep was overcoming him. He leaned his head on his fists and prayed in a whisper.

Meanwhile the ark had been opened, and the congregation began to sway like forest leaves in the wind. . . . "And the big *shofar* will be blown . . . and a still voice will be heard . . . and angels will hasten. . . ."

And a tiny angel appeared and grasped Chanina. In a matter of seconds, he too grew wings and both he and the angel soared upward.

It was quiet. Only the sound of their wings could be heard as they fanned the air. The blue sky came closer and closer to them. They passed from heaven to heaven until they reached the seventh and found themselves in front of the throne of God. A cherub hovered over the throne with the scales of justice in his hand.

Suddenly two bands of angels appeared. One band consisted of clean and white angels, the other of muddy and black angels. The speaker of the angels announced, "The clean and white angels represent the good deeds and the muddy and black angels represent the evil deeds. We will now weigh one against the other."

The black angels hurriedly crowded to one of the plates of the scales. The white angels ascended the second plate. Chanina stood terrified and trembling. Almost all the white angels were already on the scales, but the black angel side was heavier.

The last of the white angels mounted on his side. . . . The sides were evenly balanced. . . . Chanina's bad deeds matched his good ones. . . .

From somewhere came a voice, "Make way! Make way!" A tiny angel, clean and white, came flying to the scales, his eyes full of tenderness. All the angels looked at the newcomer with love and affection.

"Who is this lovely angel?" Chanina asked the speaker.

"He is the angel of forgiveness and atonement," explained the speaker. "He was created only yesterday for your good deed in forgiving your friend Menashe for his insult."

The tiny angel mounted the good deeds side of the scales, and that side went down at once to the feet of the throne of God.

"Innocent! Not guilty!" was the decision of the whole family of angels.

The chief angel grasped Chanina and both flew away. They flew until they came to a wonderful gate, the gate of the garden. The angel knocked on the gate with his fingers, "Open the gate!" . . .

And from the side of the ark in the synagogue the cantor's voice was heard, "Open the gate for us when the gate is locked!"

Chanina awoke and heard his father saying, "Wake up, my son, you have slept enough. It is time for *Neilah*."

Chanina looked through the window and saw the roofs of the houses gilded by the setting sun, their shadows becoming longer and longer. . . .

And the cantor sang, "And the day is gone. . . ."

Chanina felt reborn. His hunger was gone. He raised his voice in song together with the whole congregation.

Translated by Israel M. Goodelman[3]

A LITTLE HERO OF LONG AGO

MAMIE G. GAMORAN

(Age level eight to eleven)

This is a story of a little boy whose name was Pedro. He was a little Jewish boy. He lived in Spain about five hundred years ago.

Pedro's father was a rich Spanish Jew. His name was Don Pedro de Hernandez. His mother's name was Donna Luisa. They lived in a beautiful house. They had many servants. Don Pedro should have been happy. But he was not. He was very sad. All the Jews who lived in Spain at that time were sad, because it was very hard to be a Jew.

Many of them pretended not to be Jewish. Then they had to go to church instead of to the synagogue. They could not celebrate the Jewish holidays anymore. They could not send their children to Jewish schools. They even could not have Jewish teachers give them lessons.

Do you think that these Spanish Jews forgot that they were Jews? Do you think that they did not tell their children that they were Jews? Oh, no! They were Jews in secret. They were called Marranos.

This is what Don Pedro would do. In the evenings, the servants would go home. Donna Luisa would close the curtains. Don Pedro would lock the door.

Then little Pedro and his brother, Manuel, and his sister, Dolores, would gather around the big table in the dining room. Don Pedro would go to a secret closet. He would take out some Hebrew books. First, he would teach the children Hebrew. Then, he would teach them some prayers. After that, Donna Luisa in a low whisper would tell them some Bible stories.

Sometimes there would be a knock at the door. Quickly the books would be put away. The children would scamper to bed. Don Pedro would go to the door to let in the visitor. They had to be careful. They could not take any chances. It might be another Spanish Jew, who was their friend. But who could tell, it might be an enemy. He might have come to see if Don Pedro was still trying to be a Jew.

One evening Don Pedro called little Pedro to him.

"Pedro," he said, "if you will be a brave boy, you can help the Jews of our city who must say their prayers in secret."

"Tell me what to do, Father," said Pedro, "I am ready."

"Are you not afraid?" asked Don Pedro.

"No," said Pedro bravely, "I am not afraid."

"Tonight," said Don Pedro, "it is Yom Kippur eve. All the Jews are going to the secret synagogue. We want to sing *Kol Nidre*; we want to ask God to forgive us. All during the year we make promises that we cannot keep. We promise to give up our

Jewish religion, but we do not mean it. We have to say it, otherwise we will be put in prison or killed. Tonight we will say our Hebrew prayers. That will help us be good Jews, even if we are secret Jews."

"What shall I do?" asked Pedro.

"The synagogue is in a cellar. Over the cellar is a little window. You must play outside. Sometimes people pass by. Watch carefully. If some soldiers come by, drop some stones on the window. That will warn us. We can escape through another door. As soon as you drop the stones, go home as quickly as you can."

Don Pedro and little Pedro said good-bye to Donna Luisa. Donna Luisa kissed Pedro. "Be brave, my son," she whispered.

It was a long way to the secret synagogue. They walked fast. They did not talk on the way. At last they reached the cellar. Don Pedro showed little Pedro the window. It was covered with a dark cloth. The light could not shine through.

Don Pedro went down the steps to the synagogue. He knocked three times on the door. It opened a wee bit. He went inside.

Pedro stayed upstairs. He played with a ball. In his pocket were some small stones. He watched everyone who passed by. Sometimes a man would go down to the cellar. He would knock three times. "That is another Jew," thought Pedro. "I am watching for him."

An hour passed. Everything was quiet. The street was dark. Pedro began to get very cold. He began to get tired. "I must not stop playing," he thought. "I might fall asleep." He began to toss his ball in the air and catch it.

Suddenly he heard a noise. Some people were coming down the street. Pedro pretended to be asleep. Were they soldiers? They were coming nearer. But they did not pass on.

They stopped and looked around. "I wonder if this is the place," one of them said. He was their leader. "It is all in darkness."

"There's a boy against the wall," said another, "let's ask him."

"Here, boy," shouted the leader. "Have you seen any men going into any of these cellars tonight?"

"Men?" repeated Pedro. "I did not see any here. I saw some

men walking down the street. They suddenly disappeared. Whom are you looking for, Your Excellency?"

"Never mind, boy," answered the man. "If they are not here we will find them somewhere else. Come on, men."

They started to walk away. Pedro's heart was going pitty-pat as he watched them. They were not soldiers. But he was sure they were enemies of the secret Jews. What should he do?

The men reached the corner of the street. Then, they looked back at him. Suddenly they started to walk back. Pedro was afraid. Perhaps they did not believe him. He took the stones from his pocket and threw them against the window. As he did so, he heard a voice from below. It said: "Go home, Pedro." Pedro started to walk away. He was afraid to run. The men were coming closer.

"Where are you going, boy?" shouted someone. It was the leader of the Spanish nobles.

"I am going home," he answered.

"Where do you live?"

Pedro pointed down the street. "In that house on the corner."

"I think I will come with you," said the man. "I am not sure if I should believe you."

"Very well, Your Excellency," said Pedro. "We have never had such a fine visitor before. You are welcome."

"Do not bother with the boy," said one of the other men. "Let us go back to the cellar."

The leader stood still for a minute. "All right," he said. He turned to Pedro. "Go home, boy," he ordered. "It is too late for you to be out playing."

"Thank you, Excellency," said Pedro. He began to run. When he reached the corner he looked back. The young nobles could not be seen. They must have gone down into the cellar.

"I hope Father and the rest got away," thought Pedro. He started to walk as fast as he could. He passed the doorway of a large house. "Pedro, Pedro," someone was calling softly. There was his father, hiding in the doorway. "We can go home together," said Don Pedro. "Tell me what happened."

Pedro told him about the men.

"You were very brave," said Don Pedro. "You saved our lives.

Those were Spanish noblemen. Someone must have told them about the secret synagogue."

"Did you finish the Yom Kippur prayers?" asked Pedro.

"Yes, my son," said Don Pedro. "We finished our prayers just as you dropped the pebbles on the window. Now we must find a new place for our secret synagogue. When the next Jewish holiday comes, we will pray together again. As long as we have brave young Jews like you, we will not give up our religion."[4]

THE TEAR OF REPENTANCE

A YOM KIPPUR FANTASY

DOROTHY F. ZELIGS

(Age level ten to thirteen)

Once upon a time, there was an angel who disobeyed God. The angel was summoned to appear before the throne of judgment to answer for his misdeeds. He pleaded for mercy and begged God to forgive him. God looked down upon the angel kindly and said, "I shall not punish you, but you must atone for your wrongdoing. I will give you a task to perform. Go down to earth and bring to Me the most precious thing in the world."

The angel sped down to earth, happy to have a chance to win God's forgiveness. Over many countries he roamed, for many years, looking for the most precious thing in the world. One day, he came upon a great battlefield. He saw a young soldier lying there, badly wounded. This young man had fought bravely in the defense of his country, and was now dying. The angel caught up the last drop of blood from the soldier's wound and hastened back to heaven with it.

"This is indeed a precious thing which you have brought back," God said to the angel. "A soldier who gives his life for his country is very dear to Me. But return, and search once more."

So the angel returned to earth and continued his quest. For many years he roamed, through cities, woods, and plains. Then, one day, he saw a nurse in a great hospital. She was dying of a dread disease. She had nursed others through this disease, working so hard that she had worn down her own strength and so caught the illness herself. She lay pale and gasping upon her cot. As she was dying, the angel caught up her last breath and hastened to heaven with it.

"Surely, God," said the angel, "the last breath of this unselfish nurse is the most precious thing in the world."

"It is a very precious thing that you have brought to Me." God replied. "One who gives his life for another is indeed worthy in My sight. But return, and search again."

Then the angel returned to earth again to search once more. Far and wide he roamed, for many years. One night, he saw a villainous-looking man on horseback, riding through a dark forest. The man was armed with a sword and a spear. The angel guessed on what wicked errand this man was bound. He was going to avenge himself on the keeper of the forest, who would not permit him to poach on the king's game. The man came to the small hut where the forester and his family lived. Light streamed from the window. Getting down from his horse, the villain peered through the window. He saw the wife of the forester putting her little son to bed. He heard her teaching him how to say his evening prayers. Something within his hard heart seemed to melt. Did the scene bring back memories of his own faraway childhood and his own mother, who had also taught him to pray? Tears filled the man's eyes and he turned away from his evil deed and repented of his ways. The angel caught up one of his tears and flew back to heaven with it.

"This," said God, "is the most precious thing in the world, for it is the tear of a repentant sinner. And repentance opens the gates of heaven."[5]

HAYM SALOMON—SON OF LIBERTY

HOWARD FAST

(Age level eleven to fourteen)

Haym Salomon waited. Now he knew that the time for him to serve was near, and he waited—with strange patience for him—to see how it would come.

He studied the exchange, watched the prices on bills. He realized something of the trouble Robert Morris would encounter in his efforts to convert bills of exchange into funds with which to run the government and the war. The price on bills of exchange was dropping lower and lower.

Many of these bills came from the French army in America. They were drawn on banks in France and sold by French officers so that they might raise cash to feed their men. But so little skilled were these officers in disposing of the bills that the price dropped lower and lower. No person of repute would endorse the bills. The market was flooded with them, and dishonest brokers were demanding commissions of ten and twenty and thirty percent.

This drove down the price of American loans, which were sent from France in the form of bills of exchange. No one trusted these loans, and no one desired to convert them into cash.

Haym Salomon lost no opportunity to say to friends of Morris, "If he is ever in need, tell him to call on Haym Salomon."

And at long last the time came.

Another summer was over. The colors of fall were in the trees and in the sky, and the cold nip of fall was in the air. The High Holy Days of the Jews were approaching, and once again they gathered in their synagogue for prayer.

It was Yom Kippur, the holiest day of the year for a Jew, the Day of Atonement, when Jews fast for twenty-four hours and remain all day in the synagogue at their prayers.

The little hall was full to overflowing. Not only were the Jews of Philadelphia there, but also the men who had come from the armies in the field, men in torn, faded regimentals. They stood with the others, the striped prayer shawls over their shoulders, asking the forgiveness and mercy of God.

In the midst of the prayers, there was a knocking at the door. The sexton answered, and then a hushed whisper ran through the congregation. Haym Salomon was wanted.

He went to the door. A messenger stood there.

"This is our holiest of days," Salomon said impatiently. "Couldn't this have waited? From whom are you?"

21. Blessing the children on the eve of Yom Kippur. Israel Information Services, New York.

"From Robert Morris."

"Give me that," Salomon said. He snatched the package, and found two bills of exchange and a note.

The note was brief. It said:

My dear Mr. Salomon:

Here are two notes which must be discounted immediately. I have tried to raise the money, but found it impossible to procure within the time I have at my disposal. The need is great, the cause urgent. I have turned to you only because our distress could be satisfied in no other manner.

Sincerely,
Robert Morris

"And today, on Yom Kippur," Salomon thought. "He turns to a Jew on our holiest day, when even the thought of money is forbidden. And he turns to a Jew only when everything else has failed."

A moment he hesitated, then tightened his lips. He looked at the bills of exchange and saw that each was for ten thousand dollars. Where could he raise twenty thousand dollars? Most of his money was tied up in privateers, in blockade runners. At the most, he had at his disposal a few thousand dollars in cash.

"Wait here," he told the messenger.

He walked through the congregation, which had returned to its prayer, and up to the pulpit. He touched the rabbi on the shoulder and said:

"I must talk to the people."

"But Salomon, have you lost your mind? This is Yom Kippur."

"And this is the cause," Salomon said grimly. "I must talk to them."

There was no withstanding the fire in his eyes. The rabbi gave place to him, and Salomon said, simply and quietly:

"The superintendent of finance has called on us. He has sent us two bills, which represent twenty thousand dollars. This money he must have immediately. I need not tell you what depends on it. If you will look around and see those of your number who are wearing the uniform of our country, you will know."

Murmurs came. "But Yom Kippur—"

"But the *cause*," Salomon said harshly.

It is as much of a sin for a Jew to write on that day as to speak of money, yet check after check was written. Salomon took them, one after another, his face hard and strange.

His own check was for three thousand dollars, all the cash he could raise at the moment. Not ten minutes had passed before the twenty thousand dollars was subscribed. The Jews turned back to their prayer.

He went to the messenger and gave him the money, and the man counted it quickly.

"But you've no provision for interest," he protested.

"Tell Mr. Morris there will be no interest," Haym Salomon said.[6]

FORGIVEN

JUDAH STEINBERG

(Age level eleven to fourteen)

Abraham Jose Karminski is one of the richest men in town. He has so many people in his employ that he can sleep till three in the afternoon. But there are two days a year when he rises with the sun. No matter how early he gets up on those days, he complains of being late. They are the day of Passover and the one that ushers in the Day of Atonement. He is in such a great hurry on the day before the Day of Atonement that he literally rouses the dawn!

There is so much to do that day, not counting the *kapparah* ritual and the special prayers of penitence that are really said after midnight. It is a day that is part holy and yet somewhat of a workday too, for there are mundane matters to be attended to, such as the settling of debts that have fallen due, appeasing those whom you have offended and accepting apologies from those who have provoked quarrels with you. Then, there is the eating and drinking—it is considered a *mitzvah* to indulge yourself on that day because of the long fast that follows. You have only till midday to do all this, for the afternoon is devoted to an accounting of the soul—a reckoning that must cover the entire year that passed. Is this a trifling matter? How many days are there in each year and how many footprints of sin does man make as he lives through each day? Indeed, the very time in which you are preparing yourself for the great and awesome Day of Atonement is veritably reckoned a holy day itself.

It was the day before the Day of Atonement when the following incident took place. The first thing that Abraham Jose did that morning was to rush to the bathhouse, scrub himself in the tub, and dip himself in the *mikvah*. Then he ran trembling to ths synagogue and after a hasty prayer returned home. On the way, he reviewed the tasks that were still undone. He counted them off on his fingers, but there was one specific chore for which he had no finger.

"No!" He was emphatic. "I won't do it. It's no concern of mine!"

He entered the house in a holiday mood. "Good day!" he called out to his wife. "Let's have some refreshments."

"Good day," Sarah Leah answered with a sigh that belied her jollity, and she placed some sweets on the table. "May the holy Name bring a sweet year to all of Israel. May He give strength to fast on the holy day—the pregnant women . . ." and she stopped short.

Abraham Jose was aware of the fact that the wife of his only son was pregnant. "No one came?" he asked casually, as he nibbled at some pastry.

"No one," his wife answered in offhand manner, as if she didn't know what he referred to and whom he meant.

"Is it possible," Abraham Jose mused, "that he won't come? Not even today? No respect for a parent? And what of fear of heaven and of the Day of Judgment? Even if he does come and does apologize, I won't forgive him. He insulted his mother and me. He talked back to us most shamefully. No! Though he would leave humiliated and embarrassed, I cannot forgive him. Maybe this hurt will cleanse his soul and the Holy One, blessed be He, will forgive him.

"A generation of barbarians, these youngsters! But they are really good at heart—merely stubborn. He'll probably send a relative as peacemaker. But it won't help. It will be of no use. I won't forgive him. Let the youngster feel how deeply he has provoked us.

"And for such a reason—he came to his wife's defense! Who is she? A baby that hasn't finished teething. What manners! No respect for one's elders.

"What was all the rumpus about? What did Sarah Leah want of her? And all for her own good, too. Is it not unseemly for a daughter of Israel to appear out of doors with her locks exposed? And how can a woman permit herself not to step into the synagogue on the Sabbath when the new month is blessed? Is it possible that she doesn't know the laws that a Jewish woman should know? And, to top it all, she takes no interest in housework. She should do something to keep from being bored, even if she has no desire to help her mother-in-law.

"How angry that young fool of a husband became! Ignoramus! he shouted! Imagine! A son calling a father ignoramus! You couldn't really tell at whom he was directing his insults. He was so furious that he didn't look at me. The truth is, that in his fury he didn't know what he was saying. But yet, it was the height of impudence."

Abraham Jose busied himself listlessly, interrupting his work constantly to look out of the window, or to turn toward the entrance hall with a feeling that someone was there. Time and again, he would call out to his wife, "Who's there?"

"No one!" The answer was always the same.

"I thought I heard someone," he would justify his question.

He kept pulling his watch out of his vest pocket and looking at it. "It's getting late. Time doesn't stand still."

Suddenly, he remembered that he had to meet with a debtor who had promised to pay, though he was not certain if it was to be before or after the Day of Atonement.

"I'll go and see him. If he will pay, well and good. If not, nothing lost. But I'll have to pass the house of those young brats. How irresponsible is this new generation! They just scooped up their belongings and moved into an apartment with a stranger, as if my house wasn't big enough. Well, what does it matter? I'll walk on the other side of the street."

But Abraham Jose found himself walking on the side of the street where his children lived. He did not do it intentionally, certainly not. He just happened to forget. The door was open, and his grandchildren were playing in front of the house. When he saw them, he stopped, turned to the north, and thought he detected a cool wind blowing.

"The children are naked and barefoot," he called out angrily. "They could catch their death of cold. That's a mother and father for you! What can you expect? They are still babies themselves. I must go inside and reprimand them. It's a matter of life and death."

He picked up his little grandchildren, pressed them to his bosom, and entered the house with bold steps and obvious anger.

"How mean can you be—not to take pity on your own children!" he shouted. "The north wind is blowing and the children are practically naked."

His son, on seeing him, got to his feet and lowered his eyes in embarrassment.

"How penitent!" thought Abraham Jose, and his heart was filled with compassion for his son.

"Better not to sin than to sin and repent," he chided gently.

"But father . . ." the son started to answer.

"Enough, enough! Let's not go back to how it all began."

"But . . ."

"I said I forgive you."

"I forgive you," the daughter-in-law repeated the words in a tone of disparagement. "And what about the insult to me?"

"Sarah Leah will forgive you, I am sure. You needn't worry about that. Where's the maid? Run fetch Sarah Leah. Tell her I'm here!"

The maid dashed out of the house to call Sarah Leah while Abraham Jose continued chiding the parents for not knowing how to care for their young.

"You think one catches cold only in winter? Spring and

autumn colds are much more treacherous. You are committing a crime against your own children."

He was still talking when his wife appeared and fell on her daughter-in-law's neck. The father embraced his son, and the house was filled with the twittering of kisses.

Toward evening, when Sarah Leah blessed her candles, tears filled her eyes to overflowing as she prayed, "Master of the Universe, give strength to my daughter-in-law to fast on this holy day. . . . Let no harm come to the unborn child."

Translated from the Hebrew[7]

THE DAY OF DECISIONS

RUBEN ROTHGIESSER

(Age level twelve to fifteen)

Josias, the giant slave of the Nassis, wearing a white shroud, his head covered with a white prayer cap, and a white prayer shawl on his shoulders, was standing next to the planters Gomez and Henriquez, next to Messias, Natino, and Simra—all of whom had lost dear ones during the year just passed. They were intoning the *Kaddish*, the prayer for the souls of the dead.

For Josias, the giant, also had lost a dear one. It was less than twenty-four hours since he had found his brother dead, under a roof of palm leaves, with an arrow in his throat and his black face turned yellow-green. Josias bowed his head. The wound on his forehead, which his master had burned with gunpowder, was still painful. Josias bowed his head and, next to him, five white men bowed their heads before the ark of the Torah. Josias could neither read nor write. He did not know much about the customs of the faith which his father had adopted, his father who, as a young man, had perhaps hunted gazelles in African jungles. But Josias was circumcised, he was a Jew, and this was the day of repentance on which God's judgments were sealed. As for his brother, the judgment had already been spoken and executed. And now, before the holy ark, he was praying for his dead brother. A year ago, when

Josias's mother had died, his master had taught him the prayer in Hebrew.

"Remember, O merciful God," his lips murmured, "my brother who has entered eternal life. May God's Name be sanctified throughout the world which He created by His will. May His kingdom come in our time, and in the life of the people Israel and in our own day!"

He did not know what the strange words meant, but a shudder of deep emotion passed through him. Once again Josias bowed his head, then left the holy ark and walked on the toes of his naked feet back to the other slaves, who were huddled back of the seats of the congregation.

The rabbi, Samuel Nieto, a graybeard of seventy who had been installed by David Nassi's father, Isaac, now closed the ark of cedar, and the prayer leader, Joseph Medigo, began to intone the verse of Judah Halevi, who had composed them as part of the long service on the Day of Atonement.

Jubilant yet beseeching as well, the tones reechoed from the walls of the little synagogue built in a wilderness on the American continent, two thousand miles from Spain where, in almost forgotten times, the poet had written them. It was still early in the afternoon. The last service of the day, *Neilah*, was still a long way off; but since the evening before, the oil wicks had been burning in a crown-shaped cluster of copper, and in front of each place a candle glowed in its copper holder. They burned quietly and steadily, for neither door nor window had been open for hours. In the absence of any ventilation, the air was close and damp.

The reading of Halevi's verses continued.

The ark was made of cedar, the crown-shaped candelabrum was made of copper, beautifully etched, as were the candlesticks, while the Torah accessories were of silver. But what were all these costly things compared with the splendor of the Temple which once stood in Jerusalem! Here, in a wilderness synagogue in America, Jews of Spanish and Portuguese descent were singing of a Temple, long ago destroyed, in a city in Asia. And here were Negroes, descendants of others sold into slavery and brought here from Africa generations ago, listening to, not comprehending but moved by, these songs of praise!

In the place of honor reserved for *parnasim*, near the holy ark, sat David Nassi. His heart heard about Jerusalem's splendor, but his thoughts were on the Savannah, for whose safety he was fearful. In the sixth row of benches sat his son Isaac, fourth of the Nassi line to be settled in the Savannah, who had no eyes for anything except his father's sorrowful face.

> Then happiness blossomed, so longingly entreated,
> All the chosen were glad and rejoiced
> When Zion again rose up in youthful splendor

chanted Medigo, the *hazzan*.

Just then Isaac noticed that the candle in front of him flickered; so did the lamps in other places and the lights in the crown-shaped cluster. All were agitated by a draft. Someone must have opened the door. Isaac turned his head and saw, standing next to Josias in the group of slaves, the sergeant Eckhout, who commanded the detail of soldiers assigned to protect the Savannah. David Nassi also saw the sergeant. He stood up at once and walked through the room to the soldier.

"O heavens!" rang Medigo's strong voice. "Despise not our supplications! Have pity on Thy people, O God!"

Isaac saw his father leave the synagogue, leaving the synagogue on the most solemn holy day of the year! The sergeant followed Nassi, and Josias and all the other slaves crowded out the door. Also Tudela and Carvalho had risen and had hastily made for the door. All the men became restless, as did the women behind their wooden screen. Even the voice of Medigo began to falter, and nothing in the world could have persuaded Isaac to remain in the synagogue. Just as he reached the stoop, between the two great columns, he heard the first loud, sharp explosion, followed immediately by a second and a third. The reports seemed to come from close by, and not from a distance as in the days and even weeks past, when the soldiers had fired near the edge of the woods, to frighten raiders or alert the settlement. No, these explosions came from the vicinity of the village, from the nearest plantation, or, perhaps, even the mills. The Marrons, the escaped, angry slaves, no longer content with burning fields and harvests and then taking to their heels, were attacking the settlement itself on the most solemn holy day of the Jews, when their fields were unattended and their mills empty!

Fortunately, David Nassi was able, after the first quarter of an hour, to overcome the worst confusion. How the Marrons had been able to reach the village without having been observed could not for the moment be explained. Apparently, the soldier on duty at the watchtower had fallen asleep in the noonday heat. In any case, Eckhout, the sergeant, had been awakened by the screams of Cava, a young slave of the Nassis. The sergeant had been resting on his bed in the small house in which he and his men stayed. A few minutes passed before Eckhout could get the girl to speak intelligibly. Then he learned that she had seen a group of almost naked Negroes attack the Nassi mill and begin to overturn the vats containing the sugar syrup.

The sergeant had acted quickly. He sent five of his men to the mill. He had no more available because the rest were on sentry duty or on patrol and they, apparently, had been tricked by the Negroes. He himself ran, as fast as his feet could carry him, to the synagogue.

As soon as Nassi had a fair idea of what had happened, he drove the female slaves back to their huts, from which they had run screaming into the streets; then he had weapons distributed to the males. Similar action was taken by the other planters who, unaware of the facts, came out of the synagogue one after the other. Unfortunately, not all of Nassi's and Carvalho's slaves could be provided with firearms; of the fifty or sixty slaves available to Nassi, only some forty knew how to shoot. Added to these were the other planters and their male relatives and the sergeant with his little band of five soldiers, who had tried to drive the Marrons from the mill, but had had to retreat before the more numerous frenzied and fanatical Negroes.

Isaac was there too, and this time David did not turn his son away.

Nassi ordered the door of the synagogue closed. None of the women had left their places, and the old men and boys had remained in the section of the room reserved for males. Medigo, the *hazzan*, stood before the pulpit, and the old rabbi had risen and was standing near the ark of the Torah. From mouth to mouth the news was whispered. The service continued as if nothing had happened. No one had ordered or even suggested it, but everybody knew that this was the proper course.

In the meantime, Josias, who had ventured outside the village, came running back and reported that the Marrons were innumerable, and that they had fallen upon Tudela's and Carvalho's mills. During their stay in the bush, they had become even more vicious and bestial than their ancestors had been in Africa. Besides, for some time past, they had had a leader, Joli Coeur, who seemed to have a supernatural influence over them. The damage resulting from the Marrons' attack on the mills was incalculable; but even worse could happen. The danger to life and limb, to women and children, was extreme.

Not a second could be lost. In feverish haste, Nassi divided his little troop into four parts—three to attempt to drive the raiders from the three mills, and one to serve as a reserve. Eckhout approved of Nassi's plan. He knew that Nassi had had more experience in such affairs than he, and willingly placed himself under David's command.

Nassi led the column which was to storm his own mill, and the sergeant Eckhout and the corporal Terveen led the two other attacking detachments, while Carvalho headed the reserve to which, despite the rapidity of events, Isaac had been assigned by his father.

The sun was beginning to sink. The hour for the *Neilah* prayer had come. Half the places in the synagogue were empty; but, undistracted, the *hazzan* chanted on and, undistracted, the congregation responded in chorus. The lips moved, the eyes were fastened on the prayer books. Medigo's voice grew hoarse and dry, but he did not stop. The response of the women, the old men and the boys was no longer a chant; it was a single pleading wail. And in the midst of the discordant melodies bursts of gunfire came from outside.

The letters in the holy books danced before the eyes of Rebecca Nassi, Miriam Carvalho, and many others. Tears and sighs of anxiety were mixed with the recital of the text. But the service on this great Day of Atonement pursued its course, entirely as prescribed by law! Sweat was pouring from the forehead of Medigo. The feeble voice of Rabbi Nieto supported that of the *hazzan*, so that the prayer would have all the power and devotion that were requisite.

Outside, full of rage at the destruction of their mills and sugar refineries and the burning of their fields, the men, whose fathers and grandfathers before them had been planters in the Savannah, rushed to attack the rebellious Negroes. These men advanced with guns in their hands, with powder horns and bullet sacks secured to their waists. Most of them had not had time to remove the ceremonial garments they had worn in the synagogue, and went into battle dressed in the traditional shrouds and prayer shawls. With them advanced their slaves, many of whom had adopted the faith taught them by their masters. Through a chain of inscrutable circumstances, these slaves were now fighting brother Africans on another continent. . . .

The Marrons had been driven off and were being pursued. Dead and wounded lay about. The head of an almost naked black lay in the millstream, which was red with his blood. The cistern in which the pressed sugar sap was collected before it went to the cooking department had been overturned. It had been almost empty, but what sap had remained had spilled onto the floor, where it was mixed with blood and filth. . . .

David spoke quietly, but he grasped the strap of his gun, and Isaac saw that his hand was trembling. Never before had he seen his father so agitated. He wanted to say something; he felt it was his duty to back up his father; but before he could say anything, his father turned to him.

"See that the wounded slaves are removed to the village," he said, his tone quite composed. "Carvalho will look after them. He'll have to call out some of the women from the synagogue to help him care for the wounded."

And without adding a word, Nassi left the mill.

Isaac called Josias and several other slaves and passed his father's orders on to them. Six slaves dragged the captured Joli Coeur away. Others busied themselves with the task of carrying the wounded and fallen to the village.

None of the planters in Nassi's column or in the reserves had been killed or wounded. How the other detachments had fared Isaac did not know. . . .

In the meantime, Isaac had gone to his father's mill to appraise the damage caused by the raid. He soon established that only one of the beams and a wooden wheel were broken. The smooth, upper wooden rollers, the heart of the entire installation, which would have required considerable time and money to replace, were undamaged. It would require less time than Isaac had at first thought to repair the mill.

And now Isaac suddenly remembered that his father had gone away. His remark that the wells may have been poisoned suggested to Isaac that his father had gone to the plantation Sukkoth to see about the wells. . . .

Isaac went neither to the synagogue nor to the house of Carvalho, where the wounded were being nursed. He had to go to his father! As soon as the village was behind him, he began to run to the plantation Beer Sheba. Beyond this lay Sukkoth, and Isaac was sure his father would be there.

The sugar-cane plantings resounded with the cries of the fleeing and the shouts of the pursuers. Slowly these noises were left behind and, in the first shadows of the rapidly approaching twilight, Isaac saw, among the high stalks, neither friend nor foe. He knew every step of every plantation. He sprang over the ditch which separated Beer Sheba from Sukkoth and continued along a path between man-high stalks of sugar plants. Nearby, a short time before, a new well had been dug. It was the nearest well in Sukkoth. A narrow path, scarcely a foot wide, led into the plantation. Isaac kept on, running as if pursued, and soon espied a low structure of brick. The little round place, in the midst of the stalks, seemed forsaken and empty, but as Isaac stopped directly in front of the low wall of the well, he saw the body of a man in a white coat lying on the ground, on the other side.

Without thinking of any other possibility, Isaac knew it was his father. He felt in his chest a pain as of the point of a knife. He ran to the other side of the well. It was his father; it was David Nassi. He was lying face down, an arrow sticking out of his back.

Everything Isaac now did he did mechanically, without the aid of his reason, just as he had inexplicably been driven hither. Carefully he withdrew the arrow. It came away easily; the wound could not be very deep; besides, there had been very little bleeding. Isaac began to feel relieved. Very cautiously he turned the body over—he had to use both arms, the strong as well as the weak one—and lifted his father's head. David Nassi was alive. His breathing was spasmodic. He recognized his son, but he could speak only in a whisper. "Poisoned!" he murmured. And, after a pause, "What time is it? I can't see anything! It is so dark!"

"Yes," said his son, "it is twilight, almost night."

"Night!" whispered Nassi. And he began, very weakly at first but with increasing clearness and distinctness, to recite the closing prayer of the Yom Kippur service:

"O Eternal One, before I was created I was as naught, and now since I was created I am as if I had never been created. I am but dust in my lifetime, how much the more after my death. Praised be the Eternal! In His hand are the souls of the living and of the dead . . . the spirit of every human body. Rule over us . . . forever and ever. . . !"

More slowly and hesitatingly, but still distinctly and understandably came the last words from his lips. Isaac bent over him hopefully. But his father was silent, and Isaac saw how the light went out of his eyes, how the mouth opened; and, in spite of the darkness, that the color of the skin was greenish-yellow.

Isaac allowed the body of his father to slip slowly out of his arms. With a gentle hand he closed the eyes of the dead and then stood up. He remained erect only with difficulty; he swayed, and some phrases of the *Kaddish*, the prayer of the dead, ran through his mind. After a while, he came to himself. He looked toward the village. It was only a few thousand paces away, but the tropical darkness had already spread over the plantations; night had fallen quickly. Only one sound came to Isaac's ear. It was not very loud, but recognizable: the shrill blast of a horn. The *shofar* was being blown in the synagogue to mark the end of Yom Kippur, the day on which the decisions of life and death are sealed, but also the day which should usher in freedom and harmony. Freedom and harmony! Freedom and peace!

Once more Isaac raised himself on his toes, but he saw nothing except, at arm's length from him, the dark stalks which were swaying in the evening breeze. The village of the Savannah, the broad fields, had vanished in the darkness. Everything was extinguished.

Translated by Harry Schneiderman[8]

XVIII

CHILDREN'S POEMS

FOR YOM KIPPUR

KOL NIDRE

Ben Aronin

> I heard the cantor singing
> He sang the *Kol Nidre*.
>
> And as he sang the people prayed.
> I heard my father say,
>
> "Dear God, if I've done anything
> That hurt some other man,
>
> I'll try to make it up to him
> The best way that I can.
>
> If I forgot a promise made
> Forgive me, God, this day.
>
> Oh, hear with love, dear God above,
> My prayer, the *Kol Nidre*."[1]

FASTING

Sadie Rose Weilerstein

> I'm hungry when it's breakfast time;
>   I'm hungrier at noon;
> And when it's time for supper
>   I could almost eat the moon.
>
> But next week on Yom Kippur
>   I'm going to try to fast
> Till suppertime—or noon time—
>   Or at least till breakfast's past.[2]

ATONEMENT

Jessie E. Sampter

> Day by day, through all the year,
>   In the Book that none may read
> All my thoughts and deeds appear;
> Now I count with hope and fear
>   Every thought and deed.
>
> Day by day, through all this year
>   That is coming clean and new,
> Let my heart Thy precepts hear,
> And then written page appear
>   Worthy of a Jew.[3]

A DREAM

Jessie E. Sampter

> I shall not taste of food today,
>   Nor think of food at all,
> But all the day I mean to pray—
>   Although they say I'm small—
> I mean to pray among the crowd,
> That ask forgiveness low or loud.

Last night I heard *Kol Nidre* sung;
　The cantor's voice was deep,
And back and forth the people swung—
　I think I fell asleep;
I dreamed my mother took my hand
And led me through a desert land.

But on the ground were cookies round
　As white as milk and sweet;
Enough for all the day I found,
　I seemed to eat and eat.
Then Mother said, "By this 'tis known
Man does not live by bread alone."

"Awake, my pet," my mother said,
　When all the prayers were through.
"I know the Lord who gives us bread
　Will grant us pardon, too."
I shall not wish to eat today;
My dream will feed me while I pray.[4]

YOM KIPPUR EVE

CONSTANTINE A. SHAPIRO

Before the burning candles in
　The six-branched candlesticks, there stands
My mother filled with reverence,
　Her face all covered with her hands.

She pours her heart in humble prayer,
　In accents soft my mother speaks;
From her black eyes tears trickle down
　And flow upon her swarthy cheeks.

Lo, Father comes from out his room,
　Upon his clothes he wears a shroud;
The children all, both big and small,
　Against him press, against him crowd.

I shake and tremble then all o'er,
  And stand beside him silently;
His eyes are filled with kindly grace,
  His face is beaming radiantly.

He puts his hand upon my head,
  And blesses me softly (none can hear).
A tear then falls upon my brow,
  From Father's eye a loving tear.

Translated by Harry H. Fein[5]

ATONEMENT

ALEXANDER M. DUSHKIN

O Sabbath of Sabbaths—thou awesome and holiest day of the
    year,
Unearthly the spirit thou castest on mankind, exalted thy fear.
Somber thy mood and expectant, like beacon thou art whereunto
All hearts turn uneasy for judgment of year that is coming
    anew;
Like sailors aloft on the masts for the blackening storm prepare,
Like prisoner watching the lips which for death or for life will
    declare,
Like lover a-tremble at word that will spell his rejoicing or gloom,
Like mother at bedside of child seeks for signs of health or of
    doom.

Thirty the days were and ten for repentant return and weal,
And this the awaited dread hour of judgment, for testing and
    seal.
Thirty the *Selihot*—the vigils at midnight, when sleep was
    denied,
And piercing the stillness of night, they exhorted and pleaded
    and cried.
Ten were the Days of Repentance from New Year to Kippurim
    night;

All hatred and spite then forgiven, all grievance and wrong
     set aright.
And now in the deepest denial of body's demands and of food,
The night and the day are abandoned to fasting in penitent
     mood. . . .

At sunset in home and in temple tall candles like torches are lit,
And barefoot on holiest day in the synagogue humbly they sit.
Filled with emotions intense, like a stream that is swollen to
          burst,
Each with his soul in his corner, together like symphony re-
     hearsed.
The scrolls of the Law are brought forth to join their people
     in need,
Crescendo the *hazzan* intones the *Kol Nidre*, majestic and sweet;
That prayer so ancient and quaint, which enjoins against words
          that are vows,
Is keynote—each promise and prayer with honor, sincereness
     endows.

Martialed, united, all Israel, the righteous, the wicked, the stray,
Together in fast and in pleading, together Confession they say,
Together their sorrows and joys they must bear, for Israel is kin,
And now, as in past, for each sinner the whole has responsible
     been;
Together appeal for the covenant, He with their sires had made,
And grant them His grace, as of yore, to all penitent sinners
     displayed.
For the love He their ancestors bore they plead that from wrath
          they be spared,
For martyrs who bled for His Name, for prophets who suffered
          and dared.

As sons they beseech the great Father, as servants their Master,
          their King,
Their lives and their destinies humbly entrusting, submissive
          they sing:

"Like clay in the hand of the potter our lives in Thy hands we
    deliver,
Like rudder in hands of the pilot, like web in the hands of the
    weaver;
Like glass is blown and fashioned, do fashion our fate, O our
    Lord,
Like smithy refining the silver, refine Thou our souls, O
    Adored! . . .
In Thy glorious Temple the high priest atonement to wilderness
    sent,
Now prostrate we kneel in Thy presence, let prayers like incense
    ascend."

Their prayers ascend in the morning, their songs in the eventide,
When sun sets on closing of gates, in purity, love they abide;
Their life, the uncertain tomorrow, with trust and with courage
    they see,
For prayer, repentance, *tzedakah*, avert the most dreaded decree.
As symbol of struggle now won, comes the *shofar*'s long rallying
    call:
"The Lord alone is God, He is God, the Eternal Unique, He
    is All."
"This day He shall strengthen and bless us, this day shall exalt
    us again;
This year shall Jerusalem prosper, and peace be on Israel,
    Amen!"[6]

NOTES

I YOM KIPPUR IN THE BIBLE

1. Selections from the Pentateuch in this chapter are from *The Torah: The Five Books of Moses: A New Translation . . . according to the Masoretic Text*, Jewish Publication Society of America (Philadelphia, 1962).
2. *The Holy Scriptures according to the Masoretic Text*, Jewish Publication Society of America (Philadelphia, 1917), pp. 611–612.
3. *The Five Megilloth and Jonah: A New Translation*, introductions by H. L. Ginsberg, Jewish Publication Society of America (Philadelphia, 1969), pp. 117–121.

II YOM KIPPUR IN POSTBIBLICAL WRITINGS

1. *The Apocrypha*, trans. by Edgar J. Goodspeed, University of Chicago Press (Chicago, 1938), pp. 323–325. This selection is the source of *Mareh Khohen*, a *piyyut* recited on Yom Kippur.
2. Charles, R. H., ed., *The Apocrypha and Pseudepigrapha of the Old Testament*, Clarendon Press (Oxford, 1913), vol. 2, p. 64.
3. *Philo*, with an English translation by F. H. Colson (Loeb Classical Library), Harvard University Press (Cambridge, Mass., 1937), vol. 7, pp. 427–435.

III YOM KIPPUR IN TALMUD AND MIDRASH

1. Selections from the *Midrash Rabbah* are from the translation under the editorship of H. Freedman and Maurice Simon, Soncino Press (London, 1939–1951).

2. Newman, Louis I., and Samuel Spitz, eds., *The Talmudic Anthology*, Behrman House (New York, 1945), p. 555.
3. *Pesikta Rabbati: Discourses for Feasts, Fasts and Special Sabbaths*, trans. by William G. Braude, Yale University Press (New Haven, 1968), vol. 1, p. 473.
4. *The Mishnah*, trans. by Herbert Danby, Clarendon Press (Oxford, 1933), pp. 200–201.
5. Ibid., p. 171.
6. Ibid., p. 172.
7. Selections from *The Babylonian Talmud* are from the translation under the editorship of Isidore Epstein, Soncino Press (London, 1935–1950).
8. *Pesikta Rabbati*, vol. 1, pp. 484–485.
9. *The Mishnah*, p. 172.
10. *The Fathers according to Rabbi Nathan*, trans. by Judah Goldin, Yale University Press (New Haven, 1955), p. 164.
11. *Pesikta Rabbati*, vol. 2, p. 711.
12. *The Fathers according to Rabbi Nathan*, pp. 121–122.
13. *The Midrash on Psalms*, trans. by William G. Braude, Yale University Press (New Haven, 1959), vol. 1, p. 192.
14. *Pesikta Rabbati*, vol. 2, pp. 783–784.
15. Ibid., pp. 849–850.
16. *The Midrash on Psalms*, vol. 1, pp. 370–371.
17. Ibid., p. 350.
18. *The Fathers according to Rabbi Nathan*, pp. 34–35.
19. *The Mishnah*, pp. 162–163.
20. Ibid., p. 169.

IV YOM KIPPUR IN MEDIEVAL JEWISH LITERATURE

1. Halevi, Judah, *Kitab Al Khazari*, trans. by Hartwig Hirschfeld, Bernard G. Richards Co. (New York, 1927), pp. 140–141.
2. Abraham Bar Hayya, *The Meditation of the Sad Soul*, trans. by Geoffrey Wigoder, Schocken Books (New York, 1969), pp. 70–71. (The author's name is usually spelled Hiyya.)
3. Yonah ben Avraham of Gerona, *The Gates of Repentance*, trans. by Shraga Silverstein, Yaakov Feldheim (Boys Town, Jerusalem, 1967), pp. 95–97.
4. Israel ibn Al-Nakawa, *Menorat ha-Maor*, ed. by H. G. Enelow, Bloch Publishing Co. (New York, 1931), pp. 37–39.
5. *Zohar*, trans. by Harry Sperling and Maurice Simon, Soncino Press (London, 1931–1934), vol. 5, pp. 35, 37.

V YOM KIPPUR IN JEWISH LAW

1. *Maimonides' Mishneh Torah*, ed. and trans. by Philip Birnbaum, Hebrew Publishing Co. (New York, 1967), pp. 36–37.

VI SELECTED PRAYERS

1. *The Union Prayer Book for Jewish Worship,* newly revised edition, part 2, Central Conference of American Rabbis (New York, 1962), pp. 212–214.
2. Glatzer, Nahum N., ed., *The Dynamics of Emancipation: The Jew in the Modern Age,* Beacon Press (Boston, 1965), pp. 109–110.
3. *The High Holyday Prayer Book: Rosh Hashanah and Yom Kippur,* trans. and arranged by Ben Zion Bokser, Hebrew Publishing Co. (New York, 1959), p. 255.
4. Ibid., pp. 258–259.
5. Arzt, Max, *Justice and Mercy: Commentary on the Liturgy of the New Year and the Day of Atonement,* Holt, Rinehart and Winston (New York, 1963), pp. 201–202.
6. Bokser, pp. 269–274.
7. Cohen, Hermann, "The Day of Atonement: I," *Judaism,* vol. 17, no. 3 (Summer, 1968), pp. 354–355.
8. Bokser, p. 278.
9. *High Holiday Prayer Book . . . ,* compiled and arranged by Morris Silverman, Prayer Book Press (Hartford, 1951), p. 227.
10. Jacobs, Joseph, *The Jews of Angevin England,* David Nutt (London, 1893), pp. 109–111.
11. Martin, Bernard, *Prayer in Judaism,* Basic Books (New York, 1968), p. 221.
12. Bokser, p. 285.
13. Jacobs, Louis, *A Guide to Yom Kippur,* Jewish Chronicle Publications (London, 1957), pp. 34–35.
14. Glatzer, Nahum N., ed., *Language of Faith,* Schocken Books (New York, 1967), p. 124.
15. Arzt, p. 214.
16. Bokser, p. 290.
17. Arzt, pp. 214–215.
18. Jacobs, Louis, pp. 44–46.
19. David, Arthur, and Herbert M. Adler, eds., *Service of the Synagogue: Day of Atonement,* George Routledge & Sons (London, 1904), pp. 178–181.
20. Jacobs, Louis, pp. 52–53.
21. Bokser, pp. 501–502.
22. Arzt, pp. 278–280.
23. Solis-Cohen, Solomon, *When Love Passed By and Other Verses,* Rosenbach Co. (Philadelphia, 1929), pp. 54–55.
24. Greenstone, Julius H., *Jewish Feasts and Fasts* (Philadelphia, 1945), p. 54.
25. Glatzer, *Language of Faith,* p. 296.
26. Arzt, pp. 271–272, 277.
27. Salaman, Nina Davis, trans., *Songs of Exile by Hebrew Poets,* Jewish Publication Society of America (Philadelphia, 1901), p. 69.
28. Arzt, p. 278.
29. Solis-Cohen, p. 65.

30. Munk, Elie, *The World of Prayer*, trans. by Gertrude Hirschler, Philipp Feldheim (New York, 1963), vol. 2, p. 265.
31. *The Union Prayer Book*, pp. 262–264.

VII THE PARADOX OF "KOL NIDRE"

1. In some Ashkenazic congregations in Israel it has become a practice to combine the two versions thus: "From the previous Yom Kippur until this Yom Kippur and from this Yom Kippur until next Yom Kippur. . . ."
2. "The Curious Case of *Kol Nidre*," *Commentary*, vol. 46, no. 4 (October, 1968), pp. 53–58.

VIII THE MUSIC OF THE YOM KIPPUR LITURGY

1. The mystics found a good omen in this verse. The last letters of the first words are those of *kera* in the familiar phrase calling for the defeat of Satan. The concluding letters of the remaining words add up to 17 = *tov*, good.
2. Among the earliest efforts are *Auswahl Alter Hebraischer Synagogal-Melodien*, by A. Marksohn, W. Wolf (Leipzig, 1875); *Sind Originale Synagogen Und Volks-Melodien Bei Den Juden Nachweisbar?*, by E. Breslaur (Leipzig, 1898); "*Kol Nidre*," by F. L. Cohen, *The Jewish Encyclopedia*, vol. 7 (1904), pp. 539–545.
3. *Hebrew Union College Annual*, vol. 8/9 (1931–1932), pp. 493–501.
4. *Jewish Music Notes*, October, 1950, pp. 3–4.
5. The earliest notation of the *Kol Nidre* melody is by Ahron Beer. See *Jewish Music*, by A. Z. Idelsohn, Henry Holt & Co. (New York, 1929), p. 154.
6. As *Misinai* tunes often appear joined to different texts, the particular application of a given tune to a specific text may be in dispute. Thus I have found thirteen different settings for *Darkekha*.
7. See example 13 in *The Rosh Hashanah Anthology*, by Philip Goodman, Jewish Publication Society of America (Philadelphia, 1970), p. 181.
8. Sung to the melody of *Adonai Melekh*. See example 17, ibid., p. 182.

IX HASIDIC TALES AND TEACHINGS

1. Parts of this chapter are reprinted, in revised form, from *Rejoice in Thy Festival: A Treasury of Wisdom, Wit and Humor for the Sabbath and Jewish Holidays*, by Philip Goodman, Bloch Publishing Co. (New York, 1956).

X YOM KIPPUR IN MODERN PROSE

1. Anski, S., "The Dybbuk," *The Dybbuk and Other Great Yiddish Plays*, trans. and ed. by Joseph C. Landis, Bantam Books (New York, 1966), pp. 51–52.

2. Barth, Aron, *The Modern Jew Faces Eternal Problems*, trans. by Haim Shachter, Zionist Organization Youth and Hechalutz Department, Religious Section (Jerusalem, 1965), pp. 218–219.
3. Greenstone, Julius H., *Jewish Feasts and Fasts* (Philadelphia, 1945), pp. 27–29.
4. Jacobs, Louis, *A Guide to Yom Kippur*, Jewish Chronicle Publications (London, 1957), pp. 17–20.
5. Johannesburg *Jewish Affairs*, vol. 7, no. 9 (September, 1952), pp. 8–9; translated from "Pages Retrouvées," by Edmond Fleg, Paris *Evidences*, no. 23 (January, 1952), pp. 16–17.
6. Glatzer, Nahum N., ed., *Franz Rosenzweig: His Life and Thought*, Schocken Books and Farrar, Straus and Young (New York, 1953), pp. 328–329.
7. *Universal Jewish Encyclopedia*, vol. 9, pp. 134–135.
8. Hirsch, Samson Raphael, *Judaism Eternal: Selected Essays*, trans. by I. Grunfeld, Soncino Press (London, 1956), vol. 1, pp. 11–12.
9. Wouk, Herman, *This Is My God*, Doubleday & Co. (Garden City, N.Y., 1959), pp. 89–92.
10. Baeck, Leo, *The Essence of Judaism*, Schocken Books (New York, 1948), pp. 166–167.
11. Belkin, Samuel, *In His Image: The Jewish Philosophy of Man as Expressed in Rabbinic Tradition*, Abelard-Schuman (New York, 1960), pp. 54–55.
12. Soloveichik, Joseph B., "Sacred and Profane," *Hazedek*, vol. 2, no. 2/3 (May–June, 1945), pp. 4–20; reprinted, in a slightly revised version, in *Gesher*, vol. 3, no. 1 (June, 1966), pp. 5–29.
13. Greenberg, Hayim, *The Inner Eye: Selected Essays*, Jewish Frontier Association (New York, 1953), pp. 57–61.
14. The second and third paragraphs are from *A.D. Gordon: Selected Essays*, trans. by Frances Burnce, League for Labor Palestine (New York, 1938), pp. 284–286; the balance is from *The Zionist Idea: A Historical Analysis and Reader*, ed. by Arthur Hertzberg, Herzl Press (New York, 1959), pp. 383–384.
15. Glatzer, Nahum N., "Franz Rosenzweig," *Great Jewish Thinkers of the Twentieth Century*, ed. by Simon Noveck, B'nai B'rith Department of Adult Jewish Education (Washington, D.C., 1963), pp. 161–163.
16. Pallière, Aimé, *The Unknown Sanctuary: A Pilgrimage from Rome to Israel*, trans. by Louise Waterman Wise, Bloch Publishing Co. (New York, 1928), pp. 17–27.

XI   YOM KIPPUR IN ART

1. Plessner, Martin, "Eine illustrierte deutsche Machsorhandschrift in Breslau," *Menorah*, vol. 5, no. 2 (1927), pp. 85–91.
2. Narkiss, Bezalel, "Introduction to the Mahzor Lipsiae," *Machsor Lipsiae*, ed. by E. Katz (Leipzig, 1964), pp. 97–99.
3. Gutmann, Joseph, *Jewish Ceremonial Art* (New York, 1964), plate III; Kayser, Stephen S., *Jewish Ceremonial Art* (Philadelphia, 1959), pp. 117–118.

4. *Sefer Terumat ha-Deshen* (New York, 1957), no. 68.
5. Kirchner, Paul C., *Jüdisches Ceremoniel* (Nürnberg, 1726), pp. 116–124; Bodenschatz, Johann C. G., *Kirchliche Verfassung der heutigen Juden* (Erlang, 1748), vol. 2, pp. 199–224; Rubens, Alfred, *A Jewish Iconography* (London, 1954), pp. 5 ff.; Lauterbach, Jacob Z., *"Tashlikh: A Study in Jewish Ceremonies,"* *Rabbinic Essays* (Cincinnati, 1951), pp. 355 ff. on the *Kapparot* ceremony; Ben-Ezra, Akiva, *Minhage Hagim* (Jerusalem, 1962), pp. 36–63.

XII   YOM KIPPUR IN MANY LANDS

1. Agnon, Shmuel Yosef, *Days of Awe: Being a Treasury of Traditions, Legends . . .* , Schocken Books (New York, 1948), pp. 255–258.
2. Roth, Cecil, *A History of the Marranos*, Jewish Publication Society of America (Philadelphia, 1932), pp. 182–184.
3. Leslau, Wolf, *Falasha Anthology*, Yale University Press (New Haven, 1951), p. xxxiv.
4. Kehimkar, Haeem Samuel, *The History of the Bene-Israel of India* (Tel Aviv, 1937), pp. 18, 172–175, 180.
5. Hacohen, Devora and Menahem, *One People: The Story of the Eastern Jews*, trans. by Israel I. Taslitt, Sabra Books (New York, 1969), pp. 101–102.
6. Ibid., pp. 34–35.
7. *Igeret Lagolah*, no. 28 (August, 1946), pp. 16–22.
8. Schauss, Hayyim, *The Jewish Festivals: From Their Beginnings to Our Own Day*, trans. by Samuel Jaffe, Union of American Hebrew Congregations (Cincinnati, 1938), pp. 149–155.
9. Chagall, Bella, *Burning Lights*, trans. by Norbert Guterman, Schocken Books (New York, 1946), pp. 82–95.
10. Samuel, Maurice, *The World of Sholom Aleichem*, Alfred A. Knopf (New York, 1943), pp. 68–71.
11. Schwab, Hermann, *Memories of Frankfort*, Jewish Post Publications (London, 1955), pp. 11–12.
12. Zangwill, Israel, *Children of the Ghetto*, Jewish Publication Society of America (Philadelphia, 1892), pp. 542–546.
13. Levy, Harriet Lane, *920 O'Farrell Street*, Doubleday & Co. (Garden City, New York, 1947), pp. 241–244, 250–256.
14. Rosenfeld, Max, ed. and trans., *"Gershon,"* *A Union for Shabbos and Other Stories of Jewish Life in America*, Sholom Aleichem Club Press (Philadelphia, 1967), pp. 209–211; reprinted under title *Pushcarts and Dreamers: Stories of Jewish Life in America*, Thomas Yoseloff (New York, 1969), pp. 209–211.
15. Kranzler, David, "The Jewish Community of Shanghai, 1937–1945," unpublished doctoral thesis, Yeshiva University, 1970.
16. London *Jewish Chronicle*, no. 4,196 (September 23, 1949), p. 19.
17. *High Holy Days Program*, Mizrachi Women's Organization of America, September–October, 1954, pp. 8–10; translated from Munich *Unzer Velt*, October 12, 1948, p. 3. The author was an inmate of the Dachau concentration camp.

18. New York *Daily News*, October 2, 1950, p. 8.
19. *New York Post*, September 24, 1966, p. 4.
20. Wiesel, Elie, *The Jews of Silence*, trans. by Neal Kozodoy, Holt, Rinehart and Winston (New York, 1966), pp. 19–22, 78–80.

XIII   YOM KIPPUR IN POETRY

1. Golomb, Mollie R., *How Fair My Faith and Other Poems*, Dorrance & Co. (Philadelphia, 1968), p. 51.
2. Learsi, Rufus, *The Wedding Song: A Book of Chassidic Ballads*, Behrman's Jewish Book House (New York, 1938), pp. 22–28.
3. Harlow, Jules, ed., *Yearnings: Prayer and Meditation for the Days of Awe*, Rabbinical Assembly (New York, 1968), p. 18.
4. Zangwill, Israel, *Blind Children*, William Heinemann (London, 1903), pp. 123–125.
5. Sampter, Jessie, *Brand Plucked from the Fire*, Jewish Publication Society of America (Philadelphia, 1937), pp. 189–193.
6. Brin, Ruth F., *Interpretations for the Weekly Torah Reading*, Lerner Publications Co. (Minneapolis, 1965), pp. 156–157.
7. Lucas, Alice, trans., *The Jewish Year*, Macmillan Co. (London, 1898), pp. 145–148. This selection is from "The Royal Crown" which is included in the Sephardic *Maariv* service for Yom Kippur.
8. Misch, Marion L., ed., *Selections for Homes and Schools*, Jewish Publication Society of America (Philadelphia, 1911), pp. 238–239.
9. Leftwich, Joseph, ed., *The Golden Peacock: An Anthology of Yiddish Poetry*, Sci-Art Publishers (Cambridge, Mass., 1939), p. 673.
10. Steinbach, Alexander Alan, *Supplementary Prayers and Meditations for the High Holy Days*, Temple Ahavath Sholom (Brooklyn, 1961), p. 46.
11. Reznikoff, Charles, *By the Waters of Manhattan: Selected Verse*, San Francisco Review and New Directions (New York, 1962), pp. 90–91.
12. *Commentary*, vol. 20, no. 4 (October, 1955), p. 355.
13. Leftwich, pp. 704–706.
14. Kruger, Fania, *The Tenth Jew*, Kaleidograph Press (Dallas, 1949), p. 76.

XIV   YOM KIPPUR IN THE SHORT STORY

1. Schwarz, Leo W., ed., *The Menorah Treasury: Harvest of Half a Century*, Jewish Publication Society of America (Philadelphia, 1964), pp. 351–354; reprinted from *The Menorah Journal*, vol. 24, no. 3 (October–December, 1936), pp. 272–275.
2. Levin, Meyer, *Classic Hassidic Tales*, Citadel Press (New York, 1966), pp. 132–134.
3. London *Jewish Chronicle*, no. 5,136 (September 29, 1967), pp. 42–43.
4. Schwarz, Leo W., ed., *The Jewish Caravan: Great Stories of Twenty-five Centuries*, Farrar & Rinehart (New York, 1935), pp. 300–304.
5. Leftwich, Joseph, ed., *Yisroel: The First Jewish Omnibus*, rev. ed., Thomas Yoseloff (New York, 1963), pp. 423–428.

6. Howe, Irving, and Greenberg, Eliezer, eds., *A Treasury of Yiddish Stories*, Viking Press (New York, 1954), pp. 213–219.
7. Franzos, Karl Emil, *The Jews of Barnow*, trans. by M. W. Macdowall, D. Appleton and Co. (New York, 1883), pp. 136–146.
8. *Yiddish Tales*, trans. by Helena Frank, Jewish Publication Society of America (Philadelphia, 1912), pp. 189–208.
9. Wiesel, Elie, *Legends of Our Time*, Holt, Rinehart and Winston (New York, 1968), pp. 31–38.
10. Barwin, Victor, *Millionaires and Tatterdemalions: Stories of Jewish Life in South Africa*, Edward Goldston & Son (London, 1952), pp. 101–111.
11. Howe and Greenberg, pp. 182–187.

XV PRE-YOM KIPPUR FEASTING

1. Finkelstein, Louis, *The Pharisees: The Sociological Background of Their Faith*, Jewish Publication Society of America (Philadelphia, 1940), vol. 1, pp. 55–58.
2. *Yoma* 81b, *Berakhot* 8b.
3. *Sefer Maharil, Erev Yom Kippur; Orah Hayyim* 604.
4. Glis, Yaakov, "Mi-Minhage Yamim Noraim be-Paras," *Mahanaim*, no. 49 (5721), p. 68.
5. *Hagigah* 27a.
6. Based on Jerusalem *Peah* 8.9.
7. Kosover, Mordecai, "Yidishe Makholim," *Yuda A. Yaffe-Buch*, ed. by Yudel Mark, YIVO Institute for Jewish Research (New York, 1958), p. 125.
8. Briggs, Lloyd Cabot, and Guede, Nornia Lami, *No More For Ever: A Saharan Jewish Town*, Peabody Museum (Cambridge, Mass., 1964), pp. 43–44.
9. Adler, Elkan Nathan, *Jews in Many Lands*, Jewish Publication Society of America (Philadelphia, 1905), p. 17.
10. *Orah Hayyim* 524, Rama.
11. *Ecclesiastes Rabbah* 9.3.

XVI YOM KIPPUR MISCELLANY

1. *Rosh Hashanah* 21a.
2. Jerusalem *Rosh Hashanah* 4.1.
3. Leshem, Hayyim, *Shabbat u-Moade Yisrael*, Niv (Tel Aviv, 1965), vol. 1, pp. 186–187.
4. Rivlin, Joseph J., "Yamim Noraim Etzel Edot ha-Mizrah," *Mahanaim*, no. 60 (5722), p. 166.
5. Graetz, Heinrich, *History of the Jews*, Jewish Publication Society of America (Philadelphia, 1894), vol. 4, p. 626.
6. *Rosh Hashanah* 21a.
7. Levinsky, Yom-Tov, "Yom Kippur Sheni Shel Galuyot," *Sefer Moadim: Rosh Hashanah ve-Yom ha-Kippurim*, ed. by I. L. Barukh, Dvir (Tel Aviv, 5707), pp. 372–374.

8. *Jewish Encyclopedia*, vol. 12, p. 618.
9. Rosenthal, Erwin J., *Judaism and Islam*, Thomas Yoseloff (New York, 1961), pp. 24-25; Leshem, pp. 202-209.
10. *Rosh Hashanah* 11a-b.
11. *Mahanaim*, no. 49 (5721), p. 88.
12. Preshel, Tuviah, "*Tekiat ha-Herut*," *Hadoar*, vol. 48, no. 39 (October 4, 1968), p. 731.
13. Kieval, Herman, *The High Holy Days*, Book One: *Rosh Hashanah*, Burning Bush Press (New York, 1959), p. 126.
14. Preshel.
15. *Yevamot* 63b.
16. Goodman, Philip, and Goodman, Hanna, *The Jewish Marriage Anthology*, Jewish Publication Society of America (Philadelphia, 1965), p. 309.
17. *Keritot* 5b.
18. Wahrmann, Nahum, *Hage Yisrael u-Moadav*, Ahiasaf (Jerusalem, 1959), pp. 52-54.
19. Brauer, Erich, *Yehude Kurdistan*, Palestine Institute of Folklore and Ethnology (Jerusalem, 1947), pp. 258-259.
20. Glenn, Menahem G., *Israel Salanter: Religious-Ethical Thinker*, Bloch Publishing Co. (New York, 1953), pp. 56, 76.
21. *Yoma* 39b.
22. *Pesikta Rabbati* 40.5.
23. Liebman, Seymour B., trans. and ed., *The Enlightened: The Writings of Luis de Carvajal, El Mozo*, University of Miami Press (Coral Gables, Fla., 1967), pp. 45-46.
24. Breuer, Mordecai, "Samson Raphael Hirsch," *Guardians of Our Heritage (1724-1953)*, ed. by Leo Jung, Bloch Publishing Co. (New York, 1958), p. 272. See also Petuchowski, Jacob J., *Prayerbook Reform in Europe*, World Union for Progressive Judaism (New York, 1968), p. 337.
25. *Yamim Noraim: Yalkut le-Rosh Hashanah vele-Yom ha-Kippurim*, Israel Defense Forces (Jerusalem, 5710), p. 26.
26. *Sefer Maharil*, Yom Kippur.
27. Schwab, Hermann, *A World in Ruins: History, Life and Work of German Jewry*, trans. by Charles Fullman, Edward Goldston (London, 1946), p. 202.
28. Rischin, Moses, *The Promised City: New York's Jews, 1870-1914*, Harvard University Press (Cambridge, Mass., 1962), pp. 154-158; Kopeloff, Israel, "The Yom Kippur Balls," *The Golden Land: A Literary Portrait of American Jewry, 1654 to the Present*, ed. by Azriel Eisenberg, Thomas Yoseloff (New York, 1964), pp. 211-213.
29. Eisenstein, Judah David, *Otzar Zikhronotai* (New York, 1929), p. 72.
30. Levy, A. B., *East End Story*, Vallentine, Mitchell & Co. (London, n.d.), p. 89.
31. Bogen, Boris D., with Alfred Segal, *Born a Jew*, Macmillan Co. (New York, 1930), p. 60. See also Landesman, Alter F., *Brownsville: The Birth, Development and Passing of a Jewish Community in New York*, Bloch Publishing Co. (New York, 1969), pp. 109-110.

32. *American Jewish Year Book*, vol. 31 (1929–1930), pp. 21–22, 347–352; *New York Times*, October 3, 1928, p. 34, October 5, p. 27, October 6, p. 21, October 7, p. 31.
33. *Yedion*, Vaadat ha-Tarbut ha-Benkibbutzi, vol. 2, no. 7 (September, 1967), p. 17.
34. Spiro, Melford E., *Kibbutz: Venture in Utopia*, Harvard University Press (Cambridge, Mass., 1956), p. 143; *Yedion*, no. 9 (September, 1965), p. 15.
35. Y. Carmel in *Yedion*, ibid., pp. 10–11.
36. Nahum Mendel in *Yedion*, no. 9 (September, 1965), p. 16.
37. Benari, Nahum, *Shabbat u-Moed: Nisyonot, Haarakhot ve-Tzione Derekh le-Itzuv ha-Demut shel Shabbat u-Moed*, Ha-Histadrut ha-Kelalit shel ha-Ovadim ha-Ivrim (Tel Aviv, 5707), pp. 39–40.
38. *Yedion*, no. 9 (September, 1965), pp. 11–15; ibid., vol. 2, no. 7 (September, 1967), pp. 17–18; *Mikrae Yom ha-Kippurim*, Mishmarot, 1965.
39. Krieger, Yosef, "*Nisyonot Lehahayaat ha-Masoret be-Kibbutz Lo Dati,*" Jerusalem *Petahim*, no. 3 (March, 1968), pp. 47–49.
40. *Hadashot* (Hechal Shlomo, Jerusalem), nos. 72–73 (March–April, 1969), p. 25.

XVII   CHILDREN'S STORIES FOR YOM KIPPUR

1. Weilerstein, Sadie Rose, *The Adventures of K'tonton: A Little Jewish Tom Thumb*, National Women's League of the United Synagogue (New York, 1935), pp. 76–80.
2. Weilerstein, Sadie Rose, *What the Moon Brought*, Jewish Publication Society of America (Philadelphia, 1942), pp. 21–27.
3. Unpublished ms.
4. Gamoran, Mamie G., *Hillel's Happy Holidays*, Union of American Hebrew Congregations (Cincinnati, 1939), pp. 46–57.
5. Zeligs, Dorothy F., *The Story of Jewish Holidays and Customs for Young People*, Bloch Publishing Co. (New York, 1942), pp. 36–38.
6. Fast, Howard, *Haym Salomon: Son of Liberty*, Julian Messner (New York, 1941), pp. 136–139.
7. Eisenberg, Azriel, and Globe, Leah Ain, eds., *The Bas Mitzvah Treasury*, Twayne Publishers (New York, 1965), pp. 141–145.
8. Rothgiesser, Rubin, *The Well of Gerar*, trans. by Harry Schneiderman, Jewish Publication Society of America (Philadelphia, 1953), pp. 37–50.

XVIII   CHILDREN'S POEMS FOR YOM KIPPUR

1. Aronin, Ben, *Jolly Jingles for the Jewish Child*, Behrman House (New York, 1947), n.p.
2. Weilerstein, Sadie Rose, *The Singing Way: Poems for Jewish Children*, illus. by Jessie B. Robinson, National Women's League of the United Synagogue (New York, 1946), p. 8.

3. Sampter, Jessie E., *Around the Year in Rhymes for the Jewish Child*, Bloch Publishing Co. (New York, 1920), p. 16.
4. Ibid., p. 15.
5. Fein, Harry H., trans., *Gems of Hebrew Verse: Poems for Young People*, Bruce Humphries (Boston, 1940), p. 20.
6. Glicenstein, Enrico, and Dushkin, Alexander M., *The Tree of Life: Sketches of Jewish Life of Yesterday and Today in Drawing, Prose and Verse*, L. M. Stein (Chicago, 1933), pp. 27–29.

GLOSSARY OF YOM KIPPUR

TERMS

AL HET (for the sin). The confession recited on Yom Kippur.

ALL VOWS. See KOL NIDRE.

AMIDAH (standing). The prayer recited silently while standing.

DAY OF ATONEMENT. See YOM KIPPUR.

DAYS OF AWE. See YAMIM NORAIM.

GEMAR HATIMAH TOVAH (may the final sealing [verdict] be good). The traditional greeting on Yom Kippur.

HAZKARAT NESHAMOT (remembrance of souls [of the departed]). See YIZKOR.

HIGH HOLY DAYS. See YAMIM NORAIM.

KAAROT (plates). Plates used in the synagogue on the afternoon preceding Yom Kippur for collecting funds for charity.

KAPPAROT (atonement). A symbolic ceremony, reminiscent of the offering of a sacrifice in the Temple, in which charity is given; observed on the day before Yom Kippur.

KEROVAH (approach). Poetical interpolation in the *Amidah*.

KITTEL. A white robe worn on Yom Kippur and other solemn occasions.

KOL NIDRE (all vows). The first two words of the Aramaic formula for the absolution from vows, chanted before the evening service of Yom Kippur. The evening is often designated as *Kol Nidre* evening.

MAHZOR (cycle). Book of prayers for the cycle of holy days and festivals throughout the year; also applied to the individual parts of the yearly liturgy in which *piyyutim* are included.

NEILAH (closing). The concluding service of Yom Kippur.

PIYYUT, pl. PIYYUTIM (poetry). A liturgical poem of praise recited on Rosh Hashanah and Yom Kippur.

SEUDAH MAFSEKET (dividing meal). The final meal before the fast of Yom Kippur.

VIDDUI (confession). The prayer of confession that recurs in the Yom Kippur liturgy.

YAMIM NORAIM (Days of Awe). The ten-day penitential period from Rosh Hashanah through Yom Kippur.

YIZKOR (may He remember). Memorial prayer for the departed recited on Yom Kippur.

YOM KIPPUR (Day of Atonement). The culmination of the penitential days devoted to fasting and prayer; it falls on the tenth day of Tishri and is the most sacred day of the Jewish year.

BIBLIOGRAPHY

GENERAL REFERENCES

ABRAHAMS, ISRAEL, *Festival Studies: Being Thoughts on the Jewish Year*, Julius H. Greenstone, Philadelphia, 1906, pp. 25–31, 96–102.

AGNON, SHMUEL YOSEF, *Yamim Noraim: Sefer Minhagot ve-Midrashot ve-Aggadot le-Yeme ha-Rahamim veha-Selihot le-Rosh ha-Shanah vele-Yom ha-Kippurim vele-Yamim she-Bentaim*, Schocken, Berlin, 5698, pp. 255–382.

———, *Days of Awe: Being a Treasury of Traditions, Legends and Learned Commentaries Concerning Rosh Hashanah, Yom Kippur and the Days Between, Culled from Three Hundred Volumes Old and New*, introduction by Judah Goldin, Schocken Books, New York, 1965, pp. 147–279.

AMORAI, Y., and ARIEL, Z., eds. *Moreshet Avot* (*Entziklopediah "Mayan"*), Joseph Sreberk, Tel Aviv, n.d., pp. 64–74.

ARIEL, Z., ed., *Sefer ha-Hag veha-Moed*, Am Oved, Tel Aviv, 1962, pp. 35–76.

ASAF, A., *Sefer Yamim Noraim*, Joshua Chachik, Tel Aviv, 5715, pp. 98–200.

AUSUBEL, NATHAN, *The Book of Jewish Knowledge*, Crown Publishers, New York, 1964.

AYALI, MEIR, ed., *Hagim u-Zemanim: Mahzore Kriah le-Moade Yisrael*, Gazit, Tel Aviv, 5715, vol. 2, pp. 81–216.

BARUCH, Y. L., ed., *Sefer ha-Moadim: Rosh ha-Shanah ve-Yom ha-Kippurim*, "Oneg Shabbat" Society and Dvir, Tel Aviv, 1946, pp. 191–397.

BEN-EZRA, AKIBA, *Minhage Hagim*, M. Newman, Tel Aviv, 5723, pp. 27–63.

———, ed. *Yamim Noraim ve-Sukkot*, Mizrachi National Education Committee, New York, 1949, pp. 20–35.

BEN YEHOSHUA, HAGI, ed., *Yamim Noraim: Reshimah Bibliografit*, Municipality of Jerusalem Department of Education and Culture, Jerusalem, 1966.

BERNARDS, SOLOMON S., *The Living Heritage of the High Holy Days*, Anti-Defamation League of B'nai B'rith, New York, n.d., pp. 15–31.

BIAL, MORRISON DAVID, *Liberal Judaism at Home: The Practice of Modern Reform Judaism*, Temple Sinai, Summit, N. J., 1967, pp. 111–115.

BIRNBAUM, PHILIP, *A Book of Jewish Concepts*, Hebrew Publishing Co., New York, 1964.

BÜCHLER, A., *Studies in Sin and Atonement in the Rabbinic Literature of the First Century*, Ktav Publishing House, New York, 1967.

CHAGALL, BELLA, *Burning Lights*, Schocken Books, New York, 1946, pp. 82–95.

CHOMSKY, WILLIAM, *Ha-Yamim ha-Noraim: Rosh ha-Shanah ve-Yom ha-Kippurim*, Jewish Education Committee of New York, 1960, pp. 3–32.

EHRMANN, ELIESER L., *Rosch Ha-Schana und Jom Kippur: Ein Quellenheft*, Schocken Verlag, Berlin, 1938, pp. 36–70.

EISENSTEIN, IRA, *What We Mean by Religion: A Modern Interpretation of the Sabbath and Festivals*. Reconstructionist Press, New York, 1958, pp. 62–80.

ELINER, ELIEZER, ed., *Keseh ve-Asor*, Religious Section of the Department of Education and Culture in the Diaspora, World Zionist Organization, Jerusalem, 1951, pp. 69–205.

FREEHOF, LILLIAN S., and BANDMAN, LOTTIE C., *Flowers and Festivals of the Jewish Year*, Hearthside Press, New York, 1964, pp. 56–61.

GASTER, THEODOR H., *Festivals of the Jewish Year: A Modern Interpretation and Guide*, William Sloane Associates, New York, 1953, pp. 135–186.

GOLDIN, HYMAN E., *The Jewish Woman and Her Home*, Jewish Culture Publishing Co., Brooklyn, N.Y., 1941, pp. 203–216.

GOLDMAN, ALEX J., *A Handbook for the Jewish Family: Understanding and Enjoying the Sabbath and Holidays*, Bloch Publishing Co., New York, 1958, pp. 35–48.

GOODMAN, PHILIP, ed., *New Year and Day of Atonement Program Material for Youth and Adults*, National Jewish Welfare Board, New York, 1952, pp. 1–90.

GREENBERG, BETTY D., and SILVERMAN, ALTHEA O., *The Jewish Home Beautiful*, National Women's League of the United Synagogue of America, New York, 1941, pp. 44–47.

GREENSTONE, JULIUS H., *The Jewish Religion*, Jewish Chautauqua Society, Philadelphia, 1929, pp. 87–100.

———, *Jewish Feasts and Fasts*, Philadelphia, 1945, pp. 25–56.

HAKOHEN, SHMUEL, SHRAGAI, ELIAHU, and PELI, PINHAS, eds., *Yamim Noraim: Yalkut le-Rosh ha-Shanah ve-Yom ha-Kippurim*, Tzava Haganah le-Yisrael, no. 6 (5710), pp. 63–80.

JACOBS, LOUIS, *A Guide to Yom Kippur*, Jewish Chronicle Publications, London, 1951, pp. 1–83.

The Jewish Encyclopedia, 12 vols., Ktav Publishing House, New York; articles on *Al Het*, Atonement, Azazel, Confession of Sin, *Hazkarat Neshamot, Kapparah, Kol Nidre, Neilah.*

JOSEPH, MORRIS, *Judaism as Creed and Life*, George Routledge and Sons, London, 1903, pp. 255–274.

KAPLAN, MORDECAI M., *The Meaning of God in Modern Jewish Religion*, Jewish Reconstructionist Foundation, New York, 1947, pp. 149–187.

KITOV, ELIYAHU, *Sefer ha-Todaah: La-Daat Huke ha-Elokim u-Mitzvotav Hage Yisrael u-Moadav*, Alef Makhon le-Hatzaat Sefarim, Jerusalem, 1964, pp. 29–66.

———, *The Book of Our Heritage: The Jewish Year and Its Days of Significance*, vol. 1: *Tishrey-Shevat*, trans. by Nathan Bulman, 'A' Publishers, Jerusalem, 1968, pp. 61–128.

LAUTERBACH, JACOB Z., "The Ritual for the *Kapparot* Ceremony," *Jewish Studies in Memory of George A. Kohut*, ed. by Salo W. Baron and Alexander Marx, Alexander Kohut Memorial Foundation, New York, 1935, pp. 413–422.

LEHRMAN, S. M., *The Jewish Festivals*, Shapiro, Vallentine & Co., London, 1938, pp. 109–124.

LESHEM, HAIM, *Shabbat u-Moade Yisrael be-Halakhah, be-Aggadah, be-Historiah, be-Hivui, uve-Folklor*, Niv, Tel Aviv, 1965, pp. 155–212.

MAIMON (FISHMAN), YEHUDAH LEB HAKOHEN, *Hagim u-Moadim*, Mosad Harav Kook, Jerusalem, 1944, pp. 40–52.

MARKOWITZ, S. H., *Leading a Jewish Life in the Modern World*, rev. ed., Union of American Hebrew Congregations, New York, 1958, pp. 160–179.

MAX MOSHEH, *The Way of God*, Feldheim Publishers, New York, 1968, pp. 206–224.

MELAMED, DEBORAH M., *The Three Pillars: Thought, Worship and Practice for the Jewish Woman*, National Women's League of United Synagogue of America, New York, 1927, pp. 89–96.

Messekhet Yoma, Talmud Bavli, Wilna, 1895.

Midrash on Psalms (Midrash Tehillim), trans. by William G. Braude, Yale University Press, New Haven, 1959.

The Mishnah, trans. by Herbert Danby, Clarendon Press, Oxford, 1933, pp. 162–172.

MONTEFIORE, C. G., and LOEWE, H., *A Rabbinic Anthology*, Macmillan and Co., London, 1938.

MOORE, GEORGE FOOT, *Judaism in the First Centuries of the Christian Era*, Harvard University Press, Cambridge, Mass., 1927, vol. 1, pp. 497–534.

MORGENSTERN, JULIAN, "Two Ancient Israelite Agricultural Festivals," *Jewish Quarterly Review*, vol. 8 (1917), pp. 31–54.

———, "Two Prophecies of the Fourth Century B.C. and the Evolution of Yom Kippur," *Hebrew Union College Annual*, vol. 24 (1952–1953), pp. 1–74.

NADICH, JUDAH, *Yom Kippur*, National Jewish Welfare Board, New York, 1954, pp. 1–11.

NEWMAN, LOUIS I., and SPITZ, SAMUEL, *The Talmudic Anthology*, Behrman House, New York, 1945, pp. 553–560.

PEARLMUTTER, JACOB, ed., *Themes for Daily Study: Selections from the Bible, Talmud, Midrash and Shulchan-Aruch for Study*, part 1: *Rosh Hashanah and Yom Kippur*, Bloch Publishing Co., New York, 1941, pp. 1–21, 43–53.

PIRKE DE-RABBI ELIEZER, trans. by Gerald Friedlander, Kegan Paul, Trench, Trubner and Co., London, 1916.

PRESS, CHAIM, *What Is the Reason: An Anthology of Questions and Answers on the Jewish Holidays*, vol. 2: *Yom Kippur*, Bloch Publishing Co., New York, 1965, pp. 1–84.

ROTH, CECIL, ed., *The Standard Jewish Encyclopedia*, Doubleday & Co., Garden City, N.Y., 1959; articles on Atonement, Azazel, *Kol Nidre, Neilah.*

SACHS, A. S., *Worlds That Passed*, Jewish Publication Society of America, Philadelphia, 1928, pp. 172–183, 236–241.

SCHAUSS, HAYYIM, *The Jewish Festivals: From Their Beginnings to Our Own Day*, Union of American Hebrew Congregations, Cincinnati, 1938, pp. 119–142, 149–155.

SEIDMAN, HILLEL, *The Glory of the Jewish Holidays*, ed. by Moses Zalesky, Shengold Publishers, New York, 1969, pp. 93–99.

SHECHTER, S. ZVI, ed., *Moade Yisrael: Pirke Kriah ve-Nigun*, Ministry of Education and Culture Youth Department and Henrietta Szold Institute, Jerusalem, 1966, pp. 65–80.

SHRAGAI, ELIYAHU, and ALFASI, YITZHAK, eds., *Be-Yeme Din: Perakim le-Yamim Noraim*, Tzava Haganah le-Yisrael, no. 11 (5711), pp. 53–95.

SPERLING, ABRAHAM ISAAC, *Reasons for Jewish Customs and Traditions*, trans. by Abraham Matts, Bloch Publishing Co., New York, 1968, pp. 232–246.

Tishri: Textes pour Servir à la Préparation des Fêtes de Rosh Hashanah, Kippour et Soukkoth, Editions des E.I.F., Paris, 1945, pp. 65–143.

TVERSKI, SHIMON, ed., *Moadim: Massekhet le-Yamim Noraim vele-Hag Sukkot*, Tzava Haganah le-Yisrael, no. 15 (5713), pp. 28–45.

The Universal Jewish Encyclopedia, 10 vols., ed. by Isaac Landman, Ktav Publishing House, New York, 1968; articles on Atonement, Azazel, Confession, Fasting and Fast Days, Forgiveness, *Kappores, Kol Nidre*, Memorial Service, *Neilah*, Penance, Repentance, Yom Kippur.

UNTERMAN, ISAAC, *The Jewish Holidays*, 2nd ed., Bloch Publishing Co., New York, 1950, pp. 59–77.

VAINSTEIN, YAACOV, *The Cycle of the Jewish Year: A Study of the Festivals and of Selections from the Liturgy*, World Zionist Organization, Jerusalem, 1964, pp. 105–115.

WAHRMANN, NAHUM, *Hage Yisrael u-Moadav: Minhagehem u-Semelehem*, Ahiasaf, Jerusalem, 1959, pp. 41–60.

———, ed., *Moadim: Pirke Halakhah, Aggadah ve-Tefilah le-Khol Moade ha-Shanah*, Kiryat Sefer, Jerusalem, 1957, pp. 39–47, 174–177, 233–234.

WERBLOWSKY, R. J. ZWI, and WIGODER, GEOFFREY, eds., *The Encyclopedia of the Jewish Religion*, Holt, Rinehart and Winston, New York, 1966; articles on Atonement, *Kol Nidre.*

Yoma, trans. by Leo Jung, *The Babylonian Talmud*, ed. by Isidore Epstein, Soncino Press, London, 1938.

ZOBEL, MORITZ, *Das Jahr des Juden in Brauch und Liturgie*, Schocken Verlag, Berlin, 1963, pp. 77–93.

YOM KIPPUR IN JEWISH LAW

BERMAN, YAAKOV, *Halakhah la-Am*, Avraham Zioni, Tel Aviv, 1962, pp. 187–218.

CARO, JOSEPH, *Shulhan Arukh, Orah Hayyim*, "Hilkhot Yom Kippur," 604–624.

EISENSTEIN, JUDAH D., *Otzar Dinim u-Minhagim*, New York, 1917.

GANZFRIED, SOLOMON, *Code of Jewish Law*, trans. by Hyman E. Goldin, Hebrew Publishing Co., New York, 1927, vol. 3, pp. 81–93.

HURWITZ, S. L., *Sefer Dine Yisrael u-Minhagav le-Yamim Noraim*, New York, 1924.

Laws and Customs of Israel, trans. by Gerald Friedlander, Shapiro, Vallentine & Co., London, 1934, pp. 368–376.

MOSES BEN MAIMON, *Mishneh Torah*, Amsterdam, 1702, "Hilkhot Shevitat Asor."

SHPRILING, ABRAHAM ISAAC, *Sefer Taame ha-Minhagim u-Mekor ha-Dinim*, Eshkol, Jerusalem, 5721, pp. 325–342.

ZEVIN, SHLOMOH YOSEF, *Ha-Moadim be-Halakhah*, 2nd ed., Betan Hasefer, Tel Aviv, 5707, pp. 62–89.

THE LITURGY OF YOM KIPPUR

ADLER, HERBERT M., and DAVIS, ARTHUR, trans., *Service of the Synagogue: Day of Atonement*, George Routledge & Sons, London, 1904.

ARZT, MAX, *Justice and Mercy: Commentary on the Liturgy of the New Year and the Day of Atonement*, Holt, Rinehart and Winston, New York, 1963, pp. 189–287.

BARISH, LOUIS, *High Holiday Liturgy*, Jonathan David, New York, 1959, pp. 96–170.

BAUMGARDT, DAVID, "Yom Kippur and the Jew of Today: The Time of Renewal," *Commentary*, XXVIII (October, 1959), pp. 299–306.

BIRNBAUM, PHILIP, trans., *High Holyday Prayer Book*, Hebrew Publishing Co., New York, 1951, pp. 463–1042.

BOKSER, BEN ZION, trans., *The High Holiday Prayer Book: Rosh Hashanah and Yom Kippur*, Hebrew Publishing Co., New York, 1959, pp. 238–537.

DAVIDSON, ISRAEL, "Kol Nidre," *American Jewish Year Book 5684*, XXV (1923), pp. 180–194.

DEMBITZ, LEWIS N., *Jewish Service in Synagogue and Home*, Jewish Publication Society of America, Philadelphia, 1898, pp. 165–179.

ELBOGEN, ISAAC M., *Toldot ha-Tefilah veha-Avodah be-Yisrael*, Dvir, Jerusalem/Berlin, 5684, part 1, pp. 134–140.

FREEHOF, SOLOMON B., *The Small Sanctuary: Judaism in the Prayerbook*, Union of American Hebrew Congregations, New York, 1942, pp. 171–173, 192–195, 248–249.

———, "Hazkarath Neshamoth," *Hebrew Union College Annual*, XXXVI (1965), pp. 179–189.

GLATZER, NAHUM N., ed., *Language of Faith: A Selection from the Most Expressive Jewish Prayers*, Schocken Books, New York, 1967, pp. 280–291, 294–299.

HERTZ, JOSEPH HERMAN, *The Authorised Daily Prayer Book*, Bloch Publishing Co., New York, 1952, pp. 890–937.

IDELSOHN, A. Z., *Jewish Liturgy and Its Development*, Henry Holt and Co., New York, 1932, pp. 223–256, 287–294.

——, "The *Kol Nidre* Tune," *Hebrew Union College Annual*, VIII–IX (1931–1932), pp. 493–509.

KAPLAN, MORDECAI M., KOHN, EUGENE, and EISENSTEIN, IRA, eds., *High Holiday Prayer Book with Supplementary Prayers and Readings and with a New English Translation*, Jewish Reconstructionist Foundation, New York, 1948, vol. 2.

——, *Supplementary Prayers and Readings for the High Holidays*, part 1—*Rosh Hashanah*; part 2—*Yom Kippur*, Jewish Reconstructionist Foundation, New York, 1960.

KLEIN, MAX D., trans., *Seder Avodah: Service Book for Rosh Hashanah and Yom Kippur*, Philadelphia, 1960, pp. 379–865.

LEVY, ELIEZER, *Yesodot ha-Tefilah*, Betan Hasefer, Tel Aviv, 5712, pp. 256–264.

MARMORSTEIN, ARTHUR, "The Confession of Sins for the Day of Atonement," *Essays in Honour of . . . J. H. Hertz*, ed. by I. Epstein, E. Levine, and C. Roth, Edward Goldston, London, n.d., pp. 293–305.

MARTIN, BERNARD, *Prayer in Judaism*, Basic Books, New York, 1968, pp. 181–231, 249–256.

MUNK, ELIE, *The World of Prayer*, vol. 2: *Commentary and Translation of the Sabbath and Festival Prayers*, Philipp Feldheim, New York, 1963, pp. 217–269.

POOL, DAVID DE SOLA, ed. and trans., *Prayers for the Day of Atonement according to the Custom of the Spanish and Portuguese Jews*, Union of Sephardic Congregations, New York, 1939.

RUBINSTEIN, A. L., *A Companion to the Rosh Hashanah & Yom Kippur Machzor*, Glasgow, 1957, pp. 63–122.

SILVERMAN, MORRIS, ed., *High Holiday Prayer Book*, Prayer Book Press, Hartford, 1951, pp. 191–499.

STEINBACH, ALEXANDER ALAN, ed., *Supplementary Prayers and Meditations for the High Holy Days*, Temple Ahavath Sholom, Brooklyn, 1961, pp. 45–88.

The Union Prayer Book for Jewish Worship, newly rev. ed., part 2, Central Conference of American Rabbis, New York, 1962, pp. 123–350.

YOM KIPPUR IN THE SHORT STORY

AGNON, SHMUEL YOSEF, "The Dusk of the Day," trans. by T. Kardom, *Israel Argosy*, no. 9, ed. by Isaac Halevy-Levin, Thomas Yoseloff, New York, 1968, pp. 173–182.

——, "Chemdat," *Israel Argosy*, ed. by Isaac Halevy-Levin, Youth and Hechalutz Department of the Zionist Organization, Jerusalem, Autumn, 1962, pp. 82–111.

——, "The Story of the Cantor," *The Bridal Canopy*, trans. by I. M. Lask, Schocken Books, New York, 1967, pp. 262–272.

——, "As Evening Falls," *Hadassah Magazine*, XLVIII (May, 1967), pp. 8–9, 25.

——, *Sippure Yom ha-Kippurim*, ed. by Naftali Ginton, Schocken Publishing House, Tel Aviv, 1967.

BARWIN, VICTOR, "The Call," *Millionaires and Tatterdemalions: Stories of Jewish Life in South Africa*, Edward Goldston & Son, London, 1952, pp. 101–111.

BUBER, MARTIN, "The Prayer Book," trans. by Simon Chasen, *The Menorah Treasury: Harvest of Half a Century*, ed. by Leo W. Schwarz, Jewish Publication Society of America, Philadelphia, 1964, pp. 351–354; *Jewish Literature since the Bible: Book Two*, by Leon I. Feuer and Azriel Eisenberg, Union of American Hebrew Congregations, Cincinnati, 1941, pp. 21–27.

FERBER, EDNA, "The Fast," *A Golden Treasury of Jewish Literature*, ed. by Leo W. Schwarz, Farrar and Rinehart, New York, 1937, pp. 57–68; *Tales of Our People: Great Stories of the Jew in America*, ed. by Jerry D. Lewis, Bernard Geis Associates, New York, 1969, pp. 17–29.

FRANZOS, KARL EMIL, "The Saviour of Barnow," trans. by M. W. Macdowall, *Jewish Short Stories*, ed. by Ludwig Lewisohn, Behrman House, New York, 1945, pp. 54–64; *Yisroel: The First Jewish Omnibus*, rev. ed., ed. by Joseph Leftwich, Thomas Yoseloff, New York, 1952, pp. 242–246.

FRISHMAN, DAVID, "Three Who Ate," *Yiddish Tales*, trans. by Helena Frank, Jewish Publication Society of America, Philadelphia, 1912, pp. 267–278; *The Jewish Caravan*, ed. by Leo W. Schwarz, Farrar and Rinehart, New York, 1935, pp. 300–304; *Modern Jewish Life in Literature*, by Azriel Eisenberg, United Synagogue Commission on Jewish Education, New York, 1948, pp. 29–33.

GOLDSMITH, MILTON, "Yom Kippur," *Rabbi and Priest: A Story*, Jewish Publication Society of America, Philadelphia, 1936, pp. 172–179.

LEVIN, MEYER, "The Burning of the Torah," "The Boy's Song," *Classic Hassidic Tales*, Citadel Press, New York, 1966, pp. 125–131, 132–134.

ORNITZ, SAMUEL, "Yom Kippur Fressers," *A Treasury of Jewish Humor*, ed. by Nathan Ausubel, Doubleday & Co., Garden City, N. Y., 1951, pp. 272–274.

PERETZ, ISAAC LOEB, "The New Tune," *Stories and Pictures*, trans. by Helena Frank, Jewish Publication Society of America, Philadelphia, 1906, pp. 53–55.

——, "Neilah in Gehenna," trans. by A. M. Klein, *A Treasury of Yiddish Stories*, ed. by Irving Howe and Eliezer Greenberg, Viking Press, New York, 1954, pp. 213–219.

——, "Miracles on the Sea," *Stories from Peretz*, trans. by Sol Liptzin, Hebrew Publishing Co., New York, 1947, pp. 104–112; *A Treasury of Jewish Sea Stories*, ed. by Samuel Sobel, Jonathan David, New York, 1965, pp. 133–140.

——, "Miracles on the Sea," "Neilah," "Beryl the Tailor," *In This World and the Next: Selected Writings*, trans. by Moshe Spiegel, Thomas Yoseloff, New York, 1958, pp. 143–149, 156–166, 251–255.

——, "The Miracle on the Sea," trans. by Joseph Leftwich, *Yisroel: The First Jewish Omnibus*, rev. ed., ed. by Joseph Leftwich, Thomas Yoseloff, New York, 1952, pp. 423–428.

RABINOWITZ, S. J., see Sholom Aleichem.

RAPHAELSON, SAMSON, "The Day of Atonement," *Everybody's Magazine*, XLVI (January, 1922), pp. 44–55.

ROSENTHAL, ELIEZER DAVID, "Yom Kippur," *Yiddish Tales*, trans. by Helena Frank, Jewish Publication Society of America, Philadelphia, 1912, pp. 189–208.

ROTHBERG, ABRAHAM, "The Very Presence of God," *The Bar Mitzvah Treasury*, ed. by Azriel Eisenberg, Behrman House, New York, 1952, pp. 55–68.

RUGEL, MIRIAM, "The Flower," *Tales of Our People: Great Stories of the Jew in America*, ed. by Jerry D. Lewis, Bernard Geis Associates, New York, 1969, pp. 283–294.

SACHER-MASOCH, LEOPOLD VON, "Bair and Wolff," *Jewish Tales*, trans. by Harriet Lieber Cohen, A. C. McClurg and Co., Chicago, 1894, pp. 298–308.

SHOLOM ALEICHEM, "A Yom Kippur Scandal," "Tit for Tat," "The Day before Yom Kippur," *The Old Country*, trans. by Julius and Frances Butwin, Crown Publishers, New York, 1946, pp. 138–144, 214–217, 319–328.

————, "The Search," trans. by Norbert Guterman, *A Treasury of Yiddish Stories*, ed. by Irving Howe and Eliezer Greenberg, Viking Press, New York, 1954, pp. 182–187.

————, "A Yom Kippur Scandal," "The Day before Yom Kippur," trans. by Julius and Frances Butwin, *Selected Stories of Sholom Aleichem*, ed. by Alfred Kazin, Modern Library, New York, 1956, pp. 155–161, 324–332.

————, "A Yom Kippur Scandal," *The Tevye Stories and Others*, trans. by Julius and Frances Butwin, Pocket Books, New York, 1965, pp. 178–183.

SINGER, ISRAEL JOSHUA, "Repentance," trans. by Maurice Samuel, *A Treasury of Yiddish Stories*, ed. by Irving Howe and Eliezer Greenberg, Viking Press, New York, 1954, pp. 350–357; *Great Jewish Short Stories*, ed. by Saul Bellow, Dell Publishing Co., New York, 1963, pp. 198–208.

ZANGWILL, ISRAEL, "Hopes and Dreams," *Children of the Ghetto*, Jewish Publication Society of America, Philadelphia, 1892, pp. 542–549.

————, "Satan Mekatrig," *Ghetto Tragedies*, Jewish Publication Society of America, Philadelphia, 1899, pp. 345–400.

CHILDREN'S STORIES AND DESCRIPTIONS OF YOM KIPPUR

ABRAMSON, LILLIAN S., "Rosh Hashanah and Yom Kippur in Spain," *Join Us for the Holidays*, illus. by Jessie B. Robinson, National Women's League of the United Synagogue of America, New York, 1958, pp. 5–6.

BREGOFF, JACQUELINE, "Yom Kippur," *Holiday Time*, Bookman Associates, New York, 1957, n.p.

BURSTEIN, ABRAHAM, "The Yom Kippur Stomach Treatment," *The Ghetto Messenger*, Bloch Publishing Co., New York, 1928, pp. 220–225.

CEDARBAUM, SOPHIA N., *Rosh Ha-Shono: Yom Kippur: The High Holy Days*, illus. by Clare and John Ross, Union of American Hebrew Congregations, New York, 1962, pp. 18–30.

EDIDIN, BEN M., *Jewish Holidays and Festivals*, illus. by Kyra Markham, Hebrew Publishing Co., New York, 1940, pp. 55–68.

EINHORN, DAVID, "The Miracle of the Echo," *The Seventh Candle and Other Folk Tales of Eastern Europe*, trans. by Gertrude Pashin, illus. by Ezekiel Schloss, Ktav Publishing House, New York, 1968, pp. 88–94.

EISENBERG, AZRIEL, and ROBINSON, JESSIE B., *My Jewish Holidays*, United Synagogue Commission on Jewish Education, N. Y., 1958, pp. 27–37.

EISENBERG, AZRIEL, "Rabbi Joshua Is Disciplined on Yom Kippur," *The Story of the Jewish Calendar*, Abelard-Schuman, New York, 1958, pp. 33–35.

———, ed., "Why the Rabbi Rode on Yom Kippur," *Tzedakah: A Way of Life*, Behrman House, New York, 1963, pp. 106–109.

EPSTEIN, MORRIS, *All about Jewish Holidays and Customs*, illus. by Arnold Lobel, Ktav Publishing House, New York, 1959, pp. 24–27.

———, *A Pictorial Treasury of Jewish Holidays and Customs*, Ktav Publishing House, New York, 1959, pp. 31–35.

———, "The Boy's Prayer," *My Holiday Story Book*, illus. by Arnold Lobel, Ktav Publishing House, New York, 1958, pp. 9–13.

FAST, HOWARD M., *Haym Salomon: Son of Liberty*, Julian Messner, New York, 1941, pp. 136–139.

FINE, HELEN, "Please Forgive G'dee," *G'dee*, Union of American Hebrew Congregations, New York, 1958, pp. 28–35.

FREEHOF, LILLIAN S., "The Goldfish and the Whale," *Star Light Stories: Holiday and Sabbath Tales*, Bloch Publishing Co., New York, 1952, pp. 23–32.

FRISHMAN, DAVID, "The Three Who Ate," trans. by Helena Frank, *Modern Jewish Life in Literature*, ed. by Azriel Eisenberg, United Synagogue Commission on Jewish Education, New York, 1948, pp. 29–33.

GAMORAN, MAMIE G., *Days and Ways: The Story of Jewish Holidays and Customs*, Union of American Hebrew Congregations, Cincinnati, 1941, pp. 39–50.

———, "A Good Deed," *Hillel's Calendar*, illus. by Ida Libby Dengrove, Union of American Hebrew Congregations, New York, 1960, pp. 37–43.

———, "A Different Holiday," "A Yom Kippur Song," "A Little Hero of Long Ago," *Hillel's Happy Holidays*, illus. by Temima N. Gezari, Union of American Hebrew Congregations, Cincinnati, 1939, pp. 37–57.

GINSBURG, MARVELL, and PINS, ARNULF M., *My Yom Kippur Prayerbook: A Picture Prayerbook for the Very Young*, illus. by Robin King, Behrman House, New York, 1962.

GOLDIN, HYMAN E., *A Treasury of Jewish Holidays*, illus. by Resko, Twayne Publishers, New York, 1952, pp. 30–39.

GOLUB, ROSE W., "A Yom Kippur Surprise," *Down Holiday Lane*, illus. by Louis Kobrin, Union of American Hebrew Congregations, Cincinnati, 1947, pp. 11–17.

HALPERIN, Y., "Pardon," *Gan-Gani: Let Us Play in Israel*, ed. by Levin Kipnis and Yemima Tchernovitz, N. Tversky, Tel Aviv, 1952, pp. 30–31.

HALPERN, SALOMON ALTER, "The Tenth Jew," *Tales of Faith*, Boys Town, Jerusalem, 1968, pp. 149–153.

ISAACS, ABRAM S., "Born Again," *Under the Sabbath Lamp: Stories of Our Time for Old and Young*, Jewish Publication Society of America, Philadelphia, 1919, pp. 39–52.

ISH-KISHOR, SULAMITH, "The Good Miser," *The Palace of Eagles and Other Stories*, Shoulson Press, New York, 1948, pp. 57–65.

KATSH, ABRAHAM I., ed., *Bar Mitzvah: Illustrated*, Shengold Publishers, New York, 1955, pp. 66–68.

KRANZLER, GERSHON, ed., *Jewish Youth Companion: Stories, Poems . . .* , Merkos L'Inyonei Chinuch, Brooklyn, 1957, pp. 73–78.

KRIPKE, DOROTHY K., "Debbie on Trial," *Debbie in Dreamland: Her Holiday Adventures*, illus. by Bill Giacalone, National Women's League of United Synagogue, New York, 1960, pp. 13–18.

LEARSI, RUFUS, "Shimmele Finds a Solution," *Shimmele and His Friends*, Behrman's Jewish Book House, New York, 1940, pp. 95–113.

LEVINGER, ELMA EHRLICH, "The Borrowed Garment," *Playmates in Egypt*, Jewish Publication Society of America, Philadelphia, 1940, pp. 41–54.

——, "A Big Mistake," *Jewish Holyday Stories: Modern Tales of the American Jewish Youth*, Bloch Publishing Co., New York, 1932, pp. 43–53.

——, "The Day of Return," *In Many Lands*, Bloch Publishing Co., New York, 1923, pp. 25–33.

——, "The Day of Forgiveness," *Tales Old and New*, Bloch Publishing Co., New York, 1926, pp. 33–39.

MARGOLIS, ISIDOR, and MARKOWITZ, SIDNEY L., *Jewish Holidays and Festivals*, illus. by John Teppich, Citadel Press, New York, 1962, pp. 37–42.

MARKOWITZ, SAMUEL H., *Leading a Jewish Life in the Modern World*, Union of American Hebrew Congregations, New York, 1958, pp. 160–179.

MINDEL, NISSAN, *The Complete Story of Tishrei*, Merkos L'Inyonei Chinuch, Brooklyn, 1961, pp. 99–140.

MORROW, BETTY, and HARTMAN, LOUIS, *Jewish Holidays*, illus. by Nathan Goldstein, Garrard Publishing Co., Champaign, Ill., 1967, pp. 26–32.

"The Most Precious Thing: A Yom Kippur Fantasy," *A Handbook for the Jewish Family*, by Alex J. Goldman, Bloch Publishing Co., New York, 1958, pp. 43–46.

SHOLOM ALEICHEM, "Kaporos," trans. by Benjamin Efron, *Yiddish Stories for Young People*, ed. by Itche Goldberg, Kinderbuch Publishers, New York, 1966, pp. 57–71.

SIMON, NORMA, *Yom Kippur*, illus. by Ayala Gordon, United Synagogue Commission on Jewish Education, New York, 1959.

SIMON, SHIRLEY, "Ruth Is Never Bad," *Once Upon a Jewish Holiday*, by Bea Stadtler, illus. by Bill Giacalone, Ktav Publishing House, New York, 1965, pp. 18–20.

SMITH, HAROLD P., "Yom Kippur," *A Treasure Hunt in Judaism*, Hebrew Publishing Co., New York, 1950, pp. 58–66.

SOKOLOW, HELENA, "The Day of Atonement," *Bible Rhapsodies*, Massadah, Tel Aviv, 1956, pp. 33–36.

SPIRO, SAUL S., and SPIRO, RENA M., *The Joy of Jewish Living*, Bureau of Jewish Education, Cleveland, 1965, pp. 65–73, 191–192.

STEINBERG, JUDAH, "Forgiven," *The Bas Mitzvah Treasury*, ed. by Azriel Eisenberg and Leah Ain Globe, National Women's League of the United Synagogue of America, New York, 1965, pp. 141–145.

TAYLOR, SYDNEY, "Yom Kippur, Day of Atonement," *More All-of-a-Kind Family*, illus. by Mary Stevens, Wilcox and Follett, Chicago, 1954, pp. 25–38.

WEILERSTEIN, SADIE ROSE, "What Happened to Debby," *Little New Angel*, Jewish Publication Society of America, Philadelphia, 1947, pp. 17–26.

———, "I'm Sorry," *What the Moon Brought*, illus. by Mathilda Keller, Jewish Publication Society of America, Philadelphia, 1942, pp. 21–27.

———, "How K'tonton Was Forgiven on Yom Kippur," *The Adventures of K'tonton: A Little Jewish Tom Thumb*, Women's League Press, New York, 1935, pp. 76–80.

"The Wicked Official Who Insulted R. Samuel Hasid and Later Repented," *Ma'aseh Book*, trans. by Moses Gaster, Jewish Publication Society of America, Philadelphia, 1934, vol. 2, pp. 332–335.

ZELIGS, DOROTHY F., *The Story of Jewish Holidays and Customs for Young People*, Bloch Publishing Co., New York, 1942, pp. 32–42.

COLLECTIONS WITH YOM KIPPUR MUSIC

BAER, A., *Baal Tefillah*, J. Bulka, Nürnberg, 1930, pp. 215–346.

BINDER, A. W., *The Jewish Year in Song*, G. Schirmer, New York, 1928, p. 8.

COOK, RAY M., *Sing for Fun*, book 1, Union of American Hebrew Congregations, New York, 1957, p. 2.

COOPERSMITH, HARRY, ed., *The Songs We Sing*, United Synagogue Commission on Jewish Education, New York, 1950, pp. 91–93.

EISENSTEIN, JUDITH, and PRENSKY, FRIEDA, eds., *Songs of Childhood*, United Synagogue Commission on Jewish Education, New York, 1955, pp. 198–200.

EPHROS, GERSHON, ed., *Cantorial Anthology of Traditional and Modern Synagogue Music*, vol. 2: *Yom Kippur*, Bloch Publishing Co., New York, 1948.

GOLDFARB, ISRAEL, and GOLDFARB, SAMUEL E., *Synagogue Melodies for the High Holy Days: Arranged for Congregational Singing*, Brooklyn, 1926, pp. 18, 20–29, 50–63.

IDELSOHN, ABRAHAM ZEVI, *The Jewish Song Book*, Publications for Judaism, Cincinnati, 1938, pp. 248–342, 411–418.

SAMINSKY, LAZARE, *A Song Treasury of Old Israel*, Bloch Publishing Co., New York, 1951, pp. 5, 21–22, 29, 39–42.

Union Hymnal: Songs and Prayers for Jewish Worship, 3rd ed., Central Conference of American Rabbis, New York, 1940, pp. 172–196, 526–540.

Union Hymnal: Songs and Prayers for Jewish Worship, part 2—*Musical Services*, Central Conference of American Rabbis, New York, 1936, pp. 362, 366–374, 383–428.
Union Songster: Songs and Prayers for Jewish Youth, Central Conference of American Rabbis, New York, 1960, pp. 142–150, 157–162.
VINAVER, CHEMJO, ed., *Anthology of Jewish Music*, Edward B. Marks Music Corp., New York, 1955, pp. 137–175.
WOHLBERG, MAX, *High Holyday Hymns Set to Music*, Hebrew Publishing Co., New York, 1959, pp. 4–17.

RECORDINGS

The Art of David Roitman. Collectors Guild 626.
Avodas Yosef. Sung by Joseph Rosenblatt. Greater Recording Co. 44.
Cantor Pierre Pinchik Sings. Menorah 213.
Cantorial Masterpieces. Sung by Maurice Ganchoff. Tikva Records. T 35.
Cantorials for the High Holidays. Sung by Abraham Brun. MFW 940.
Days of Awe. Sung by Zavel Kwartin. Collectors Guild 620.
Gates of Prayer. By Ben Zion Kapov-Kagan. Collectors Guild 617.
Gems of the Synagogue. Sung by David Kusevitzky. Tikva Records 55.
Great Voices of the Synagogue. Sung by Berele Chagy, Mordecai Hershman, Zavel Kwartin, David Roitman, Joseph Rosenblatt, and Gershon Sirota. Collectors Guild 590.
Hebrew Melodies (includes "*Kol Nidre*" and "A Plea to God of Levi Yitzhak of Berditchev"). Sung by Jan Peerce. Victor LSC 2498.
Kol Nidre. Composed by Max Bruch for cello and orchestra. Mace S 10033.
Kol Nidre. By Richard Tucker. CBS Mono 72394.
Liturgical Classics. Sung by Samuel Vigoda. MABC 355.

PROGRAM AND AUDIO-VISUAL MATERIALS

PLAYS

m = *number of male parts;* f = *number of female parts*
min. = *approximate performance time in minutes*

MINDEL, JOSEPH, *Hour of Forgiveness.* Eternal Light radio script, no. 477, September 25, 1955. Jewish Theological Seminary of America, New York. 25 min. Youth and adults. An account of the last survivor of a Polish ghetto in 1943 and his effort to conceal his observance of Yom Kippur from the Nazis.

———, *The Third Confession.* Eternal Light radio script, no. 672, September 25, 1960. Jewish Theological Seminary of America, New York. 25 min. Youth and adults. A Yom Kippur script based on the reading of part of the Holy Day's service.

———, *Throne of Mercy.* Eternal Light radio script, no. 394, September 13, 1953. Jewish Theological Seminary of America, New York. 25 min. Youth and adults. An allegorical tale of a man's search for punishment for his failure to aid another man, only to find that there is remorse and repentance, justice and mercy.

———, *To Begin Again.* Eternal Light radio script, no. 599, September 21, 1958. Jewish Theological Seminary of America, New York. 25 min.

Youth and adults. Honoring Yom Kippur, this program shows how one man learns to accept the pain and disappointment of life as well as the happiness and blessings.

RAPHAELSON, SAMSON, *The Jazz Singer*, Brentano's, New York, 1925. 14 m, 3 f, extras, adults. 2 hours. The conflict of a jazz singer who is a cantor's son.

SAMUEL, MAURICE, *At Home with the Almighty*, based on story by I. L. Peretz, dramatized by Mark Feder, in *Isaac Loeb Peretz: A Source Book for Programming*, ed. by Philip Goodman, National Jewish Welfare Board, New York, 1951. 4 m, extras, ages 13–16. 15 min. A tailor complains to Rabbi Levi Isaac of Berditchev about the Almighty.

SEGAL, SAMUEL M., "It Happened on *Kol Nidre* Night," *On Stage Everyone*, Jonathan David Co., New York, 1957. 3 m, 2 f, extras, ages 10–13. 15 min. A fantasy.

WISHENGRAD, MORTON, *The Fourth Confession*. Eternal Light radio script, no. 241, October 2, 1949. Jewish Theological Seminary of America, New York. 25 min. Youth and adults. A modern interpretation of *Al Het*.

———, *Rabbi Israel Salanter*. Eternal Light radio script, no. 964, January 19, 1969. Jewish Theological Seminary of America, New York. (Also in his *The Eternal Light*, Crown Publishers, New York, 1947, pp. 335–350.) 25 min. Youth and adults. The rabbi enjoins his congregation to eat on Yom Kippur.

———, *Song of Berditchev*. Eternal Light radio script, no. 275, September 17, 1950. Jewish Theological Seminary of America, New York, 25 min. Youth and adults. An interpretation of the song of Rabbi Levi Yitzhak of Berditchev in which he complains about the Almighty.

KINESCOPE

The Sin of Virtue, by Morton Wishengrad. 16 mm, sound, black and white. 30 min. National Academy for Adult Jewish Studies of the United Synagogue of America, New York. A story about Rabbi Israel Salanter, who persuaded his congregation to break the Yom Kippur fast during a plague.

FILMSTRIP

The Story of Yom Kippur, by Samuel J. Citron. Jewish Education Committee of New York, 1952. 45 frames, black and white, narration. A portrayal of the spirit of soul-searching and repentance associated with Yom Kippur, including a story by S. Ansky dealing with repentance, prayer, and charity.

MOTION PICTURE

The Fast I Have Chosen. 16 mm, sound, black and white, 28½ min. Jewish Chautauqua Society, New York. A documentary narrated by Melvin Douglas; relates Judaism's moral mandates for the war on poverty in the Yom Kippur liturgy.

ARTS AND CRAFTS

SHARON, RUTH, *Arts and Crafts the Year Round*, United Synagogue Commission on Jewish Education, New York, 1965, vol. 1, pp. 78–83.

Make books your companion
Let your bookshelf be your garden–
Judah Ibn Tibbon

to become a member –
to present a gift –

call 1 (800) 234-3151
or write:
The Jewish Publication Society
1930 Chestnut Street
Philadelphia, Pennsylvania 19103

A Jewish Tradition